Sun™

Java™ 2 Enterprise Edition (J2EE™) Web Component Developer Exam

Exam 310-080

Alain Trottier

Training Guide

Sun™ Certification Training Guide (310-080): Java™ 2 Enterprise Edition (J2EE™) Web Component Developer Exam

International Standard Book Number: 0-7897-2821-4

Library of Congress Catalog Card Number: 2002110900

Printed in the United States of America

First Printing: October 2002

04 03 02 01 4 3 2 1

Trademarks

Warning and Disclaimer

PUBLISHER
David Culverwell

EXECUTIVE EDITOR
Jeff Riley

ACQUISITIONS EDITOR
Jeff Riley

DEVELOPMENT EDITOR
Susan Brown Zahn

MANAGING EDITOR
Thomas Hayes

PROJECT EDITOR
Tricia Liebig

COPY EDITORS
Benjamin Berg
Kezia Endsley

INDEXER
Larry Sweazy

PROOFREADER
Suzanne Thomas

TECHNICAL EDITORS
Bryan Basham
Steve Heckler
Marcus Green

MEDIA SPECIALIST
Michael Hunter

TEAM COORDINATOR
Rosemary Lewis

INTERIOR DESIGNER
Louisa Klucznik

COVER DESIGNER
Anne Jones

PAGE LAYOUT
Cheryl Lynch

GRAPHICS
Tammy Graham
Oliver Jackson

Contents at a Glance

Table of Contents

PART I: Becoming a Sun Certified J2EE Web Component Developer

PART II: Final Review

PART III: Appendixes

Preface

Hi. I'm glad you decided to prepare for this exam. Earning a certification is a career spike. Sure, it is work, but it is also a fun, quantifiable step forward. Clean steps like this one are rare in a software job. I'll work awfully hard to help you.

In one way I don't like this book. It is designed to speed up the preparation phase, so the facts fly across the pages rapidly. I would rather take more time to explain every last detail of the technology, but that is for another long book. So, if you want to focus on and sprint to your certification then this book is for you. I kept out non-essential material and laser-focused on the exam objectives. I know you'll like the book because it is concise. In a few places I comment about a matter not directly on the exam (for example, there's a little more about encryption than you need for the exam), but when I do that I say so.

I suppose the idea is to tell you what I discovered, experienced, and saw on my way to my own certification. That is a nice way to spread a good thing. However, I must tell you that a lot of research went into these pages. I am indebted to so many. I tried to give credit by including links to those resources that were helpful, occasionally giving a name.

There is efficiency to being deadpan honest. I'm impatient with appearances, but not to the point of being a derelict. I write bluntly. I'm like that in real life, so it wasn't a stretch. I don't get invited to many parties, but I'm tolerable and, more important to me, I'm reliable. If I help you, your money makes us even. If I erred or you simply didn't like something then—arghhhh!—I hate that. Please, email me about it (see the book's Web site at `www.inforobo.com/scwcd`). I promise not to sin twice. I'll get you the right answer.

By the way, there is much more to do with Java than has been done. Join me as we light the wick to the next explosion in software. I see two markets that are fast building up demand for your skills. The more flamboyant is the Web services arena. They still don't have it right, but they are getting close. Don't wait, you be the one who fixes the complex problems (nice idea but few portals actually talk to each other). The other one is the small device market. The sheer momentum behind the PDA, phone and appliance movement is like a trillion-gallon reservoir: The dam is about to break. Jump in the water with your Java gear now because, later, that torrent will be brutal on procrastinators.

The editorial process filters out sarcasm and puns that I enjoy. Still, I'm having so much fun talking with managers, developers, and students about this stuff. It is all fascinating to me. Remember that you are an adult prodigy so get tired, but not bored. I invite you to take a solid stance and just kick the heck out of anything that gets in your path to passing this Sun Certified Web Component Developer exam!

About the Author

Alain Trottier observes the .com warfare of Southern California as a technology management consultant (Strategic Business Resources) and adjunct professor at Vanguard University. He has been in the tech sector for two decades. He has been on the electronics side, working with RF gear, Nuclear Power Plants, and electro-mechanical devices. On the IT side he has had roles as technologist, developer support specialist, programmer, architect, and manager. He got a kick out of being in the U.S. Submarine Navy (nuclear power division). He was impressed with his bosses at Chevron's world-class research center. He was astonished by the .com bubble while at Adforce, and then Winfire, where he experienced a meteoric IPO, but subsequent flame-out. He has been through get-it-right-at-all-cost in a Fortune 30 company, but also the other extreme where one bets it all on a get-it-out-there-at-no-cost venture. He enjoys a difficult technology challenge and likes the people even better. He feels his degrees in religion (B.A., M.A. with specialization in the linguistics of ancient religious texts) is a terrific way to broaden one's abilities. He has certifications from both Microsoft and Sun so his bias is simply what works best for a given situation. If you have a question, comment, or even a challenge, the author would be delighted to hear from you. Please contact him (think Chief Technology Ambassador) from the book's Web site at `www.inforobo.com/scwcd`.

About the Technical Reviewers

Steve Heckler is a freelance programmer and IT trainer specializing in .NET, Java, ColdFusion, Flash ActionScript, and XML. Based in Atlanta, Georgia, he works with clients nationwide. In addition, he is the author of the *Sun Certification Instructor Resource Kit (310-025, 310-027): Java 2 Programmer and Developer Exams* and *Sun Certification Instructor Resource Kit (310-080): Java 2 Web Component Developer Exam*, and is currently writing an ASP.NET-related book for Addison-Wesley.

Prior to being self-employed, he served nearly seven years as vice president and president of a leading East Coast IT training firm. He holds bachelor's and masters degrees from Stanford University.

Marcus Green has been working with PCs since 1986 and with Internet technologies since 1992. He has written extensively on Java Programmer Certification and runs a Web site on that subject at `http://www.jchq.net`. He has written database-backed Web sites using Perl, PHP, and JSP, and he uses Linux as his default operating system.

Bryan Basham is a courseware developer for Sun Microsystems concentrating on Java technology and object-oriented design principles. In the 1980s, Bryan worked for NASA in Houston, Texas, developing advanced automation software using Artificial Intelligence techniques. In the 1990s, he worked for a medium-sized software engineering consulting firm. His development expertise has focused on the design and development of database business applications. Bryan has worked for Sun Educational Services for three years. In that time, he has worked on a large range of Java courses, including Sun's core Java programming course, the JDBC course, the J2EE overview seminar, and the Servlet/JSP course. Bryan is a practicing Zen Buddhist, Ultimate Frisbee player, audiophile, and telemark skier.

Dedication

This book is dedicated to my wife Patricia, the love of my life, and to my son Devyn who brings us tremendous joy and is already my hero.

Acknowledgments

I would like to thank Jeff Riley (acquisitions editor) and Margot Malley (agent) who made this book possible. Thank you Susan Brown Zahn (development editor) for your valuable guidance and encouragement. It was a terrific experience working with Que's team. Their contributions added much to the book. I admit having fun talking about and even sparring over the details. Every book purchase is a nod to Que's preeminent team.

We Want to Hear from You!

As the reader of this book, *you* are our most important critic and commentator. We value your opinion and want to know what we're doing right, what we could do better, what areas you'd like to see us publish in, and any other words of wisdom you're willing to pass our way.

As an associate publisher for Que, I welcome your comments. You can email or write me directly to let me know what you did or didn't like about this book—as well as what we can do to make our books better.

Please note that I cannot help you with technical problems related to the *topic* of this book. We do have a User Services group, however, where I will forward specific technical questions related to the book.

When you write, please be sure to include this book's title and author as well as your name, email address, and phone number. I will carefully review your comments and share them with the author and editors who worked on the book.

Email: `feedback@quepublishing.com`

Mail: Jeff Riley
Que Publishing
201 West 103rd Street
Indianapolis, IN 46290 USA

For more information about this book or another Que title, visit our Web site at `www.quepublishing.com`. Type the ISBN (excluding hyphens) or the title of a book in the Search field to find the page you're looking for.

How to Use This Book

Que Certification has made an effort in its Training Guide series to make the information as accessible as possible for the purposes of learning the certification material. Here, you have an opportunity to view the many instructional features that have been incorporated into the books to achieve that goal.

Chapter Opener

Each chapter begins with a set of features designed to allow you to maximize study time for that material.

List of Objectives: Each chapter begins with a list of the objectives as stated by the exam's vendor.

Objective Explanations: Immediately following each objective is an explanation of it, providing context that defines it more meaningfully in relation to the exam. Because vendors can sometimes be vague in their objectives list, the objective explanations are designed to clarify any vagueness by relying on the authors' test-taking experience.

Objectives

This chapter covers the following objectives listed by Sun in "Section 1—The Servlet Model" and "Section 3—The Servlet Container Model."

1.1 For each of the HTTP methods, GET, POST, and PUT, identify the corresponding method in the HttpServlet class.

- The HTTP methods GET, POST, and PUT are how browsers and Web servers communicate the purpose of communication. A GET simply wants to retrieve a page without providing much information. A POST, however, can package lots of form or file information with its request. A PUT is for uploading a file. The HttpServlet class has a corresponding method for each HTTP method, including doGet(), doPost(), and doPut().

1.2 For each of the HTTP methods, GET, POST, and HEAD, identify triggers that might cause a browser to use the method, and identify benefits or functionality of the method.

- This objective asks you to understand the events associated with each type of request. For example, clicking a hyperlink will send a GET request to a Web server, but clicking a Submit button (when the action is set to "post") will send a POST request.

CHAPTER 4

Servlet Container Model

Objectives

1.3 For each of the following operations, identify the interface and method name that should be used to

- **Retrieve HTML form parameters from the request**
- **Retrieve a servlet initialization parameter**
- **Retrieve HTTP request header information**
- **Set an HTTP response header; set the content type of the response**
- **Acquire a text stream for the response**
- **Acquire a binary stream for the response**
- **Redirect an HTTP request to another URL**

This objective is huge. It encompasses the heart of a servlet process, especially the request and response objects. The request parameters for the servlet are the strings sent by the client to the Servlet Container. The container parses the request and puts the information in an `HttpServletRequest` object which is passed to the servlet. Going the other way, the container wraps the response parameters in an `HttpServletResponse` object which is passed back to the container. The associated chapter section later in this chapter ("Overriding HttpServlet `GET`, `POST`, and `PUT` methods") goes into much detail on the methods involved.

1.4 Identify the interface and method to access values and resources and to set object attributes within the following three Web scopes:

- **Request**
- **Session**
- **Context**

This objective addresses the idea of scope. When something has Context scope, it is application-wide and all users can share data. Session scope means one user can share data across page views, but other users can't. Request scope restricts data to only that page.

1.5 Given a life-cycle method, identify correct statements about its purpose or about how and when it is invoked. These methods are

- `init`
- `service`
- `destroy`

The container manages the servlet life-cycle. This part of the chapter explains, with examples, how the container initializes a servlet with a call to the `init()` method. Then it calls the `service()` method upon every request. Finally, when the servlet is about to be removed from memory, the container calls its `destroy()` method. This gives the servlet one last chance to clean up resources.

1.6 Use a `RequestDispatcher` to include or forward to a Web resource.

The `RequestDispatcher` object is the servlet forwarding mechanism. You will see in the section "Servlet Life-cycle" how you can transfer processing of the request from one servlet to another (which the browser will be unaware of). This is how a servlet can pass the request to some other Web component within the same Web container.

3.1 Identify the uses for and the interfaces (or classes) and methods to achieve the following features:

- **Servlet context initialization parameters**
- **Servlet context listener**
- **Servlet context attribute listener**
- **Session attribute listeners**

These elements let you get and monitor servlet attributes. Not only can you get them and change them too, but you can actually put in place behavior to occur when an attribute changes. The listeners are event-driven triggers. When an attribute changes, special targeted methods are called.

Chapter Outline: Learning always gets a boost when you can see both the forest and the trees. To give you a visual image of how the topics in a chapter fit together, you will find a chapter outline at the beginning of each chapter. You will also be able to use this for easy reference when looking for a particular topic.

Outline

Study Strategies

- The key to this section of the exam is understanding how servlets implement the Servlet interface, which defines life-cycle methods. The Servlet Container (such as Apache Tomcat) is itself an application that monitors a port on a given IP address. Servlets generate responses to HTTP requests. To do so, the container loads your servlet (if it isn't in memory already) and calls the methods defined in the interface. This is the foundation of servlet and JSP architecture.
- There are many methods to know. It is easier if you learn the methods in groups according to theme. For example, write a servlet that has HttpServlet methods which handle all three `GET`, `POST`, and `PUT` types of request.
- Each JavaServer Page is transformed into a servlet that is compiled and then loaded. Therefore much of what you learn here applies to the JSP section of the exam too.

Study Strategies: Each topic presents its own learning challenge. To support you through this, Que Certification has included strategies for how to best approach studying in order to retain the material in the chapter, particularly as it is addressed on the exam.

INSTRUCTIONAL FEATURES WITHIN THE CHAPTER

These books include a large amount and different kinds of information. The many different elements are designed to help you identify information by its purpose and importance to the exam and also to provide you with varied ways to learn the material. You will be able to determine how much attention to devote to certain elements, depending on what your goals are. By becoming familiar with the different presentations of information, you will know what information will be important to you as a test-taker and which information will be important to you as a practitioner.

EXAM TIP

When is `INIT()` called? A common question on the exam tests your understanding of when `init()` is called. Knowledge of a servlet's life-cycle is crucial to answering these types of questions. Remember, `init()` may be called when the server starts (tell `web.xml` to load servlet upon startup), when first requested, and sometimes the container management console will allow you to call it as part of the server administration. The exam expects you to know that `init()` will only be called once per servlet instance, that it is not used to send information back to the browser (`HttpServletResponse` is not a parameter), and that it throws a `ServletException` to the container that called the servlet if anything goes wrong.

Exam Tip: Exam Tips appear in the margins to provide specific exam-related advice. Such tips may address what material is covered (or not covered) on the exam, how it is covered, mnemonic devices, or particular quirks of that exam.

Note: Notes appear in the margins and contain various kinds of useful information, such as tips on the technology or administrative practices, historical background on terms and technologies, or side commentary on industry issues.

NOTE

Servlet Reloading! Servlets are loaded in one of three ways. The first way is when the Web server starts. You can set this in the configuration file. Reload can happen automatically after the container detects that its class file (under servlet dir, for example, WEB-INF/classes) has changes. The third way, with some containers, is through an administrator interface.

Objective Coverage Text: In the text before an exam objective is specifically addressed, you will notice the objective is listed to help call your attention to that particular material.

OVERRIDING HTTPSERVLET GET, POST, AND PUT METHODS

1.1 For each of the HTTP methods, `GET`, `POST`, and `PUT`, identify the corresponding method in the `HttpServlet` class.

- `GET`
- `POST`
- `PUT`

Warning: In using sophisticated information technology, there is always potential for mistakes or even catastrophes that can occur through improper application of the technology. Warnings appear in the margins to alert you to such potential problems.

WARNING

`DESTROY()` is not called if the container crashes! You should log activity from somewhere other than the `destroy()` method if a given piece of information is essential, but might not be logged if the logging functionality is placed in the `destroy()` method. This is because the `destroy()` method is not called if the Servlet Container quits abruptly (crashes).

STEP BY STEP

9.1 Creating a New Tag Library

1. Write and compile a simple tag handler similar to the `ColorTagHandler` example that services the custom tag in your JSP (JSP custom tag attribute invokes a setter method in tag handler). Place the tag handler Java class files for your tags in the WEB-INF/classes directory of your Web application.
2. Write the tag library descriptor (TLD), which defines the tag library including the name of the tag handler class and attributes. Place it in its directory, which you declare in the deployment descriptor (`CATALINA_HOME/webapps/examples/WEB-INF/veltag.tld`). An example is given earlier in this chapter.

continues

FIGURE 4.2
You can create dynamic content using a servlet.

Step by Step: Step by Steps are hands-on tutorial instructions that walk you through a particular task or function relevant to the exam objectives.

Figure: To improve readability, the figures have been placed in the margins wherever possible so they do not interrupt the main flow of text.

IN THE FIELD

HOW DOES A SERVLET WORK?

You write a servlet and compile it, and then place it in the appropriate directory. When the Servlet Container starts, it will preload your servlet in memory if specified in the web.xml configuration file. If your servlet is not already loaded (not listed in the web.xml configuration file), its instance will be created as soon as a request for it is received by the Servlet Container. The first time it is loaded, the container calls your servlet's `init()` method, if there is one. Notice that it gets called only once, so place one-off functionality in this method (such as database connection, file object). Now that your servlet is ready, it waits for requests. The container will call your `service()` method each time a request is received for your servlet. The `HttpServlet` class (which your servlet must extend) already has this method, so you don't have to write one, but you can override it. The `service()` method then passes the request on to the appropriate method (usually `GET` for simple requests and `POST` to submit data, say a Web page form) such as the `doGet()` method if it is a `GET` request, or the `doPost()` method if it is a `POST` request. The `doXXX()` methods are the ones you need to override and where you will spend most of your effort. The servlet processes the request (code you write in `doGet()`), returning a response to the container. The container sends the text of the response back to the browser.

The preceding JSP and servlet examples are part of a Web application. A Web application is a collection of servlets, JSP pages, HTML documents, and other Web resources (such as image files, compressed archives, and other data). This collection may be packaged into an archive or exist as separate files in an open directory structure. Since you have many servlet classes, JSP pages, HTML pages, and other supporting libraries and files for a given Web application, there are many dependencies. These are not trivial to manage. It is vital that all parts go in their correct locations in the Web application archive or in an open directory structure. Once you get the dependencies resolved, it is a good idea to package the collection into a Web application archive, a single file with the .war extension that contains all of the components of a Web application. You can do this using standard JAR tools.

In the Field Sidebar: These more extensive discussions cover material that perhaps is not as directly relevant to the exam, but which is useful as reference material or in everyday practice. In the Field may also provide useful background or contextual information necessary for understanding the larger topic under consideration.

KEY TERMS

- Redirection
- Servlet Life-Cycle
- Servlet Forwarding and Includes
- Servlet attribute
- Context parameters
- Application session
- listeners

CHAPTER SUMMARY

The HTTP methods GET, POST, and PUT are how browsers and Web servers trade data with each other. The GET retrieves a page without providing much information, while a POST can package huge amounts of information with its request. A PUT is for uploading a file. There are events associated with each type of request, such as clicking a hyperlink sending a GET request, but clicking a form button sends a POST request.

Key Terms: A list of key terms appears at the end of each chapter. These are terms that you should be sure you know and are comfortable defining and understanding when you go in to take the exam.

Chapter Summary: Before the Apply Your Knowledge section, you will find a chapter summary that wraps up the chapter and reviews what you should have learned.

EXTENSIVE REVIEW AND SELF-TEST OPTIONS

At the end of each chapter, along with some summary elements, you will find a section called "Apply Your Knowledge" that gives you several different methods with which to test your understanding of the material and review what you have learned.

126 Part I BECOMING A SUN CERTIFIED J2EE WEB COMPONENT DEVELOPER

APPLY YOUR KNOWLEDGE

Review Questions

1. What methods of the `Servlet` interface are invoked at different points in the servlet life cycle?
2. What HTTP methods are supported by `HttpServlet`?
3. What objects are passed to the servlet's `service()` method?
4. What is a distributable application?
5. Why is it a bad idea to synchronize a servlet's `service()` method?
6. What is the relationship between an application's `ServletConfig` object and `ServletContext` object?
7. What mechanisms are used by a Servlet Container to maintain session information?
8. What are the four events that are defined in the Servlet API?
9. How are request dispatchers used?

Exam Questions

1. Which of the following methods are defined in the `Servlet` interface?

   A. `init()`

   B. `service()`

   C. `finalize()`

   D. `destroy()`

2. Which of the following objects are passed to a servlet's `service()` method?

   A. `ServletRequest`

   B. `HttpServletRequest`

   C. `ServletResponse`

   D. `HttpServletResponse`

3. By default, how many instances of a servlet are created by a Servlet Container?

   A. One

   B. One per request

   C. One per session

   D. None of the above

4. Which of the following exceptions are defined by the Servlet API?

   A. `ServletException`

   B. `InitializationException`

   C. `UnavailableException`

   D. `ServletContextException`

5. Which of the following are used by Servlet Containers to maintain session information?

   A. cookies

   B. hidden form fields

   C. HTTPS protocol information

   D. URL rewriting

Review Questions: These open-ended, short-answer questions allow you to quickly assess your comprehension of what you just read in the chapter. Instead of asking you to choose from a list of options, these questions require you to state the correct answers in your own words. Although you will not experience these kinds of questions on the exam, these questions will indeed test your level of comprehension of key concepts.

126 Part I BECOMING A SUN CERTIFIED J2EE WEB COMPONENT DEVELOPER

Apply Your Knowledge

Review Questions

1. What methods of the Servlet interface are invoked at different points in the servlet life cycle?
2. What HTTP methods are supported by HttpServlet?
3. What objects are passed to the servlet's service() method?
4. What is a distributable application?
5. Why is it a bad idea to synchronize a servlet's service() method?
6. What is the relationship between an application's ServletConfig object and ServletContext object?
7. What mechanisms are used by a Servlet Container to maintain session information?
8. What are the four events that are defined in the Servlet API?
9. How are request dispatchers used?

Exam Questions

1. Which of the following methods are defined in the Servlet interface?
   A. init()
   B. service()
   C. finalize()
   D. destroy()
2. Which of the following objects are passed to a servlet's service() method?
   A. ServletRequest
   B. HttpServletRequest
   C. ServletResponse
   D. HttpServletResponse
3. By default, how many instances of a servlet are created by a Servlet Container?
   A. One
   B. One per request
   C. One per session
   D. None of the above
4. Which of the following exceptions are defined by the Servlet API?
   A. ServletException
   B. InitializationException
   C. UnavailableException
   D. ServletContextException
5. Which of the following are used by Servlet Containers to maintain session information?
   A. cookies
   B. hidden form fields
   C. HTTPS protocol information
   D. URL rewriting

Exam Questions: These questions reflect the kinds of questions that appear on the actual vendor exam. Use them to become familiar with the exam question formats and to help you determine what you know and what you need to review or study more.

Answers and Explanations: For each of the Review and Exam questions, you will find thorough explanations located at the end of the section.

Suggested Readings and Resources

1. Sun's excellent J2EE Tutorial—java.sun.com/j2ee/tutorial/1_3-fcs/doc/J2eeTutorialTOC.html.
2. The Java Language Specification—(java.sun.com/docs/books/jls/second_edition/html/j.title.doc.html).
3. Exam objectives for the Sun Certified Web Component Developer for J2EE Platform—http://suned.sun.com/US/certification/java/exam_objectives.html.
4. The Java Servlet 2.3 Specification—http://jcp.org/aboutJava/communityprocess/first/jsr053/index.html.
5. Sun's official Servlet page—http://java.sun.com/products/servlet/.

Suggested Readings and Resources: The very last element in every chapter is a list of additional resources you can use if you want to go above and beyond certification-level material or if you need to spend more time on a particular subject that you are having trouble understanding.

Introduction

In just a few years, Java has become one of the world's most popular programming languages. Java's initial popularity stemmed from its association with the Web and its capability to deliver executable content to Web pages. This popularity increased as programmers discovered that Java's power, simplicity, and rich APIs could tackle the challenges of backend systems. Java's popularity increased further as both large and small companies invested in building Java-based information infrastructures.

One of the results of Java's popularity is the high demand for skilled Java programmers and developers. However, due to Java's brief existence, experienced Java programmers are hard to find. Few in the field have more than five years of experience in developing Java applications. This is a problem for both employers and programmers. Employers cannot rely on the traditional number of years of experience in selecting senior-level Java programmers and software engineers. Star Java programmers have a hard time differentiating themselves from entry-level Java programmers.

The Java certification exams provide a solution for both employers and programmers. Employers can identify skilled Java programmers by their certification level. Programmers and software engineers can attest to their knowledge of Java by citing their certification credentials.

The Java certification program consists of four certification exams:

- Programmer exam—The Programmer exam tests the candidate's knowledge of the Java language and basic API packages. The exam consists of 59 multiple choice questions.
- Developer exam—The Developer exam tests the candidate's ability to complete an extended programming assignment and answer questions concerning the issues and tradeoffs that are involved in the assignment's completion. Programmer certification is a prerequisite to Developer certification.
- Web Component Developer exam—The Component Developer exam tests the candidate's knowledge of developing Java Web applications using Java servlets and Java Server Pages (JSP). The exam consists of 60 multiple choice questions. Programmer certification is a prerequisite to Web Component Developer certification. This book prepares you for this exam.
- Architect exam—The Architect exam test a candidate's familiarity with the technologies that are used to build Java-based enterprise applications and the candidate's ability to resolve issues in Java application design. This exam focuses on much higher-level software and system engineering skills than the other exams. It consists of a 48-question multiple choice exam, an architecture and design project, and a 4-question essay exam.

Being on the dark side (Microsoft Certified Solution Developer) for many years, I was intrigued by how Sun could have invented a new language and convinced enough people to use it. I was surprised by its hybrid nature (best parts of several languages) and its thorough rethinking of what a language is supposed to be. While there are many areas that will continue to be implemented better (faster, more efficient and so on), I'm impressed with the structure of Java. It actually feels good to use and there are few messy aspects to it.

Furthermore, the portability of Java should be credited to world-class design and effective marketing. The computer language industry is fractured, so I am amazed that Sun was able to convince so many to build Java Virtual Machines for all the operating systems. Without this cooperation Java would be dead.

Having taken many Microsoft exams, it was very interesting to take Sun's exam. The quality of the exam itself was no better or worse than MS exams, but because the technology was cleaner to begin with I felt Sun's test was somehow better representative of my Java skill level. I am confident that this book will help you pass the Sun Certification Web Component Developer (SCWCD) exam.

Attaining Java certification is not easy. As you saw with the basic certification exam, the Programmer exam, it is difficult, even for an experienced Java programmer. The SCWCD exam covers every aspect of the Java language associated with Web site building. This includes the core classes and interfaces of the servlet API packages. To pass this exam, you must acquire both a breadth and depth of experience with servlets and JSP. This book is organized to help you prepare for the Web Component Developer exam as follows:

- Part I of this book is dedicated to the exam objectives, organized according to Sun's published exam topics and objectives, except for a few juggled items that seemed to fit better in a section different from Sun's original structure. It contains a detailed and focused description of the topics that are covered by the exam, numerous questions that review your understanding of these topics, and even more questions that you can use to measure your progress and determine when you are ready to take the exam.
- Part II prepares you for the exam by providing you with Fast Facts, Practice Exams, and Study and Exam Preparation Tips to help you successfully take the exam. A detailed study plan explaining all the tasks necessary to prepare for and taking the exam is also provided. Sample exam questions are examined and answers to these questions are provided.
- Part III includes helpful reference information. For example, you need to practice the code listings in the book. To help you do that I've added Appendix D, "Setting Up a Servlet Environment." Also, you'll find other appendices including an API snapshot, a JSP syntax snapshot, and an extensive section on resources.

WHO SHOULD READ THIS BOOK

This book is for anyone who wants to take and pass the Sun Certification Web Component Developer for J2EE certification exam. If you are an experienced Java programmer and you want to pass the SCWCD exam, this book will show you how. It will fill any gaps that you might have in your knowledge of the Java language or servlet API packages. It will cover all that you need to know to do well on the exam and help you assess your test readiness through hundreds of review and sample exam questions. If you study the material that is presented in each chapter, use the review questions to identify areas in which you need to improve, and continue your study until you get high grades in the sample exam questions, you will be on a direct path to passing the exam.

If you are not an experienced Java programmer, you will need to learn how to program in Java and then pass the Programmer exam. I suggest that you start with Sun's online Java tutorial at `http://www.javasoft.com/docs/books/tutorial/index.html` and work your way through an intermediate-to-advanced Java book, such as *Java 2 Unleashed* from Sams Publishing. Then read Que's *Sun Certification Training Guide: Java 2 Programmer and Developer Exams* which will prepare you for the Programmer exam.

When you successfully pass the Java Programmer exam, you might want to achieve a higher level of certification by taking and passing the Java Developer exam. The Java Developer exam is a two-part exam that consists of a programming assignment and an essay exam. The programming assignment requires you to complete a partially developed Java application according to specific instructions. The essay exam consists of (5–10) short-answer essay questions.

Like the Developer exam, the SCWCD exam this book covers requires successfully passing the Java Programmer exam first. If you are not yet a certified Java Programmer, you should focus on successfully completing that exam before moving on to the SCWCD or Developer exams.

Getting Started

To use this book, you will need a computer and operating system that support the Java 2 Platform. Many operating systems support the Java 2 Platform, including Windows, Linux, and Solaris. Ports of the Java 2 Platform to many other operating systems are in the works. The examples used in this book were developed under Tomcat running on Windows 2000. However, they will run under all servlet containers that are implemented according to specification on the Java 2 Platform.

The CD-ROM that accompanies this book contains all the source and compiled code for all examples presented in this book. The CD-ROM is a hybrid that works on Windows, Linux, Unix, and Macintosh platforms. In addition, it contains an exam preparation program that helps you review the material presented in each chapter and a Simulated Exam program that tests your knowledge of this material. Appendix E, "What's on the CD-ROM," outlines what is on the CD-ROM.

How to Use This Book

Start with Chapter 1 and proceed through each chapter of the book in order, working through all review and exam questions. As noted previously, passing the Programmer exam is a prerequisite to taking the Developer exam, so that level of familiarity is assumed.

How This Book Helps You

This book takes you on a self-guided tour of all the areas that are covered by the SCWCD for Java 2 Platform exam and teaches you the specific skills you will need to achieve your Sun certification. You will also find helpful hints, tips, and real-world examples, as well as references to additional study materials. Specifically, this book is set up to help you in the following ways:

- Organization—The book is organized by individual exam objectives. Every objective you need to know for the SCWCD J2EE exams is covered in this book. The objectives are in an order that is similar to that listed by Sun. However, sometimes this book presents the objectives in a different order from Sun to make the material as easy as possible for you to learn. The information is accessible in the following ways:
  - The full list of the Sun testing objectives is included in the introductory chapter for each part.

  - Each chapter begins with a list of the Sun testing objectives to be covered. For some chapters, this book has created additional "learning objectives" to complement or extend the ones that Sun lists. These additional objectives are introduced when it is necessary for you to understand additional or related material to succeed in the exams.
  - Each chapter also begins with an outline that provides you with an overview of the material and the page numbers where particular topics can be found.

- Instructional Features—This book has been designed to provide you with multiple ways to learn and reinforce the exam material. Following are some of the helpful methods:
  - *Objective Explanations*—As mentioned previously, each chapter begins with a list of the objectives covered in the chapter. In addition, immediately following each objective is an explanation in a context that defines the objective more meaningfully.
  - *Study Strategies*—The beginning of the chapter also includes strategies for approaching how to study and retain the material in the chapter, particularly as it is addressed on the exam.
  - *Exam Tips*—Exam Tips appear in the margin to provide specific exam-related advice. Such tips might address what material is covered (or not covered) on the exam, how it is covered, mnemonic devices, or particular quirks of that exam.
  - *Key Terms*—A list of key terms appears at the end of each chapter.
  - *Notes*—These appear in the margin and contain various kinds of useful information such as tips on technology or administrative practices, historical background on terms and technologies, or side commentary on industry issues.
  - *Warnings*—When using sophisticated information technology, there is always the potential for mistakes or even catastrophes that occur because of improper application of the technology. Warnings appear in the margin to alert you to such potential problems.
  - *Suggested Readings and Resources*—Each chapter ends with a reference to additional information that you can use to learn more about the material that you just studied.

- Extensive practice test options—This book provides numerous opportunities for you to assess your knowledge and practice for the exam. The practice options include the following:
  - *Review Questions*—These open-ended questions appear in the "Apply Your Knowledge" section at the end of each chapter. They allow you to quickly assess your comprehension of what you just read in the chapter. Answers to the questions are provided later in a separate section titled "Answers to Review Questions."
  - *Exam Questions*—These questions also appear in the "Apply Your Knowledge" section. Use them to help you determine what you know and what you need to review or study further. Answers and explanations for these questions are provided in a separate section titled "Answers to Exam Questions."

- *Practice Exam*—Three Practice Exams are included in Part II, "Final Review." The "Final Review" section and the Practice Exams are discussed further later in this Introduction.
- *PrepLogic*. The special Training Guide version of the *PrepLogic Practice Tests, Preview Edition* software included on the CD-ROM provides further practice questions.

◆ Final Review—This part of the book provides you with three valuable tools for preparing for the exam.

- *Fast Facts*—This condensed version of the information contained in the book will prove extremely useful for last-minute review.
- *Study and Exam Prep Tips*—Read this section early on to help you develop study strategies. This section also provides you with valuable exam-day tips and information on exam/question formats.
- *Practice Exam*—Three practice exams offer multiple opportunities for you to assess your learning. Questions are written in styles similar to those used on the actual exams. Use the practice exams to assess your understanding of the material in the book.

CONVENTIONS USED IN THIS BOOK

Italic is used in this book when a key term is introduced. A `monospaced font` identifies program code. An *`italic monospaced font`* identifies placeholders used in Java syntax descriptions.

An arrow at the beginning of a line of code means that a single line of code is too long to fit on the printed page. Continue typing all characters after the ➥ as though they were a part of the preceding line.

THE BOOK'S WEB SITE

To help you with your certification studies, a Java certification Web site has been put together to supplement the information presented in this book. The Web site provides a forum for feedback on the certification exams and contains any corrections for errors that are discovered after the book's printing. The URL for this Web site is `http://www.inforobo.com/java/scwcd/`. If you have any questions, comments, or suggestions concerning the book, its Web site, or the certification exams, please direct them to `atrottier@hotmail.com`.

QUE PUBLISHING

The staff of Que Certification is committed to bringing you the very best in computer reference material. Each Que Certification book is the result of months of work by authors and staff who research and refine the information contained within its covers.

As part of this commitment to you, the reader, Que invites your input. Please let us know if you enjoy this book, if you have trouble with the information or examples presented, or if you have a suggestion for the next edition.

Please note, however, that Que staff cannot serve as a technical resource during your preparation for the Java certification exams or for questions about software- or hardware-related problems. Please refer instead to the documentation that accompanies the Java products or to the applications' Help systems.

If you have a question or comment about any Que book, there are several ways to contact Que Publishing. We will respond to as many readers as we can. Your name, address, or phone number will never become part of a mailing list or be used for any purpose other than to help us continue to bring you the best books possible. You can write to us at the following address:

Que Certification
Attn: Jeff Riley
201 W. 103rd Street
Indianapolis, IN 46290

If you prefer, you can fax Que at 317-581-4663.

You also can send email to Que at the following Internet address:

`feedback@quepublishing.com`

Que is an imprint of Pearson Technical Group. To purchase a Que book, call 800-428-5331.

Thank you for selecting *Sun Certification Training Guide (310-080): Sun Certified Web Component Developer Exam.*

PART I

Becoming a Sun Certified J2EE Web Component Developer

OBJECTIVES

There are no formal Sun exam objectives covered in this chapter. This chapter just introduces you to the Web Component Developer exam.

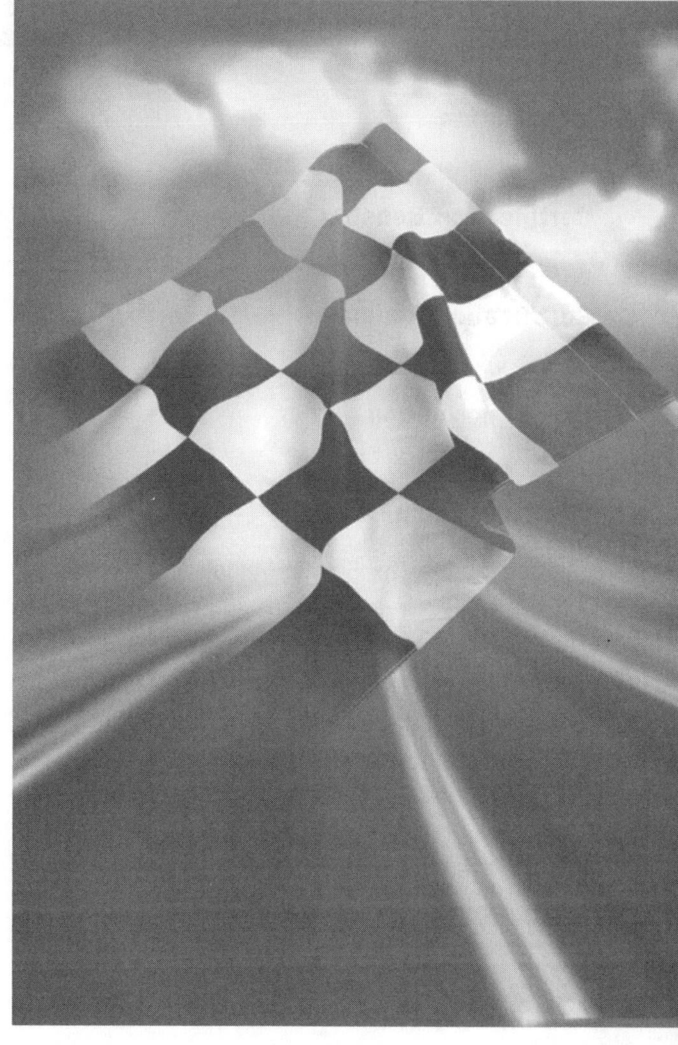

CHAPTER 1

The Java Web Component Developer for J2EE Platform Exam

OUTLINE

INTRODUCTION

This chapter introduces you to the Sun Certified Web Component Developer for the J2EE Platform Examination. It identifies the topics that the exam covers, discusses how the exam is given, and provides you with tips and other information on how to take the exam.

The technologies the certification covers are servlets and JavaServer Pages (JSP). Servlets are classes that look like those you use in J2SE, except they extend special purpose classes that enable them to respond to Web server requests. JSP pages extend servlet technology with a simple HTML (or XML) syntax. You can also include normal Java statements. The servlet container actually compiles JSP pages into a servlet the first time it is requested.

Let's look at the official definitions for these. The specification says, "JavaServer Pages is the Java 2 Platform, Enterprise Edition (J2EE) technology for building applications for generating dynamic Web content, such as HTML, DHTML, XHTML and XML. The JavaServer Pages technology enables the easy authoring of web pages that create dynamic content with maximum power and flexibility." So, it is a Web page with a mixture of HTML and Java. This mixture makes JSP useful for the following primary reasons:

- Write Once, Run Anywhere
- High quality tool support
- Separation of roles
- Reuse of components and tag libraries
- Separation of dynamic and static content
- Support for scripting and actions
- Web access layer for N-tier enterprise application architecture(s)

Sun publishes a specification for servlets, too. I have modified slightly Sun's definition for a servlet as a Java technology-based Web component, managed by a container that generates dynamic content. Containers, sometimes called servlet engines, are Web server extensions that provide servlet functionality. Servlets interact with Web clients via a request/response paradigm implemented by the servlet container.

The servlet container is a part of a Web server or application server that provides the network services over which requests and responses are sent, decodes MIME-based requests, and formats MIME-based responses. A servlet container also contains and manages servlets through their lifecycle. According to the specification, the primary advantages of servlets are

- They are faster than CGI scripts because each CGI script produces an entirely new process that takes time to execute while a servlet is only another thread.
- The API is standard and public, unlike some proprietary APIs, server-side languages, and scripts. For example, Microsoft's excellent Active Server Pages is a so-called proprietary API, which means it only works on Windows (although there are third-party plug-ins that enable you to run it on other platforms).
- Servlets have the Java advantages of ease of development and platform independence.
- They can access all the huge J2SE and J2EE APIs. This is not true of, say, JavaScript. JavaScript can run on many servers, but normally has limited access to the backend. Not so with JSP and servlets, which can take full advantage of the full power of Java.

The advantages of JSP and servlets are many, as stated previously. However, how can you convince a recruiter that he or she should hire you to take advantage of them? Nothing is more convincing than real examples. While these are best, you can also interest the recruiter with a certification. The next section explains why you should get certified.

CERTIFICATION BENEFITS

There are many benefits to getting certified. Many major industries use certification as a quality control mechanism. Would you go to an uncertified doctor? Of course not! Think of the mess roads would be without the driver's license infrastructure. Road deaths would skyrocket if the government didn't enforce its license laws.

The Department of Motor Vehicles uses the word "license" instead of "certification," but it is the same thing. It's a way to gauge competency, granting permission to some and restricting the rest.

Many occupations regulate activity through state-required certifications, licenses, and permits. There are Certified Public Accountants, Commercial Driver's Licenses (CDL) for truck drivers, Residential Building Contractors, Pharmacist Licenses, Electrical Contractors, and many more. The closest one to software would be Professional Engineer. The software industry is still trying to figure out objective ways to gauge competency. The best we have are vendor certifications. It isn't that software people don't want certification, but rather, it is hard to build a certification or license process that is practical. The electricians have a system where each state regulates the wiring for buildings so it is all the same. In this situation, it is straightforward to design a test for everyone. In software, the "wiring" (software language) varies. Also, while the building codes for wiring don't change much, software languages change yearly. For example, J2SE recently was upgraded from 1.3 to 1.4 (Merlin), introducing big changes.

The software industry would be better off if we had a Software Professional Engineer license that would be required of every commercial developer. This would focus on the language-independent ideas which we all should know, from bits/bytes to algorithms, from requirements to design, and from programming to life cycle. I realize a computer science degree covers much of this, but we need a government-run license program too. The board certification is a big reason physicians in countries that require certifications for its practicing doctors are some of the best in the world.

The Software Professional Engineer license doesn't exist, so there is pent-up demand for another measuring stick. Sun's certification is one such stick, which makes it very valuable. I've seen it happen so many times where a programmer making about $50,000 gets a huge ($10,000) increase after getting a certification. Sometimes they get the raise from their current employer, or they switch companies and get the raise that way. Certification is that valuable. Often, it's not the salary, but a responsibility hike that results. Eventually, that translates into more money too.

Why do people hang their framed certification, diploma, or license on the wall? It is powerful; that is why. One glance tells others

- Certification preparation improved their skill set.
- They convinced a board they know what they are doing.
- They understand process, invaluable for big projects.
- They know what they know, and aren't shy about it.
- They are making money.
- They follow standards and procedures (team player).
- They have credibility.
- They demonstrates professionalism.

Certification Roadmap

This section illustrates where the SCWCD certification fits in Sun's certification program. Figure 1.1 presents a sort of "roadmap" of Sun certifications. The Sun Certified Web Component Developer certification requires that you first obtain the Sun Certified Programmer for Java certification. However, it does not require the Sun Certified Developer or the Sun Certified Enterprise Architect for J2EE Technology certifications.

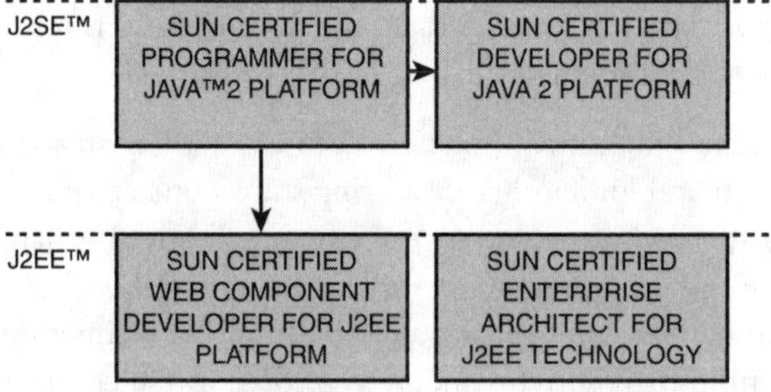

FIGURE 1.1
Roadmap to Sun certification.

Exam Information

This section covers practical details about the exam itself. For example, it tells you how much the exam costs and how many questions are on it. More links and resources are provided at the end of the chapter, but Table 1.1 provides a crisp list of exam details.

TABLE 1.1

EXAM DETAILS

Category	*Description*
Purchase	Sun Educational Services: `http://suned.sun.com/US/certification/register/index.html`. Note: You must call, not buy online! You can purchase an exam voucher by calling (800) 422-8020.
Objectives	`suned.sun.com/US/certification/java/exam_objectives.html`
SCWCD Home	`suned.sun.com/US/certification/java/java_web.html`
Prometric Testing Center	`www.2test.com/`
Legal	`suned.sun.com/US/certification/register/policies.html`
Sun's "My Certification"	`suned.sun.com/US/certification/my_certification/index.html`
Prerequisites	Sun Certified Programmer for Java 2 Platform status
Exam type	Multiple choice, short answer, and drag and drop
Questions	60
Pass score	61% or 37 questions
Time limit	90 minutes
Cost	US $150 or as priced in the country where the exam is taken
Difficulty	Easy-----------------x-------Hard
JSP	Version 1.2 (September, 2001 spec). JCP Expert Group—JSR053 (`jcp.org/jsr/detail/53.jsp`)
Servlet	Version 2.3 (August, 2001). JCP Expert Group—JSR053 (`jcp.org/jsr/detail/53.jsp`)
Based upon	Servlet containers must be built with J2SE 1.2+ and J2EE 1.2+
ePractice Exam	`suned.sun.com/US/catalog/courses/WGS-PREX-J080B.html` (pay). `tmn.sun.com/WLC/servlet/GuestLoginServlet?id=programmer` (free)

WHAT THE EXAM COVERS

The Java 2 Web Component Developer exam covers a wide range of topics related to servlets and JavaServer Pages, servlets and JSP API classes and interfaces, Web application design patterns, and topics related to application deployment and configuration. It contains 60 questions on programming topics that you are expected to understand. These questions cover the following exam objectives (defined by Sun) and are presented in random order on the test.

Section 1—The Servlet Model

1.1 For each of the HTTP methods, `GET`, `POST`, and `PUT`, identify the corresponding method in the `HttpServlet` class.

1.2 For each of the HTTP methods, `GET`, `POST`, and `HEAD`, identify triggers that might cause a browser to use the method, and identify benefits or functionality of the method.

1.3 For each of the following operations, identify the interface and method name that should be used:

- Retrieve HTML form parameters from the request
- Retrieve a servlet initialization parameter
- Retrieve HTTP request header information
- Set an HTTP response header; set the content type of the response
- Acquire a text stream for the response
- Acquire a binary stream for the response
- Redirect an HTTP request to another URL

1.4 Identify the interface and method to access values and resources and to set object attributes within the following three Web scopes:

- Request
- Session
- Context

1.5 Given a life-cycle method: `init`, `service`, or `destroy`, identify correct statements about its purpose or about how and when it is invoked.

1.6 Use a `RequestDispatcher` to include or forward to a Web resource.

Section 2—The Structure and Deployment of Modern Servlet Web Applications

2.1 Identify the structure of a Web Application and Web Archive file, the name of the WebApp deployment descriptor, and the name of the directories where you place the following:

- The WebApp deployment descriptor
- The WebApp class files
- Any auxiliary JAR files

2.2 Match the name with a description of purpose or functionality for each of the following deployment descriptor elements:

- Servlet instance
- Servlet name
- Servlet class
- Initialization parameters
- URL to named servlet mapping

Section 3—The Servlet Container Model

3.1 Identify the uses for and the interfaces (or classes) and methods to achieve the following features:

- Servlet context init. parameters
- Servlet context listener

- Servlet context attribute listener
- Session attribute listeners

3.2 Identify the WebApp deployment descriptor element name that declares the following features:

- Servlet context init. parameters
- Servlet context listener
- Servlet context attribute listener
- Session attribute listeners

3.3 Distinguish the behavior of the following in a distributable:

- Servlet context init. parameters
- Servlet context listener
- Servlet context attribute listener
- Session attribute listeners

Section 4—Designing and Developing Servlets to Handle Server-side Exceptions

4.1 For each of several cases described on the exam, identify correctly constructed code for handling business logic exceptions, and match that code with correct statements about the code's behavior: Return an HTTP error using the `sendError` response method; Return an HTTP error using the `setStatus` method.

4.2 Given a set of business logic exceptions, identify the following: The configuration that the deployment descriptor uses to handle each exception; how to use a `RequestDispatcher` to forward the request to an error page; specify the handling declaratively in the deployment descriptor.

4.3 Identify the method used for the following: Write a message to the WebApp log; write a message and an exception to the WebApp log.

Section 5—Designing and Developing Servlets Using Session Management

5.1 Identify the interface and method for each of the following:

- Retrieve a session object across multiple requests to the same or different servlets within the same WebApp
- Store objects into a session object
- Retrieve objects from a session object
- Respond to the event when a particular object is added to a session
- Respond to the event when a session is created and destroyed
- Expunge a session object

5.2 Given a scenario, state whether a session object will be invalidated.

5.3 Given that URL-rewriting must be used for session management, identify the design requirement on session-related HTML pages.

Section 6—Designing and Developing Secure Web Applications

6.1 Identify correct descriptions or statements about the security issues:

- Authentication, authorization
- Data integrity
- Auditing
- Malicious code
- Web site attacks

6.2 Identify the deployment descriptor element names, and their structure, that declare the following:

- A security constraint
- A Web resource
- The login configuration
- A security role

6.3 Given an authentication type: BASIC, DIGEST, FORM, and CLIENT-CERT, identify the correct definition of its mechanism.

Section 7—Designing and Developing Thread-safe Servlets

7.1 Identify which attribute scopes are thread-safe:

- Local variables
- Instance variables
- Class variables
- Request attributes
- Session attributes
- Context attributes

7.2 Identify correct statements about differences between the multi-threaded and single-threaded servlet models.

7.3 Identify the interface used to declare that a servlet must use the single thread model.

Section 8—The JavaServer Pages (JSP) Technology Model

8.1 Write the opening and closing tags for the following JSP tag types:

- Directive
- Declaration
- Scriptlet
- Expression

8.2 Given a type of JSP tag, identify correct statements about its purpose or use.

8.3 Given a JSP tag type, identify the equivalent XML-based tags.

8.4 Identify the page directive attribute, and its values, that:

- Import a Java class into the JSP page
- Declare that a JSP page exists within a session
- Declare that a JSP page uses an error page
- Declare that a JSP page is an error page

8.5 Identify and put in sequence the following elements of the JSP page lifecycle:

- Page translation
- JSP page compilation
- Load class
- Create instance
- Call jspInit
- Call _jspService
- Call jspDestroy

8.6 Match correct descriptions about purpose, function, or use with any of the following implicit objects:

- request
- response
- out
- session
- config
- application
- page
- pageContext
- exception

8.7 Distinguish correct and incorrect scriptlet code for:

- A conditional statement
- An iteration statement

Section 9—Designing and Developing Reusable Web Components

9.1 Given a description of required functionality, identify the JSP page directive or standard tag in the correct format with the correct attributes required to specify the inclusion of a Web component into the JSP page.

Section 10—Designing and Developing JSP Pages Using JavaBean Components

10.1 For any of the following tag functions, match the correctly constructed tag, with attributes and values as appropriate, with the corresponding description of the tag's functionality:

- Declare the use of a JavaBean component within the page.
- Specify, for `jsp:useBean` or `jsp:getProperty` tags, the name of an attribute.
- Specify, for a `jsp:useBean` tag, the class of the attribute.
- Specify, for a `jsp:useBean` tag, the scope of the attribute.
- Access or mutate a property from a declared JavaBean.
- Specify, for a `jsp:getProperty` tag, the property of the attribute.
- Specify, for a `jsp:setProperty` tag, the property of the attribute to mutate, and the new value.

10.2 Given JSP page attribute scopes: request, session, and application, identify the equivalent servlet code.

10.3 Identify techniques that access a declared JavaBean component.

Section 11—Designing and Developing JSP Pages Using Custom Tags

11.1 Identify properly formatted tag library declarations in the Web application deployment descriptor.

11.2 Identify properly formatted taglib directives in a JSP page.

11.3 Given a custom tag library, identify properly formatted custom tag usage in a JSP page. Uses include:

- An empty custom tag
- A custom tag with attributes
- A custom tag that surrounds other JSP code
- Nested custom tags

Section 12—Designing and Developing a Custom Tag Library

12.1 Identify the tag library descriptor element names that declare the following:

- The name of the tag
- The class of the tag handler
- The type of content that the tag accepts
- Any attributes of the tag

12.2 Identify the tag library descriptor element names that declare the following:

- The name of a tag attribute
- Whether a tag attribute is required
- Whether or not the attribute's value can be dynamically specified

12.3 Given a custom tag, identify the necessary value for the body-content TLD element for any of the following tag types:

- Empty-tag
- Custom tag that surrounds other JSP code
- Custom tag that surrounds content that is used only by the tag handler

12.4 Given a tag event method (doStartTag, doAfterBody, and doEndTag), identify the correct description of the methods trigger.

12.5 Identify valid return values for the following methods:

- `doStartTag`
- `doAfterBody`
- `doEndTag`
- `PageConext.getOut`

12.6 Given a "BODY" or "PAGE" constant, identify a correct description of the constant's use in the following methods:

- `doStartTag`
- `doAfterBody`
- `doEndTag`

12.7 Identify the method in the custom tag handler that accesses:

- A given JSP page's implicit variable
- The JSP page's attributes

12.8 Identify methods that return an outer tag handler from within an inner tag handler.

Section 13—Design Patterns

13.1 Given a scenario description with a list of issues, select the design pattern (Value Objects, MVC, Data Access Object, or Business Delegate) that would best solve those issues.

13.2 Match design patterns with statements describing potential benefits that accrue from the use of the pattern, for any of the following patterns:

- Value Objects
- MVC
- Data Access Object
- Business Delegate

The previous topics and exam objectives are specific, so they will guide you in selecting what details to concentrate on while preparing for the exam. The chapters of this book are organized according to these topics and objectives. While all the objectives are addressed in the book, they have been reorganized to make the topics easier to study, as shown in Table 1.2.

TABLE 1.2

CHAPTER TO EXAM TOPIC MAPPING

Chapter	*Title*	*Exam Topics*
4	Servlet & Container Model	Section 1.1–1.6, 3.1–3.2—The Servlet Model
5	Servlet Exceptions	Section 4.1, 4.3—Handling Server-side Exceptions
6	Session Management	Section 5—Using Session Management
7	JavaServer Pages (JSP) Technology Model	Section 8—The JavaServer Pages (JSP) Technology Model and Section 9—Designing and Developing Reusable Web Components
8	Extend JSP with JavaBeans	Section 10—Designing and Developing JSP Pages Using JavaBean Components
9	Customize JSP with Tag Libraries and Including Components	Section 12, 11.2–11.3—Designing and Developing JSP Pages Using Custom Tags
10	Web Applications	Section 2.1–2.2, 3.2, 4.2, 11.1—The Structure and Deployment of Modern Servlet Web Applications
		Section 6—Designing and Developing Secure Web Applications
		Section 7—Designing and Developing Thread-Safe Servlets
11	Design Patterns	Section 13—Design Patterns

HOW THE EXAM IS GIVEN

The exam is a computer-based test consisting of 60 multiple-choice and short-answer questions. The tests are given at Sylvan Prometric Testing Centers. You first call Sun (yes, no online purchase for this) for an exam voucher. You can purchase an exam voucher by calling (800) 422-8020. Then you schedule the exam with Prometric (call or online).

Certification exam question count and time limits have been known to change over time, but Sun has been consistent. The current format gives you 90 minutes to complete the 60-question exam.

The multiple-choice questions are either single-answer questions or multiple-answer (choose all that apply) questions. Single-answer questions are indicated by radio buttons. Multiple-answer questions have check boxes. You must choose all that apply to get multiple-answer questions correct. For example, suppose question 28 has stated answers A, C, and D as correct options. You must select all three to get credit for this question. You will not receive partial credit for choosing A and D (which are correct), but omitting C (which is also correct). The exam questions on the actual exam tell you exactly how many answers you must supply.

The short-answer questions ask you to enter a word or line of text. Typically these are class/method names or a code statement. There aren't many of these questions (<10%). However, you have to type it exactly as expected because the testing software simply compares your answer to an internal string; it isn't parsed, so a typed answer with correct syntax is wrong if it isn't an exact string match. Also, be careful in that the answers are case-sensitive. Sun won't try to trick you with an answer that looks correct, but the case is wrong. However, case does matter on all questions so be careful.

When you arrive at the testing center, you will sign in and show *two* forms of ID. One must have a picture, but both must have signatures. Although I once arrived early and was allowed to take an exam ahead of schedule, Prometric frowns on early or late arrivals, so arrive at least 10 minutes before your scheduled time and expect the administrator to allow you to sit for the exam exactly on schedule. You can't bring any paper into or out of the testing area. They will provide you with paper and pencil/pen, but you will leave that at the test center. Of course, you can't take any electronic device (PDA, phone) into the testing area.

The test software presents only one exam question on the screen at a time. It allows you to mark a question if you would rather return to it later. You can also move backward and forward between the questions you've answered and those you have yet to answer.

The testing software gives you all the instructions, so it's easy to get through the test. At the conclusion of your test, you will click the "Had enough of this?" button (it's not really marked "Had enough of this?"!). This will cause the software to grade your test. Next, there will be a button on the screen to print the results. You can click it twice, or just copy the printout the test administrator provides to you. One copy will be stamped with an "Authorized Testing Center" seal. The testing center software automatically notifies Sun of your test results. You walk out knowing how you did. You can also go to the official test database Web site (`suned.sun.com/US/certification/my_certification/index.html`) to verify your score.

Exam Preparation

This exam is moderately difficult. You won't pass if you simply study the API. The chapters in this book will provide you with all the information you need to get a perfect score. However, you'll probably fail if all you do is do is read the pages. I strongly recommend installing and practicing with Tomcat (see Appendix D, "Setting Up a Servlet Environment," for more on Tomcat) or similar servlet engine (such as JRun, Resin, WebLogic, Websphere, JBoss, and so on). Writing JSP and servlets then testing them with Tomcat is crucial. You must both write/run code and study the book to obtain a high score on the exam.

Once you have installed and configured a servlet engine such as Tomcat, you can then practice with all the sample code of the book. This is really the best and fastest way to understand JSP and servlets.

How to Take the Exam

You will soon be ready. The testing software is designed to make it simple, and it is. Remember that you need 37 correct answers to pass the test, but be prepared to do much better. Wrong answers are not penalized, so answer them all. First go through and answer the ones you know well, skipping anything too hard. You will probably answer about 90% of the exam on first pass. Then return to the hard questions and answer a few of those. Next, eliminate the bad answers on the stumpers and just guess. Lastly, make sure all questions are answered.

So, the steps to take overall are

- Install and set up SDK 1.3+.
- Install and set up Tomcat 4.0+.
- Download the JSP 1.2 and servlets 2.3 specifications.
- Page through the specifications.
- Read through the book and do the exercises.
- Take the book's practice exams.
- Take other practice exams.
- Review the objectives, making sure you covered them all.
- Take the real exam.
- Answer easy questions first, skipping tough ones.
- Return to skipped questions.
- Make sure all questions are answered.
- Get your certification diploma.

CODING STYLE

This section discusses code conventions used in this book and which I recommend for several reasons. Without them we can't share code well. Did you know that convincing studies show that the majority of software lifetime (80%) is spent in maintenance, not original build? Likewise, the people doing the maintenance are usually not the original author. The efficiency of code work improves when code conventions are enforced. Lastly, while this applies to a minority, it looks more professional to ship code with product that complies with a clean convention.

Much of the following is a condensation, with a few modifications, of "Code Conventions for the Java Programming Language," published by Sun (April 20, 1999).

Files

There can be just one file or thousands of files that comprise a given application. Table 1.3 presents naming conventions for the files.

TABLE 1.3

FILE CONVENTIONS

File	*Convention*	*Note*
MyClass.java	.java	Java source always has this extension.
MyClass.class	.class	The compiler creates a new bytecode file by the same name, but with this extension.
README.TXT	README.TXT; README.HTML	Preferred name for a file with a summary of the contents of a particular directory.

Comments

All source files should start with a descriptive note including the class name, version information, date, and copyright notice. The following example shows the minimum:

```
/*
 * Classname
 *
 * Version information
 *
 * Date
 *
 * Copyright notice
 */
```

Other items that are often helpful are Author, Filename, Purpose, Version History or Revision, Deprecated, Link, See, and Since. Remember, these comments are meant to guide programmers, not users or management. In fact, there is a whole style guide just for code comments. If you go to `http://java.sun.com/j2se/javadoc/writingdoccomments/index.html#styleguide` you'll find a guide on how to use javadoc style comments. I recommend following this guide. One day you will want to generate the documentation for your code, and javadoc does it well, so take advantage of it by marking your comments in a way that it can correctly parse them. Notice that javadoc produces HTML documentation, so you can embed HTML markup right in your code comments and it will pass through to the final documentation.

Do comment all the non-obvious portions. Marking another loop index is useless, but noting that the exit condition of a given loop is reached when the customer has attempted more than five successive logons is informative.

Breaking Lines

Try to keep code lines under 70 characters. If you have a line that is longer, break it following these rules:

- Break after a comma.
- Break before an operator.
- Prefer higher-level breaks to lower-level breaks.
- Align the new line with the beginning of previous line.
- Otherwise just indent some spaces.

Break outside the parenthesized expression (higher level), rather than, say, between `varName4` and `varName5`. For example

```
varName1 = varName2 * (varName3 + varName4 - varName5)
                + varName6 - methoCall();
```

Opening and Closing Curly Braces

I disagree with Sun and many programmers on this topic. They recommend placing the opening brace "{" at the end of the same line as the declaration statement, like so:

```
class MyClass implements MyInterface {
    String sName;
    int count;

    myMethod(String firstName, String lastName) {
        int start = 0;
        int end = 99;
    }
    ...
}
```

No matter how much I try, I can't easily match the braces, so it is difficult to see if any are missing. It also obscures field scope, although indentation is a better indication for scope. I've talked to my students many times about this. A few like the style above, but most learn Java faster when I use the following convention that I use throughout the book:

```
class MyClass implements MyInterface
{
    String sName;
    int count;

    myMethod(String firstName, String lastName)
    {
        int start = 0;
        int end = 99;
    }
    ...
}
```

if, if-else, if else-if else, and switch Statements

The `if-else` style is fine either Sun's way or my preferred open-closing brace alignment way. The book uses this form:

```
if (condition)
{
    statements;
}

if (condition)
{
    statements;
} else
{
    statements;
}

if (condition)
{
    statements;
} else if (condition)
{
    statements;
} else
{
    statements;
}
```

Likewise, use this format for the `switch`:

```
switch (condition)
{
   case CONSTANT1:
      statements;
      /* falls through */

   case CONSTANT2:
      statements;
      break;

   case CONSTANT3:
      statements;
      break;

   default:
      statements;
      break;
}
```

Naming Conventions

How you name things is very important. There is information in the naming convention. For example, use all uppercase for constants. That way, when you come across a field spelled in all uppercase you know it's a constant; you'll avoid the temptation to change its value. One common mistake programmers make is to use cryptic names. This is a holdover from the ancient days when the number of characters you used in a name actually impacted the memory resources. It's also easier to simply type something that works and move on. Names don't affect memory anymore, so make the effort to be descriptive. A simple glance tells you what `customerCount` is, but what is `iCus` or, worse, `i`? Table 1.4 describes the naming conventions you'll find on the exam and throughout this book:

TABLE 1.4

NAMING CONVENTIONS

Identifier	*Example*	*Rule*
Package	`com.sun.security`	All-lowercase ASCII letters. Most use domain name (ending in com, edu, gov, mil, net, org) to ensure uniqueness.
Class, Interface	`System`	Capitalize
Method, Variable	`myMethod`, `customerCount`	Lowercase first letter, but internal words start with capital letters.

SPECIFICATIONS

The specifications are how Sun defines JSP and servlet technology. Notice that Sun is only just starting to sell software based on its specifications. Sun realizes that its best competitive position stems from defining and publishing the specifications. For example, early on Sun built a reference implementation for servlets, but then decided to give the servlet container building to others (Apache). Tomcat is the best free JSP and servlet environment on the market. It is 100% compliant with Sun's specifications. In fact, you can get the source code from Apache and learn how they did it.

There are two specifications. Sun's two specifications (JSR-000053) for Servlet 2.3 and JavaServer Pages 1.2 are at `jcp.org/aboutJava/communityprocess/first/jsr053/index.html`. I strongly recommend you download them and read through each of them. It's an outstanding way to start studying for the exam.

COURSES

There are many paths leading to a certification. One viable path is taking courses before sitting for the exam. Many vendors offer exam preparation courses, although most are for the other exams; this one is still rare. You can take a course at a technical training center or at a college. The best way is to have a private tutor. Few of us can afford that, so the next best approach is taking courses. Some of us can't afford that either, so use a good book and prepare yourself. When it comes to software, the last option isn't bad. Sun offers three courses that together will get you ready for the Certified Web Component exam. Given the huge range of course quality and the stiff price tag, I encourage you to talk to recent graduates of these courses and to ask to sit in on a class for one meeting at no charge in order to see if the quality is satisfactory.

The first course they recommend you take is *Developing J2EE Compliant Applications* (FJ-310) [`suned.sun.com/US/catalog/courses/FJ-310.html`]. It teaches you how to build and deploy enterprise applications that comply with Java 2 Enterprise Edition (J2EE). Remember that you can focus on handhelds (J2ME), PCs (J2SE), or the big enterprise applications (J2EE), which this course teaches.

The key technologies taught are Enterprise JavaBeans (EJB), servlets, and JavaServer Pages (JSP) to the HTML and Java-based clients that use them. You learn to build the clients as HTML pages, applets, and standalone applications that access server pieces which you also build through labs that build an end-to-end, distributed business application. This enterprise training also covers database interaction from session EJB components using Java Database Connectivity (JDBC). You will learn how entity EJB components can use both bean-managed and container-managed persistence. Finally, you are taught how to assemble an application from reusable components and deploy an application into the J2EE runtime environment.

The second one is *Web Component Development with Java Technology* (SL-314) [`suned.sun.com/US/catalog/courses/SL-314.html`]. This is a hands-on course that teaches you how to build Web tier components from JavaServer Pages and servlet technologies using the Tomcat server environment. Sun promises that its real-world lab exercises provide students experience with constructing and deploying small- to medium-scale Web applications found in intranet and low-volume commercial sites. This one is probably the best one at Sun to prepare for the Sun Certified Web Component Developer certification examination.

The third one is *Java Servlets: A Technical Introduction* (WJB-305-180) [`http://suned.sun.com/US/catalog/courses/WJB-305-180.html`]. This course provides an introduction to servlets.

CHAPTER SUMMARY

This section introduced you to the Sun Certified Web Component Developer for the J2EE Platform Examination. It identified the topics that the exam covers, discussed how the exam is given, and provided you with tips and other information on how to take the exam. You should now be able to go on to study the remaining chapters of Part I.

Suggested Readings and Resources

1. Details of the Sun Certified Web Component Developer for the J2EE Platform (`http://suned.sun.com/US/certification/java/java_web.html`).
2. Details of the Sun Certified Web Component Developer for the J2EE Platform (`http://suned.sun.com/US/certification/java/java_web.html`).
3. JSP home page (`java.sun.com/products/jsp`).
4. Servlet home page (`java.sun.com/products/servlet`).
5. Java 2 Platform, Standard Edition (`java.sun.com/products/jdk/1.4`).
6. Java 2 Platform, Enterprise Edition (`java.sun.com/j2ee`).
7. XML in the Java Platform home page (`java.sun.com/xml`).
8. JavaBeans technology home page (`java.sun.com/beans`).
9. XML home page at W3C (`www.w3.org/XML`).
10. HTML home page at W3C (`www.w3.org/MarkUp`).
11. XML.org home page (`www.xml.org`).
12. Expert group JSR053, who wrote the JSP and servlet specifications under the Java Community Process (`jcp.org/jsr/detail/53.jsp`).
13. Sun Educational Services (`suned.sun.com/US/certification/register/index.html`).
14. Exam Objectives (`suned.sun.com/US/certification/java/exam_objectives.html`).
15. Exam home page (`suned.sun.com/US/certification/java/java_web.html`).
16. Prometric Testing Center (`www.2test.com`).
17. Check your scores at Sun's "My Certification" (`suned.sun.com/US/certification/my_certification/index.html`).
18. Fee-based ePractice exam at Sun (`suned.sun.com/US/catalog/courses/WGS-PREX-J080B.html`).
19. Free ePractice exam at Sun (`https://tmn.sun.com/WLC/servlet/GuestLoginServlet?id=programmer`).
20. SCWCD@Whiz—SCWCD Test (Sun Certified Web Component Developer Certification) Simulator (`http://www.whizlabs.com/products/scwcd/scwcd.html`).
21. JWeb—SCWCD Test (Sun Certified Web Component Developer Certification) Simulator (`http://enthuware.com/jwebplus/index.html`).
22. IBM's jCentral (`www.ibm.com/java/`).
23. jGuru (`www.jguru.com/`).
24. jRoundup (`www.jroundup.com`).
25. JavaWorld (`http://www.javaworld.com/index`).
26. Java Developers Journal (`www.sys-con.com/java/`).
27. Exam home page (`suned.sun.com/US/certification/java/java_web.html`).

OBJECTIVES

This chapter does not address any specific exam objectives, but instead helps you plan your preparation activities for the SCWCD exam. If a project takes more than a week, then you need a plan. If it takes a month or more then you also need a strategy. This chapter answers the question, "What is the best way to approach Sun's exam, and what are the steps necessary to pass it?"

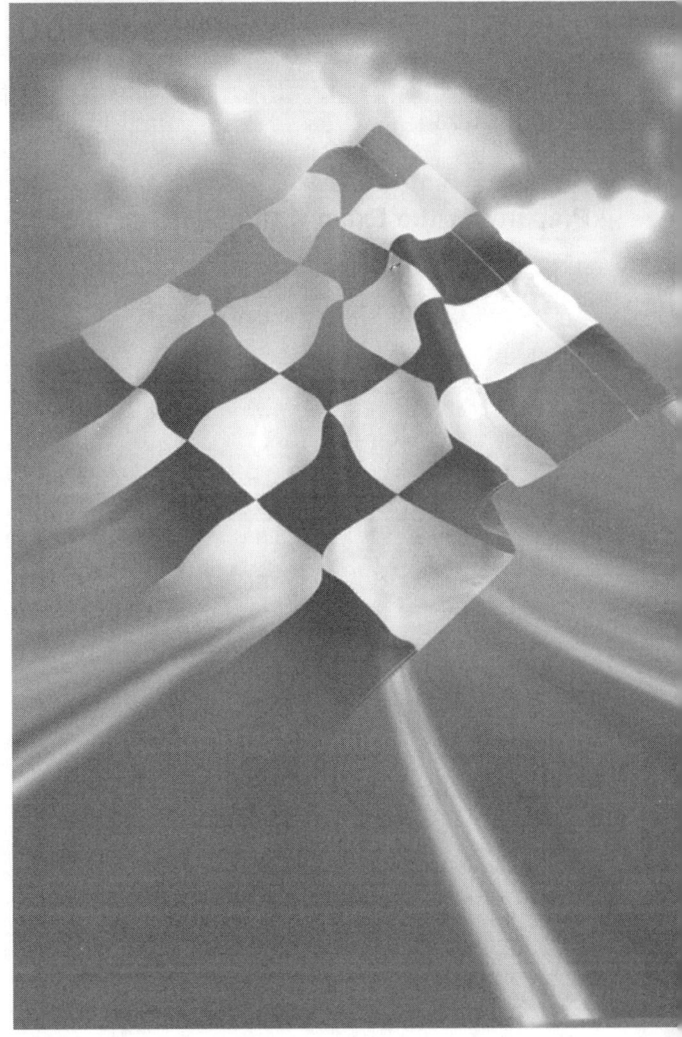

CHAPTER 2

Exam Preparation Strategy

Outline

Study Strategies

- The study plan in this chapter eliminates the uncertainty of passing the exam. You will definitely pass with a high score if you complete the tasks in Table 2.1. Don't rely on just a few mock exams. Retaking them until you get 100% won't translate to a good performance on the real thing.
- Make sure you don't sprint through the process. You are trying to do more than hang a plaque. Completing all the steps in Table 2.1 will make you a legitimate Web component developer.
- Take a deep breath, but then don't let anything stop you. March like a soldier through all tasks listed below. If you are an experienced guru, you will still run into trouble if you don't study; the answers to the exam questions are not all obvious. Many of them are difficult to guess, but straightforward if you are prepared. Even if you have designed remarkable products, the exam will spear you for not being very familiar with the specifications.

INTRODUCTION

If you are already deep into servlet development at work then you might still like the schedule as an outline for your test preparation. Otherwise, everything here will help. There are no specific exam objectives addressed here. The following information is a blueprint for your preparation efforts. I acknowledge that most people don't plan their preparation. They just buy a book like this one, take a few mock exams until they have good scores, and then sit for the real thing. Sun won't disclose exact figures, but anecdotal evidence and industry experts peg a 25%–50% failure rate for major certification exams. These numbers are bloated with the toe-in-the-water and just-practicing folk. That still leaves a lot of well-intentioned people without a certification who paid $150 for the privilege of letting Sun tell them they don't know what they are doing.

PREPARE FOR THE EXAM WITH A PLAN

Having the attitude that you are going to study hard will help, but if you don't have a good plan then it will take longer and you risk failure. Here is a plan that will ensure you pass the exam. The following ten-week schedule in Table 2.1 offers a concise list of tasks you should complete. You can pass with less effort, but then you'll be like a lot of people out there who have diplomas, but don't know anything. These people are found out eventually. If you follow this plan you'll do great and have fun learning.

TABLE 2.1

EXAM PREPARATION SCHEDULE

Task	*Activity*	*Chapter and Other Resources*	*Week*	*Date*
1	Make and commit to schedule	2	1	
2	Review Sun's SCWCD home page	Sun	1	
3	Buy exam voucher, schedule exam	Sun, Prometric	1	
4	Take Sun's free example exam	Sun	1	
5	Choose container and editor	Appendix D	1	
6	Set up container and editor	Appendix D	1	
7	Test environment (compile test servlet, browse to it)	Your PC	1	
8	Review JSP & Servlets	1–3	1	
9	Take Practice Exam 1	Part 2	1	
10	Read "Servlet & Container Model"	4	2	
11	Compile/run Chapter 3 listings	3	2	
12	Do Chapter 4 review questions	4	2	
13	Scan Sun's servlet tutorial	Sun	2	
14	Read "Servlet Exceptions"	5	3	
15	Compile/run Chapter 5 listings	5	3	
16	Do Chapter 5 review questions	5	3	
17	Get a host and hang a shingle		3	
18	Take JavaRanch's SCWCD Mock Exam		3	
19	Read "Session Management"	6	4	
20	Compile/run Chapter 6 listings	6	4	
21	Do Chapter 6 review questions	6	4	
22	Read the Servlet Specification	Sun Web site	4	
23	Take Practice Exam 2	Part 2	4	
24	Post a few servlets to Web site		4	
25	Read "JavaServer Pages (JSP) Technology Model"	7	5	
26	Code Chapter 7 listings	7	5	
27	Do Chapter 7 review questions	7	5	
28	Read Sun's JSP tutorial		5	
29	Read JSP Specification		5	

Task	*Activity*	*Chapter and Other Resources*	*Week*	*Date*
30	Take withmilk.com—SCWCD exam		5	
31	Read "Extend JSP with JavaBeans"	8	6	
32	Code Chapter 8 listings	8	6	
33	Do Chapter 8 review questions	8	6	
34	Post a few JSPs to Web site		6	
35	Read "Customize JSP with Tag Libraries"	9	6	
36	Code Chapter 9 listings	9	6	
37	Do Chapter 9 review questions	9	6	
38	Read "Web Applications"	10	7	
39	Code Chapter 10 listings	10	7	
40	Do Chapter 10 review questions	10	7	
41	Take Practice Exam 3	Part 2	7	
42	Take Anand Chawla's Mock Exam		8	
43	Take Practice Exam 1	Part 2	8	
44	Take Practice Exam 2	Part 2	8	
45	Take Practice Exam 3	Part 2	8	
46	Scan Servlet Specification	Sun	9	
47	Take the real exam	Prometric	9	
48	Revise resume	Home PC	1	
49	Ask for promotion; get new job	Work	10	
50	Visit jCert Initiative	Work	10	
51	Celebrate with family and friends	Park/Beach	10	

The following are notes on the tasks in Table 2.1:

- **Task 1.** This task is crucial to the success of this project. Don't underestimate the commitment; it is a serious project. Declare to yourself when you will take this exam. Don't leave it as simply "I will do it when I can find time"; set a date. Free time won't find its way to you. You have to make free time. You can set a schedule (daily, weekly, or monthly) for when to accomplish the specified tasks. Take an hour to coordinate these tasks with your calendar, and don't waiver from it.

EXAM TIP

Stick to the Schedule Sun's exams are not easy. Regardless of your towering IQ, you can ace the exam only by training for it. Use what is useful here and make your schedule: Stick to it and don't let anything knock you off track.

- **Task 2.** You want to review Sun's SCWCD home page to make sure you have the latest official information. At the very least, compare the exam number and objectives to what is in this book.

- **Task 3. Verify The Exam Numbers And Register.** Make sure you have the right number (Sun Certified Web Component Developer for J2EE Platform: 310-080). Purchase an exam voucher from your local Sun Educational Services office. To find your local office, go to `http://www.sun.com/service/suned` and choose the country in which you want to take the test. Then contact Prometric to schedule your exam. The exams take place at authorized Prometric Testing Centers. To register go to `http://www.2test.com` for information on your local Prometric office. In some countries, you may register for exams online. While most of us automatically just agree, you might have a reason to review the Certification Candidate Pre-Test Agreement, which can be viewed at `http://suned.sun.com/US/certification/register/policies.html`. After all, if you do not sign the agreement, you will not be allowed to take the exam.

- **Task 4.** Take Sun's free practice exam (ePractice Sample Questions for Sun Certified Web Component Developer for J2EE Platform: WGS-PREX-J000; `https://tmn.sun.com/WLC/servlet/GuestLoginServlet?id=programmer`). While this test is short, the expectations and content are exactly right. If you have money falling out of your pocket, then buy and take the ePractice Preview Exam for Sun Certified Web Component Developer for J2EE Platform (WGS-PREX-J080B; `http://suned.sun.com/US/catalog/courses/WGS-PREX-J080B.html`). Now you'll know the challenge you are facing.

- **Task 5.** While this should be painless, you do have to choose a container to practice with. Even if they have one for you at work, I strongly recommend you get your own. The installation and configuration tasks themselves are instructive. There are many to choose from. Unlike other areas in our industry, there are several excellent servlet- and JSP-capable servers on the market. They are reliable, conform to Sun's specifications, are free, and, best of all, ship with the source so you can see how they were created.

One comprehensive listing is at Java Skyline (`www.javaskyline.com/serv.html`). Pick one on that list that is open source, doesn't support EJB (which muddies the waters at this point), and uses Servlets 2.3 and JSP 1.2. Tomcat meets these requirements.

◆ **Task 6.** Try Tomcat. It is free, runs well, and is built to Sun's specifications. To do this, you should read the get/setup instructions at `http://jakarta.apache.org/tomcat/tomcat-4.0-doc/RUNNING.txt`). You will:

STEP BY STEP

2.1 Set up Tomcat (`jakarta.apache.org/tomcat/`).

1. Download a Java Development Kit (JDK) release (version 1.2 or later) from `java.sun.com/j2se/`.
2. Download a binary distribution of Tomcat. Go to `http://jakarta.apache.org/site/binindex.html`. Under "Release Builds," pick the latest version of Tomcat. The final release of Apache Tomcat is available in both binary and source versions. Download both.
3. Unpack the binary distribution (default directory is "`jakarta-tomcat-4.0`"). Refer to "`RUNNING.txt`" for more information. This file, specific to the platform, will provide instructions on how to set up Tomcat, including setting up environment variables.
4. Create shortcuts to the startup and shutdown scripts (`startup.sh`—Unix and `startup.bat`—Windows; `shudown.sh`—Unix, and `shutdown.bat`—Windows) to ease starting and stopping Tomcat.
5. Shut down your other Web servers.
6. Start up Tomcat 4.0 with `startup.bat` or `startup.sh`.
7. Test your new servlet and JSP environment by pointing your browser to `http://localhost:8080/`. You should see the screen shown in Figure 2.1.

continues

continued

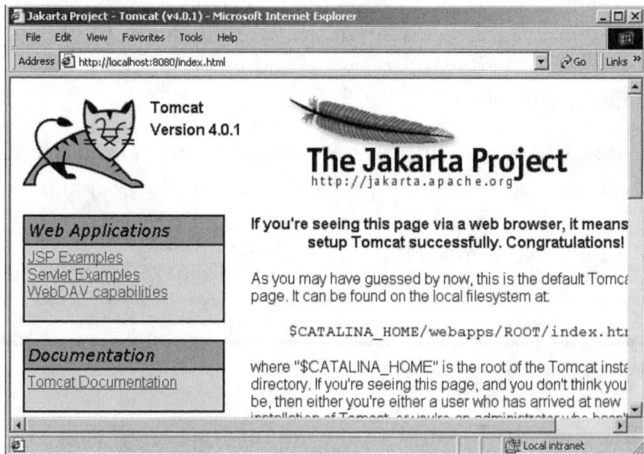

FIGURE 2.1
The default (index.html) Web page returned by Tomcat after initial installation.

8. Modify the configuration, such as changing the default home page or setting up multiple Tomcat 4 instances.

- **Task 9.** Test yourself with Practice Exam 1. Unless you are ready for the exam and this is just review, you'll fail. The point is to expose yourself to your first real exam. Time it and don't look up answers.
- **Task 13.** Briefly read Sun's tutorial. It is skimpy, but it hits the main points. It is a helpful review.
- **Task 17.** Rent some space on the Web from a commercial host. Even if your pal has a server, pass. Buy real space. You'll learn a lot the first time your servlet crashes and you have to call/email their technical help. There are many free hosting services, but these rarely support servlets and JSP. I use EZpublishing (`http://www.ezpublishing.com/`). At first I had trouble because their servers were not configured properly. Also, they didn't do a good job of describing their environment (that is, I couldn't figure out how to import because their package paths were weird). A couple times they moved things around and broke my internal references (darn imports again).

They should be out of beta for Tomcat 4 (Servlet 2.3 and JSP 1.2) by the time you read this. However, *EVERY* time I called, they jumped up to help me. I haven't had to call for months now, so I'm happy. You can go to `http://www.adrenalinegroup.com/jwsisp.html` or `http://www.servlets.com/isps/servlet/ISPViewAll` to check out two strong lists of hosts to consider. You can also read the servlet ISP thread (`http://www.jguru.com/faq/view.jsp?EID=155`) at the outstanding jGuru (`www.jguru.com`). Some hosting firms allow you a free trial. For example, WebAppCabaret (`http://www.webappcabaret.com/webhosting.html`) provides a free 15-day trial for EJB 1.1, JavaServer Pages (JSP) 1.1/1.2, and Servlets 2.2/2.3.

- **Task 18.** Take JavaRanch's SCWCD mock exam. Because someone is paying attention, it continues to improve.
- **Task 22.** Download and read Sun's Servlet Specification. It is now time to wade through the Java Servlet Specification 2.3 (`java.sun.com/products/servlet/index.html`).
- **Task 24.** Post a few servlets to your Web site. Doing this makes it all real. Each problem you run into will teach you another trick.
- **Task 29.** Read the JSP Specification 1.2 (`java.sun.com/products/jsp/`).
- **Tasks 42–46.** This is the last phase of preparation. Take all these exams and then scan the Servlet Specification one last time. This should be the last step you do before taking the real exam—the night before, not the same day.
- **Task 47.** If you have followed this chapter's advice, you will score +90%. Upon completing your exam, you will print your score sheet. It has section-by-section and overall scores. You can also view your exam results at `suned.sun.com/US/certification/my_certification/index.html` within three to five business days. You won't fail, but if your less fortunate buddy does not pass the exam, they must wait two weeks before taking it again.

WARNING

Do Not Merely Take Mock Exams! Do not set your hopes on passing a few mock exams. Many people do that, and are surprised when the real thing is much harder. There is no shortcut; you have to study and write code. There are too many details for normal folk to memorize. Sun can easily dice your memory with nuance. However, if you actually code this book's servlet and JSP code listings and play with them under Tomcat, then Sun is the one who had better look out (you might find a mistake or ambiguity on the exam).

- **Tasks 48–50.** You accomplished much these weeks. Leverage this achievement while it is hot. Revise your resume first. Then tell your boss (in a professionally written email). Finally, ask for a hike in responsibility so you can better apply your new credentials. Even if you get rejected, it is a reasonable request. Also, without threatening or demanding, you have now served notice that you are doing what they asked you to do when you were first hired (motivated, standards complying, leadership tendencies, and so on). You can even change jobs now. Don't get the idea that your certification is a winning lottery ticket. Still, it is significant and hard to deny due to market forces.
- **Task 51.** Congratulations, from all of us at Que!

Table 2.1 is a suggested week-to-week schedule. Modify it as you wish. For example, perhaps you have written a thousand JSPs. In that case, spend less time on JSP and more time on servlets. Then make a spreadsheet similar to Table 2.1. Fill in actual dates; this is important. Take notes as you move through the tasks.

CHAPTER SUMMARY

KEY TERMS

- Apache Jakarta Tomcat
- Certification exam voucher
- Development environment
- Study Plan
- Practice/mock exam
- Servlet hosting
- ISP
- JSP
- Prometric Testing Center
- Servlet and JSP specifications

One of the first steps a Java programmer must take in order to make more money is to differentiate him/herself from colleagues. I'm sorry, it doesn't sound nice, but that is the reality of the ultra-competitive development career. Bragging rarely wins promotions. Continued improvement in code production, problem solving, and professional maturity (no kidding, I once was promoted past a higher-skilled colleague because he was a slob) earns more bucks. The certification is, in many ways, a convenience for beleaguered managers because it is a significant filter mechanism. This certificate doesn't always produce immediate raises, but it often does.

Suggested Readings and Resources

1. SQL Server Books Online
   - JavaRanch: `http://www.javaranch.com/scwcdlinks.jsp`
   - servlets.com: `http://www.servlets.com`
   - Java Skyline: `http://www.javaskyline.com`
   - jGuru: `http://www.jguru.com/forums/Servlets`
   - jspinsider: `http://www.jspinsider.com`

OBJECTIVES

No formal objectives are covered in this chapter. It serves as background material for subsequent chapters.

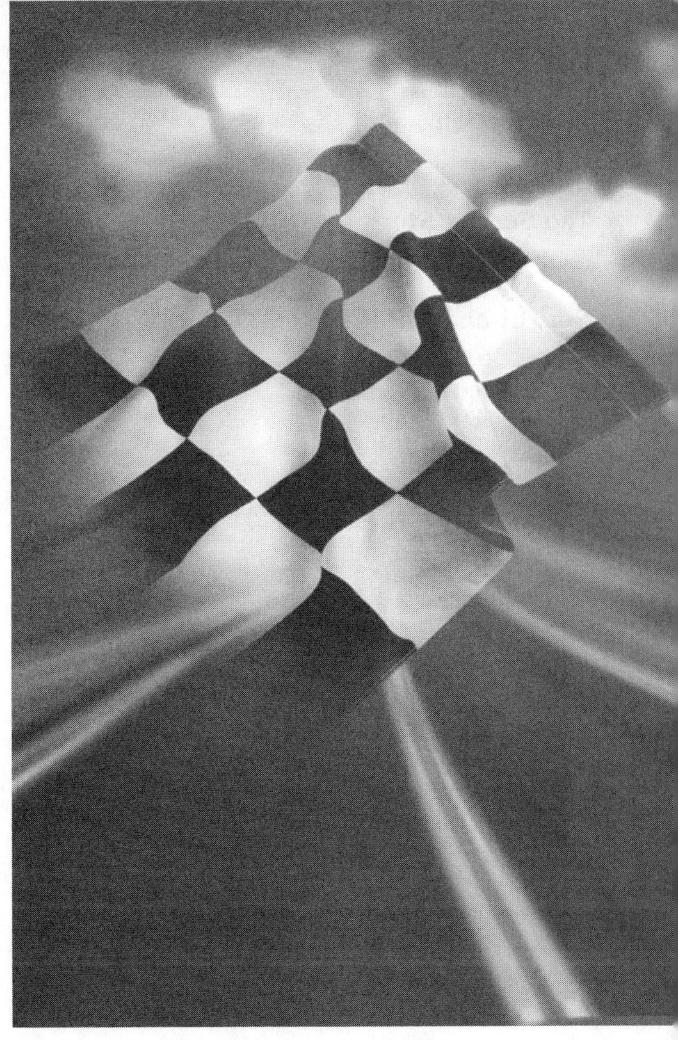

CHAPTER 3

JSP and Servlet Overview

OUTLINE

INTRODUCTION

This chapter helps you to prepare for the exam by providing an overview of JSP and servlet technologies. It does not directly address any of the objectives listed by Sun. It is general in scope, leaving the technical details to subsequent chapters. To pass the exam, you have to go deeper than just learning syntax. Memorizing without hands-on practice won't work. There are times when it helps to study how Sun designed its classes. Likewise, there are several places throughout the book where I offer a snippet from Tomcat's (or another open source container's) implementation and walk through its source code. You'll discover first-hand how a servlet container works. This chapter also helps you understand the market forces that shaped Java in general and servlets in particular. It also discusses where JSPs fit in the server-side pantheon of scripting technologies. Why even have JSP, since servlets are the real thing? The overview below will answer this question and others, answers that will demystify important issues.

THE SERVLET STORY

Once upon a time there was a lot of political testosterone. Responding to USSR's superpower-defining Sputnik satellite, the U.S. formed the Advanced Research Projects Agency (ARPA) in 1957. In those days computers were living in digital Babylon as none could understand its neighbor. Four years later, Leonard Kleinrock (MIT) wrote "Information Flow in Large Communication Nets," the first paper on packet-switching theory. MIT kept leading the way when in 1966 Lawrence G. Roberts proposed the first wide-scale network, known as the ARPANET plan. The Department of Defense (DoD) acknowledged the academics by, what turned out to be pivotal, commissioning the ARPANET in 1969. The ARPANET team rewarded the DoD by establishing the Network Control Protocol (NCP), the first host-to-host protocol, making it possible for university and research center computers to call each other.

Glad for the new business, AT&T installed the first cross-country link between UCLA and BBN. The world didn't know it at the time, but a vortex was born; something other than people was causing busy signals. By 1973, hundreds of computers between organizations, even across the ocean, were shoveling data to each other.

While the cross-country communication gap between industrial goliaths shortened, market pressure mounted for a way to connect PCs in the same room. That is when Bob Metcalfe invented Ethernet, which Xerox PARC helped to build. Then in 1974, Vint Cerf and Bob Kahn published a distance network scheme that eventually became the TCP/IP standard (1982). In this standard, several ideas found solid footing including Usenet, email, and others. In a related development, the Domain Name System established itself, which kicked the number of hosts up past 1,000 (1984).

In 1987, the National Science Foundation signed a cooperative agreement to manage the nascent Internet (NSFNET) backbone, weakened by multiplying hosts which had shot past 10,000 that year but reached several hundred thousand hosts by 1991. There was nobody in charge and the digital anarchy irritated one scientist. In 1991, Tim Berners-Lee was fed up with the way electronic documents worked, so he created hyperlinks. Not one to go partway, he needed links to talk to each other, so to make that possible he invented a whole protocol which he christened the World Wide Web.

The WWW crawled into a crowd as Gopher, WAIS, telnet, email, and many other services ruled the networks. All the activity and growth numbers were impressive, but no one was ready for what came next. In 1993, Marc Andersen and pals wanted to see what was on the Internet, so they developed a new computer program called the NCSA Mosaic (National Center for Supercomputing Applications at the University of Illinois) based on Berners-Lee's contraption. They gave it away!

Mosaic started a worldwide frenzy: The Internet exploded. Even the most optimistic proponents were shocked. In less than a decade, the number of hosts snowballed to nearly 200 million and the number of users approached one billion!

There is more news in the making. The Net is being invaded by a swarm of aliens that will dwarf the human user count. With the advent of Internet capability in non-PC devices including phones, GPS, PDAs, and even cars and refrigerators, the Internet is about to mushroom again as devices using the Net multiply, outnumbering people by several orders of magnitude.

Remarkably, the Internet is only a teenager. Our prodigy has no idea what it will do when it grows up. So, let's help it decide. As you will see in the next chapters, servlets and JSPs are tools we can use to direct all those bytes down the straight and narrow path. It is at the juncture between users and repositories where the Internet struggles most. If we could just close this distance, even a little, then our contribution will be very valuable. Admittedly, Java has its disappointments (Gosling and gang simply copied switch blocks from C without adding value such as allowing strings), but servlets are mighty because they have access to the entire Java API. Since JSPs metamorphose into servlets, the technology is very effective. It gives us intelligent bricks to build a wall around embattled OS warlords, rendering all their wares into one virtual platform.

SERVLET AND JSP HISTORY

The Internet's original purpose was to access and copy files from one computer to another far away (they already had short distance networks by then, but they were expensive, proprietary, and not ready for mass consumption). While TCP/IP provided a highway layer, the File Transfer Protocol (FTP) specification provided a standard way to exchange those files. It defined a way of shuttling them back and forth, but said nothing about looking at the content. HyperText Markup Language (HTML) allowed us to see the documents on the Internet. FTP can transmit HTML files just as easily as HTTP can. But we use Hypertext Transfer Protocol (HTTP) to act as an FTP specifically for HTML documents because it is a connectionless/ stateless protocol which makes having many short connections more efficient.

Now that we have discussed the plumbing, our attention turns to the content. What files should be published? Perhaps our data isn't in files, but in databases. Some of the content is old, but the majority of data is only days old. This immediacy drives traffic on the Internet.

With HTML running over HTTP, an end user can browse files housed on a distant server. This is useful, but live data is even better.

The Common Gateway Interface (CGI) specification allowed a Web server to reach beyond the file server and grab data from corporate databases. This also meant that CGI could change the HTML on-the-fly. The CGI specification was a major breakthrough in Web application development. The standard made sure that the same CGI program worked on different Web servers.

CGI became the most common means of delivering dynamic content. Alas, the pressure of the Internet was too much. CGI's performance just couldn't keep up because of a technical glitch where each request for a CGI script spawned a separate process. This design nibbled server resources off-hours but devoured them during peak loads. Further demand came, but, fortunately, better solutions came also. Functionality and scalability became key. Plain file-returning Web servers, even CGI-enabled ones, needed to mature into true application servers.

Many CGI derivatives sprouted as server-side programming solutions that implement business logic, including ASP, ColdFusion, PHP, and Perl. Java surpassed them all due to portability and its object oriented programming design.

Java has come a long way since its inception in 1991 when Sun launched "Project Green," which tried to integrate digitally controlled consumer devices like TV sets, CD players, and computers. OAK (a name which comes from an oak tree outside Gosling's window!) was born, but didn't come to life until HotJava and applets. This was a humble beginning. Sun threw the gauntlet down in 1995 by releasing Java as open source. The feedback was tremendous, and fixed more than just a few bugs. This drove Java deep into the server-side development industry.

Naturally, Sun packed Java with Internet functionality, and in June 1997 Sun announced the servlet interface. Servlets targeted CGI. Unlike CGI, which starts a process for each request, Servlets run in a single process using finer grain threads instead. Servlets represent a more efficient architecture, helping them withstand the Internet's mercurial crush. How can we possibly keep up? It's hard, but we can do it with Java servlets, which provide the foundation for developing Java Web components. One advantage to servlets is that the additional overhead for each additional simultaneous request the servlet handles is very small.

Servlets require real Java programming skills. However, the look and feel belongs to the marketing team. So, what can the graphics people do? They can thank Sun for JavaServer Pages (JSP), which was released in 1998. Inspired, some say copied, by the immensely successful Microsoft ASP, Sun made it easy to write dynamic HTML pages. With JSP, the marketing team can do their work, and with servlets the engineers can do theirs. Together, servlets and JSPs pages enable you to develop modular, maintainable, scalable, and portable Web applications. Another advantage is how Java provides a separation between JSPs, which are created by the marketers, and the JavaBeans they use, which are created by the engineers.

Web Servers and Servlet Containers

A servlet is a Java-coded Web component that runs in a container. It generates HTML content. It is pure Java, so the benefits and restrictions of regular Java classes apply. Servlets are compiled to platform-neutral bytecode. Upon request, this bytecode file is loaded into a container. Some containers (servlet engines) are integrated with the Web server, while others are plug-ins or extensions to Web servers that run inside the JVM. Servlets look the same as static Web pages (just a URL to the browser) to the client, but are really complete programs capable of complex operations.

The servlet container is an extension of a Web server in the same way CGI, ASP, and PHP are. A servlet functions like these, but the language is Java. The servlet doesn't talk to the client directly. The Web server does that. In a chain of processes, the client sends a request to the Web server, which hands it to the container, which hands it to the servlet (which sometimes hands it off yet again to a database or a JavaBean). The response retraces the course from the servlet to the container to the Web server to the client. Of course there are several other steps that happen too (JSP may need to be converted to servlet, and the TCP/IP packet hops from node to node). A snapshot of these steps is: Web server-> container-> servlet-> JavaBean-> DB.

The servlet architecture makes the container manage servlets through their lifecycle. The container invokes a servlet upon an HTTP request, providing that servlet with request information (stored in a request object) and the container configuration. The servlet goes about its deed. When finished, it hands back HTML and objects that hold information about the response. The container then forms an HTTP response and returns it to the client (see Figure 3.1).

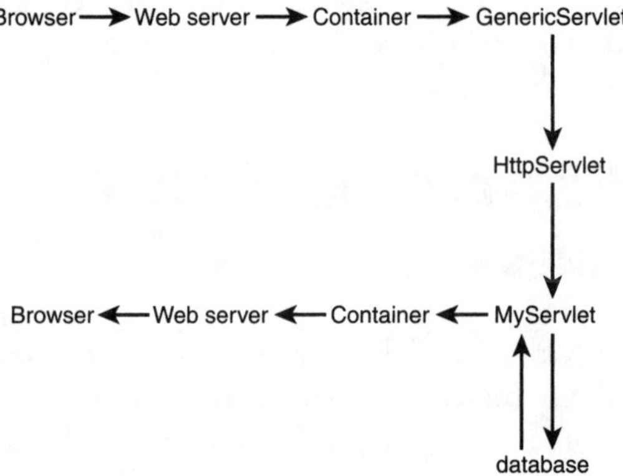

FIGURE 3.1
This is an example Web page.

The container itself is often written in Java, since the specification defines it as operating inside a JVM. Not surprisingly, vendors vary in their implementation, including writing their containers in other languages (C++ is popular) mimicking a Java environment. They argue the application server is faster that way.

Listing 3.1 is a template for your servlets. It won't compile as-is, but shows the main outline to get you started.

LISTING 3.1

A SERVLET TEMPLATE

```
/*
 * servlet name
 *
 * copyright notice
 *
 * author
 * date
 * version
 *
```

```
 * servlet description
 *
 */

//package declaration

//import statements

public class MyServlet
    extends HttpServlet {
{

//class member declarations

// Instance Variables

// Static Initializer

// Public Methods. Optional doHead, & other doXXX not
shown.

    /**
     * Initialize this servlet. Called only once in
➥lifetime
     */
    public void init() throws ServletException
    {
        // handle initialization chores
    }

    /**
     * This gets called with every request.
     * It is called first. The parent class already has
     * this method so you don't have to override it,
     * but you can.
     *
     * @param request The servlet request we are processing
     * @param response The servlet response we are creating
     *
     * @exception IOException if input/output error occurs
     * @exception ServletException if a servlet-specified
     * error occurs
     */
    protected void service(HttpServletRequest req,
                           HttpServletResponse resp)
        throws ServletException, IOException
    {
        //bypass doGet and doPost by handling request here.
        // perhaps:
            response.setContentType("text/plain");
            PrintWriter out = response.getWriter();
            StringBuffer html = new StringBuffer();
            html.append("<html>\n");
            html.append("<head><title>Servlet
➥Example</title>" +
```

continues

LISTING 3.1 *continued*

A SERVLET TEMPLATE

```
                           "</head>\n");
              html.append("<body>\n");
              html.append("Servlet Example");
              html.append("</body>");
              html.append("</html>");
              out.print( html.toString() );
              //you out.println() or use buffer as above.
      }

  /*The service method will process the request so the doGet
    and doPost methods are never called in this class. They
    are included to show you what they look like. You could
    remove the service method (the one here actually
    overrides the default one in the super class) and then
    the doGet and doPost methods will get called.
  */

      /**
       * Process a GET request for the specified resource.
       *
       * @param request The servlet request we are processing
       * @param response The servlet response we are creating
       *
       * @exception IOException if input/output error occurs
       * @exception ServletException if a servlet-specified
       * error occurs
       */
      protected void doGet(HttpServletRequest request,
                           HttpServletResponse response)
          throws IOException, ServletException
      {
          // Serve the requested resource,
          //  including the data content.
      }

      /**
       * Process a POST request for the specified resource.
       *
       * @param request The servlet request we are processing
       * @param response The servlet response we are creating
       *
       * @exception IOException if input/output error occurs
       * @exception ServletException if a servlet-specified
       * error occurs
       */
      protected void doPost(HttpServletRequest request,
                            HttpServletResponse response)
          throws IOException, ServletException
      {
          //often just throw it at doGet()
          doGet(request, response);
```

```
    }
    /**
     * Process a PUT request for the specified resource.
     *
     * @param request The servlet request we are processing
     * @param response The servlet response we are creating
     *
     * @exception IOException if input/output error occurs
     * @exception ServletException if a servlet-specified
     * error occurs
     */
    protected void doPut(HttpServletRequest req,
                         HttpServletResponse resp)
        throws ServletException, IOException
    {
        //rarely used
    }

    /**
     * A few more convenience methods
     */

    /**
     * last thing called in a servlet, a funeral method
     */
    public void destroy()
    {
       // clean up what init starts like DB connection
    }
}
```

The template is a useful blueprint for your servlet, but they can be as short as the program in Listing 3.2:

LISTING 3.2

A Short Example of a Servlet Program

```
import javax.servlet.http.HttpServlet;
import javax.servlet.http.HttpServletRequest;
import javax.servlet.http.HttpServletResponse;
import javax.servlet.ServletException;
import java.io.PrintWriter;
import java.io.IOException;


public class MyServlet extends HttpServlet
{

  public void service(HttpServletRequest request,
                      HttpServletResponse response)
```

continues

LISTING 3.2 *continued*

A SHORT EXAMPLE OF A SERVLET PROGRAM

```
        throws ServletException, IOException
      {
        response.setContentType("text/html");
        PrintWriter out = response.getWriter();
        out.println("<html>");
        out.println("<head><title>Servlet Error Handling " +
                    "Example</title></head>");
        out.println("<body>");
        out.println("A skimpy, but complete servlet.");
        out.println("</body>");
        out.println("</html>");
        //not necessary, but this is how you couldset the
    ➥status
        response.setStatus(HttpServletResponse.SC_OK);
      }
}
```

All servlet containers must support HTTP/1.0 as a protocol for requests and responses. They are not required to support HTTPS (HTTP over SSL), but may do so. Most containers implement the HTTP/1.1 specification as well. The container provides one or more Java Virtual Machines to support servlet execution. The servlet container instantiates objects that encapsulate client requests and server responses. The servlet container manages the servlet life cycle from loading and initialization, through the processing of requests and responses, to the eventual unloading and finalization of the servlets.

The servlet interface is the central abstraction of the servlet API. All servlets implement this interface. Usually, a servlet extends the `HttpServlet` class that implements the interface. In addition, the servlet container creates the `ServletContext` object, through which a servlet can log events, set and store attributes at the application level (across browsers) or session level (across pages, but same browser), and grab file paths.

JSP

JSPs are converted to servlets before the container runs them. This is a nice trick by Sun because non-programmers can create JSP pages.

Although JSP reduces the required skill level, JSP becomes a servlet, with the nice performance and portability benefits. Let's walk through the JSP-to-servlet process.

Listing 3.3 is a trivial JSP file:

LISTING 3.3

A TRIVIAL JSP FILE

```
<!--
  Simple demonstration of how Tomcat converts
  JSP to a servlet.
-->
<html>
<body>
Devyn likes <b>R/C Buggies</b>.
</body>
</html>
```

This JSP file was placed in the ...\jakarta-tomcat-4.0.1\webapps\examples\jsp directory. I requested the file with this: `http://localhost:8080/examples/jsp/jsp_servlet.jsp`. Tomcat converted the JSP code into a servlet source file, compiled it, and then invoked it. The servlet source file is located in ...\jakarta-tomcat-4.0.1\work\localhost\examples\jsp as jsp_0005fservlet$jsp.java. The source is shown in Listing 3.4, the translation of a trivial JSP file (see Listing 3.3):

LISTING 3.4

TRANSLATION OF JSP FILE INTO A SERVLET

```
package org.apache.jsp;

import javax.servlet.*;
import javax.servlet.http.*;
import javax.servlet.jsp.*;
import org.apache.jasper.runtime.*;


public class jsp_0005fservlet$jsp extends HttpJspBase {


    static {
    }
    public jsp_0005fservlet$jsp( ) {
```

continues

LISTING 3.4 *continued*

TRANSLATION OF JSP FILE INTO A SERVLET

```
    }

    private static boolean _jspx_inited = false;

    public final void _jspx_init()
          throws org.apache.jasper.runtime.JspException {
    }

    public void _jspService(HttpServletRequest request,
                            HttpServletResponse  response)
        throws java.io.IOException, ServletException {

        JspFactory _jspxFactory = null;
        PageContext pageContext = null;
        HttpSession session = null;
        ServletContext application = null;
        ServletConfig config = null;
        JspWriter out = null;
        Object page = this;
        String  _value = null;
        try {

            if (_jspx_inited == false) {
                synchronized (this) {
                    if (_jspx_inited == false) {
                        _jspx_init();
                        _jspx_inited = true;
                    }
                }
            }
            _jspxFactory = JspFactory.getDefaultFactory();
            response.setContentType("text/html;charset=" +
                                    "ISO-8859-1");
            pageContext = _jspxFactory.getPageContext(this,
                           request, response, "",
                           true, 8192, true);

            application = pageContext.getServletContext();
            config = pageContext.getServletConfig();
            session = pageContext.getSession();
            out = pageContext.getOut();

            // HTML // begin [file="/jsp/jsp_servlet.jsp"]
                out.write("<!--\r\n  Simple demonstration"+
                " of how Tomcat converts\r\n  JSP to a "+
                "servlet.\r\n-->\r\n<html>\r\n<body>"+
                "\r\nDevyn likes <b>R/C Buggies</b>."+
                "\r\n</body>\r\n</html>\r\n");

            // end
```

```
        } catch (Throwable t) {
            if (out != null && out.getBufferSize() != 0)
                out.clearBuffer();
            if (pageContext != null)
                   pageContext.handlePageException(t);
        } finally {
            if (_jspxFactory != null)
               jspxFactory.releasePageContext(pageContext);
        }
    }
}
   // servlet code generated from JSP source may vary
//from container to container
```

As you can see, Tomcat does a lot of work when it converts a JSP to a servlet. If you look at the source that is sent to your browser, you will see the original HTML in the JSP file. The plain HTML in a JSP is always passed through. What happens when we throw in a little Java syntax? I revised the JSP so that it contains two lines of Java code, as shown in Listing 3.5.

LISTING 3.5

JAVA CODE IN A JSP FILE

```
  <!--
    Simple demonstration of how Tomcat converts
    JSP to a servlet.
  -->
  <html>
  <body>
  Devyn likes <b>R/C Buggies</b>. <br>
  <%! int count = 100, factor=5; %>
   <%=count * factor%>
  </body>
</html>
```

Tomcat converts the Java embedded in the JSP (see Listing 3.5) to the following, which was at the top of the class:

```
  // begin [file="/jsp/jsp_servlet.jsp";from=(7,3);to=(7,31)]
         int count = 100, factor=5;
  // end
```

It also generates this version of the try block, which differed slightly from the previous servlet source:

```
  try {

      if (_jspx_inited == false) {
```

```
            synchronized (this) {
                if (_jspx_inited == false) {
                    _jspx_init();
                    _jspx_inited = true;
                }
            }
        }
        _jspxFactory = JspFactory.getDefaultFactory();
        response.setContentType("text/html;charset=ISO-8859-1");
        pageContext = _jspxFactory.getPageContext(this,
                              request, response,
                              "", true, 8192, true);

        application = pageContext.getServletContext();
        config = pageContext.getServletConfig();
        session = pageContext.getSession();
        out = pageContext.getOut();

        // HTML // begin [file="/jsp/jsp_servlet.jsp"…]
            out.write("<!--\r\n  Simple demonstration of how" +
            " Tomcat converts\r\n  JSP to a servlet.\r\n-->" +
            "\r\n<html>\r\n<body>\r\n" +
            "Devyn likes <b>R/C Buggies</b>. <br>\r\n");

        // end
        // HTML // begin [file="/jsp/jsp_servlet.jsp";from=…]
            out.write("\r\n ");

        // end
        // begin [file="/jsp/jsp_servlet.jsp";from=…]
            out.print(count * factor);
        // end
        // HTML // begin [file="/jsp/jsp_servlet.jsp";from=…]
            out.write("\r\n\r\n</body>\r\n</html>\r\n");

        // end

    }
```

You can see how Tomcat takes the top level count and factor variables declared at the top of the JSP and generates the declarations as class-level variables in the servlet. So, `<%=count * factor%>` becomes `out.print(count * factor);`.

Once the translation is completed, the servlet is compiled and loaded into memory. Every subsequent request for this JSP will trigger Tomcat to compare the modification date of the loaded servlet with the date of the JSP. If the JSP changes, Tomcat will translate and recompile it.

CHAPTER SUMMARY

In this chapter, you reviewed the history that led to servlet and JSP architecture. You learned, in broad terms, how servlet containers work. The following review and exam questions will test your knowledge of these topics and will help you to determine whether your knowledge of the API is sufficient to answer the questions you'll encounter in the certification exam.

KEY TERMS

- Servlet container
- Servlet life cycle
- Web application
- Thread safety
- Single thread model

APPLY YOUR KNOWLEDGE

Review Questions

1. What language is used to write servlets and JSP?
2. What is the servlet life cycle and what manages it?
3. What protocol do servlets and JSP use to communicate with clients?
4. What is the relationship between servlets and JSP?

Answers to Review Questions

1. Servlets are written in the Java language. JSPs on the other hand use a combination of HTML and Java. Eventually JSPs are converted into a pure Java servlet. See "Servlet and JSP History," earlier in this chapter.
2. The servlet life cycle refers to the loading, initialization, invoking, and killing of a servlet. The container manages this life cycle. See "Web Servers and Servlet Containers," earlier in this chapter.
3. Servlets use the HTTP protocol. See "Web Servers and Servlet Containers," earlier in this chapter.
4. JSPs are converted to servlets. First, the JSP source is parsed and a Java source file is generated. Then this source is compiled into a servlet. See "JSP," earlier in this chapter.

Suggested Readings and Resources

1. Java Servlet Technology, `http://java.sun.com/products/servlet/whitepaper.html`.
2. Exam objectives for the Sun Certified Web Component Developer for J2EE Platform, `http://suned.sun.com/US/certification/java/exam_objectives.html`.
3. The Java Servlet 2.3 Specification, `http://jcp.org/aboutJava/communityprocess/first/jsr053/index.html`.
4. The Java Servlet 2.3 API, `http://java.sun.com/products/servlet/2.3/javadoc/index.html`.
5. Sun's basic "Writing Servlets" tutorial: `http://developer.java.sun.com/developer/onlineTraining/Programming/BasicJava1/servlet.html`.
6. Another tutorial on learning servlets: `http://java.sun.com/docs/books/tutorial/servlets/index.html`.
7. The Servlet/JSP tutorial series by Marty Hall: `http://www.apl.jhu.edu/~hall/java/Servlet-Tutorial/`.
8. jGuru Tomcat FAQ: `http://www.jguru.com/faq/Tomcat`.

OBJECTIVES

This chapter covers the following objectives listed by Sun in "Section 1—The Servlet Model" and "Section 3—The Servlet Container Model."

1.1 For each of the HTTP methods, `GET`, `POST`, and `PUT`, identify the corresponding method in the `HttpServlet` class.

- The HTTP methods `GET`, `POST`, and `PUT` are how browsers and Web servers communicate the purpose of communication. A `GET` simply wants to retrieve a page without providing much information. A `POST`, however, can package lots of form or file information with its request. A `PUT` is for uploading a file. The `HttpServlet` class has a corresponding method for each HTTP method, including `doGet()`, `doPost()`, and `doPut()`.

1.2 For each of the HTTP methods, `GET`, `POST`, and `HEAD`, identify triggers that might cause a browser to use the method, and identify benefits or functionality of the method.

- This objective asks you to understand the events associated with each type of request. For example, clicking a hyperlink will send a `GET` request to a Web server, but clicking a Submit button (when the action is set to `"post"`) will send a `POST` request.

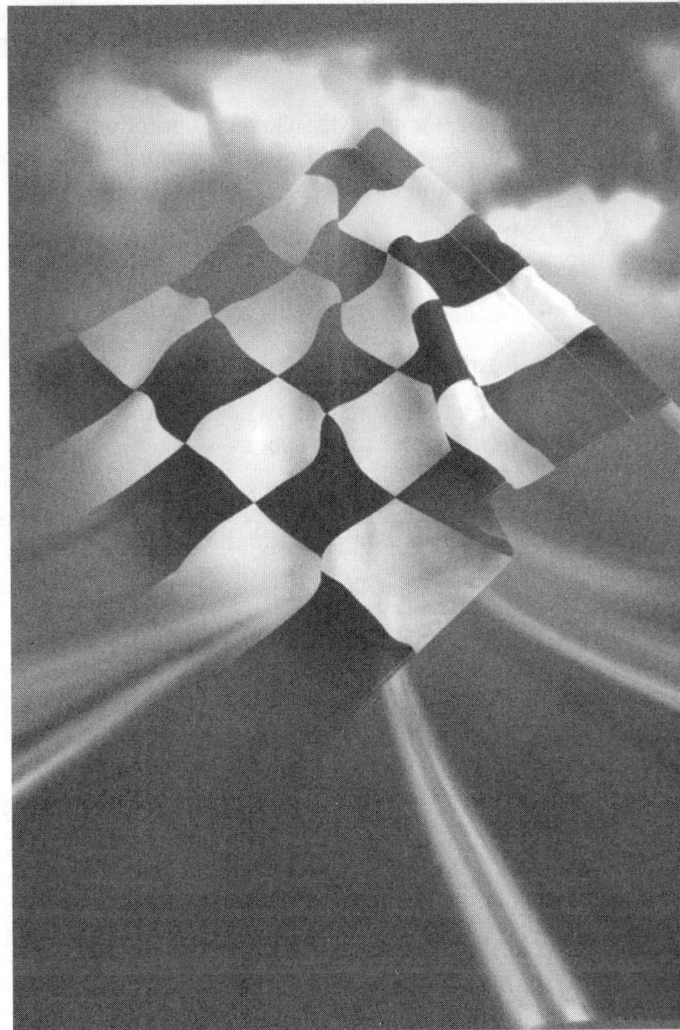

CHAPTER 4

Servlet Container Model

OBJECTIVES

1.3 For each of the following operations, identify the interface and method name that should be used to

- **Retrieve HTML form parameters from the request**
- **Retrieve a servlet initialization parameter**
- **Retrieve HTTP request header information**
- **Set an HTTP response header; set the content type of the response**
- **Acquire a text stream for the response**
- **Acquire a binary stream for the response**
- **Redirect an HTTP request to another URL**

▶ This objective is huge. It encompasses the heart of a servlet process, especially the request and response objects. The request parameters for the servlet are the strings sent by the client to the Servlet Container. The container parses the request and puts the information in an `HttpServletRequest` object which is passed to the servlet. Going the other way, the container wraps the response parameters in an `HttpServletResponse` object which is passed back to the container. The associated chapter section later in this chapter ("Overriding HttpServlet `GET`, `POST`, and `PUT` methods") goes into much detail on the methods involved.

1.4 Identify the interface and method to access values and resources and to set object attributes within the following three Web scopes:

- **Request**
- **Session**
- **Context**

▶ This objective addresses the idea of scope. When something has Context scope, it is application-wide and all users can share data. Session scope means one user can share data across page views, but other users can't. Request scope restricts data to only that page.

1.5 Given a life-cycle method, identify correct statements about its purpose or about how and when it is invoked. These methods are

- **`init`**
- **`service`**
- **`destroy`**

▶ The container manages the servlet life-cycle. This part of the chapter explains, with examples, how the container initializes a servlet with a call to the `init()` method. Then it calls the `service()` method upon every request. Finally, when the servlet is about to be removed from memory, the container calls its `destroy()` method. This gives the servlet one last chance to clean up resources.

1.6 Use a `RequestDispatcher` to include or forward to a Web resource.

▶ The `RequestDispatcher` object is the servlet forwarding mechanism. You will see in the section "Servlet Life-cycle" how you can transfer processing of the request from one servlet to another (which the browser will be unaware of). This is how a servlet can pass the request to some other Web component within the same Web container.

3.1 Identify the uses for and the interfaces (or classes) and methods to achieve the following features:

- **Servlet context initialization parameters**
- **Servlet context listener**
- **Servlet context attribute listener**
- **Session attribute listeners**

▶ These elements let you get and monitor servlet attributes. Not only can you get them and change them too, but you can actually put in place behavior to occur when an attribute changes. The listeners are event-driven triggers. When an attribute changes, special targeted methods are called.

OBJECTIVES

In them, you can define special actions, such as adding a note to the log every time the user count changes (perhaps a context attribute called counter).

3.3 Distinguish the behavior of the following in a distributable:

- **Servlet context initialization parameters**
- **Servlet context listener**
- **Servlet context attribute listener**
- **Session attribute listeners**

▶ As explained in the previous objective, these elements let you get and monitor Servlet attributes. There is a difference here in that Sun wants you to understand how this works in a distributable Web application.

OUTLINE

Outline

Study Strategies

- The key to this section of the exam is understanding how servlets implement the Servlet interface, which defines life-cycle methods. The Servlet Container (such as Apache Tomcat) is itself an application that monitors a port on a given IP address. Servlets generate responses to HTTP requests. To do so, the container loads your servlet (if it isn't in memory already) and calls the methods defined in the interface. This is the foundation of servlet and JSP architecture.
- There are many methods to know. It is easier if you learn the methods in groups according to theme. For example, write a servlet that has HttpServlet methods which handle all three GET, POST, and PUT types of request.
- Each JavaServer Page is transformed into a servlet that is compiled and then loaded. Therefore much of what you learn here applies to the JSP section of the exam too.

INTRODUCTION

JSP and servlets have greatly enhanced the way in which you can create and manage Web pages. The difficulty level of coding JSP is between that of coding HTML and pure Java. Servlets are pure Java. The idea behind having both is providing a way for non-programmers to contribute functionality through JSP. You can "program" a JSP page almost as easily as you can write an HTML page. For simple tasks like displaying the current date, you write a normal HTML page and add only a small amount of Java as a scriptlet. For big tasks like processing a shopping cart, you use JSP as the mediator between the Web form and a component(s) (bean or servlet) that has all the horsepower. Most of the code in a Web application will go into servlets. The JSP portion is a soft front end to the application that, typically, marketing can use comfortably.

There is a lot that happens when a servlet is invoked. This chapter covers much material that explains each step of the process. At this point, it will help to provide an overview of what happens in a typical JSP/servlet request. The sequence of events starts with a browser sending a request to a Web server. The server hands the request to a Servlet Container. The container loads the servlet (if it isn't already loaded), instantiates a request and response objects, and then hands these objects to the servlet by calling first its `init()` method, then its `service()` method, and lastly the `destroy()` method. The `service()` method will typically call one of the `doXXX()` methods such as `doGet()`.

All these steps are covered in detail later in this chapter. Presently, just review the overall process presented in Figure 4.1.

Let's study an example of a servlet. The following is a fully functioning, albeit trivial, servlet example. Listing 4.1 represents all that is required to have a complete servlet.

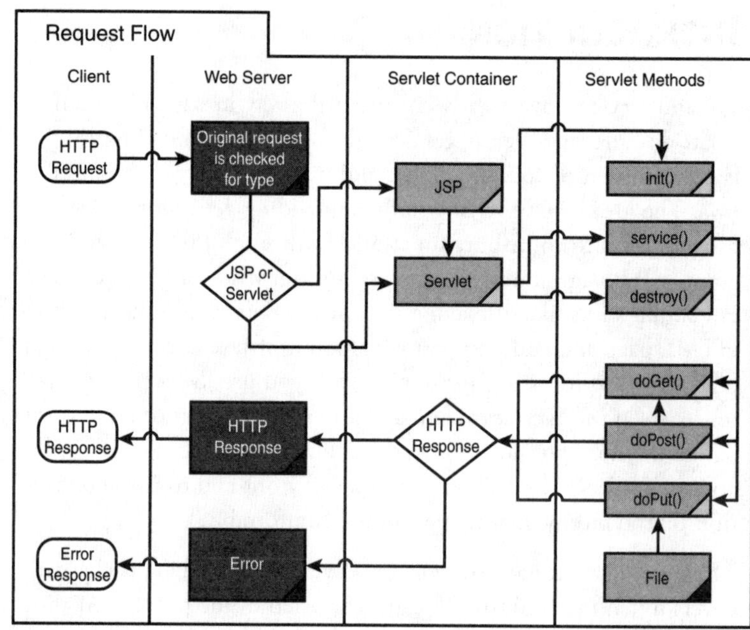

FIGURE 4.1
Servlet handling of an HTTP Request.

LISTING 4.1

The Source Code of a Minimum Servlet

```
/* SimpleServletExample.java, v 1.0
 *
 */

import java.io.*;
import javax.servlet.*;
import javax.servlet.http.*;

/**
 * A simple servlet.
 * SCWCD Exam Objective 1.1 = doGet(), doPost(), doPut()
 *
 * @author Reader@Que
 */

public class SimpleServletExample extends HttpServlet
{
    // doGet() - SCWCD Exam Objective 1.1
    public void doGet(HttpServletRequest request,
                      HttpServletResponse response)
        throws IOException, ServletException
    {
```

```
        // set the MIME type
        response.setContentType("text/html");

        // use this to print to browser
        PrintWriter out = response.getWriter();

        out.println("<html>");
        out.println("<head>");
        out.println("<title> A simple servlet. </title>");
        out.println("</head>");
        out.println("<body>");
        out.println("<h1>Simple Servlet</h1>");
        out.println("This is a trivial " +
                    "example of a servlet.");
        out.println("</body>");
        out.println("</html>");
    }
}
```

Listing 4.1 showed you an example of a servlet. The code is ordinary, but notice one small thing about printing to the browser. This example uses `PrintWriter` instead of using `ServletOutputStream`. The former is used for text, while the latter is used for bytes. See Figure 4.2 for a picture of the output. Listing 4.2 is the HTML the servlet generates and sends to the browser.

LISTING 4.2

THE SOURCE CODE RETURNED TO THE BROWSER BY LISTING 4.1

```
  <html>
  <head>
  <title> A simple servlet. </title>
  </head>
  <body>
  <h1>Simple Servlet</h1>
  This is a trivial example of a servlet.
  </body>
</html>
```

The HTML in Listing 4.2 is rendered by a browser so that it looks like Figure 4.2.

FIGURE 4.2
You can create dynamic content using a servlet.

IN THE FIELD

HOW DOES A SERVLET WORK?

You write a servlet and compile it, and then place it in the appropriate directory. When the Servlet Container starts, it will preload your servlet in memory if specified in the web.xml configuration file. If your servlet is not already loaded (not listed in the web.xml configuration file), its instance will be created as soon as a request for it is received by the Servlet Container. The first time it is loaded, the container calls your servlet's `init()` method, if there is one. Notice that it gets called only once, so place one-off functionality in this method (such as database connection, file object). Now that your servlet is ready, it waits for requests. The container will call your `service()` method each time a request is received for your servlet. The `HttpServlet` class (which your servlet must extend) already has this method, so you don't have to write one, but you can override it. The `service()` method then passes the request on to the appropriate method (usually `GET` for simple requests and `POST` to submit data, say a Web page form) such as the `doGet()` method if it is a `GET` request, or the `doPost()` method if it is a `POST` request. The `doXXX()` methods are the ones you need to override and where you will spend most of your effort. The servlet processes the request (code you write in `doGet()`), returning a response to the container. The container sends the text of the response back to the browser.

The preceding JSP and servlet examples are part of a Web application. A Web application is a collection of servlets, JSP pages, HTML documents, and other Web resources (such as image files, compressed archives, and other data). This collection may be packaged into an archive or exist as separate files in an open directory structure. Since you have many servlet classes, JSP pages, HTML pages, and other supporting libraries and files for a given Web application, there are many dependencies. These are not trivial to manage. It is vital that all parts go in their correct locations in the Web application archive or in an open directory structure. Once you get the dependencies resolved, it is a good idea to package the collection into a Web application archive, a single file with the .war extension that contains all of the components of a Web application. You can do this using standard JAR tools.

Now, we need to define what is meant regarding deploying a Web application. Normally, Web applications run on only one VM at any one time. When we talk about deploying a Web application, we mean that the collection of files that comprise a Web application is placed into a Web server's runtime (at least one part goes into JVM, which can then link to or grab other parts). What happens if you want to deploy your Web application in a Web farm? In this case, your Web application will run on several VMs simultaneously.

A distributable Web application is written so that it can be deployed in a Web container, distributed across multiple Java virtual machines running on the same host or different hosts. The two keys to making this possible are how you thread the servlets and what you tell the deployment descriptor. With the right combination of these, your Web application will run on several VMs simultaneously. The servlet declaration, which is part of the deployment descriptor, controls how the Servlet Container provides instances of the servlet. Normally, the Servlet Container uses only one instance per servlet declaration. However, for a servlet implementing the SingleThreadModel interface, the Servlet Container may instantiate multiple instances to handle a heavy request load and serialize requests to a particular instance.

In the case where a servlet is marked in the deployment descriptor as distributable and the application implements the SingleThreadModel interface, the container may instantiate multiple instances of that servlet in each VM of the container or across many machines (clustering servlets usually through serialization). The container has a complicated task in managing requests, sessions, and contexts across JVMs. How each vendor accomplishes this is beyond the scope of this book. You do need to know that to convert your Web application into a distributable one, you must implement the SingleThreadModel interface and mark the servlet as distributable in the deployment descriptor (see Chapter 10, "Web Applications," for more about web.xml).

OVERRIDING HTTPSERVLET GET, POST, AND PUT METHODS

1.1 For each of the HTTP methods, `GET`, `POST`, and `PUT`, identify the corresponding method in the `HttpServlet` class.

- **`GET`**
- **`POST`**
- **`PUT`**

This exam objective addresses the most-used feature of servlets, namely, responding to HTTP requests. The exam will have several questions on this topic. These three types of requests dominate browser-server traffic.

The following code is a minimal template showing you how to use the GET, POST, and PUT methods. GET appends data to the URL before the URL is submitted to the server, whereas POST sends the data to the server separately from the URL. GET submissions can only be 1KB in length in most cases, whereas POST submissions can be arbitrarily large. The results of a GET submission can be reliably bookmarked, whereas the results of a POST submission can't. There are several differences between them which are explained later in this section.

These methods are called by the service method (not required in your servlet as it is in HttpServlet, as this method is inherited from HttpServlet). Together they can look like Listing 4.3.

LISTING 4.4

SERVLET THAT HANDLES GET, POST, AND PUT REQUESTS

```
/* doGetdoPostdoPutServlet.java, v 1.0
* SCWCD Exam Objective 1.1 = doGet(), doPost(), doPut()
 *
 */

import java.io.*;
import javax.servlet.*;
import javax.servlet.http.*;

/**
 * A servlet that reports back to the browser
 * the type of request received.
 *
 * @author Reader@Que
 */

public class doGetdoPostdoPutServlet extends HttpServlet
{
    // doGet() - SCWCD Exam Objective 1.1
    public void doGet(HttpServletRequest request,
                      HttpServletResponse response)
        throws IOException, ServletException
    {
        reportType("doGet", response);
    }
```

```
    // doPost() - SCWCD Exam Objective 1.1
    public void doPost(HttpServletRequest request,
                      HttpServletResponse response)
        throws IOException, ServletException
    {
        reportType("doPost", response);
    }

    // doPut() - SCWCD Exam Objective 1.1
    public void doPut(HttpServletRequest request,
                      HttpServletResponse response)
        throws IOException, ServletException
    {
        reportType("doPut", response);
    }

    public void reportType(String requestType,
                           HttpServletResponse response)
        throws IOException, ServletException
    {
        // set the MIME type
        response.setContentType("text/html");

        // use this to print to browser
        PrintWriter out = response.getWriter();

        out.println("<html>");
        out.println("<head>");
        out.println("<title>doGetdoPostdoPutServlet" +
                    "</title>");
        out.println("</head>");
        out.println("<body>");
        out.println("<h1>Your Request</h1>");
        out.println("Your request type: " + requestType);
        out.println("</body>");
        out.println("</html>");
    }
}
```

Listing 4.3 sends a basic HTML message back to the browser that looks like Figure 4.3.

FIGURE 4.3
Filtering request types using a servlet.

It is the service method that calls the `doXXX()` methods. While you normally wouldn't override the service method, Listing 4.4 presents a skeleton example of what you could do with it. You might want to preprocess the request before sending it on to the appropriate `doXXX()` method.

LISTING 4.4

SERVICE METHOD EXAMPLE

```
  protected void service(HttpServletRequest req,
                         HttpServletResponse resp)
      throws ServletException, IOException
  {
       String method = req.getMethod();

       if (method.equals(METHOD_GET))
       {
           doGet(req, resp);
       } else if (method.equals(METHOD_POST))
       {
           doPost(req, resp);
       } else if (method.equals(METHOD_PUT))
       {
           doPut(req, resp);
       } else
       {
          // Servlet doesn't currently support
          // other types of request.
          String errMsg = "Method Not Supported");
          resp.sendError(
             HttpServletResponse.SC_NOT_IMPLEMENTED, errMsg);
       }
}
```

GET

The `GET` type request is normally used for simple HTML page requests. It has this syntax:

```
public void doGet(HttpServletRequest request,
                  HttpServletResponse response)
    throws IOException, ServletException
   { //your code here}
```

When you write a servlet, this is the one method that you will start with. If this method is all you had in your servlet, it would handle the majority of your Web server's needs regarding this servlet.

Notice, that the `init()` and `service()` methods involved in a request are already provided by the `HttpServlet` class, so they don't need to be overridden, although you can do so.

The `GET` is the most common type of browser request. According to the Hypertext Transfer Protocol standard, the `GET` method means "retrieve whatever information (in the form of an entity) is identified by the Request-URI." For a full discussion on naming and addressing (URL vs. URI) please see `http://www.w3.org/Addressing/`. If the Request-URI refers to a data-producing process, it is the produced data which shall be returned as the entity in the response and not the source text of the process, unless that text happens to be the output of the process." In our example, the test message is the entity.

IN THE FIELD

GET METHOD

The `GET` is the most common type of browser request. The `GET` request is defined by the Internet Society's RFC 2616: Hypertext Transfer Protocol—HTTP/1.1. See section 9.3 of RFC 2616 at `ftp://ftp.isi.edu/in-notes/rfc2616.txt`.

This method is where your servlet does most of its labor. You could process a simple HTML response or hit a database with a query.

Table 4.1 provides a list of differences between `GET` and `POST` requests.

TABLE 4.1

GET VS. POST REQUEST

GET	*POST*
Query string or form data is simply appended to the URL as name-value pairs.	Form name-value pairs are sent in the body of the request, not in the URL itself.
Query length is limited (~1KB).	Query length is unlimited.
Users can see data in address bar.	Data hidden from users.

continues

TABLE 4.1 *continued*

GET VS. POST REQUEST

GET	*POST*
`http://mycompany.com/support?Name=John+Smith&Product=go+kart&Complaint=the+engine+is+sputtering+oil`.	`http://mycompany.com/support` <values of Name, Product, and Complaint are in request body>.
`doGet()`.	`doPost()`.
For getting (retrieving) data only.	For causing a change on the server (store data in DB).
ASCII.	ASCII + Binary.
Easy to bookmark.	Hard to bookmark.
Used more.	Used less.

The following short listings exemplify the `GET` and `POST` requests

```
<html>
 <body>
  <form method="GET" action="/myservlet/process">
   <input type="text" name="product" size="25"
    maxlength="35" value="type product name here">
   <input type="submit" name="submitButton" value="Submit">
  </form>
 </body>
</html>
```

```
<html>
 <body>
  <form method="post" action="/myservlet/process">
   <input type="text" name="product" size="25"
    maxlength="35" value="type product name here">
   <input type="submit" name="submitButton" value="Submit">
  </form>
 </body>
</html>
```

POST

The `POST` type request is most often used by HTML forms. It has this syntax:

```
public void doPost(HttpServletRequest request,
                   HttpServletResponse response)
    throws IOException, ServletException
   { //your code here}
```

The POST method is more sophisticated than a GET request. Normally, a Web form has fields whose names and values are sent to the server in key-value pairs. The POST is designed for posting long messages (for example, to a bulletin board, newsgroup, mailing list); providing a block of data, such as the result of submitting a form; and submitting long data fields to a database (such as a SQL insert of lengthy string). Sometimes the action performed by the POST method doesn't return a standard HTML page. Suppose you updated a database table. The database doesn't send back an HTML confirmation on its own. You would have to wrap the database results in HTML manually. You also have the option of sending back an empty response with a header status of either 200 (OK) or 204 (No Content). A No Content status tells the browser that it shouldn't expect any HTML. You might want to do this if it is software to software interaction and no eyeballs are waiting to see a Web page.

IN THE FIELD

POST METHOD

The POST is the most sophisticated of the methods covered by this part of the exam. The POST request is defined by the Internet Society's RFC 2616: Hypertext Transfer Protocol—HTTP/1.1. See section 9.5 of RFC 2616 at ftp://ftp.isi.edu/in-notes/rfc2616.txt.

Normally, this method is used to process a form submitted by a browser. You will very likely be looking for form field names and values. For example, the following snippet is how you would grab the value of the field formCountField that the user supplied a value for:

```
//read the query string
int customerRequest = 0;
String count = request.getParameter("formCountField");
try
{
    customerRequest = Integer.parseInt(count);
} catch (Exception e)
{ // NumberFormat or NullPointerException
    processError(e);
}
```

PUT

The PUT type request is a means of uploading files to the server. While uploading is its original intent, I have not seen it used much. Instead, POST is generally used to upload files. The PUT handler has this syntax:

```
public void doPut(HttpServletRequest request,
                  HttpServletResponse response)
    throws IOException, ServletException
   { //your code here}
```

The doPut() method is called by the server (via the service method) to handle a PUT request. Uploading files from a browser has always been difficult. The idea behind the PUT operation is to make uploading straightforward. It is supposed to allow a client to place a file on the server, just like sending a file by FTP. The javadoc for this method warns that when overriding this method, you should leave intact any content headers sent with the request (including Content-Length, Content-Type, Content-Transfer-Encoding, Content-Encoding, Content-Base, Content-Language, Content-Location, Content-MD5, and Content-Range). This method is rarely used, but it is powerful if you need it.

Listing 4.5 is a simplified HTML page that creates a file upload page that will direct the file contents to a servlet.

LISTING 4.5

HTML Form Example

```
   <html>
   <body>
   <form enctype="multipart/form-data" method="PUT"
   action="localhost:8080/examples/servlet/UploadServlet">
   <input type="file" size="20" name="FileToUpload"
   value="Select File">
   <input type="submit" name="UploadFile" value="Upload">
   <input type="reset" value="Reset">
   </form>
   </body>
</html>
```

Listing 4.6 is a servlet that can accept an uploaded file.

LISTING 4.6

SERVLET THAT HANDLES A FILE UPLOAD FROM THE CLIENT

```
import java.io.*;
import java.util.*;
import java.net.*;
import javax.servlet.*;
import javax.servlet.http.*;

public class UploadServlet extends HttpServlet
{
        static final String dir="C:/temp";

        public void doPut(HttpServletRequest req,
        HttpServletResponse res)
        throws ServletException, IOException
        {
          PrintWriter outHTML = res.getWriter();
          outHTML.println("done");

          try
          {
                int i;
                InputStream input;
                input = req.getInputStream();
                BufferedInputStream in =
                      new BufferedInputStream(input);
                BufferedReader reader =
                      new BufferedReader(
                          new InputStreamReader(in));
                File outputFile =
                      new File("c:/temp/out.txt");
                FileWriter out =
                      new FileWriter(outputFile);

                while ((i = reader.read()) != -1)
                {
                    out.write(i);
                }

                out.close();
                in.close();

            }
            catch (IOException e) {}
        }
}
```

You need to account for the header and footer lines that the stream attaches to the actual file contents. The stream looks like this:

```
------------BB1rHqKAOHkiUoiFS3VI6v
Content-Disposition: form-data; name="FileToUpload";
                                 filename="Candle.txt"
Content-Type: application/octet-stream; name="Candle. txt"

// ...
//actual file content here
// ...

------------BB1rHqKAOHkiUoiFS3VI6v
Content-Disposition: form-data; name="UploadFile"

Upload
------------BB1rHqKAOHkiUoiFS3VI6v
```

Therefore, you will need to search (`indexOf`) for the start of the actual file content by looking for the Content-Type and subsequent name parameters like so:

```
int headerEnd = line.indexOf("Content-Type: ");
headerEnd = line.indexOf("name=\"", headerEnd);
headerEnd = line.indexOf("\"", headerEnd + 7); //last quote
```

Likewise, you need to search the end of the file for the telltale Content-Disposition and preceding "------------" marker like so:

```
int footerStart =
              line.lastIndexOf ("Content- Disposition: ");
footerStart = line.lastIndexOf ("---------", footerStart);
```

Lastly, you will grab the text between the two like so:

```
fileContent = line.substring(headerEnd, footerStart);
```

You can refer to RFC 1867 to learn more about uploading files through an HTML form (`www.servlets.com/rfcs/rfc1867.html`). This is all tedious, so you might just grab an open source (`http://www.servlets.com/cos/index.html`) or commercial Bean that uploads files such as uploadBean (`www.javazoom.net/jzservlets/uploadbean/uploadbean.html`) or jspSmartUpload (`www.jspsmart.com/`).

Listing 4.6 worked when placed in the `doPost()` method (and the form method of Listing 4.5 is set to post), but did not work in the `doPut()` method using IE or Opera against Tomcat (version 4). I verified that the `doPut()` method is called as expected in the servlet. However, even after much tweaking, this file upload code failed when placed in the `doPut` method as shown previously.

If you only change `doPut` to `doPost` it works?! Although I need to research this problem with Tomcat, you do need to understand that `PUT` is used to upload files to a Web server and that this is usually done by non-browser, client-side Web content development tools.

Triggering HttpServlet GET, POST, and PUT Methods

1.2 For each of the HTTP methods, GET, POST, and HEAD, identify triggers that might cause a browser to use the method, and identify benefits or functionality of the method.

- **GET**
- **POST**
- **HEAD**

This exam objective focuses on what triggers the events or methods in your servlets. For example, what action can a client take that results in the `doGet()` method being called in your servlet?

GET

As noted previously, the `GET` type request is normally used for simple HTML page requests. The types of events that generate this type of request are clicking on a hyperlink, changing the address directly by typing in the address textbox on a browser or application that has HTML functionality, and submitting an HTML form where the method header is set to `get` as in `method=get`. Also, a `GET` request is triggered when selecting a favorite from the Favorites list and using JavaScript to change `location.href`. Usually the browser is configured to send a `GET` request even if no method is set explicitly by the HTML.

The benefits of the `GET` method are

- It retrieves information such as a simple HTML page or the results of a database query.
- It supports query strings (name-value pairs appended to URL). Servers usually limit query strings to about 1,000 characters.
- It allows bookmarks.

POST

This occurs when a browser or application submits an HTML form with the method attribute set to post as in `method=post`.

The benefits of the `POST` method are

- It sends information to the server such as form fields, large text bodies, and key-value pairs.
- It hides form data because it isn't passed as a query string, but in the message body.
- It sends unlimited length data as part of its HTTP request body.
- It disallows bookmarks.

HEAD

A browser or application will sometimes send a request to a server just to check the status or get information (for example, "can you handle file upload?") from the server.

The `HEAD` method returns the same header lines that a `GET` method would return; however, no body or content is returned. This is often accomplished by calling `doGet()`, setting the headers but not setting any output, and then returning the response (without any body) to the requester.

The primary benefit of this method is message size. The `HEAD` method receives and returns very small messages. Therefore it is fast and lightweight on both ends.

INTERFACING WITH HTML REQUESTS

In this section we deal with interfacing with HTML requests: how to process them and how to return a response to one. Since the HTTP client is sending the request, how do you know what it wants? While the container handles things like parsing the request and placing the information into a Request object, sometimes you have manually code processing routines. This section tells you how to write these routines that perform actions such as retrieve HTML form parameters, request headers, servlet initialization parameters, and redirects.

1.3 For each of the following operations, identify the interface and method name that should be used to

- **Retrieve HTML form parameters from the request**
- **Retrieve a servlet initialization parameter**
- **Retrieve HTTP request header information**
- **Set an HTTP response header; set the content type of the response**
- **Acquire a text stream for the response**
- **Acquire a binary stream for the response**
- **Redirect an HTTP request to another URL**

This is a broad-stroke objective. It is asking you to be familiar with the most important servlet interfaces and their methods. Thankfully, this objective reduces the task from remembering almost 1,000 methods to just a few of them, which happen to be the most interesting ones.

Form Parameters

The interface that defines the form parameter methods is `ServletRequest`. This interface is implemented by the Web container to get the parameters from a request. Parameters are sent in the query string or posted form data. The four methods associated with getting parameters are

- `getParameter(String)`. You use this method if you know the particular parameter name. It returns the value of a request parameter as a string, or null if the parameter does not exist. Use this method when you are sure the parameter has only one value; otherwise use `getParameterValues()`. Be careful: If you use this method with a multivalued parameter, you won't get an error. You will get the first value in the array returned by `getParameterValues()`.
- `getParameterMap()`. You use this method to create a map of the form parameters supplied with this request.
- `getParameterNames()`. This one returns an `Enumeration` of string objects containing the names of the parameters contained in this request, or an empty `Enumeration` if the request has no parameters.

- `getParameterValues(String)`. This method returns an array of values as strings, or null if the parameter does not exist. If the parameter has a single value, the array has a length of 1. One of the common uses of `getParameterValues()` is for processing <select> lists that have their "multiple" attribute set.

Listing 4.7, the following code snippet, demonstrates how you would grab the parameters from a request.

LISTING 4.7

SERVLET THAT WALKS THE REQUEST PARAMETER LIST

```
import java.io.*;
import java.util.*;
import javax.servlet.*;
import javax.servlet.http.*;

public class ShowRequestParameters extends HttpServlet
{
    public void doPost(HttpServletRequest request,
                       HttpServletResponse response)
    throws IOException, ServletException
    {
        Enumeration parameterNames =
                    request.getParameterNames();

        // acquire text stream for response
        PrintWriter out = res.getWriter ();

        while (parameterNames.hasMoreElements()) {
            String name =
                (String)parameterNames.nextElement();
            String value = request.getParameter(name);
            out.println(name + " = " + value + "<br/>");
        }
    }
}
```

Retrieving a Servlet Initialization Parameter

A Web application includes many parts; it rarely is just one class or file. It can be a combination of JSP pages, servlets, tag libraries, Java beans, and other class files. The Java Virtual Machine creates a memory box for all of these called a `ServletContext` object which maintains information (context) about your Web application.

You access the `ServletContext` for information about the application state. As the API states, the `ServletContext` allows you access many types of information. You can get application-level initialization parameters. You can also set and get application attributes, as well as the major and minor version of the Servlet API that this Servlet Container supports. One very interesting capability is to get hold of `RequestDispatcher` object to forward requests to other application components within the server, or to include responses from certain components within the servlet and to log a message to application log file. The `ServletContext` object is how you can set, get, and change application (not session) level attributes and talk to the Servlet Container.

Context means application scope. The `getInitParameter` and `getInitParameterNames` methods retrieve context-wide, application-wide, or "Web application" parameters. The `getInitParameter` method returns a string containing the value of the parameter (you provide the name), or null if the parameter does not exist.

Some parameters have no information, so this method will return a string containing at least the Servlet Container name and version number. The `getInitParameterNames` method retrieves the names of the servlet's initialization parameters as an Enumeration of string objects. If there aren't any, it returns an empty Enumeration. Be careful; don't confuse this with session-wide attributes.

Listing 4.8 shows an example of displaying servlet initialization parameters.

LISTING 4.8

SERVLET THAT WALKS THE CONTEXT INITIALIZATION PARAMETER LIST

```
import java.io.IOException;
import java.io.PrintWriter;
import java.util.Enumeration;
import javax.servlet.*;
import javax.servlet.http.*;

public class InitializationParameters extends HttpServlet
{
    /**
     * Print servlet configuration init. parameters.
     *
     * @param request The servlet request we are processing
```

continues

LISTING 4.8 *continued*

SERVLET THAT WALKS THE CONTEXT INITIALIZATION PARAMETER LIST

```
     * @param response The servlet response we are creating
     *
     * @exception IOException if an input/output error
     * @exception ServletException for a
     * servlet-specified error
     */
    public void doGet(HttpServletRequest request,
                      HttpServletResponse response)
        throws IOException, ServletException
    {

        response.setContentType("text/html");
        PrintWriter writer = response.getWriter();

        // servlet configuration initialization parameters
        writer.println("<h1>ServletConfig " +
                       "Initialization Parameters</h1>");
        writer.println("<ul>");
        Enumeration params =
                getServletConfig().getInitParameterNames();
        while (params.hasMoreElements())
        {
            String param = (String) params.nextElement();
            String value =
                getServletConfig().getInitParameter(param);
            writer.println("<li><b>" + param +
                           "</b> = " + value);
        }
        writer.println("</ul>");
        writer.println("<hr>");
    }
}
```

Retrieving HTTP Request Header Information

The request header is where all the details of the request are bundled. This is where the browser specifies the file wanted, date, image file support, and more. Listing 4.9 shows a popular way to display the header parameters by walking through an Enumeration of them.

LISTING 4.9

SERVLET THAT DISPLAYS THE HTTP HEADER INFORMATION

```
import java.io.*;
import java.text.*;
import java.util.*;
import javax.servlet.*;
import javax.servlet.http.*;

/**
 * Displaying request headers
 *
 * @author Reader@Que
 */

public class DisplayRequestHeaders extends HttpServlet {

    public void doGet(HttpServletRequest request,
                      HttpServletResponse response)
        throws IOException, ServletException
    {
        response.setContentType("text/html");

        PrintWriter out = response.getWriter();
        out.println("<html>");
        out.println("<head>");

        String title = "Requestheader Example";
        out.println("<title>" + title + "</title>");
        out.println("</head>");
        out.println("<body>");

        out.println("<h3>" + title + "</h3>");
        out.println("<table>");
        Enumeration e = request.getHeaderNames();
        while (e.hasMoreElements())
        {
            String headerName = (String)e.nextElement();
            String headerValue =
                         request.getHeader(headerName);
            out.println("<tr><td bgcolor=\"#CCCCCC\">" +
                         headerName);
            out.println("</td><td>" + headerValue +
                        "</td></tr>");
        }
        out.println("</table>");
        out.println("</body>");
        out.println("</html>");
    }
}
```

The output of this listing looks like Figure 4.4.

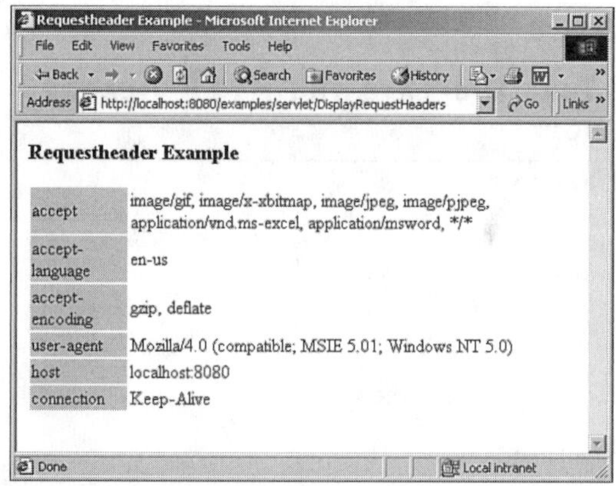

FIGURE 4.4
You can retrieve request header information using a servlet.

Acquiring a Binary Stream for the Response

Suppose you want to open a binary file in a browser from a servlet. It isn't text so you have to write the file to the servlet's output stream. Let's practice with a PDF document. First, you get the servlet's output stream with:

```
ServletOutputStream out = res.getOutputStream();
```

Next, you set the file type in the response object using one of the standard MIME (Multipurpose Internet Mail Extension) protocols. Several listings of content type names are available on the Internet including one at `ftp://ftp.isi.edu/in-notes/iana/assignments/media-types`. Then you use an HTTP response header named content-disposition. This header allows the servlet to specify information about the file's presentation. Using that header, you can indicate that the content should be opened separately (not actually in the browser) and that it should not be displayed automatically, but rather upon some further action by the user. You can also suggest the filename to be used if the content is to be saved to a file. That filename would be the name of the file that appears in the Save As dialog box. If you don't specify the filename, you are likely to get the name of your servlet in that box. To find out more about the content-disposition header, check out Resources or go to `http://www.alternic.org/rfcs/rfc2100/rfc2183.txt`.

Sending a binary stream to the client is not easy. Listing 4.10 will help you do it right.

LISTING 4.10

SERVLET THAT SENDS A FILE TO THE CLIENT

```
public class BinaryResponse extends HttpServlet {

   /**Set global variables*/
   public void init(ServletConfig config)
          throws ServletException
   {
     super.init(config);
   }

   /**Process HTTP Post request with doPost*/
   public void doPost(HttpServletRequest request,
                      HttpServletResponse response)
       throws ServletException, IOException
   {

      String fileName = "index.html";  //set file name
      String contentType = getContentType(fileName);
      //contentType = getType(); //get the content type

      // get the file
      File file = new File(fileName);
      long length = file.length();
      if(length > Integer.MAX_VALUE)
      {
          //handle too large file error
          //perhaps log and return error message to client

      }
      byte[] bytes = new byte[(long)length];
      BufferedInputStream in =
        new BufferedInputStream(new FileInputStream(file));
      // then place it into a byte array
      if(length != in.read(bytes))
      {
          //handle too large file error
          //perhaps log and return error message to client
      }

      //get the servlet's output stream
      BufferedOutputStream out =
      new BufferedOutputStream(response.getOutputStream());
      //set the content type of the response
      response.setContentType( contentType );
      //send the file to the client
      out.write( bytes );
    }
  }

   /**Clean up resources*/
```

continues

LISTING 4.10 *continued*

SERVLET THAT SENDS A FILE TO THE CLIENT

```
    public void destroy()
    {
       //If you need to clean up resources.
       //Otherwise don't override.
    }
    String getContentType(String fileName)
    {
       String extension[] =
       {                             // File Extensions
          "txt",                         //0 - plain text
          "htm",                         //1 - hypertext
          "jpg",                         //2 - JPEG image
          "gif",                         //3 - gif image
          "pdf",                         //4 - adobe pdf
          "doc",                         //5 - Microsoft Word
       },                                // you can add more
       mimeType[] =
       {                            // mime types
          "text/plain",                  //0 - plain text
          "text/html",                   //1 - hypertext
          "image/jpg",                   //2 - image
          "image/gif",                   //3 - image
          "application/pdf",             //4 - Adobe pdf
          "application/msword",          //5 - Microsoft Word
       },                                // you can add more
       contentType = "text/html";        // default type

       // dot + file extension
       int dotPosition = fileName.lastIndexOf('.');
       // get file extension
       String fileExtension =
               fileName.substring(dotPosition + 1);
       // match mime type to extension
       for(int index = 0; index < MT.length; index++)
       {
          if(fileExtension.equalsIgnoreCase(
                                    extension[index]))
          {
             contentType = mimeType[index];
             break;
          }
       }

       return contentType;
    }
}
```

Redirecting an HTTP Request to Another URL

It often happens that pages move around and a URL becomes invalid. Throwing back a 404 error isn't nice. The response object has the `sendRedirect` method, which sends a temporary redirect response to the client sending with it a new location URL. You can use relative or absolute URLs, because the Servlet Container translates a relative URL to an absolute URL before sending the response to the client.

The two potential problems with this method are sending a bad URL to the client and using this method after the response has already been committed. The bad URL will look bad, but not produce an error. The latter, though, will throw an `IllegalStateException`. Furthermore, after using this method, the response is committed and can't be written to, or you'll get an error. One nice feature is that this method writes a short response body including a hyperlink to the new location. This way, if the browser doesn't support redirects, it will still get the new link. Use the following syntax for this method:

```
// Suppose this portion of the server is down.
// Redirect the user to an explanation page.
redirectPath = "./error/notAvailable.html";
response.sendRedirect(redirectPath);
```

WEB APPLICATION SCOPE

This section discusses scope. There are three scopes to worry about for the exam: namely, Request, Session, and Context. Suppose you had to keep track of all your customer visits to your support Web site. Where would you place the counter? You would place it in Context scope. To better understand what I mean, please study the following objective.

1.4 Identify the interface and method to access values and resources and to set object attributes within the following three Web scopes:

- **Request**
- **Session**
- **Context**

This objective requires you to understand how to set and get name-value attributes at three different levels. The breadth of scope increases from Request to Session to Context, the widest scope.

Table 4.2 provides a definition of the three object scopes of concern under this objective, namely, Request, Session, and Application.

TABLE 4.2

REQUEST, SESSION, AND APPLICATION SCOPE

Name	*Accessibility*	*Lifetime*
Request	Current, included, or forwarded pages	Until the response is returned to the user.
Session	All requests from same browser within session timeout	Until session timeout or session ID invalidated (such as user quits browser).
application	All request to same Web application	Life of container or explicitly killed (such as container administration action).

The idea here is if you set an attribute (that is, `request.setAttribute()`), when can you access it? The answer depends on which object was used to the attribute. So, if you set an attribute with the request object, then the scope of that specific attribute is only Request. You can't access it once the request is complete. You can't see this attribute in another request even if it is in the same session. Conversely, any attribute set with the ServletContext object can be seen in all sessions and all requests.

Listing 4.11 is a program that demonstrates how you could use access attributes from the three primary scopes of Request, Session, and Application. You can also use `setAttribute()` for each of these scopes.

LISTING 4.11

ATTRIBUTES FROM REQUEST, SESSION, AND APPLICATION SCOPES

```
import java.io.IOException;
import java.io.PrintWriter;
import java.text.SimpleDateFormat;
import java.util.Date;
import java.util.Enumeration;
```

```
import javax.servlet.*;
import javax.servlet.http.*;

public class AttributeScope extends HttpServlet {

   public void printHeader(PrintWriter out, String header)
{
        out.println("   <tr>");
        out.println("    <td bgcolor=\"#999999\" " +
                    "colspan=\"2\">");
        out.println("     <b>"+header+"</b>");
        out.println("    </td>");
        out.println("   </tr>");
    }

    public void printValue(PrintWriter out, String key,
           String val)
    {
       if (val!=null)
       {
           if (val.length()>255)
            val=val.substring(0,128)+" <i>(... more)</i>";
       }
       out.println("<tr>");
       out.println("<td bgcolor=\"#cccccc\">"+key+"</td>");
       out.println("<td bgcolor=\"#ffffff\">"+val+"</td>");
       out.println("</tr>");
   }

    public void printVoid(PrintWriter out)
    {
        out.println("   <tr><td bgcolor=\"#ffffff\" " +
                    "colspan=\"2\"> </td></tr>");
    }

    public void doPost(HttpServletRequest request,
           HttpServletResponse response)
      throws ServletException, IOException
    {
        doGet(request,response);
    }

    public void doGet(HttpServletRequest request,
           HttpServletResponse response)
      throws ServletException, IOException
    {

        Enumeration enum = getInitParameterNames();
        ServletContext context = getServletContext();
        PrintWriter out = response.getWriter();
        response.setContentType("text/html");

        out.println("<html>");
        out.println(" <head>");
        out.println("  <title>Attribute Scope Example" +
```

continues

LISTING 4.11 *continued*

ATTRIBUTES FROM REQUEST, SESSION, AND APPLICATION SCOPES

```
                "</title>");
out.println(" </head>");
out.println(" <body>");
out.println("  <p align=center>");
out.println("    <h2>Attribute Scope Example</h2>");

String url=request.getScheme()+"://"+
           request.getServerName()+":"+
           request.getServerPort()+
           request.getRequestURI();

out.println("    <table border=\"0\" cellspacing=" +
                \"2\" cellpadding=\"2\">");
out.println("     <tr>");
out.println("      <td>");

out.println("        <form action=\""+url+
                  "\" method=\"GET\">");
out.println("         <input type=\"hidden\" " +
                  "name=\"hiddenName\" " +
                  "value=\"hiddenValue\">");
out.println("         <input type=\"submit\" " +
                  "name=\"submitName\" " +
                  "value=\"Submit using GET\">");
out.println("        </form>");

out.println("      </td>");
out.println("     </tr>");
out.println("    </table>");

out.println("  </p>");
out.println("  <br>");

out.println("  <table width=\"100%\" border=\"1\""+
         " cellspacing=\"0\" cellpadding=\"1\">");

printHeader(out,"Context attributes:");
enum = context.getAttributeNames();
while (enum.hasMoreElements()) {
    String key = (String)enum.nextElement();
    Object val = context.getAttribute(key);
    printValue(out,key,val.toString());
}
printVoid(out);

printHeader(out,"Request attributes:");
enum = request.getAttributeNames();
while (enum.hasMoreElements()) {
    String key = (String)enum.nextElement();
    Object val = request.getAttribute(key);
    printValue(out,key,val.toString());
```

```
        }
        printVoid(out);

        printHeader(out,"Parameter names in request:");
        enum = request.getParameterNames();
        while (enum.hasMoreElements()) {
            String key = (String)enum.nextElement();
            String[] val = request.getParameterValues(key);
            for(int i = 0; i < val.length; i++)
                printValue(out,key,val[i]);
        }
        printVoid(out);


        printHeader(out,"Session information:");
        SimpleDateFormat format =
         new SimpleDateFormat("yyyy/MM/dd hh:mm:ss.SSS z");
        HttpSession session = request.getSession();
        if (session!=null) {
        printValue(out,"Requested Session Id:",
                          request.getRequestedSessionId());
            printValue(out,"Current Session Id:",
                                         session.getId());
            printValue(out,"Current Time:",
                                   format.format(new Date()));
            printValue(out,"Session Created Time:",
       format.format(new Date(session.getCreationTime())));
            printValue(out,"Session Last Accessed Time:",
   format.format(new Date(session.getLastAccessedTime())));
            printValue(out,"Session Max Inactive Interval"+
                        " Seconds:",
       Integer.toString(session.getMaxInactiveInterval()));
            printVoid(out);

            printHeader(out,"Session values:");
            enum = session.getAttributeNames();
            while (enum.hasMoreElements()) {
                String key = (String) enum.nextElement();
                Object val = session.getAttribute(key);
                printValue(out,key,val.toString());
            }
        }
        printVoid(out);

        out.println("</pre>");
        out.println("    </td>");
        out.println("   </tr>");

        out.println("  </table>");
        out.println(" </body>");
        out.println("</html>");
        out.flush();
    }
}
```

The output of this listing looks like Figure 4.5.

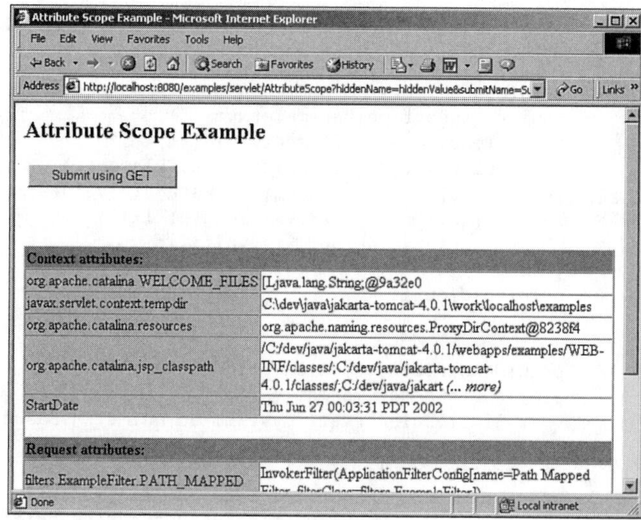

FIGURE 4.5
You can get attributes with Request, Session, or Application scope.

The previous listing demonstrates how to retrieve attributes from the three primary scopes. Let us now focus on the Request object.

Request

When a user hits a URL with a servlet at the other end, the Servlet Container creates an `HttpServletRequest` object. It passes this object as an argument to the servlet's service methods (`doPut()`, `doGet()`, and `doPost()`). There is a lot of information in this object, including the login of the user making this request (`getRemoteUser()`) and the name of the HTTP method with which this request was made (`getMethod()`). However, this exam objective is restricted to header information. Therefore, you need to know the following `HttpServletRequest` methods.

The following list of methods summarizes the Request (Interfaces: `ServletRequest` and `HttpServletRequest`) methods you need to be familiar with. While, strictly speaking, all are fair game, I marked with an asterisk those that are more likely to be on the exam:

- *`getAttribute(`*`String name`*`)`. Returns the value of the named attribute as an Object, or null if no attribute of the given name exists.

- *`getAttributeNames()`. Returns an Enumeration containing the names of the attributes available to this request.
- `getAuthType()`. Returns the name of the authentication scheme used to protect the servlet.
- `getCharacterEncoding()`. Returns the name of the character encoding used in the body of this request.
- `getContentLength()`. Returns the length, in bytes, of the request body if made available by the input stream, or -1 if the length is not known.
- `getContentType()`. Returns the MIME type of the body of the request, or null if the type is not known.
- `getContextPath()`. Returns the portion of the request URI that indicates the context of the request.
- `getCookies()`. Returns an array containing all of the Cookie objects the client sent with this request.
- `getDateHeader(java.lang.String name)`. Returns the value of the specified request header as a long value that represents a Date object.
- *`getHeader(java.lang.String name)`. Returns the value of the specified request header as a String.
- *`getHeaderNames()`. Returns an enumeration of all the header names this request contains.
- `getHeaders(java.lang.String name)`. Returns all the values of the specified request header as an Enumeration of String objects.
- `getInputStream()`. Retrieves the body of the request as binary data using a `ServletInputStream`.
- `getIntHeader(java.lang.String name)`. Returns the value of the specified request header as an int.
- `getLocale()`. Returns the preferred Locale that the client will accept content in, based on the Accept-Language header.
- `getLocales()`. Returns an Enumeration of Locale objects indicating, in decreasing order starting with the preferred locale, the locales that are acceptable to the client based on the Accept-Language header.

- *getMethod(). Returns the name of the HTTP method with which this request was made; for example, GET, POST, or PUT.
- *getParameter(java.lang.String name). Returns the value of a request parameter as a string, or null if the parameter does not exist.
- getParameterMap(). Returns a java.util.Map of the parameters of this request.
- *getParameterNames(). Returns an Enumeration of string objects containing the names of the parameters contained in this request.
- *getParameterValues(java.lang.String name). Returns an array of string objects containing all of the values the given request parameter has, or null if the parameter does not exist.
- getPathInfo(). Returns any extra path information associated with the URL the client sent when it made this request.
- getPathTranslated(). Returns any extra path information after the servlet name but before the query string, and translates it to a real path.
- getProtocol(). Returns the name and version of the protocol the request uses in the form protocol/majorVersion.minorVersion, for example, HTTP/1.1.
- *getQueryString(). Returns the query string that is contained in the request URL after the path.
- getReader(). Retrieves the body of the request as character data using a BufferedReader.
- getRemoteAddr(). Returns the Internet Protocol (IP) address of the client that sent the request.
- getRemoteHost(). Returns the fully qualified name of the client that sent the request.
- getRemoteUser(). Returns the login of the user making this request, if the user has been authenticated, or null if the user has not been authenticated.
- *getRequestDispatcher(java.lang.String path). Returns a RequestDispatcher object that acts as a wrapper for the resource located at the given path.

- `getRequestURI()`. Returns the part of this request's URL from the protocol name up to the query string in the first line of the HTTP request.
- `getRequestURL()`. Reconstructs the URL the client used to make the request.
- `getRequestedSessionId()`. Returns the session ID specified by the client.
- `getScheme()`. Returns the name of the scheme used to make this request; for example, http, https, or ftp.
- `getServerName()`. Returns the host name of the server that received the request.
- `getServerPort()`. Returns the port number on which this request was received.
- `getServletPath()`. Returns the part of this request's URL that calls the servlet.
- `*getSession()`. Returns the current session (HttpSession) associated with this request, or if the request does not have a session, creates one.
- `*getSession(boolean create)`. Returns the current `HttpSession` associated with this request, or, if there is no current session and create is true, returns a new session.
- `getUserPrincipal()`. Returns a `java.security.Principal` object containing the name of the current authenticated user.
- `isRequestedSessionIdFromCookie()`. Checks whether the requested session ID came in as a cookie.
- `isRequestedSessionIdFromURL()`. Checks whether the requested session ID came in as part of the request URL.
- `isRequestedSessionIdValid()`. Checks whether the requested session ID is still valid.
- `isSecure()`. Returns a boolean indicating whether this request was made using a secure channel, such as HTTPS.
- `isUserInRole(java.lang.String role)`. Returns a boolean indicating whether the authenticated user is included in the specified logical "role".

- *removeAttribute(java.lang.String name). Removes an attribute from this request.
- *setAttribute(java.lang.String name, java.lang.Object o). Stores an attribute in this request.
- setCharacterEncoding(java.lang.String env). Overrides the name of the character encoding used in the body of this request.

Several of the HttpServletRequest methods are not mentioned specifically in the objectives, but you should be familiar with them. Listing 4.11 is a program that demonstrates how you would retrieve attributes from the Request object, the main concern in the current exam objective. However, I thought you might also like to see what else you can do with this object. Listing 4.12 uses the Request object's methods to retrieve HTTP request header information (similar to Listing 4.10). Of course, the information you get out of the Request object has only Request scope.

LISTING 4.12

SERVLET THAT RETRIEVES REQUEST HEADER INFORMATION

```
import java.io.*;
import java.util.*;
import javax.servlet.*;
import javax.servlet.http.*;

/**
 * set request attributes
 *
 * @author Reader@Que
 */

public class RequestDislay extends HttpServlet
{
    public void doGet(HttpServletRequest request,
                      HttpServletResponse response)
        throws IOException, ServletException
    {

   // Set MIME type response header
   response.setContentType("text/html");

   // Acquire a text stream for the response
   PrintWriter out = response.getWriter();
```

```
//prefer to buffer html then print all at once
StringBuffer html = new StringBuffer();

// HTML header
html.append("<html>");
html.append("<head>");
html.append("<title>");
html.append("Servlet Header Example");
html.append("</title>");
html.append("<head>");
html.append("<body>");

// begin the HTML body
html.append("<h1>Request info</h1>");

// build list of header name-value pairs
String headerName;
String headerValue;
Enumeration headerNames = request.getHeaderNames();
while (headerNames.hasMoreElements())
{
   //enumeration returns object so cast as String
   headerName = (String) headerNames.nextElement();
   headerValue = request.getHeader(headerName);
   html.append("  " + headerName + " : " + headerValue +
               "<br/>");
}

//These methods are not named by objectives, but are
// good to know.
//A simple march down the API:
html.append("Auth Type: " + request.getAuthType());
html.append("Character Encoding: " +
                        request.getCharacterEncoding());
html.append("Content Length: " +
                            request.getContentLength());
html.append("Content Type: "+ request.getContentType());
html.append("Method: " + request.getMethod());
html.append("Path Info: " + request.getPathInfo());
html.append("Path Translated: " +
                           request.getPathTranslated());
html.append("Protocol: " + request.getProtocol());
html.append("Query String: "+ request.getQueryString());
html.append("Remote Address: "+request.getRemoteAddr());
html.append("Remote Host: " + request.getRemoteHost());
html.append("Request URI: " + request.getRequestURI());
html.append("Remote User: " + request.getRemoteUser());
html.append("Scheme: " + request.getScheme());
html.append("Server Name: " + request.getServerName());
html.append("Servlet Path: "+ request.getServletPath());
html.append("Server Port: " + request.getServerPort());
```

continues

LISTING 4.12 *continued*

SERVLET THAT RETRIEVES REQUEST HEADER INFORMATION

```
        // build list of parameter name-value pairs
        html.append("Parameters:");
        Enumeration parameterNames =request.getParameterNames();
        while (parameterNames.hasMoreElements())
        {
           String parameterName =
                      (String) parameterNames.nextElement();
           String[] parameterValues =
                   request.getParameterValues(parameterName);
           html.append("    " + parameterName + ":");
           for (int i = 0; i < parameterValues.length; i++)
           {
              html.append("      " + parameterValues[i]);
           }
        }

        // build list of cookie name-value pairs
        html.append("Cookies:");
        Cookie[] cookies = request.getCookies();
        for (int i = 0; i < cookies.length; i++)
        {
           String cookieName = cookies[i].getName();
           String cookieValue = cookies[i].getValue();
           html.append("  " + cookieName + " : " + cookieValue);
        }
        html.append("</body>");
        html.append("</html>");

        // optional use descriptive elements to clarify code
        final String BEGIN_TAG = "<";
        final String CLOSE_TAG = "/";
        final String END_TAG = ">";

        // Print the HTML footer
        html.append(BEGIN_TAG + CLOSE_TAG + "body" + END_TAG);
        html.append(BEGIN_TAG + CLOSE_TAG + "html" + END_TAG);

        // Sometimes it is better (performance improvement)
        // to send html to stream all at once.
        out.print( html );
        out.close();
      }
}
```

Session

A Session is made up of multiple hits from the same browser across some period of time. The session scope includes all hits from a single machine (multiple browser windows if they share cookies). Servlets maintain state with sessions. Listing 4.13 is a modification of a sample servlet that ships with Tomcat. It demonstrates how you can use session attributes.

LISTING 4.13

SERVLET THAT DEMONSTRATES SESSION ATTRIBUTES

```
import java.io.*;
import java.text.*;
import java.util.*;
import javax.servlet.*;
import javax.servlet.http.*;

public class SessionExample extends HttpServlet
{

    public void doGet(HttpServletRequest request,
                      HttpServletResponse response)
        throws IOException, ServletException
    {
        response.setContentType("text/html");

        PrintWriter out = response.getWriter();
        out.println("<html>");
        out.println("<body bgcolor=\"white\">");
        out.println("<head>");

        String title = "Session Servlet";
        out.println("<title>" + title + "</title>");
        out.println("</head>");
        out.println("<body>");

         out.println("<h3>" + title + "</h3>");

        HttpSession session = request.getSession();
        out.println("session id" + " " + session.getId());
        out.println("<br/>");
        out.println("session created" + " ");
        out.println(new Date(session.getCreationTime()) +
                    "<br/>");
        out.println("session lastaccessed" + " ");
        out.println(
                new Date(session.getLastAccessedTime()));
```

continues

LISTING 4.13 *continued*

SERVLET THAT DEMONSTRATES SESSION ATTRIBUTES

```
        //get these from the HTML form or query string
        String dataName = request.getParameter("dataname");
        String dataValue
➥=request.getParameter("datavalue");
        if (dataName != null && dataValue != null)
        {
            session.setAttribute(dataName, dataValue);
        }

        out.println("<p/>");
        out.println("session data" + "<br/>");
        Enumeration names = session.getAttributeNames();
        while (names.hasMoreElements())
        {
            String name = (String) names.nextElement();
            String value =
                    session.getAttribute(name).toString();
            out.println(name + " = " + value + "<br/>");
        }

        out.println("<p/>");
        out.print("<form action=\"");
        out.print(response.encodeURL("SessionExample"));
        out.print("\" ");
        out.println("method=POST>");
        out.println("Name of Session Attribute:");
        out.println("<input type=text size=20 " +
                    "name=dataname>");
        out.println("<br/>");
        out.println("Value of Session Attribute:");
        out.println("<input type=text size=20 " +
                    "name=datavalue>");
        out.println("<br/>");
        out.println("<input type=submit>");
        out.println("</form>");

        out.println("<p/>GET based form:<br/>");
        out.print("<form action=\"");
        out.print(response.encodeURL("SessionExample"));
        out.print("\" ");
        out.println("method=GET>");
        out.println("Name of Session Attribute:");
        out.println("<input type=text size=20 " +
                    "name=dataname>");
        out.println("<br/>");
        out.println("Value of Session Attribute:");
        out.println("<input type=text size=20 " +
                    "name=datavalue>");
        out.println("<br/>");
        out.println("<input type=submit>");
        out.println("</form>");
```

```
        out.print("<p/><a href=\"");
        String url = "SessionExample?dataname=scwcd&" +
                     "datavalue=pass!";
        out.print(response.encodeURL(url));
        out.println("\" >URL encoded </a>");

        out.println("</body>");
        out.println("</html>");

        out.println("</body>");
        out.println("</html>");
    }

    public void doPost(HttpServletRequest request,
                       HttpServletResponse response)
        throws IOException, ServletException
    {
        doGet(request, response);
    }

}
//returns a page that looks like:
//Session Servlet
//
//session id 9805A5C4C084F5B47788242406C22455
//session created Tue Apr 16 22:11:06 PDT 2002
//session lastaccessed Tue Apr 16 22:13:27 PDT 2002
//
//session data
//publisher = Que
//author = trottier
//scwcd = pass!
```

To summarize, sessions are what you can use to track a single user over a short time. You get the session object (HttpSession) from the request object. To track multiple users over time you must jump to context, covered next.

Context

A Web application includes many parts; it rarely is just one class or one JSP. To help manage an application, you will sometimes need to set and get information that all of the servlets share together, which we say is context-wide. An example would be using a login servlet to create an application-level attribute such as application name like so:

```
public void init(ServletConfig config)
     throws ServletException
{
       super.init(config);
```

```
        // set application scope parameter
        // to "Certification by Que"
        ServletContext context =config.getServletContext();
        context.setAttribute(
            "applicationName", "Certification by Que");
  }
```

Later, in another servlet you may use the application name as demonstrated in Listing 4.14.

LISTING 4.14

SERVLET doGet METHOD DEMONSTRATION

```
  public void doGet(HttpServletRequest request,
                  HttpServletResponse response)
        throws ServletException, IOException
  {
        response.setContentType("text/html");

        PrintWriter out = response.getWriter();
        out.print("<html>");
        out.print("<head>");
        out.print("<title>");

        // get value of applicationName from ServletContext
        out.print(getServletContext().getAttribute(
                        "applicationName").toString());

        out.print("</title>");
        out.print("<head>");
        out.print("<body>");

        //complete body content here...

        out.print("</body></html>");
        out.close();
}
```

Besides setting and retrieving your custom attributes, you can get additional information from the Servlet Container, such as its major and minor version, the path to a given servlet, and more. The following summarizes the additional methods you might use:

- `getAttributeNames()`. Returns an `Enumeration` object containing the attribute names available within this servlet context.
- `getContext(String uripath)`. Returns a `ServletContext` object that corresponds to a specified URL on the server.

- `getInitParameter(String name)`. Returns a string containing the value of the named context-wide initialization parameter, or null if the parameter does not exist.
- `getInitParameterNames()`. Returns the names of the context's initialization parameters as an Enumeration of string objects, or an empty Enumeration if the context has no initialization parameters.
- `getMajorVersion()`. Returns the major version as an int of the Java Servlet API that this Servlet Container supports.
- `getMimeType(java.lang.String file)`. Returns the MIME type as a string of the specified file, or null if the MIME type is not known.
- `getMinorVersion()`. Returns the minor version as an int of the Servlet API that this Servlet Container supports.
- `getNamedDispatcher(String name)`. Returns a `RequestDispatcher` object that acts as a wrapper for the named servlet.
- `getRealPath(String path)`. Returns a string containing the real path for a given virtual path.
- `getRequestDispatcher(String path)`. Returns a `RequestDispatcher` object that acts as a wrapper for the resource located at the given path.
- `getResource(String path)`. Returns a URL to the resource that is mapped to a specified path.
- `getResourceAsStream(String path)`. Returns the resource located at the named path as an `InputStream` object.
- `getServerInfo()`. Returns the name and version as a String of the Servlet Container on which the servlet is running.

SERVLET LIFE-CYCLE

1.5 Given a life-cycle method, `init`, `service`, or `destroy`, identify correct statements about its purpose or about how and when it is invoked.

EXAM TIP

When is INIT() called? A common question on the exam tests your understanding of when init() is called. Knowledge of a servlet's life-cycle is crucial to answering these types of questions. Remember, init() may be called when the server starts (tell web.xml to load servlet upon startup), when first requested, and sometimes the container management console will allow you to call it as part of the server administration. The exam expects you to know that init() will only be called once per servlet instance, that it is not used to send information back to the browser (HttpServletResponse is not a parameter), and that it throws a ServletException to the container that called the servlet if anything goes wrong.

WARNING

DESTROY() is not called if the container crashes! You should log activity from somewhere other than the destroy() method if a given piece of information is essential, but might not be logged if the logging functionality is placed in the destroy() method. This is because the destroy() method is not called if the Servlet Container quits abruptly (crashes).

The servlet life-cycle is not obvious. The container calls three methods—namely, init(), service() and destroy()—in that order. Ordinarily, that is how the container talks to your servlet. With some containers, you can modify this behavior, but the exam will assume this order.

The init method is called first, the first time the servlet is invoked. This happens one time. However, the service method is called every time a servlet is requested. Lastly, the destroy method is called one time, upon the removal of the servlet from memory due either to explicit removal or lack of use (for example, the session expires). You can configure the container to load certain servlets upon startup (<load-on-startup/> in web.xml), but most of them will be loaded upon first request. Either way, the init method is called first. Place in this method things you will use across requests, like database connections, and class member values such as finalized constants.

The destroy() method, like init(), is called only once. It is called when the servlet is taken out of service and all pending requests to a given servlet (that one with the mentioned destroy() method) are completed or have timed-out. This method is called by the container to give you a chance to release resources such as database connections and threads. You can always call super.destroy() (GenericServlet.destroy()) to add a note to the log about what is going on. You might want to do this even if only to place a timestamp in there.

Listings 4.15 and 4.16 are sample Web applications (HTML page and servlet combination) that demonstrate how to use the init(), service(), and destroy() methods, and when they are called. You could combine them and just have one servlet, but there are two pieces here to illustrate the relationship between static and dynamic parts of an application. The first part, Listing 4.15, is the HTML page.

LISTING 4.15

HTML PAGE THAT WORKS WITH SERVLET IN LISTING 4.16 ILLUSTRATING THE RELATIONSHIP

```
<html>
<head>
<title>LifeCycle Demonstration Using SQL Server</title>
</head>
```

```
   <body bgcolor="#FFFFFF">

   <p align=center>
   <h1>LifeCycle Demonstration Using DB</h1>
   <form name="formSearch" method="post" action=
   "localhost:8080/examples/servlet/SearchLastNameServlet">
   <table border="0" cellspacing="0" cellpadding="6">
      <tr>
         <td><h2>Search</h2></td>
         <td></td>
      </tr>
      <tr>
         <td><b>Last Name</b></td>
         <td><input type="text" name="LastName"
                    value="Fuller">
         </td>
      </tr>
      <tr>
         <td></td>
         <td align="center"><input type="submit" name="Submit"
             value="Submit">
         </td>
      </tr>
   </table>
   </form>
   </p>
   </body>
</html>
```

NOTE

Servlet Reloading! Servlets are loaded in one of three ways. The first way is when the Web server starts. You can set this in the configuration file. Reload can happen automatically after the container detects that its class file (under servlet dir, for example, WEB-INF/classes) has changes. The third way, with some containers, is through an administrator interface.

The HTML page contains a form with one field for a last name. When submitted, the container takes the lastname field and hands it to the servlet in the request object. This object is where you normally extract requester information. The servlet grabs the lastname, if any, and builds a SQL `WHERE` clause with it. Then the servlet establishes a connection with the database server (I'm using MS SQL Server) and executes the statement. Then it walks through the `resultset` getting the data from each field of every row. Finally, it builds the HTML page and sends it off to the client browser. While the database portion is not on the exam, it is an excellent example of how you can take advantage of the methods that are called by the container.

Listing 4.16 is the servlet that queries the database based on the form data. Notice that you can forgo the above HTML file by appending the FirstName parameter to the URL like so: `http://localhost:8080/examples/servlet/SearchLastNameServlet?LastName=Fuller`. Also, you need to set up a data source with system data source names (DSNs), whether to a data source that is local to your computer or remote on the network.

NOTE

Servlet Synchronizing! Servlets are run each in their own thread. When the `synchronized` keyword is used with a servlet's `service()` method, requests to that servlet are handled one at a time in a serialized manner. This means that multiple requests won't interfere with each other when accessing variables and references within one servlet. It also means the processing capabilities of the Servlet Container are reduced because the more efficient multithreaded mode has been disallowed for a given servlet that has been declared with the synchronized keyword.

LISTING 4.16

SERVLET THAT QUERIES A DATABASE BASED ON FORM INPUT FROM LISTING 4.15

```
/* Don't use "java.io.*"
   Be explicit to see which classes are expected
*/
import java.io.IOException;
import java.io.PrintWriter;
import java.sql.DriverManager;
import java.sql.Connection;
import java.sql.Statement;
import java.sql.ResultSet;

import javax.servlet.http.HttpServlet;
import javax.servlet.http.HttpServletRequest;
import javax.servlet.http.HttpServletResponse;
import javax.servlet.ServletOutputStream;
import javax.servlet.ServletException;
import javax.servlet.http.Cookie;
import javax.servlet.ServletConfig;

public class SearchLastNameServlet extends HttpServlet
{
   //These will be used across requests,
   //so declare it at class level,
   //not service or doGet level.
   //While it is common to use con,stmt,rs
   //I find these cryptic so I prefer to  spell
   //them out completely for clarity.
   private Connection _connection = null;
   //Can differentiate between attributes of a class
   //and local variables within a method
   //with preceding underscore.
   private String _driverName =
                        "sun.jdbc.odbc.JdbcOdbcDriver";
   //connects to Northwind DB in SQL Server on my machine
   private String _connectionString =
                                "jdbc:odbc:employeeDB";
   //optional, declare these in doPost() or service()
   //to avoid conflict between requests.
   private Statement statement = null;
   private ResultSet resultset = null;
   //not here, keep query local
   //private String query = null;

   //common types
   final int COMMA = 1;
   final int TABLE_COLUMN = 2;
   final int TABLE_HEADER = 3;
   final boolean DELIMITED = true;

   //This is called only once during lifecycle!
   public void init(ServletConfig _config)
```

```
  throws ServletException
{
   super.init(_config);

    //warning! userid and password is exposed:
   String username = "sa";
   String password = "sa";

   try
   {
      Class.forName(_driverName);
      //warning! userid and password is exposed:
      _connection = DriverManager.getConnection
         (_connectionString, username, password);
   } catch(Exception ex)
   {
      throw new ServletException(ex.getMessage());
   }
}

public void service(HttpServletRequest _request,
        HttpServletResponse _response)
  throws ServletException, IOException
{
   _response.setContentType("text/html");

   String table = " Employees ";
   // query string where clause constraint
   String where = "";
   if (_request.getParameter("LastName").length() > 0)
   {
      String lastName = _
                      request.getParameter("LastName");
      where = " where LastName like \'";
      where += lastName;
      where += "%\'";

   } else
   {
      where = "";
   }

   StringBuffer htmlResult = new StringBuffer();
   try
   {
      String sqlQuery = "SELECT * from "+ table + where;
      statement = _connection.createStatement();
      resultset = statement.executeQuery(sqlQuery);

      while(resultset.next())
      {
         //Not necessary to place in array, but...
         String[] field = new String[8];
         //warning! these should be in same order as
         //DB table field order
         //otherwise you can get errors, a Sun todo.
```

continues

LISTING 4.16 *continued*

SERVLET THAT QUERIES A DATABASE BASED ON FORM INPUT FROM LISTING 4.15

```
            field[0] = ""+resultset.getInt("EmployeeID");
            field[1] = resultset.getString("LastName");
            field[2] = resultset.getString("FirstName");
            field[3] = resultset.getString("Title");
            field[4] = ""+resultset.getDate("BirthDate");
            field[5] = resultset.getString("City");
            field[6] = resultset.getString("Region");
            field[7] = resultset.getString("Country");
            htmlResult.append( getTableBody(field) );
          }
      } catch(Exception ex)
      {
         throw new ServletException(ex.getMessage());
      }

      StringBuffer html = new StringBuffer();
      html.append( htmlHeader() );

      //build results
      html.append( getTableHeader() );
      html.append( htmlResult.toString() );
      html.append( getTableFooter() );

      html.append( htmlFooter() );

      ServletOutputStream out = response.getOutputStream();
      out.println( html.toString() );
   }

   public void destroy()
   {
      try
      {
       // Give connection to garbage collector
          connection.close();
          connection = null;
      } catch(Exception ex)
      {
          throw new ServletException(ex.getMessage());
      }
   }
   //
   // convenience methods providing abstraction
   //

   /*
    * Prints the table header.
    */
   public String getTableHeader()
   {
         StringBuffer header = new StringBuffer();
```

```
    header.append("<table border=\"2\">\n");
    header.append("<tr>\n");
    header.append("<th align=\"left\">EmployeeID</th>\n");
    header.append("<th align=\"left\">LastName</th>\n");
    header.append("<th align=\"left\">FirstName</th>\n");
    header.append("<th align=\"left\">Title</th>\n");
    header.append("<th align=\"left\">BirthDate</th>\n");
    header.append("<th align=\"left\">City</th>\n");
    header.append("<th align=\"left\">Region</th>\n");
    header.append("<th align=\"left\">Country</th>\n");
    header.append("</tr>\n");
      return header.toString();
  }

  /*
   * Prints the table body.
   */
  public String getTableBody(String[] field)
  {
     StringBuffer body = new StringBuffer();
     body.append("<tr>\n");

     for(int index=0; index<field.length; index++)
     {
        body.append("   <td align=\"left\">");
        body.append(field[index]);
        body.append("</td>\n");
     }
     body.append("</tr>\n");
     return body.toString();
  }

  //you would bother to have a whole method for this
  //because someone might ask you to add extra
  //stuff to the bottom of every table so it is smart
  //to separate it like this.
  public String getTableFooter()
  {
     StringBuffer footer = new StringBuffer();

     footer.append("</table>\n");

     return footer.toString();
  }

  /*
   * Prints the html file header.
   */
  public String htmlHeader()
  {
     StringBuffer html = new StringBuffer();

     html.append("<html>");
     html.append("<head>");
     html.append("<title>LifeCycle Servlet Response" +
                 "</title>");
```

continues

LISTING 4.16 *continued*

SERVLET THAT QUERIES A DATABASE BASED ON FORM INPUT FROM LISTING 4.15

```
      html.append("</head>");
      html.append("<body bgcolor=\"#FFFFFF\"> ");
      html.append("<p align=center><h1>LifeCycle Servlet "+
                  " Response</h1></p>");

      return html.toString();
   }

   /*
    * Prints the html file footer.
    * This will change often due to
    * marketing and lawyers.
    */
   public String htmlFooter()
   {
      StringBuffer html = new StringBuffer();

      html.append("<a href=\"http://localhost:8080/" +
          "examples/servlets/LifeCycle.html\">" +
          "</b>BACK</b></a>");
      html.append("</p>");
      html.append("</body>");
      html.append("</html>");

      return html.toString();
   }
}
```

Once you set up a proper System DSN, or use a fully qualified connection string, the servlet will query the database. Listing 4.15 shows how you can create an HTML form to call this servlet. The output of the servlet query looks similar to Figure 4.6.

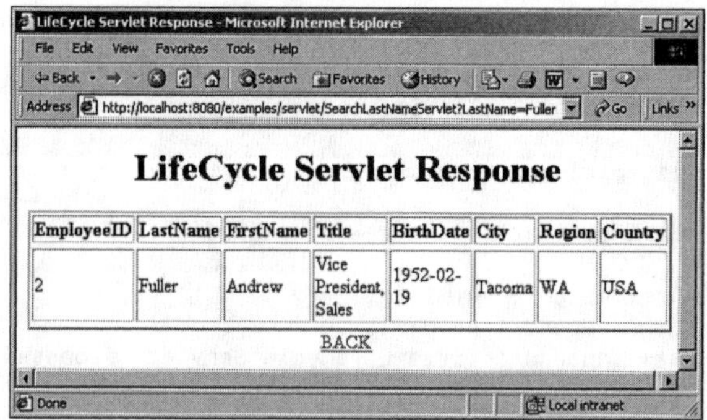

FIGURE 4.6
The result of a query by a servlet.

Listing 4.16 is just an example of when you might invoke the `destroy()` method. This code example could be improved in two ways. First, it is not thread-safe (statement and resultset variables could be local, not instance variables). That way separate instances wouldn't walk over each other's results. Second, this example doesn't make use of the Data Access Object pattern. You could do better by having separate objects for the Presentation and Database ("separation of concerns") portions of the program. I've lumped it all together here just to demonstrate the section point of how the `destroy()` method is used.

USING A REQUESTDISPATCHER

1.6 Use a RequestDispatcher to include or forward to a Web resource.

The `RequestDispatcher` is a powerful tool. You can perform programmatic server-side includes or route the whole request to another servlet or JSP with a forward. There are three ways to get the RequestDispatcher. The first two are through the Context, with `ServletContext.getRequestDispatcher(java.lang.String)` or with `ServletContext.getNamedDispatcher(java.lang.String)`. Either returns a RequestDispatcher object that acts as a wrapper for the named servlet (in web.xml, the Web application deployment descriptor). The final way is with `ServletRequest.getRequestDispatcher(java.lang.String)`. Notice that you can use a relative pathname here. You must use absolutes with `ServletContext.getRequestDispatcher(java.lang.String)`. Be careful with your paths. If the path begins with a "/", it is interpreted as relative to the current context root. You will get a null if the Servlet Container cannot return a RequestDispatcher.

A `RequestDispatcher` object can be used to forward a request to the resource or to include output from the resource in a response. The specification allows the resource to be dynamic or static. If it is dynamic, such as a servlet, the container will invoke that servlet, and then take the output and include it. If it is static, such as a text file, then the container will include the text as is. Listing 4.17 demonstrates how one servlet can transfer the request to another servlet.

LISTING 4.17

USING A REQUESTDISPATCHER TO FORWARD A REQUEST TO ANOTHER SERVLET

```
import javax.servlet.*;
import javax.servlet.http.*;
import java.io.*;

public class ServletToServlet extends HttpServlet
{
    public void doGet (HttpServletRequest request,
                       HttpServletResponse response)
           throws ServletException, IOException
    {
        try {
            getServletConfig()
                .getServletContext()
                .getRequestDispatcher("/HelloWorldExample")
                .forward(request, response);
        } catch (Exception ex) {
            ex.printStackTrace ();
        }
    }
}
```

You can also include content from a static page or another servlet. You would use a snippet like so:

```
RequestDispatcher dispatcher =
     getServletContext().getRequestDispatcher(path);
if (dispatcher == null)
{
   out.println(path + " not available");
   return;
} else
{
   dispatcher.include(request, response);
}
```

There are a few characteristics about the forward and include methods. The `ServletRequest`'s path elements and parameters remain unchanged from the caller's. The included servlet cannot set headers. This is a good candidate for a trick question. The servlet cannot change the response status code either (if you try, it will be ignored). The best way to send along information from the calling servlet to the called servlet is using a query string or, even better, using the `setAttribute()` method to set request object attributes where they are easy to access.

There is a matter of timing to consider. You can call an include anytime, but the forward has to be called before the response is committed. Otherwise you'll throw an `IllegalStateException` exception.

IN THE FIELD

REQUEST DISPATCHER PATHS

`ServletContext.getRequestDispatcher()`—This method uses absolute paths.

`ServletRequest.getRequestDispatcher(String path)`—The path may be relative, but cannot extend outside current servlet context.

`ServletRequest.getNamedDispatcher(String name)`—This name is the name of the servlet for which a dispatcher is requested, and is in the web.xml file (see Chapter 10, "Web Applications," for more about web.xml).

Regarding the forward method, one reason you may want to use it is so you can dedicate a servlet as the controller. In this way, the controller can filter, preprocess requests, and manage the transaction. The gotcha here is once a servlet forwards a request, it loses control. The controller has no capability to regain access directly. You can create an architecture where requests are returned (forwarded back by a slave servlet), but the native functionality isn't helpful for this. There is another problem. When you run Listing 4.17, you'll notice something missing—the URL in the address bar doesn't change. The client loses path information when it receives a forwarded request. That means all relative URLs in the HTML become invalid. Your browser will consider the links broken. Sometimes this doesn't matter, but when it does, use `sendRedirect()` instead.

WEB APPLICATION CONTEXT

3.1 Identify the uses for and the interfaces (or classes) and methods to achieve the following features:

- **Servlet context initialization parameters.**
- **Servlet context listener.**
- **Servlet context attribute listener.**
- **Session attribute listeners.**

Please see the section "Interfacing with HTML Requests," earlier in this chapter, where the related objective 1.3 "Retrieve a servlet initialization parameter" is discussed. Listing 4.8 is especially helpful here because it demonstrates how to enumerate the context initialization parameter list.

Regarding listeners, you can monitor and react to servlet events by defining listener objects. These objects have methods that the container invokes when life-cycle events occur. To make this happen, you define a listener class by implementing a listener interface. The container will invoke the listener method and pass it information (methods in the `HttpSessionListener` interface are passed an `HttpSessionEvent`) about that event.

Listing 4.18 demonstrates how you could use the initialization and destruction events.

LISTING 4.18

LISTENING FOR A CONTEXT INITIALIZATION AND DESTRUCTION

```
import java.util.Date;
import javax.servlet.ServletContext;
import javax.servlet.ServletContextAttributeEvent;
import javax.servlet.ServletContextAttributeListener;
import javax.servlet.ServletContextEvent;
import javax.servlet.ServletContextListener;

public final class ContextListener
   implements ServletContextListener
{
   public void contextInitialized(
                                  ServletContextEvent event)
   {
      ServletContext context = event.getServletContext();
      context.setAttribute("StartDate", Date);
   }

   public void contextDestroyed(ServletContextEvent event)
   {
      ServletContext context = event.getServletContext();
      Date startDate = context.getAttribute("StartDate");
      customLog(startDate);
      context.removeAttribute("StartDate");
   }
}
```

The attribute `StartDate` is set when the container initializes the application. Then when the application quits, the same attribute is logged and then deleted. For an excellent article that provides an overview of application life-cycle events, please see Servlet App Event Listeners by Stephanie Fesler (04/12/2001, `www.onjava.com/pub/a/onjava/2001/04/12/listeners.html`). The four interfaces that you can expect to see on the exam are these:

- When a servlet is initialized or destroyed:
  - `javax.servlet.ServletContextListener.`
  - `contextDestroyed(ServletContextEvent sce)` Notification that the servlet context is about to be shut down.
  - `contextInitialized(ServletContextEvent sce)` Notification that the Web application is ready to process requests.
- When a context attribute is added, removed, or replaced:
  - `javax.servlet.ServletContextAttributeListener.`
  - `attributeAdded(ServletContextAttributeEvent scab)` Notification that a new attribute was added to the servlet context.
  - `attributeRemoved(ServletContextAttributeEvent scab)` Notification that an existing attribute has been removed from the servlet context.
  - `attributeReplaced(ServletContextAttributeEvent scab)` Notification that an attribute on the servlet context has been replaced.
- When a session is initialized or destroyed:
  - `javax.servlet.http.HttpSessionListener.`
  - `sessionCreated(HttpSessionEvent se)` Notification that a session was created.
  - `sessionDestroyed(HttpSessionEvent se)` Notification that a session became invalid or timed out.

- When a session attribute is added, removed, or replaced:
  - `HttpSessionAttributeListener`.
  - `attributeAdded(HttpSessionBindingEvent se)` Notification that an attribute has been added to a session.
  - `attributeRemoved(HttpSessionBindingEvent se)` Notification that an attribute has been removed from a session.
  - `attributeReplaced(HttpSessionBindingEvent se)` Notification that an attribute has been replaced in a session.

CONTEXT WITHIN A DISTRIBUTABLE WEB APPLICATION

3.3 Distinguish the behavior of the following in a distributable:

- **Servlet context init. parameters.**
- **Servlet context listener.**
- **Servlet context attribute listener.**
- **Session attribute listeners.**

The behavior of these listeners in a distributable is exactly the same as those discussed in the previous section, with one notable exception: Event notification of addition, removal, or replacement will affect the listener for only that context. No other context, such as other JVMs on the same or other machine, will know about the listener events.

CHAPTER SUMMARY

The HTTP methods `GET`, `POST`, and `PUT` are how browsers and Web servers trade data with each other. The `GET` retrieves a page without providing much information, while a `POST` can package huge amounts of information with its request. A `PUT` is for uploading a file. There are events associated with each type of request, such as clicking a hyperlink sending a `GET` request, but clicking a form button sends a `POST` request.

The most important objects in the servlet process are the request and response objects. The request parameters for the servlet are the strings sent by the client to the Servlet Container. The container parses the request and puts the information in a `HttpServletRequest` object which is passed to the servlet. Going the other way, the container wraps the response parameters with the HttpServletResponse object which is passed back to the container.

Containers have the idea of scope. When something has Context scope it is application-wide and all users can share data. Session scope means one user can share data across page views, but other users can't. Request scope restricts data to only that page. The container also manages the servlet life-cycle by initializing a servlet with a call to the `init()` method, a call to the `service()` method upon every request, and by calling a servlet's `destroy()` method just prior to removing it from memory. The container also allows you to monitor context and session events with listeners that are event-driven triggers. When an attribute changes, special targeted methods are called. In them, you can define special actions such as "add a note to the log every time the user count changes."

Lastly, the servlet specifies a `RequestDispatcher` object which performs servlet forwarding. Notice that this is different from redirection, where the servlet would return a new URL to the browser that triggers the browser to try to get that page. The `RequestDispatcher` doesn't redirect; rather it "dispatches" or performs forwarding.

KEY TERMS

- Redirection
- Servlet Life-Cycle
- Servlet Forwarding and Includes
- Servlet attribute
- Context parameters
- Application session
- listeners

APPLY YOUR KNOWLEDGE

Review Questions

1. What methods of the `Servlet` interface are invoked at different points in the servlet life cycle?
2. What HTTP methods are supported by `HttpServlet`?
3. What objects are passed to the servlet's `service()` method?
4. What is a distributable application?
5. Why is it a bad idea to synchronize a servlet's `service()` method?
6. What is the relationship between an application's `ServletConfig` object and `ServletContext` object?
7. What mechanisms are used by a Servlet Container to maintain session information?
8. What are the four events that are defined in the Servlet API?
9. How are request dispatchers used?

Exam Questions

1. Which of the following methods are defined in the `Servlet` interface?

   A. `init()`

   B. `service()`

   C. `finalize()`

   D. `destroy()`

2. Which of the following objects are passed to a servlet's `service()` method?

   A. `ServletRequest`

   B. `HttpServletRequest`

   C. `ServletResponse`

   D. `HttpServletResponse`

3. By default, how many instances of a servlet are created by a Servlet Container?

   A. One

   B. One per request

   C. One per session

   D. None of the above

4. Which of the following exceptions are defined by the Servlet API?

   A. `ServletException`

   B. `InitializationException`

   C. `UnavailableException`

   D. `ServletContextException`

5. Which of the following are used by Servlet Containers to maintain session information?

   A. cookies

   B. hidden form fields

   C. HTTPS protocol information

   D. URL rewriting

APPLY YOUR KNOWLEDGE

6. Which of the following event listeners are defined by the Servlet API?

   A. `HttpSessionBindingListener`

   B. `HttpSessionEventListener`

   C. `HttpSessionParameterListener`

   D. `HttpSessionAttributeListener`

7. Which of the following methods are defined by the `RequestDispatcher` interface?

   A. `dispatch()`

   B. `include()`

   C. `redirect()`

   D. `forward()`

8. Which of the following is the name of the cookie used by Servlet Containers to maintain session information?

   A. SESSIONID

   B. SERVLETID

   C. JSESSIONID

   D. CONTAINERID

Answers to Review Questions

1. The `init()` method is invoked during the initialization phase. The `service()` method is invoked during the request processing (service) phase. In other words, `init()` is invoked the first time the servlet runs, but `service()` is invoked once for every request the servlet receives. The `destroy()` method is invoked when the servlet is to be taken out of service. Refer to the section, "Servlet Life-cycle."

2. The `GET`, `POST`, `HEAD`, `PUT`, `DELETE`, `TRACE`, and `OPTIONS` methods are supported by `HttpServlet`. Refer to the section, "Interfacing with HTML Requests."

3. `ServletRequest` and `ServletResponse` objects are passed to the servlet's service method. Refer to the section, "Interfacing with HTML Requests."

4. A distributable application is an application that is distributed over multiple JVMs. Refer to the In the Field, "How Does a Servlet Work?"

5. When the `synchronized` keyword is used with a servlet's `service()` method, requests to that servlet are handled one at a time in a serialized manner. This means that the processing capabilities of the Servlet Container are minimized. Refer to the section, "Servlet Life-cycle."

6. An application's `ServletConfig` object contains its `ServletContext` object and provides access to this object via its `getServletContext()` method. Refer to the section, "Web Application Context."

7. Cookies, URL rewriting, and HTTPS protocol information are used to maintain session information. Refer to the section, "Session."

8. The four events that are defined by the Servlet API are `HttpSessionEvent`, `HttpSessionBindingEvent`, `ServletContextEvent`, and `ServletContextAttributeEvent`. Refer to the section, "Servlet Life-cycle."

9. Request dispatchers are used to forward requests to other servlets or to include the results of other servlets. Refer to the section, "Using a RequestDispatcher."

APPLY YOUR KNOWLEDGE

Answers to Exam Questions

1. **C.** The `finalize()` method is not defined by the `Servlet` interface. Refer to the section, "Servlet Life-cycle."
2. **A, C.** `ServletRequest` and `ServletResponse` methods are passed to the `service()` method. Refer to the section, "Servlet Life-cycle."
3. **A.** By default, only one instance of a servlet is created by a Servlet Container. Refer to the section, "Servlet Life-cycle."
4. **A, C.** The Servlet API defines ServletException and UnavailableException. Refer to the section, "Servlet Life-cycle."
5. **A, C, D.** Hidden form fields are not used by Servlet Containers to maintain session information. Refer to the section, "Form Parameters."
6. **A.** Only `HttpSessionBindingListener` is defined by the Servlet API. Refer to the section, "Servlet Life-cycle."
7. **B, D.** The `RequestDispatcher` interface defines the `include()` and `forward()` methods. Refer to the section, "Using a RequestDispatcher."
8. **C.** The JSESSIONID cookie is used by Servlet Containers to maintain session information. Refer to the section, "Session."

Suggested Readings and Resources

1. Sun's excellent J2EE Tutorial—`java.sun.com/j2ee/tutorial/1_3-fcs/doc/J2eeTutorialTOC.html`.
2. The Java Language Specification—(`java.sun.com/docs/books/jls/second_edition/html/j.title.doc.html`).
3. Exam objectives for the Sun Certified Web Component Developer for J2EE Platform—`http://suned.sun.com/US/certification/java/exam_objectives.html`.
4. The Java Servlet 2.3 Specification—`http://jcp.org/aboutJava/communityprocess/first/jsr053/index.html`.
5. Sun's official Servlet page—`http://java.sun.com/products/servlet/`.
6. Java Software FAQ Index—`http://java.sun.com/docs/faqindex.html`.
7. Tomcat—an implementation of the Java Servlet 2.2 and JavaServer Pages 1.1 Specifications—`http://jakarta.apache.org/tomcat/index.html`.
8. Java Training by the MageLang Institute—`http://www.magelang.com/`.
9. Servlets.com, Web site companion to *Java Servlet Programming* by O'Reilly—`http://www.servlets.com/`.
10. Glossary of Java Technology-Related Terms—`http://java.sun.com/docs/glossary.html`.

OBJECTIVES

Servicing requests from users on the Web means you will sometimes receive bad information. Also, you may make a mistake in your code. How do you handle these conditions in servlets? This chapter discusses error and exception handling.

There are two categories of problems you will face. One is from Java itself and your code. For example, you may try to write a note to the log file, but that file is locked at the moment so the write attempt fails. That will throw an exception. The other category regards the user's request, where you might get a corrupt or incomplete request. These error codes that you will work with are based on the Hypertext Transfer Protocol (HTTP).

The main focus of this chapter is servlet exceptions and HTTPse error codes (those associated with the client), how they are used, and the effect they have on the servlet behavior. So this chapter covers objectives 4.1 and 4.3 from Section 4, "Designing and Developing Servlets to Handle Server-side Exceptions," of the Sun preparation guide.

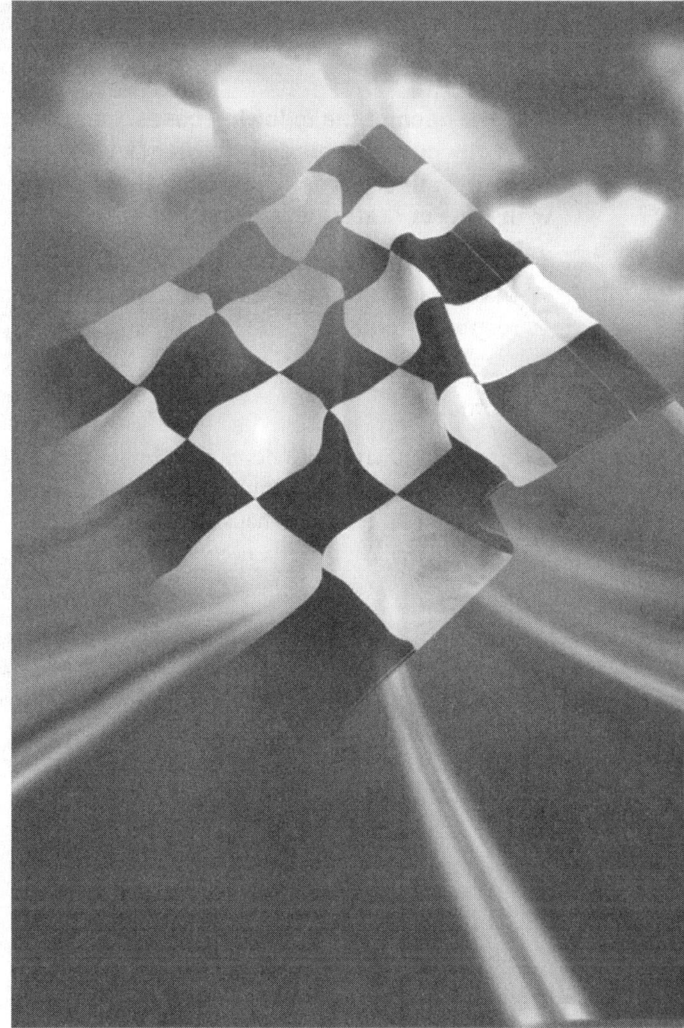

CHAPTER 5

Servlet Exceptions

Objectives

4.1 For each of the following cases, identify correctly constructed code for handling business logic exceptions, and match that code with correct statements about the code's behavior:

- **Return an HTTP error using the `sendError` response method.**
- **Return an HTTP error using the `setStatus` method.**

▶ Exceptions and errors are never nice, but with a GUI application, at least you can expect a person at the console to interact, perhaps intercept, an application's bad behavior. With a server, this isn't so. You must handle the exceptions assuming the server is operating completely on its own. This chapter introduces you to the way servlets throw and manage exceptions, including the steps you need to take to make sure your server catches exceptions properly.

4.3 Identify the method used for the following:

- **Write a message to the WebApp log.**
- **Write a message and an exception to the WebApp log.**

▶ The purpose of this objective is to teach you how to write data into the log file. This objective is related to the previous one because you often write data into a log file immediately after throwing an exception.

OUTLINE

STUDY STRATEGIES

- Throwing exceptions in servlets involves some blind work. Be sure to practice using both the `sendError` and `setStatus` methods to see what happens.
- Make sure you know the basic syntax of `sendError()` as well as `setStatus()`.
- Take some time to study the difference between the two approaches to telling the client a problem has occurred.

WARNING

The exam is looking for SENDERROR and SETSTATUS! While there are many ways to customize error handling, do not expect weird customized exception routines on the exam. Also, notice that you use the response object (`HttpServletResponse`), not the request object, to tell the browser that there is a problem.

INTRODUCTION

The way in which you create and manage exceptions with servlets is slightly different from how you do this with standalone applications.

In this chapter, we are concerned with implementing error handling routines. Because the exam includes both exceptions (caused by the servlet) and HTTP error codes (those you send back to the client), you will work with both types throughout this chapter.

According to the standard, HTTP/1.1 (HTTP uses a "<major>.<minor>" numbering scheme) is "an application-level protocol for distributed, collaborative, hypermedia information systems." These error codes for HTTP have been around for several years; they have been used by the World Wide Web since 1990. MIME-like messages were introduced with HTTP/1.0. The current HTTP/1.1 is the Internet standard which enhanced the previous requirements to ensure reliability. Since servlets communicate with clients through HTTP, it is helpful to know a little about this protocol.

The HTTP protocol is a request/response scheme where a client sends a request to the server (in this case a servlet container). There are four major portions of this request, namely, a request method (GET, POST…), URI (such as `www.que.com`), protocol version (HTTP/1.1), and finally a MIME-like message. This message can be any size, and normally includes request modifiers, client information, and body content. Below you will read how you send error information to the client using the `sendError` method, which sends a status line with the protocol version and a success or error code (this is what `sendError` affects directly). It also returns a MIME-like message containing server information, entity meta information, and body content.

You must be aware of both the severity and type of error to properly tell the client what went wrong. Just how damaging is the problem? Your error handling logic needs to determine the most appropriate severity for a particular error.

After receiving a request, the server responds. It returns an HTTP response message. The first line of this response message is called the *status line*. The status line has three parts. They are, in this order, protocol version, numeric status code, and status textual phrase.

For details, such as the fact that each element is separated by space characters, and CR or LF are disallowed except in the final CRLF sequence, please see RFC 2616. This status code is what you are setting when you use `sendError` and `setStatus` methods.

You have surely encountered the 404, NOT FOUND message at some Web sites. This tells you that the URL is bad. Notice that number 404. This is an example of a status code, a three-digit integer code. The first digit of the status code defines the class of response, while the last two digits do not have categories, although they are defined in the standard. Table 5.1 provides a list of the HTTP status codes (only the first digit is significant).

TABLE 5.1

STATUS CODES

Number	*Type*	*Description*
1XX	Informational	Request received, continuing to process.
2XX	Success	The action was successfully received, understood, and accepted.
3XX	Redirection	Further action must be taken in order to complete the request.
4XX	Client Error	The request contains bad syntax or cannot be fulfilled.
5XX	Server Error	The server failed to fulfill an apparently valid request.

While Table 5.1 describes a five-part scheme for the status codes, we will primarily be interested in the Server Error category (5XX) codes.

As mentioned previously, the HTTP protocol is a request/response scheme where a client sends a request to the server. When you need to inform the client of a problem at the server end, you call the `sendError` method. This causes the server to respond with a status line, with protocol version and a success or error code (this is what `sendError` affects directly). Of course, it also returns a MIME-like message containing server information, entity meta information, and body content.

Internally, the `sendError()` and `setStatus` are closely related. In fact, they both set the error message to be displayed by the client and the status code used by the client. The default status code is `HttpServletResponse.SC_OK ="OK"`; however, there are a few dozen standard codes.

Table 5.2 provides a list of status codes. These codes were defined by the W3C and are sanctioned by the Internet Society (ISOC). The constant names, quoted messages that get displayed in the browser, and code descriptions are a combination of the servlet specification and Tomcat's implementation of that specification. The exam will not test your memory of these directly. However, taking five minutes to study this table will help you understand what these codes do and figure out which ones you need to use with the `sendError` and `setStatus` methods. Notice that the RFC column provides the Request For Comment document and section, the Internet's way of documenting standards. Also, some browsers allow the user to hide "friendly" error messages. If they do that, they will not see many of these errors, even if they occur.

TABLE 5.2

HTTP STATUS CODES

Code	*Constant*	*RFC*	*Message*	*Description*
100	SC_CONTINUE	10.1.1	"Continue"	Client can continue.
101	SC_SWITCHING_PROTOCOLS	10.1.2	"Switching Protocols"	Server is switching protocols according to Upgrade header.
200	SC_OK	10.2.1	"OK"	Request succeeded normally.
201	SC_CREATED	10.2.2	"Created"	Request succeeded and created a new resource on the server.
202	SC_ACCEPTED	10.2.3	"Accepted"	Request was accepted for processing but was not completed.
203	SC_NON_AUTHORITATIVE_INFORMATION	10.2.4	"Non-Authoritative Information"	Meta information presented by the client did not originate from the server.
204	SC_NO_CONTENT	10.2.5	"No Content"	Request succeeded but there was no new information to return.
205	SC_RESET_CONTENT	10.2.6	"Reset Content"	Agent should reset the document view which caused the request to be sent.
206	SC_PARTIAL_CONTENT	10.2.7	"Partial Content"	Server has fulfilled the partial GET request for the resource.

Code	*Constant*	*RFC*	*Message*	*Description*
300	SC_MULTIPLE_CHOICES	10.3.1	"Multiple Choices"	Requested resource corresponds to any one of a set of representations with each with its own specific location.
301	SC_MOVED_PERMANENTLY	10.3.2	"Moved Permanently"	Resource has permanently moved to a new location and future references should use a new URI with their requests.
302	SC_MOVED_TEMPORARILY	10.3.3	"Moved Temporarily"	Resource has temporarily moved to another location but future references should still use the original URI to access the resource.
303	SC_SEE_OTHER	10.3.4	"See Other"	Response to the request can be found under a different URI.
304	SC_NOT_MODIFIED	10.3.5	"Not Modified"	Conditional GET operation found that the resource was available and not modified.
305	SC_USE_PROXY	10.3.6	"Use Proxy"	Requested resource must be accessed through the proxy given by the Location field.
307	SC_TEMPORARY_REDIRECT	10.3.8	NA	Requested resource resides temporarily under a different URI. The temporary URI should be given by the Location field in the response.
400	SC_BAD_REQUEST	10.4.1	"Bad Request"	Request sent by the client was syntactically incorrect.
401	SC_UNAUTHORIZED	10.4.2	"Unauthorized"	Request requires HTTP authentication.
402	SC_PAYMENT_REQUIRED	10.4.3	"Payment Required"	Reserved for future use.
403	SC_FORBIDDEN	10.4.4	"Forbidden"	Server understood the request but refused to fulfill it.
404	SC_NOT_FOUND	10.4.5	"Not Found"	Requested resource is not available.
405	SC_METHOD_NOT_ALLOWED	10.4.6	"Method Not Allowed"	Method specified in the Request-Line is not allowed for the resource identified by the Request-URI.
406	SC_NOT_ACCEPTABLE	10.4.7	"Not Acceptable"	Resource identified by the request is only capable of generating response entities that have content characteristics not acceptable according to the accept headers sent in the request.
407	SC_PROXY_AUTHENTICATION_REQUIRED	10.4.8	"Proxy Authentication Required"	Client must first authenticate itself with the proxy.
408	SC_REQUEST_TIMEOUT	10.4.9	"Request Timeout"	Client did not produce a request within the time that the server was prepared to wait.
409	SC_CONFLICT	10.4.10	"Conflict"	Request could not be completed due to a conflict with the current state of the resource.
410	SC_GONE	10.4.11	"Gone"	Resource is no longer available at the server and no forwarding address is known. This condition should be considered permanent.
411	SC_LENGTH_REQUIRED	10.4.12	"Length Required"	Request cannot be handled without a defined Content-Length.

continues

TABLE 5.2 *continued*

HTTP STATUS CODES

Code	*Constant*	*RFC*	*Message*	*Description*
412	SC_PRECONDITION_FAILED	10.4.13	"Precondition Failed"	A precondition given in one or more of the request-header fields evaluated to false when it was tested on the server.
413	SC_REQUEST_ENTITY_ TOO_LARGE	10.4.14	"Request Entity Too Large"	Server is refusing to process the request because the request entity is larger than the server is willing or able to process.
414	SC_REQUEST_URI_TOO_LONG	10.4.15	"Request URI Too Long"	Server is refusing to service the request because the Request-URI is longer than the server is willing to interpret.
415	SC_UNSUPPORTED_MEDIA_ TYPE	10.4.16	"Unsupported Media Type"	Server is refusing to service the request because the entity of the request is in a format not supported by the requested resource for the requested method.
416	SC_REQUESTED_RANGE_ NOT_SATISFIABLE	10.4.17	"Requested Range Not Satisfiable"	Server cannot serve the requested byte range.
417	SC_EXPECTATION_FAILED	10.4.18	"Expectation Failed"	Server could not meet the expectation given in the Expect request header.
500	SC_INTERNAL_SERVER_ERROR	10.5.1	"Internal Server Error"	Error inside the server which prevented it from fulfilling the request. This error represents many server problems such as exceptions or perhaps a database hiccup.
501	SC_NOT_IMPLEMENTED	10.5.2	"Not Implemented"	Server does not support the functionality needed to fulfill the request.
502	SC_BAD_GATEWAY	10.5.3	"Bad Gateway"	Server received an invalid response from a server it consulted when acting as a proxy or gateway.
503	SC_SERVICE_UNAVAILABLE	10.5.4	"Service Unavailable"	Server is temporarily overloaded and unable to handle the request.
504	SC_GATEWAY_TIMEOUT	10.5.5	"Gateway Timeout"	Server did not receive a timely response from the upstream server while acting as a gateway or proxy.
505	SC_HTTP_VERSION_NOT_ SUPPORTED	10.5.6	"HTTP Version Not Supported"	Server does not support or refuses to support the HTTP protocol version that was used in the request message.

RETURNING AN ERROR CODE TO THE CLIENT

4.1 For each of the following cases, identify correctly constructed code for handling business logic exceptions, and match that code with correct statements about the code's behavior:

- **Return an HTTP error using the `sendError` response method.**
- **Return an HTTP error using the `setStatus` method.**

The servlet is just as prone to logic errors and bugs as standalone applications. Java has a smart facility for handling them in both environments. Let's look at a very simple example of how you might handle an error in a servlet. The ErrorServlet servlet illustrates the use of the `sendError()` method. It takes an error code as a parameter and an optional custom message associated with that error (see Listing 5.1).

LISTING 5.1

THE SOURCE CODE OF THE ERRORSERVLET SERVLET

```
import javax.servlet.http.HttpServlet;
import javax.servlet.http.HttpServletRequest;
import javax.servlet.http.HttpServletResponse;
import javax.servlet.ServletOutputStream;
import javax.servlet.ServletException;
import java.io.PrintWriter;
import java.io.IOException;

public class ErrorServlet extends HttpServlet {

  public void service(HttpServletRequest request,
                      HttpServletResponse response)
    throws ServletException, IOException {

    response.sendError(HttpServletResponse.SC_FORBIDDEN,
                   "Sorry, restricted to geeks.");
  }
}
```

Compile the ErrorServlet file and hit the servlet with your browser.

The container will send an error message to the client. You should see a page that looks like Figure 5.1.

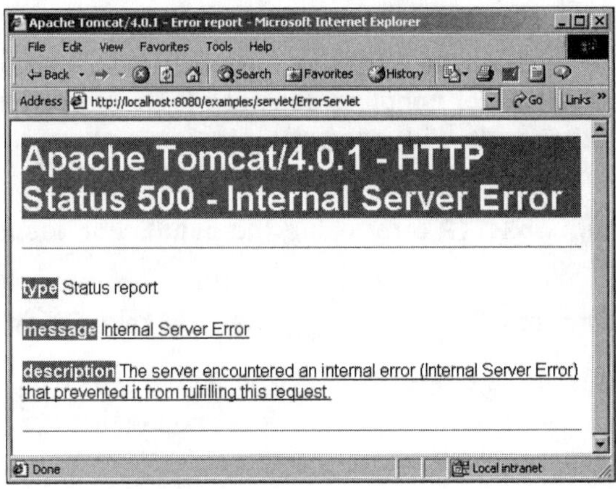

FIGURE 5.1
Result of using `sendError` to send an error message to the browser.

WARNING

Do Not Send Data to Client After SENDERROR()! Once the `sendError` method is invoked, all buffered output will be discarded. If data has been written to the response buffer but not returned to the client (not committed), the data is cleared and replaced with the data sent by the `sendError` method. The `sendError` method will commit the response, if it has not already been committed, and terminate it. Data written to the response afterward is ignored. However, if you write data to the response buffer and try to commit it *after* `sendError` has been invoked, an `IllegalStateException` will be thrown.

`sendError` Method

The `sendError` method sends an error response to the client using the specified status. Using this method clears the buffer. The server creates an HTML-formatted server error page. This page contains a default, or the message you provide, as an argument. It also sets the content type to "text/html", even if you changed this, but leaves cookies and other headers unmodified.

The `sendError` method will set the appropriate headers and content body for an error message to return to the client. An optional String argument can be provided to the `sendError` method, which can be used in the content body of the error. Using this method will commit the response (if not already committed) and terminate it. The data stacked in the output stream to the client before calling `sendError()` method is ignored.

Internally, the servlet base classes prevent you from writing to the output stream after calling `sendError()`. In the write-to-stream methods there is a test for a previous error in the servlet that looks like this:

```
//suspended is a flag set once output is committed
      if (suspended)//true if sendError has been called
         throw new IOException
            (sm.getString("responseBase.write.suspended"));
```

That is why you can't add to the outputstream after calling sendError().

The best way to understand the sendError() method is to look at it directly. Listing 5.2 (prettied a bit) is how Tomcat implements the specification on sendError():

LISTING 5.2

TOMCAT'S sendError() METHOD

```
/**
 * Send an error response with the status and message.
 *
 * @param status HTTP status code to send
 * @param message Corresponding message to send
 *
 * @exception IllegalStateException if this response has
 *  already been committed
 * @exception IOException if an input/output error occurs
 */
public void sendError(int status, String message)
       throws IOException
{
    if (isCommitted())
        throw new IllegalStateException
          (sm.getString("httpResponseBase.sendError.ise"));

    if (included)
        return;  //Ignore any call from an included servlet

    setError();

    // Record the status code and message.
    this.status = status; //class level field
    this.message = message; //class level field

    // Clear any data content that has been buffered
    resetBuffer();

    // Cause the response to be finished
    // (from the application perspective)
    setSuspended(true);
}
```

You can see from the method internals that six steps are taken. The first thing it does is throw an IllegalStateException exception if the response was already sent (committed). Then it quits if it is not being called from the outermost servlet. The third thing it does is set an internal flag with setError(). It then sets the status and message class fields. These two are what concern us the most. It next clears the buffer and, finally, suspends further output stream access.

You can make better use of this method if you create a wrapper for it. You might want to do this if you care to send custom messages to the client rather than accept the default ones provided by the container. You can write a wrapper like the one in Listing 5.3.

LISTING 5.3

A WRAPPER FOR THE sendError() METHOD

```
import javax.servlet.http.HttpServlet;
import javax.servlet.http.HttpServletRequest;
import javax.servlet.http.HttpServletResponse;
import javax.servlet.ServletException;
import java.io.PrintWriter;
import java.io.IOException;


public class ErrorManager extends HttpServlet
{
  //your own custom flag:
  static final int SC_CUSTOM_ERROR_FIRST_NAME = 3229;

  public void sendError(HttpServletResponse response,
                        int code)
     throws ServletException, IOException
  {
    // Message sent by sendError().
    String message = getErrorMessage(code);

    if(message.equals("NONE"))
    {
       response.sendError(HttpServletResponse.SC_
➥FORBIDDEN);
    } else
    {
        response.sendError(HttpServletResponse.SC_
➥FORBIDDEN,
                             message);
    }

    //perhaps your own history log:
    //internalLog(code, message);
  }

  public String getErrorMessage(int code)
  {
     String message = "NONE";
     //in Tomcat HttpResponseBase extends ResponseBase
     //        implements HttpResponse, HttpServletResponse
```

```
        //HttpServletResponse msg = new HttpServletResponse();
        switch (code)
        {
           case HttpServletResponse.SC_OK:
              return ("OK");
           case HttpServletResponse.SC_ACCEPTED:
              return ("Accepted");
           case HttpServletResponse.SC_BAD_GATEWAY:
              return ("Bad Gateway");
           case HttpServletResponse.SC_BAD_REQUEST:
              return ("Bad Request");
           case HttpServletResponse.SC_CONFLICT:
              return ("Conflict");
           case HttpServletResponse.SC_CONTINUE:
              return ("Continue");
           case HttpServletResponse.SC_CREATED:
              return ("Created");

           //many other standard codes removed for space

           //first custom message; overides default message
           case HttpServletResponse.SC_GONE:
              return ("Sorry, this resource   +
                      "is not available.");
           case
             HttpServletResponse.SC_HTTP_VERSION_NOT_
    ➥SUPPORTED:
              return ("Whoa! You are doing something funky" +
                      " and we do not support it.");
           case HttpServletResponse.SC_INTERNAL_SERVER_ERROR:
              return ("Have no idea what happened, but it "
                      "was a terrible server error");
           case HttpServletResponse.SC_MOVED_PERMANENTLY:
              return ("For the last time, this has moved "
                      "permanently!");
           case HttpServletResponse.SC_MOVED_TEMPORARILY:
              return ("Just messing around, "
                      "it will be back soon");
           case HttpServletResponse.SC_NO_CONTENT:
              return ("Duh, notin to say.");
           case HttpServletResponse.SC_PAYMENT_REQUIRED:
              return ("Hey! You think you can do that "
                      "without paying???");
           case SC_CUSTOM_ERROR_FIRST_NAME:
              return ("Terribly sorry. You must "
                      "provide a first name.");
           default:
              return ("NONE");
           }
       }
}
```

setStatus Method

The setStatus method sets the status code for a given response. Use this method, instead of sendError, when there is no exception or serious error (such as Forbidden page). If there is a serious error, the sendError method should be used; otherwise use setStatus. Like the sendError method, using this method clears the buffer, but leaves cookies and other headers unmodified.

Internally, the setStatus method looks like Listing 5.4:

LISTING 5.4

TOMCAT'S setStatus() METHOD

```
    /**
     * Set the HTTP status and message to be returned
     *  with this response.
     *
     * @param status The new HTTP status
     * @param message The associated text message
     *
     * @deprecated As of Version 2.1 of the Java Servlet
     * API, this method has been deprecated due to the
     * ambiguous meaning of the message
     *  parameter.
     */
    public void setStatus(int status, String message) {

        if (included)
            return; //Ignore any call from included servlet

        this.status = status;
        this.message = message;

}
```

As you can see, this method has been deprecated because the message functionality isn't reliable. The setStatus method will remain (the one taking only a status code), but without a message parameter in a future version, I predict. You can write a wrapper for the setStatus method like that shown in Listing 5.5.

LISTING 5.5

A setStatus() METHOD WRAPPER

```
    /**
     * statusManager Method.
     */
    void statusManager(HttpServletResponse response)
        throws ServletException
    {
        if( !isValid(firstName) )
        {
            response.setStatus(response.SC_BAD_REQUEST);
        } else if( !isValid(lastName) )
        {
            response.setStatus(response.SC_BAD_REQUEST);
        } else if( !isValid(countryName) )
        {
            response.setStatus(response.SC_BAD_REQUEST);
        } else if( !isValid(creditCardNumber) )
        {
            response.setStatus(response.SC_BAD_REQUEST);
        } else
        {
            response.setStatus(response.SC_OK);
        }
}
```

The same status codes that are used for the `sendError` method can be used for the `setStatus` method, too. The primary difference is that the former prevents any further response to the client and throws an exception if you try. This is not so for the latter. There is one point of confusion with the `setStatus` method. The specification says the buffer is cleared when called. In other words, you should set this first before you send anything back to the client. However, I looked in Tomcat and did not observe the buffer being cleared. The following snippet:

```
out.println("pre setStatus message.");
response.setStatus(HttpServletResponse.SC_OK);
out.println("post setStatus message.");
```

produced this:

```
pre setStatus message.
post setStatus message.
```

WARNING

Containers don't always follow the specification! Clearly, Tomcat does not clear the buffer as the specification notes. The specification doesn't make sense on this point; the way Tomcat implemented it is better. However, since other containers may follow the specification here and the exam will be based on the specification, assume that is how it actually works.

WEBAPP LOG

4.3 Identify the method used for the following:

- **Write a message to the WebApp log.**
- **Write a message and an exception to the WebApp log.**

The Server Configuration File defines the component elements that comprise the "Server," a singleton element that represents the entire JVM. Two of these elements are the Access log and the Activity log. These are simple text files to which the container appends messages. While containers differ, Tomcat implements the specification very closely, except for just a few things. Let's look at how Tomcat uses logs.

By default, log files are created in the "logs" directory relative to the home directory of Tomcat installation (`$CATALINA_HOME`). You can specify a different directory, using either a relative (to `$CATALINA_HOME`) or absolute path, with the "directory" attribute in the server.xml file. Different containers handle this in various ways, but Tomcat creates two new files, access and activity, every time you start the server.

Tomcat implements several log files. One of them is the Global log file (for example, catalina_log.2002-12-25.txt). Its contents look like this after starting, stopping, and starting again:

```
2002-04-25 13:52:29 HttpConnector Opening server socket ...
2002-04-25 13:52:34 HttpConnector[8080] Starting ...
2002-04-25 13:52:34 HttpProcessor[8080][0] Starting ...
2002-04-25 13:52:34 HttpProcessor[8080][1] Starting ...
2002-04-25 13:52:34 HttpProcessor[8080][2] Starting ...
2002-04-25 13:52:34 HttpProcessor[8080][3] Starting ...
2002-04-25 13:52:34 HttpProcessor[8080][4] Starting ...
2002-04-25 14:33:36 HttpProcessor[8080][4] Stopping ...
2002-04-25 14:33:36 HttpProcessor[8080][3] Stopping ...
2002-04-25 14:33:36 HttpProcessor[8080][2] Stopping ...
2002-04-25 14:33:36 HttpProcessor[8080][1] Stopping ...
2002-04-25 14:33:36 HttpProcessor[8080][0] Stopping ...
2002-04-25 14:33:36 HttpConnector[8080] Stopping ...
2002-04-25 14:34:52 HttpConnector Opening server ...
2002-04-25 14:34:55 HttpConnector[8080] Starting ...
2002-04-25 14:34:56 HttpProcessor[8080][0] Starting ...
2002-04-25 14:34:56 HttpProcessor[8080][1] Starting ...
2002-04-25 14:34:56 HttpProcessor[8080][2] Starting ...
2002-04-25 14:34:56 HttpProcessor[8080][3] Starting ...
2002-04-25 14:34:56 HttpProcessor[8080][4] Starting ...
```

When something breaks, this log is somewhat helpful in that you can see what thread is broken. A more helpful log is Tomcat's access log (such as localhost_access_log.2002-12-25.txt), which appends the following line after I request the previous servlet above with `http://localhost:8080/examples/servlet/ErrorServlet:`

```
127.0.0.1 - - [25/Dec/2002:14:23:53 -0800]
"GET /examples/servlet/ErrorServlet HTTP/1.1" 200 75
```

The log which is most interesting to us is the file localhost_examples_log.2002-04-25.txt (other containers will use a different name and perhaps a different location). This is the one that is written to when you use the logging functionality in the servlet environment.

Listing 5.6 is a logger wrapper. It creates a snapshot of the request parameters and prints it to the log file. You might not want all this information, but it illustrates what you can do.

LISTING 5.6

THE SOURCE CODE OF THE LogServlet PROGRAM

```
import javax.servlet.http.HttpServlet;
import javax.servlet.http.HttpServletRequest;
import javax.servlet.http.HttpServletResponse;
import javax.servlet.http.Cookie;
import javax.servlet.ServletContext;
import javax.servlet.ServletException;
import java.util.Enumeration;
import java.sql.Timestamp;
import java.io.PrintWriter;
import java.io.IOException;

public class LogServlet extends HttpServlet
{

  public void service(HttpServletRequest request,
                      HttpServletResponse response)
    throws ServletException, IOException {

    response.setContentType("text/html");
    PrintWriter out = response.getWriter();
    out.println("<html>");
    out.println("<head><title>Servlet Error Handling " +
                "Example</title></head>");
    out.println("<body>");

    String logMessage = getSnapshot(request);
    out.println("You are being watched. " +
               "Logging this request.");
```

continues

LISTING 5.6 *continued*

THE SOURCE CODE OF THE LogServlet PROGRAM

```
//    Context context = request.getContext();
      ServletContext context = getServletContext();
      context.log(logMessage);

      out.println(logMessage);
      out.println("</body>");
      out.println("</html>");
    }

      public String getSnapshot(HttpServletRequest request)
      throws ServletException
      {

      // get generic servlet request properties
      StringBuffer snapshot = new StringBuffer();
      snapshot.append("Activity occurred at " +
         (new Timestamp(System.currentTimeMillis())) + '\n');
      snapshot.append(" characterEncoding=" +
                      request.getCharacterEncoding() + '\n');
      snapshot.append("     contentLength=" +
                          request.getContentLength() + '\n');
      snapshot.append("       contentType=" +
                          request.getContentType() + '\n');
      snapshot.append("locale=" +request.getLocale() + '\n');

      Enumeration names = request.getParameterNames();
      while (names.hasMoreElements()) {
          String name = (String) names.nextElement();
          snapshot.append("        parameter=" + name + "=");
          String values[] = request.getParameterValues(name);
          for (int i = 0; i < values.length; i++) {
              if (i > 0)
              snapshot.append(", ");
          snapshot.append(values[i]);
          }
          snapshot.append('\n');
      }
      snapshot.append("          protocol=" +
                          request.getProtocol() + '\n');
      snapshot.append("        remoteAddr=" +
                          request.getRemoteAddr() + '\n');
      snapshot.append("        remoteHost=" +
                          request.getRemoteHost() + '\n');
      snapshot.append("            scheme=" +
                          request.getScheme() + '\n');
      snapshot.append("        serverName=" +
                          request.getServerName() + '\n');
```

```
    snapshot.append("        serverPort=" +
                     request.getServerPort() + '\n');
    snapshot.append("          isSecure=" +
                     request.isSecure() + '\n');

    // Render the HTTP servlet request properties
    if (request instanceof HttpServletRequest) {
      snapshot.append("---------------------------------");
       HttpServletRequest hrequest =
                         (HttpServletRequest) request;
       snapshot.append("       contextPath=" +
                        hrequest.getContextPath() + '\n');
       Cookie cookies[] = hrequest.getCookies();
           if (cookies == null)
               cookies = new Cookie[0];
       for (int i = 0; i < cookies.length; i++) {
           snapshot.append("            cookie=" +
                             cookies[i].getName() +
                   "=" + cookies[i].getValue());
       }
       names = hrequest.getHeaderNames();
       while (names.hasMoreElements()) {
           String name = (String) names.nextElement();
       String value = hrequest.getHeader(name);
           snapshot.append("            header=" +
                             name + "=" + value + '\n');
       }
       snapshot.append("            method=" +
                            hrequest.getMethod() + '\n');
       snapshot.append("          pathInfo=" +
                            hrequest.getPathInfo() + '\n');
       snapshot.append("       queryString=" +
                         hrequest.getQueryString() + '\n');
       snapshot.append("        remoteUser=" +
                          hrequest.getRemoteUser() + '\n');
       snapshot.append("requestedSessionId=" +
              hrequest.getRequestedSessionId());
       snapshot.append("        requestURI=" +
                          hrequest.getRequestURI() + '\n');
       snapshot.append("       servletPath=" +
                         hrequest.getServletPath() + '\n');
    }
    snapshot.append("=============================" +'\n');

    // return the information
    return snapshot.toString();
    }
}
```

Listing 5.6 will create a string of information and write it to the log file using the built-in logging facility, namely, `ServletContext.log(String)` method. After requesting this servlet, the container wrote the following to the log file (localhost_examples_log.2002-012-25.txt):

```
2002-12-25 16:09:15 Activity occurred at 2002-12-25
16:09:15
 characterEncoding=null
     contentLength=-1
       contentType=null
            locale=en_US
          protocol=HTTP/1.1
        remoteAddr=127.0.0.1
        remoteHost=127.0.0.1
            scheme=http
        serverName=localhost
        serverPort=8080
          isSecure=false
       contextPath=/examples
            header=accept=*/*
            header=accept-language=en-us
            header=accept-encoding=gzip, deflate
            header=user-agent=Mozilla/4.0 (compatible;
                     MSIE 5.01; Windows NT 5.0)
            header=host=localhost:8080
            header=connection=Keep-Alive
            method=GET
          pathInfo=null
       queryString=null
        remoteUser=null
requestedSessionId=null
requestURI=/examples/servlet/LogServlet
       servletPath=/servlet/LogServlet
=============================================

2002-12-25 16:09:15 InvokerFilter(ApplicationFilterConfig
[name=Path Mapped Filter,
filterClass=filters.ExampleFilter]): 10 milliseconds
```

The output was revised to fit on the page. You will change the information to suit your needs, but Listing 5.6 will get you started. The exam will ask about the log method so compile and play with this code.

There is one more wrinkle to the log feature that you need to know for the exam. You can pass an exception object to the log method. If you add the following code to the preceding `LogServlet` code:

```
try
{
   int zero = 0;
   int problem = 10/zero;
} catch (Exception e)
{
   log("Oops, division by zero.", e);
```

```
    //optional:
    //throw new ServletException(e);
  }
```

The logger will add the following to the log file (localhost_examples_log.2002-012-25.txt):

```
2002-04-25 22:00:09 org.apache.catalina.INVOKER.LogServlet:
 Oops, division by zero.
java.lang.ArithmeticException: / by zero
    at LogServlet.service(LogServlet.java:38)
    at javax.servlet.http.HttpServlet.service(...)
        //33 more lines of error messages removed for space
    at java.lang.Thread.run(Thread.java:536)
```

NOTE

GenericServlet has log method! The abstract GenericServlet class has a log method, `log(String)`, which writes the specified message to a servlet log file, prepended by the servlet's name.

CHAPTER SUMMARY

One of the first hurdles in servlet design you'll encounter is exception handling. The exception features of the servlet API are decent. The exam expects you to know how to handle exceptions. There won't be many questions on this, but you will see a few.

Logging your programs is a traditional approach to spying on the internals. It is often helpful to look at log files to figure out what happened, say, just before a crash. Perhaps it isn't even a dramatic event; you just need to keep an eye on who is accessing what. There are many wonderful third-party tools that will leverage log files. For example, WebTrends (`www.webtrends.com`) does many nice things for Web site administrators. It performs traffic analysis for Web sites and produces nice graphs. WebTrends and products like it started life as glorified log file readers.

There are other ways to analyze application events and performance. There is the Jylog project (`jylog.sourceforge.net/`) which is an open source logging tool built with the Java Platform Debugger Architecture (JPDA) SDK 1.3 (`java.sun.com/products/jpda/`). It eliminates the tedious logging code that will litter your source. Another excellent effort by the Apache group is the log4j project. log4j enables logging at runtime without modifying the application binary. That group is trying to design the package so that you don't incur a heavy performance cost. It has a nice architecture where the logging behavior is controlled by editing a configuration file. These applications are a boon to you when you need detailed context for application events and failures. However, for the exam, you only need to know how to call the log method, which has two signatures, both with a string message and one with an exception.

KEY TERMS

- exception
- `sendError()`
- `setStatus()`
- Logging
- Status codes
- Error codes

APPLY YOUR KNOWLEDGE

Review Questions

1. What is a status code?
2. What classifications are there for status codes?
3. How does logging work in servlets?
4. What would be the preferred storage location for application events?
5. How does `sendError()` work?
6. What is the difference between `sendError()` and `setStatus()`?

Exam Questions

1. The `sendError()` method sends what type of information to the client?

   A. Response footer.

   B. Response header.

   C. Content body.

   D. None of the above.

2. Which of the following is a correct `sendError()` call?

   A. `response.sendError(HttpServletResponse.SC_FORBIDDEN, "Sorry, restricted to geeks.");`

   B. `request.sendError(HttpServletResponse.SC_FORBIDDEN, "Sorry, restricted to geeks.");`

   C. `request.sendError(HttpServletResponse.SC_FORBIDDEN);`

   D. `response.sendError("Sorry, restricted to geeks.");`

3. The Status-Code element is a three-digit integer code. The first digit of the Status-Code defines the class of response while the last two digits do not have categories, although they are defined in the standard. What classification is used for redirect?

   A. 2XX.

   B. 3XX.

   C. 4XX.

   D. 5XX.

4. The status codes have been defined by whom?

   A. The DSN group.

   B. Sun's expert group.

   C. The Internet Society.

   D. The Apache group.

5. You need to terminate the request due to an erroneous set of credentials. What method should your servlet respond with?

   A. `addHeader(String name, String value)` method of the response object to add a response header with the given name and value.

   B. `terminate(String name, int value)` to add a response header with the given name and integer value.

   C. `doTerminate(String location)` to send a temporary redirect response to the client so they can try again.

   D. `response.sendError(HttpServletResponse.SC_NOT_ACCEPTABLE, "Sorry, your crentials are invalid. Please try again.");.`

APPLY YOUR KNOWLEDGE

6. Which method is best for telling the client that all went well and the request was processed successfully?

   A. Do nothing. This is the default.

   B. `setHeader()`

   C. `setStatus()`

   D. `setIntHeader()`

7. Which method commits the response, effectively terminating it?

   A. `sendError()`

   B. `setHeader()`

   C. `setStatus()`

   D. `finalize()`

8. How can you return an exception object to the client?

   A. You cannot do this.

   B. Use `sendError`.

   C. Use `setStatus`.

   D. Use `sendException`.

9. Which of the following will throw an `IllegalStateException` exception?

   A. `setIntHeader(long)`

   B. `setHeader(long)`

   C. Calling the destroy method before the buffer is flushed.

   D. Calling `sendError` after the response is committed.

Answers to Review Questions

1. A status code is a discrete mechanism where the server and client talk to each other employing a predefined vocabulary of codes. These codes also help the client keep the user informed on the progress of a request. See "Introduction."

2. The default status code for requests is 200 ("OK"). There are five types of status codes defined by the HTTP standard (not Sun). 1XX is informational. It indicates a request was received and is continuing to be processed. All is well. 2XX says that there was success. So, the request was successfully received, understood, and accepted. 3XX is used for redirection. It tells the browser to try somewhere else and further action must be taken in order to complete the request. 4XX is a message from the server telling the client that the request contains bad syntax or cannot be fulfilled. The last class of status codes is 5XX, which indicates a server error. The server failed to fulfill a syntactically valid request. See "Introduction."

3. The `log()` method writes a specified message to a servlet log file. This can be used as a debug log or simply an event log. The name and type of the servlet log file is specific to the servlet container. Tomcat allows you modify this. See "WebApp Log."

4. When you are working with servlets, it is hard to see what is going on. You will probably need to log servlet activity. The preferred storage location for application events is a log file. You can use your own or use the built in logging functionality in servlets. See "WebApp Log."

APPLY YOUR KNOWLEDGE

5. When you call the `sendError` method, the server responds with a status line with the protocol version and a success or error code (this is what `sendError` affects directly). Of course, it also returns a MIME-like message containing server information, entity meta information, and body content. See "Returning an Error Code to the Client."

6. The `setStatus` method sets the status code for a given response. Use this method, instead of `sendError`, when there is no exception or serious error (such as Forbidden page). If there is a serious error, the `sendError` method should be used; otherwise use `setStatus`. Like the `sendError` method, using `setStatus` clears the buffer, but leaves cookies and other headers unmodified. See "Returning an Error Code to the Client."

Answers to Exam Questions

Answers marked with an asterisk (*) indicate that the specific material covered by the question has a very low probability of being on the exam in that form. These questions were included because the concepts they tap represent important background knowledge or because they are important to developing your overall professional skills.

1. **D.** The `sendError()` method sends both header and content body type information. This method is overloaded to handle either header only or both. See "Returning an Error Code to the Client."

2. **A.** This method is overloaded with two signatures. Only A is correct. B and C are wrong because this method is part of the response object not the request object. D is wrong because you must supply a status code; you can't just send a String message. See "Returning an Error Code to the Client."

*3. **B.** 3XX is used for redirection. The other codes are 2XX for continuation, 4XX for client error, and 5XX for server error. See "Introduction."

*4. **C.** The Internet Society is the group who defined these codes. The other groups were not involved. Please see RFC 2616. See "Introduction."

5. **D.** This is the correct way to send a "Not Acceptable" status code of 406. The other answers are correct syntax, but don't send the proper status code to the client. See "Returning an Error Code to the Client."

6. **A.** This is a difficult question. B, C, and D can be used to send information to the client. C is close because it is sometimes used to send an "OK" status of 200 back to the client. However, A is the correct answer. This particular task should be left to the container. See "Returning an Error Code to the Client."

7. **A.** This is the only method that actually terminates the request. `sendError()` commits the response, if it has not already been committed, and terminates it. No further output to the client can be made because data written to the response after this method is called is ignored. See "Returning an Error Code to the Client."

8. **B.** Sending an exception object is not possible without a lot of tweaking. This action is not mentioned anywhere in the specification. See "Returning an Error Code to the Client."

9. **D.** Calling `sendError` will throw an `IllegalStateException` exception if the response was already sent (committed). None of the other choices will throw this exception. See "Returning an Error Code to the Client."

APPLY YOUR KNOWLEDGE

Suggested Readings and Resources

1. Hypertext Transfer Protocol—HTTP/1.1: `ftp://ftp.isi.edu/in-notes/rfc2616.txt`.
2. jGuru's JSP FAQ—`http://www.jguru.com/faq/JSP`.
3. jGuru's Servlet FAQ—`http://www.jguru.com/faq/Servlets`.
4. Sun's excellent J2EE Tutorial—`java.sun.com/j2ee/tutorial/1_3-fcs/doc/J2eeTutorialTOC.html`.
5. The Java Language Specification—`java.sun.com/docs/books/jls/second_edition/html/j.title.doc.html`.
6. jGuru JSP forum—`http://www.jguru.com/forums/JSP`.
7. jGuru Servlet forum—`http://www.jguru.com/forums/Servlets`.
8. Servlet 2.3 Specifications and JavaDoc—`http://java.sun.com/products/servlet/download.html`.
9. WebTrends—`http://www.webtrends.com`.

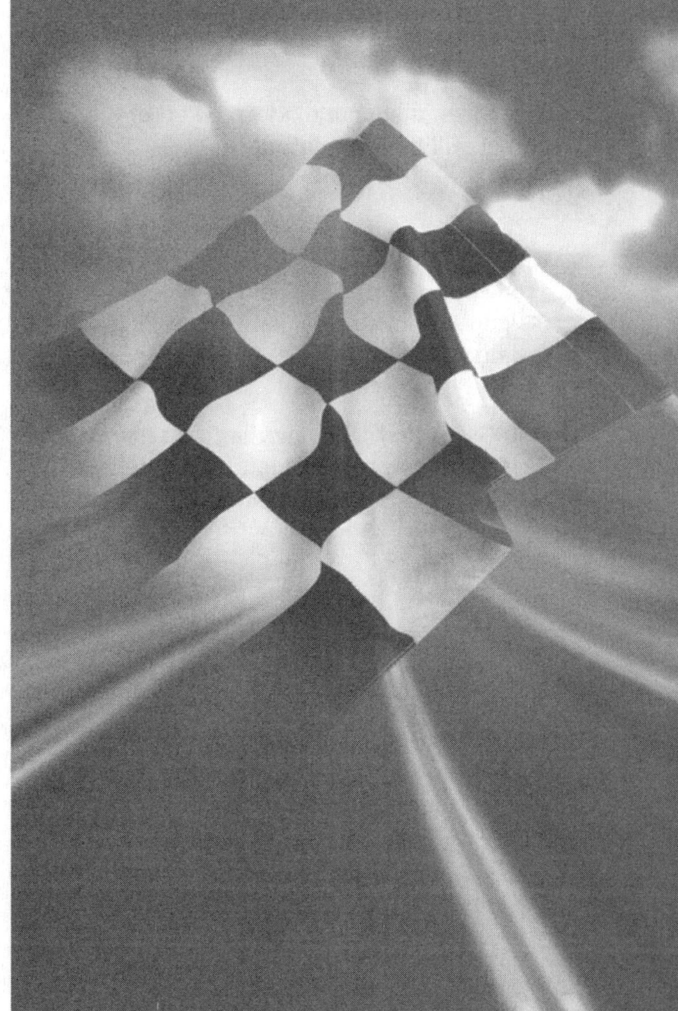

CHAPTER 6

Session Management

OBJECTIVES

This chapter covers the following Sun-specified objectives specified in Section 5, "Designing and Developing Servlets Using Session Management," of the Sun Certified Web Component Developer For J2EE Platform exam:

5.1 Identify the interface and method for each of the following:

- **Retrieve a session object across multiple requests to the same or different servlets within the same WebApp.**
- **Store objects into a session object.**
- **Retrieve objects from a session object.**
- **Respond to the event when a particular object is added to a session.**
- **Respond to the event when a session is created and destroyed.**
- **Expunge a session object.**

▶ This section of the exam covers your familiarity with session objects within servlets. Sun gave session functionality ample attention, so it is not hard to learn. For example, it is easy to retrieve a session object across multiple requests to the same or different servlets within the same WebApp. You can store and later retrieve objects from the session object. Lastly, you can respond to triggers that fire upon a change to the session object state (for example, adding an object to or removing an object from a session). Session objects help maintain client state in a consistent manner. This is a better way to maintain state than most custom approaches.

Objectives

5.2 Given a scenario, state whether a session object will be invalidated.

- The exam will present scenarios which may or may not invalidate a session object. In other words, what will kill a session? For example does viewing another page invalidate a session? Does leaving your desk do so? This section answers these questions and discusses exactly how to kill a session.

5.3 Given that URL-rewriting must be used for session management, identify the design requirement on session-related HTML pages.

- Maintaining a session between a Web container and client requires passing an identifier between the client and server. This identifier or tag usually goes into a cookie on the client. However, if the user has turned off cookies, you can pass the identifier in the query string. In this case, each link in the HTML must then include this identifier. We say the URL is rewritten because the previous string is changed to include the identifier.

Outline

STUDY STRATEGIES

- The key to this section of the exam is to understand how servlets implement the session object functionality.
- There aren't many methods to know, but scope is another matter. If you are not careful, you can get confused and lose track of what you added to a session and what you didn't.
- Each session object lives for the duration of a single client accessing the Web server. There are a few rules, such as the timeout where the session dies if inactivity lasts more than 20 minutes (time is configurable).

INTRODUCTION

When one page needs to share information with another, the scope of the data broadens beyond processing a single request. When that happens, you must send the data from one page to the server and from the server to the next requested page, whether it be the same page or another page altogether. There are several ways to share state information between requests. However, the primary way is to use sessions, the topic of this chapter.

SHARING STATE INFORMATION BETWEEN REQUESTS

There are many techniques in use today to share state information between requests. This chapter focuses on using sessions to maintain state. To appreciate sessions, let us first look at a few others ways to maintain state. One way is to persist the data in a form field between views of the same page.

Let's study an example. For example, suppose you want to maintain the first and last name of a user between page views. Listing 6.1 represents all that is required to persist data between views of the same page generated by a servlet.

LISTING 6.1

PERSISTING DATA IN FORM FIELDS

```
/* PersistDataInFormFields.java, v 1.0
 *
 */

import java.io.*;
import javax.servlet.*;
import javax.servlet.http.*;

/**
 * A simple servlet.
 * SCWCD Exam Objective 5.1 = session objects
 *
 * @author Reader@Que
 */
```

```
public class PersistDataInFormFields extends HttpServlet
{
    public void doPost(HttpServletRequest request,
                       HttpServletResponse response)
        throws IOException, ServletException
    {
        response.setContentType("text/html");

        PrintWriter out = response.getWriter();
        out.println("<html>");
        out.println("<body>");
        out.println("<head>");
        String title = "Persist Data In Form Fields
➥Example";
        out.println("<title>" + title + "</title>");
        out.println("</head>");
        out.println("<body bgcolor=\"white\">");

        out.println("<h3>" + title + "</h3>");

        // get data to persist in form fields
        String firstName=request.getParameter("firstname");
        String lastName = request.getParameter("lastname");
        out.println("<p />");
        out.print("<form action=\"");
        out.print("PersistDataInFormFields\" ");
        out.println("method=\'POST\'>");
        out.print("<input type=\'text\' " +
                  "size=20 name=\'firstname\' ");
        out.print("value=\"" + firstName + "\">");
        out.print("<input type=\'text\' " +
                  "size=20 name=\'lastname\' ");
        out.print("value=\"" + lastName + "\">");
        out.println("<br>");
        out.println("<input type=\'submit\'>");
        out.println("</form>");

        out.println("</body>");
        out.println("</html>");
    }
}
```

Listing 6.1 showed you an example of how you can persist data between views of the same page. See Figure 6.1 for a picture of the output.

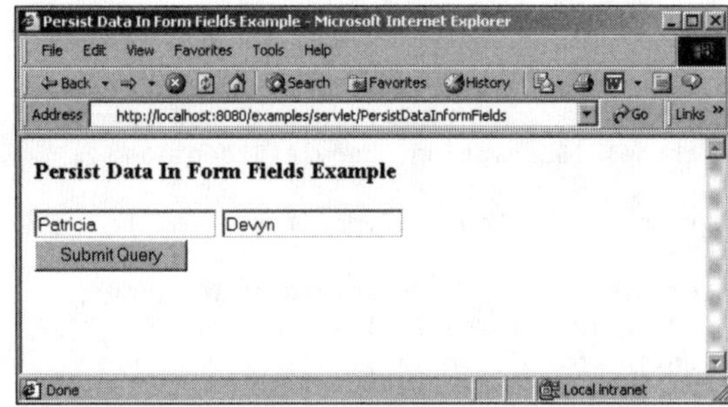

FIGURE 6.1
You can persist data between views of the same page using form fields.

Listing 6.2 is the HTML the servlet generates and sends to the browser after the user typed Patricia and Devyn in the fields.

LISTING 6.2

THE SOURCE CODE RETURNED TO THE BROWSER BY LISTING 6.1

```
<html>
<body>
<head>
<title>Persist Data In Form Fields Example</title>
</head>
<body bgcolor="white">
<h3>Persist Data In Form Fields Example</h3>
<p />
<form action="PersistDataInFormFields" method=POST>
<input type='text' size=20 name='firstname'
➥value="Patricia">
<input type='text' size=20 name='lastname'
➥value="Devyn"><br>
<input type='submit'>
</form>
</body>
</html>
```

The HTML in Listing 6.2 is rendered by the browser which requested the `PersistDataInFormFields` servlet. At least we have established communication between pages in a stateless environment. This is a first step toward maintaining client state.

HOW DO SESSIONS WORK?

The container generates a session ID. When you create a session, the server saves the session ID on the client's machine as a cookie. If cookies are turned off then it appends the ID in the URL. On the server, whatever you add to the session object gets placed in server memory—very resource intensive. The server associates that object in memory with the session ID. When the user sends a new request, the session ID is sent too. The server can then match the objects in its memory with that session ID. This is how we maintain client state.

You basically persist the data between views of the same page by receiving the field value and populating the field again with the same value when returning the form in your response. There are times when this is appropriate (don't make the user retype a field). However, this isn't a good way to persist data, because the data lives only in the field value and nowhere else. Another trick is to use hidden fields.

Another old tactic you can use is to "hide" user submitted information in a form with the `HIDDEN` tag. This tag just sits in the page, but the browser doesn't display it to the user. The following is an example:

```
<!-- formHandler is servlet that handles form submission --
➥>
<form   action="formHandler">
<input name="firstName"    value="" >
<input name="userID" value="23AX" type="hidden">
<input type=submit>
</form>
```

This HTML snippet specifies that the `firstName` and the `userID` field values be sent to the `formHandler` servlet. The `firstName` field is visible on the screen, but the `userID` field is not; it is hidden. Be careful with hidden fields. While the hidden field's value isn't displayed on the page, the user can see the value of the hidden field by viewing the HTML source of the document. Even so, at least you can persist data between pages with hidden fields. This is a very shallow method. It is insecure. Don't use it if the data is sensitive.

The next step on our ladder of sophisticated means to persist data between pages is using cookies. A cookie is a tiny text file that is maintained by the browser to do things like store unique IDs. They are normally small (~1KB) and saved in the OS cookie directory or folder. There are numerous browsers that handle cookies in various ways. For example, in Windows, the following short list shows you how a few versions of Explorer stores cookies:

- IE 4.x for Windows 98: `\%windir%\Cookies\<username>@<site name>.txt`
- IE 4.x for Windows NT: `\%systemroot%\profiles\%username%\Cookies\<username>@<site name>.txt`
- IE 5.0 for Windows 95: `\%windir%\Cookies\<username>@<site name>.txt`
- IE 5.0 for Windows 98: `\%windir%\Cookies\<username>@<site name>.txt`
- IE 5.0 for Windows NT: `\%systemroot%\profiles\%username%\Cookies\<username>@<site name>.txt`

Figure 6.2 shows you where they are on my Dell Inspiron running Windows 2000 Professional.

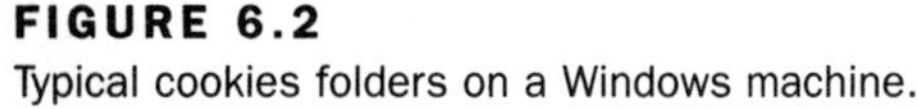

FIGURE 6.2
Typical cookies folders on a Windows machine.

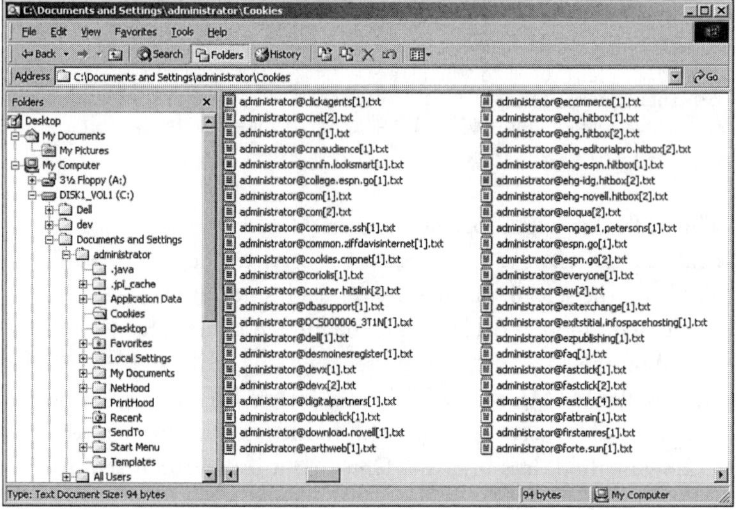

Cookies have had many lives and deaths, it seems. In the old days they were used for all manner of things, including storing personal data like passwords. The popularity of doing so has waned. Today, especially with servlets, it is better to store most information in sessions than cookies. But it is still important to understand cookies before discussing sessions.

Figure 6.2 is typical of a cookie folder. As you can see, there are many cookies on my machine. Those shown in Figure 6.2 are only a few that have been created on my Dell. Originally, folks put actual data like names and addresses in cookies because there wasn't anywhere else to save these valuable pieces of data. Today, the information in a cookie is primarily an identifier of sorts. The following cookie text was placed on my hard disk by DoubleClick. I never saw it happen. The reason it happened to me is companies (for example, Netscape) hire DoubleClick to manage their online advertisement. Companies like DoubleClick can charge more for their advertising services if they can figure out what I like. When a user visits Netscape, a DoubleClick cookie is created and an identifier is placed in it by DoubleClick. DoubleClick records which pages on Netscape you visit. Also, if you happen to visit another vendor who has a contract with DoubleClick, that movement is recorded too. Now, DoubleClick knows a little more about you so it can throw ads at you that you are more likely to like.

Vendors implement session IDs differently. Let us dig into Tomcat to see how it handles sessions IDs. The following snippet, edited for clarity, is how a session ID is generated:

```
/**
     * Generate and return a new session identifier.
     */
    protected synchronized String generateSessionId() {

        // Generate a byte array containing a session ID
        Random random = getRandom();
        //int SESSION_ID_BYTES = 16;
        byte bytes[] = new byte[SESSION_ID_BYTES];
        getRandom().nextBytes(bytes);
        bytes = getDigest().digest(bytes);

        // The remainder of routine converts
        // the byte array to a String of hexadecimal
➥digits.

        // This returns something like:
        // 62A027E37975F305B07555859780E423
        // see Listing 6.6
        return (result.toString());
    }
```

Web sites keep track of your activities (such as a shopping cart) with a standard session ID, which assigns each visitor a unique, random number. The servlet specification doesn't address how browsers are supposed to store the session ID. Some browsers store it in memory (but send/receive in request/response header as a cookie), while most store it in a cookie file. For example, when I recently visited Amazon, its servers sent my browser a new session ID which was stored in a cookie file called administrator@amazon[1].txt. In this cookie was the following session ID, among other things like datestamp:

```
session-id
002-0150365-1700034
amazon.com/
```

Cookies have been the target of privacy advocates since the beginning of Net time. Cookies are now used for many things, including the suspicious tracking of your activities as you surf the Internet. Some people call the use of cookies to track activity (as opposed to benign page to page data sharing on only one Web site) Web bugs. Some companies are paid to monitor you as much as possible to create a profile. Companies like DoubleClick and MatchLogic then sell their ability to target advertising to Internet users for a given advertising campaign. One popular tactic they employ is the use of a one-pixel image tag on a Web page they monitor. This tag is in the page, but the browser doesn't display it. You can't see it because it is too small and has the same color as the background. The browser sends a request to the watchdog company (such as DoubleClick) to retrieve the image. This one-pixel image tag results in a server being informed of your visit to a Web site, whether you like it or not. The first time you hit a page with a DoubleClick pixel image, DoubleClick places an ID in a cookie on your machine. Going forward, DoubleClick can then collect statistics on you regarding how many times you visit any Web page it monitors. The following cookie was placed on my machine by DoubleClick:

```
id
8000833313c3021
doubleclick.net/
0
9008256768
245696467
32324437008
290098027
*
```

It is an ID plus other data DoubleClick uses. Any time I visit a page that has a DoubleClick image tag (it is surprising how many do), DoubleClick logs my activity. Since it has this ID, it can more accurately build a profile on me. Without it, companies like DoubleClick have to rely on IP addresses, which can cause inaccuracy due to proxy servers, dynamic IP address schemes, and other complications DoubleClick would rather avoid.

Most of the cookies on our machines are not used for anything sinister. You can thwart all this by turning off cookies and images, but the Web suddenly becomes bland. For example, you can almost thwart companies like DoubleClick from invading on your privacy by making a change in your browser's configuration. You can do this in IE by going to View, Internet Options, Advanced, selecting Prompt before accepting Cookies, and clicking OK.

Cookies aren't all cloak and dagger, though. In fact, they are used for good far more often than bad. For example, when I go to Amazon.com, I get a familiar view because they remember what I did on my last visit. Amazon can do that because it placed a file on my machine called administrator@amazon[1].txt (the browser actually does this) containing this:

```
session-id
432-5447995-1125358
amazon.com/
0
4322765824
89901156
321345632
79444758
*
session-id-time
8731881600
amazon.com/
0
9985765824
44191156
185745632
09789758
*
ubid-main
0883061-5210078
amazon.com/
0
6796341376
69581269
777869456
29476039
*
```

```
x-main
3xBkjhwcqmPgTz7hgffU8UoFvMDSWX
amazon.com/
0
7896341376
1969969
939053232
9770408
*
```

I like the idea of Amazon tracking my activities. They are open about it and I can stop them any time I wish. I hate it when other companies do so stealthily.

It isn't just DoubleClick and Amazon that need cookies: You do, too. You can create cookies with the cookie functionality of the response object. In fact, if you want to perform any real communication between views, you need to use cookies. Cookies aren't a big focus of the exam, but I thought you might like to understand how they work in servlets.

Maintaining client state has always been important. With the Internet it is hard to do because the very nature of the Internet is packet switching, which means asynchronous communication. There is a disconnect between Web page requests due to the Internet's nuclear-war-withstanding, stateless protocol. However, some of your applications will require a series of client requests to be associated with one another. The best way we have for maintaining state, out of the Java box, is called sessions. To support applications that need to maintain state, Java Servlet technology provides an API for managing sessions and allows several mechanisms for implementing sessions.

To summarize, the following are the four most frequently used methods for persisting data between views:

- Field-field: Value of a field in a request is copied to value of same field in response.
- Hidden form field: Data is placed in the HTML in a hidden form field.
- Query string: Some data is appended to the query string or a hyperlink in the HTML.
- Cookie: A small text file created by the browser that stores data sent by the server.

These four approaches are the ones most often used; however, session technology does more for you. The following section describes how Java uses sessions to help you maintain client state.

USING SESSION OBJECTS

The primary methods associated with sessions belong to the HttpSession interface. The following summarizes the session methods you need to know for the exam:

- `getAttribute(java.lang.String name)`: Returns an Object associated with that name that was stored in the session object.
- `getAttributeNames()`: Returns an Enumeration object that lists the names of the objects stored in the session object.
- `getCreationTime()`: Returns a long containing the date stamp of creation.
- `getId()`: Returns the id of the session as a String representing the unique identifier assigned to this session.
- `getLastAccessedTime()`: Returns a long containing the date stamp of the last time the session was accessed.
- `getMaxInactiveInterval()`: Returns an integer representing the maximum time interval, in seconds, that the servlet container will keep this session open between client accesses.
- `invalidate()`: This destroys a session. It can't be referenced after this method has been called.
- `isNew()`: This tells you whether the client knows about the session. In other words, the has session been created by the server, but the client hasn't acknowledged receiving the session ID yet.
- `removeAttribute(java.lang.String name)`: This removes an attribute. It deletes it from the session object.
- `setAttribute(java.lang.String name, java.lang.Object value)`: You use this method to add objects to a session.
- `setMaxInactiveInterval(int interval)`: Specifies the time, in seconds, between client requests before the servlet container will invalidate this session.

- `getValue(java.lang.String name)`: Returns an Object associated with that name that was stored in the session object. As of Version 2.2, this method is replaced by `getAttribute()`. The `getAttribute()` method will be on the exam, not this one, but it is here for completeness.
- `getValueNames()`: Returns a String array with a list of names associated with the objects added to a given session. As of Version 2.2, this method is replaced by `getAttributeNames()`. The `getAttributeNames()` method will be on the exam, not this one, but it is here for completeness.
- `putValue(java.lang.String name, java.lang.Object value)`: You use this method to add objects to a session. This has been deprecated. As of Version 2.2, this method is replaced by `setAttribute(java.lang.String, java.lang.Object)`. The `setAttribute()` method will be on the exam, not this one, but it is here for completeness.
- `removeValue(java.lang.String name)`: This removes a value, but retains an attribute name in the session. The name is valid but the object is null. This has been deprecated. As of Version 2.2, this method is replaced by `removeAttribute()`. The `removeAttribute()` method will be on the exam, not this one, but it is here for completeness.

The preceding methods are the ones that will appear on the exam. The following sections will show you how to use them and in what context they are best suited.

Storing and Retrieving Session Objects

5.1 Identify the interface and method for each of the following:

- **Retrieve a session object across multiple requests to the same or different servlets within the same WebApp.**
- **Store objects into a session object.**
- **Retrieve objects from a session object.**

- **Respond to the event when a particular object is added to a session.**
- **Respond to the event when a session is created and destroyed.**
- **Expunge a session object.**

This exam objective addresses the manner in which you use sessions in servlets; namely, to set and get information into and out of a session object while processing a request. Listing 6.3 is a guest listing of sorts. This is how Tomcat implements the capability to create a session. It usually helps to look under the hood to see how something is done before we discuss how to use that same functionality.

LISTING 6.3

TOMCAT'S IMPLEMENTATION OF CREATING SESSION OBJECTS

```
/**
 * Return the session associated with this Request,
 * creating one if necessary and requested.
 *
 * @param create Create a new session if none exist
 */
public HttpSession getSession(boolean create)
{
    if( System.getSecurityManager() != null )
    {
        PrivilegedGetSession dp =
                            new PrivilegedGetSession(create);
        return (HttpSession)AccessController
                                          .doPrivileged(dp);
    }
    return doGetSession(create);
}

private HttpSession doGetSession(boolean create)
{
    // There cannot be a session if
    // no context has been assigned yet
    if (context == null)
        return (null);

    // Return the current session if it exists and is valid
    if ((session != null) && !session.isValid())
        session = null;
    if (session != null)
        return (session.getSession());
```

continues

LISTING 6.3 *continued*

TOMCAT'S IMPLEMENTATION OF CREATING SESSION OBJECTS

```
        // Return the requested session if
        //it exists and is valid
        Manager manager = null;
        if (context != null)
            manager = context.getManager();
        if (manager == null)
            return (null);      // Sessions are not supported
        if (requestedSessionId != null)
        {
           try
           {
             session = manager.findSession(requestedSessionId);
           } catch (IOException e) {
                session = null;
           }
           if ((session != null) && !session.isValid())
               session = null;
           if (session != null) {
               return (session.getSession());
           }
        }

        // Create a new session if requested and
        //the response is not committed
        if (!create)
            return (null);
        if ((context != null) && (response != null) &&
            context.getCookies() &&
            response.getResponse().isCommitted())
        {
            throw new IllegalStateException
              (sm.getString("httpRequestBase.createCommitted"));
        }

        session = manager.createSession();
        if (session != null)
           return (session.getSession());
        else
           return (null);
    }

    /**
     * Return <code>true</code> if the session identifier
     * included in this request came from a cookie.
     */
    public boolean isRequestedSessionIdFromCookie()
    {
        if (requestedSessionId != null)
            return (requestedSessionCookie);
        else
```

```
        return (false);
    }

    /**
     * Return <code>true</code> if the session identifier
     * included in this request came from the request URI.
     */
    public boolean isRequestedSessionIdFromURL()
    {
        if (requestedSessionId != null)
            return (requestedSessionURL);
        else
            return (false);
}
```

Listing 6.3 shows you how Tomcat handles your request to create a session object. Now let us make use of that functionality. Listing 6.4 demonstrates some basic techniques of how to create a cookie and session, place data into them, and finally get that same data back out. This is a derivation of several excellent code samples I found in the Tomcat source distribution.

LISTING 6.4

Manipulating Cookie and Session Objects

```
import java.io.IOException;
import java.io.PrintWriter;
import java.text.SimpleDateFormat;
import java.util.Date;
import java.util.Enumeration;
import javax.servlet.*;
import javax.servlet.http.*;

/* some version/OS combinations throw an
exception when manipulating sessions. For
example, some versions of Linux return a
setAttribute nomethodfound error when this
servlet is requested.
*/

public class SessionDetailReporter extends HttpServlet
{
    public void doPost(HttpServletRequest request,
                       HttpServletResponse response)
            throws ServletException, IOException
    {
        doGet(request,response);
    }

    public void doGet(HttpServletRequest request,
```

continues

LISTING 6.4 *continued*

MANIPULATING COOKIE AND SESSION OBJECTS

```
                        HttpServletResponse response)
            throws ServletException, IOException
    {

      /**
        * Return the session associated with this Request,
        * creating one if necessary and requested.
        *
        * @param create Create a new session if none exist
        *
        * To make sure the session is properly maintained,
        * you must call this method before the response is
        * committed. If the container is using cookies to
        * maintain session integrity and is asked to create
        * a new session when the response is committed,
        * an IllegalStateException is thrown.
        */
        HttpSession session = request.getSession(true);

        //If you don't set an attribute, you might not see
        //the session. That happened to me when I placed
➥this
        //line AFTER sending HTML to the response object.
        //It works now that it is at the top.

        //If buffering is off and the HTTP header
        //(which contains the cookie information)
        //has already been sent, you can't do any
        //other operations that would send cookie headers.
session.setAttribute("sessionNumber", new Integer(22));

        String cookieName =
                  request.getParameter("cookiename");
        String cookieValue =
                  request.getParameter("cookievalue");
        if (cookieName != null && cookieValue != null)
        {
            Cookie cookie =
                  new Cookie(cookieName, cookieValue);
            response.addCookie(cookie);
        }

        PrintWriter out = response.getWriter();
        response.setContentType("text/html");

        out.println("<html>");
        out.println(" <head>");
        out.println(" <title>Session Detail " +
                            "Report</title>");
        out.println(" </head>");
        out.println(" <body>");
        out.println("  <center>");
        out.println("   <h2>Session Detail Report</h2>");
```

```
    String url=request.getScheme()+
               "://"+request.getServerName()+
               ":"+request.getServerPort()+
               request.getRequestURI();

    out.println("  <table width=\"100%\" border=\"1\" +
              " cellspacing=\"0\" cellpadding=\"1\">");
    out.println("    <tr>");
    out.println("     <td colspan=2>"+url+"</td>");
    out.println("    </tr>");
    printVoid(out);

    out.println("    <tr>");
    out.println("     <td colspan=2>");
    out.print("<form action=\"");
    out.println(url + "\" method=POST>");
    out.println("Attribute Name:<input type=text " +
               "length=20 name=cookiename><br>");
    out.println("Attribute Value:<input type=text" +
               " length=20 name=cookievalue><br>");
    out.println("<input type=submit></form>");
    out.println("     </td>");
    out.println("    </tr>");

    printHeader(out,"Cookies in this request:");
    Cookie[] cookies = request.getCookies();
    if (cookies!=null)
      for (int i = 0; i < cookies.length; i++) {
        Cookie cookie = cookies[i];
        printValue(out,cookie.getName(),
                   cookie.getValue());
    }
    printVoid(out);

    printHeader(out,"Session information:");
    SimpleDateFormat format = new
        SimpleDateFormat("yyyy/MM/dd hh:mm:ss.SSS z");
    printValue(out,"Requested Session Id:",
                     request.getRequestedSessionId());
    printValue(out,"Current Session Id:",
                     session.getId());
    printValue(out,"Current Time:",
                     format.format(new Date()));
    printValue(out,"Session Created Time:",
format.format(new Date(session.getCreationTime())));
    printValue(out,"Session Last Accessed Time:",
format.format(new Date(session.getLastAccessedTime())));
    printValue(out,"Session Max Inactive " +
    "Interval Seconds:",
Integer.toString(session.getMaxInactiveInterval()));
    printVoid(out);

    printHeader(out,"Session values:");
    Enumeration enum = session.getAttributeNames();
    while (enum.hasMoreElements())
    {
```

continues

LISTING 6.4 *continued*

MANIPULATING COOKIE AND SESSION OBJECTS

```
            String key = (String) enum.nextElement();
            Object val = session.getAttribute(key);
            printValue(out,key,val.toString());
        }
        printVoid(out);

        out.println("    </td>");
        out.println("   </tr>");
        out.println("  </table>");
        out.println(" </body>");
        out.println("</html>");
        out.flush();
    }

    public void printHeader(PrintWriter out, String header)
    {
        out.println("   <tr>");
        out.println("    <td bgcolor=\"#999999\" ");
        out.println("    "colspan=\"2\">");
        out.println("     <b>"+header+"</b>");
        out.println("    </td>");
        out.println("   </tr>");
    }

    public void printValue(PrintWriter out,
                           String key, String val)
    {
        if (val!=null) {
            if (val.length()>255)
             val=val.substring(0,128)+" <i>(... more)</i>";
        }
        out.println("   <tr>");
        out.println("    <td bgcolor=\"#cccccc\">"+
                                        key + "</td>");
        out.println("    <td bgcolor=\"#ffffff\">"+
                                        val + "</td>");
        out.println("   </tr>");
    }

    public void printVoid(PrintWriter out)
    {
        out.println("   <tr><td bgcolor=\"#ffffff\" " +
                       "colspan=\"2\"> </td></tr>");
    }
}
 /*
 Of course, you could do more useful things
 with cookies like use them to facilitate shopping carts.
*/
```

Figure 6.3 shows you the output from Listing 6.4.

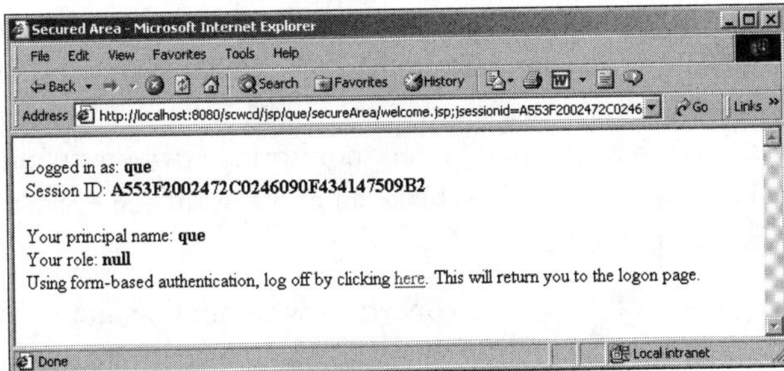

FIGURE 6.3
Output from Listing 6.4.

Event Listeners

JDK 1.1 introduced a new event-handling paradigm for Java. This functionality allowed the generation and handling of AWT events. These events include a delegation event model, with such events as `ActionEvent`, `AdjustmentEvent`, and `FocusEvent`. There is similar functionality in version 2.3 of the servlets specification. There are four interfaces and several methods that comprise the primary event-related methods you need to know for the exam.

We will first look at how objects bound to a session may listen to container events, notifying them that sessions will be passivated or sessions will be activated. This interface is `HttpSessionActivationListener extends java.util.EventListener`. The methods are

- `sessionDidActivate(HttpSessionEvent se)`: This is the notification that the session has just been activated.
- `sessionWillPassivate(HttpSessionEvent se)`: This is the notification that the session is about to be passivated.

> **NOTE**
>
> **Session Moving Between JVMs** The specification dictates that a container that migrates a session between VMs or persists sessions is required to notify all attributes bound to sessions implementing `HttpSessionActivationListener`. This has to do with distributed Web apps, covered in Chapter 10, "Web Applications."

These two methods call the method by the same name in the listener when the session is created or destroyed.

The listener interface that enables an object to monitor changes to the attribute lists of sessions within a given Web application is `HttpSessionAttributeListener extends java.util.EventListener`. The methods that concern us here are

- `attributeAdded(HttpSessionBindingEvent se)`: This is the notification that an attribute has been added to a session.
- `attributeRemoved(HttpSessionBindingEvent se)`: This is the notification that an attribute has been removed from a session.

- `attributeReplaced(HttpSessionBindingEvent se)`: This is the notification that an attribute has been replaced in a session.

You would use these methods when monitoring attributes within a session. Perhaps you'll want to make an entry in the log every time a user visits a certain URL.

The last group of listeners are concerned with binding and unbinding to a session. This event listener causes an object to be notified when it is bound to or unbound from a session. The interface is `HttpSessionBindingListener extends java.util.EventListener`. This will be triggered when a servlet is coded to explicitly unbind an attribute from a session, due to a session being invalidated or a session timeout. The methods that concern us here are

- `valueBound(HttpSessionBindingEvent event)`: This is the notification to the object that it is being bound to a session and identifies the session.
- `valueUnbound(HttpSessionBindingEvent event)`: This is the notification to the object that it is being unbound from a session and identifies the session.

You might want to know when an object is added or removed from a session to handle, say, a shopping cart checkout.

Listing 6.5 shows you a small snippet of creating a session, binding and unbinding attributes to it, and then destroying the session. Use it with Listing 6.6 to see how to monitor attributes with listeners.

LISTING 6.5

INTENTIONALLY CREATING EVENTS TO TRIGGER LISTENER CALLS

```
import java.io.*;
import javax.servlet.*;
import javax.servlet.http.*;

public class SessionEventTriggers extends HttpServlet {

    public void doGet(HttpServletRequest request,
                      HttpServletResponse response)
        throws IOException, ServletException
    {
```

```
        // These activities trigger listener events
        HttpSession session = request.getSession(true);
        session.setAttribute("attributeName", "firstValue");
        session.setAttribute("attributeName", "firstValue");
        session.removeAttribute("attributeName");
        session.invalidate();
    }
}
```

This little servlet simply creates the events. Listing 6.6 captures the event triggers. You might log these or set off an alarm, for example.

LISTING 6.6

CAPTURING THE EVENTS TRIGGERED BY LISTING 6.5

```
import java.io.*;
import javax.servlet.*;
import javax.servlet.http.*;

public class SessionActivityListener
  implements HttpSessionListener,
  HttpSessionAttributeListener
{
  public void attributeAdded(HttpSessionBindingEvent event)
  {
     //do something with event.getName() & event.getValue()
  }

  public void attributeRemoved(HttpSessionBindingEvent
                                  event) {
  {
     //do something with event.getName() & event.getValue()
  }

  public void attributeReplaced(HttpSessionBindingEvent
                                  event) {
  {
     //do something with event.getName() & event.getValue()
  }

  public void sessionCreated(HttpSessionEvent event) {
  {
     //do something with event.getName() & event.getValue()
  }
```

continues

LISTING 6.6 *continued*

CAPTURING THE EVENTS TRIGGERED BY LISTING 6.5

```
    public void sessionDestroyed(HttpSessionEvent event) {
    {
       //do something with event.getName() & event.getValue()
    }
  }
  /*
  One reason you might listen to an attribute is to keep
  track of when a user logs on and off, for example.
*/
```

Invalidating Sessions

5.2 Given a scenario, state whether a session object will be invalidated.

This section helps you answer exam questions regarding what invalidates a session. The exam will present a scenario and ask you whether a session object will be invalidated. This can be tricky. For example, what happens when the user leaves her desk or closes her browser?

The six most frequent ways to invalidate a session are

- Calling `HttpSession.setMaxInactiveInterval(int secs)` method, explicitly setting how many minutes the session will last.
- The session will automatically be invalid after a certain time of inactivity (Tomcat default is 30 minutes).
- The user closes all browser windows. Notice, that the session will timeout rather than directly triggering a session invalidation.
- The session will expire when it is explicitly invalidated by a servlet by calling `invalidate()`.
- The server is stopped or crashes. Notice that this event might not trigger a session invalidation. A Web container that permits failover might persist the session and allow a backup Web container to take over when the original server fails.

EXAM TIP

When is session invalid Surfing to another Web site does not invalidate a session, but quitting the browser does. The user can surf from your page to somewhere else and back again without losing the session. The session will remain intact unless the user was away longer than the timeout.

WARNING

Default Timeouts Vary! You should be careful about the default timeout value. Some containers come configured for 20-minute timeouts, but this is not a hard rule. Tomcat is configured for 30-minute timeouts, for example. All containers are configurable though.

- You can set the default timeout in the web.xml file (`<web-app><session-config><session-timeout>`). (See Chapter 10 for more information about the deploy descriptor file, web.xml.)

Session Tracking Through a URL Rather Than a Cookie

5.3 Given that URL-rewriting must be used for session management, identify the design requirement on session-related HTML pages.

A Web container associates a session with a user by sending and receiving an identifier. This session ID is passed between the client and server. You could place this identifier in the HTML, but servlets are already designed to track this identifier if it is placed in a cookie or in the query string. The cookie is the easiest and happens automatically for you when you create a session. If the user turns off cookies then you can send the identifier back and forth in the query string by including it in every URL that is returned to the client.

You append the session ID in URLs by calling the response's `encodeURL(URL)` (or `encodeRedirectURL()`) method on all URLs returned by a servlet. This method includes the session ID in the URL only if cookies are disabled; otherwise, it returns the URL unchanged. The following snippet shows you how to do this:

LISTING 6.7

APPENDING SESSION IDs

```
import java.io.*;
import javax.servlet.*;
import javax.servlet.http.*;


public class SessionIdInUrl extends HttpServlet
{
    public void doGet(HttpServletRequest request,
                      HttpServletResponse response)
        throws IOException, ServletException
    {
        //these lines commented to force encodeURL to
        //append the session ID.
        HttpSession session = request.getSession(true);
```

continues

LISTING 6.7 *continued*

APPENDING SESSION IDS

```
        session.setAttribute("sessionNumber",
                             new Integer(22));

        response.setContentType("text/html");

        PrintWriter out = response.getWriter();
        out.println("<html>");
        out.println("<body bgcolor=\"white\">");
        out.println("<head>");

        String title = "Session ID Is In URL";
        out.println("<title>" + title + "</title>");
        out.println("</head>");
        out.println("<body>");
        out.println("<center>");

        out.println("<h1>" + title + "</h1>");


        out.println("<P>");
        out.print(response.encodeURL("ExampleURL"));
        out.println("<P>");
        out.print(response.encodeURL("ExampleURL?name=" +
                  "university&value=Vanguard"));

        out.println("</center>");
        out.println("</body>");
        out.println("</html>");

        out.println("</body>");
        out.println("</html>");
    }

    public void doPost(HttpServletRequest request,
                       HttpServletResponse response)
        throws IOException, ServletException
    {
        doGet(request, response);
    }
}
```

> **NOTE**
>
> **JSESSIONID!** Session tracking is maintained when cookies are off, with the `jsessionid` attribute being appended to query strings using the `encodeURL()` and `encodeRedirectURL()` methods.

When I first ran Listing 6.7, my cookies were turned on. I saw this in the browser:

```
ExampleURL?name=university&value=Vanguard
```

I then turned off cookies and received this on the next visit:

```
ExampleURL;jsessionid=62A027E37975F305B07555859780E423?name
=university&value=Vanguard
```

As you can see, the `jsessionid` attribute gets added. You will probably see this attribute mentioned on the exam.

CHAPTER SUMMARY

KEY TERMS

- Session
- Session ID
- Session Timeout
- Session Attribute
- Session Events
- Listeners

The session functionality is not extensive in servlets. However, it is enough to get most jobs done. You can use a session in servlets to maintain state between visits. There is a time limit (usually less than an hour). To get the current session in a servlet, you call the `getSession()` method of `HttpServletRequest`. You have one parameter to think about. If you don't provide a boolean (no-arg variation of getSession) then this method will create a session if no session exists. However, if you provide a true boolean, the container will automatically create a new session if it doesn't already exist. The point of providing a true boolean is to make your intentions explicit even though providing no argument has the same effect. You can provide a false to make sure a session is not created should one not exist. You get a session like so:

```
HttpSession session = request.getSession(true);
```

It is easy to retrieve a session object across multiple requests to the same or different servlets within the same WebApp. Likewise, Sun has made it a trivial matter to store and later retrieve objects from the session object. Another nice feature is the ability respond to triggers that fire upon a change to the session object state (such as adding an object to or removing an object from a session). Session objects help maintain client state in a consistent manner.

APPLY YOUR KNOWLEDGE

Review Questions

1. What are frequently used methods of persisting data between views?
2. What is the purpose of the `HttpSession` object?
3. We use sessions now. Are cookies still important?
4. How do you know when an event has occurred?
5. What are the events that are defined for sessions?

Exam Questions

1. Which of the following two methods are used to track or store the session ID?

   A. `encodeURL()`

   B. `sessionTrack()`

   C. `sessionUpdate()`

   D. `encodeRedirectURL()`

2. How do you create a session?

   A. `createSession()`

   B. `makeSession()`

   C. `callSession()`

   D. `getSession()`

3. How do you retrieve a session object across multiple requests to the same or different servlets within the same WebApp?

   A. `retrieveSession()`

   B. `findSession()`

   C. `getSession()`

   D. `callSession()`

4. How do you store objects into a session object?

   A. `put(String, Object)`

   B. `setAttribute(String, Object)`

   C. `addObject(Object)`

   D. `putObject(String, Object)`

5. How do you know if a session is alive?

   A. Look in the cookies.

   B. `getSession(false)`

   C. `isSessionAlive()`

   D. Exception thrown if you try to create one when one already exists.

6. How do you destroy or expunge a session?

   A. `Session.isAlive = false;`

   B. `Session.isNew(false)`

   C. `invalidate()`

   D. `removeSession()`

7. How do you know when a particular object is added to a session?

   A. `getCreationTime()`

   B. `getAttribute(Date)`

   C. `Session.attributeDate(index)`

   D. `attributeAdded(HttpSessionBindingEvent)`

8. How do you know when a session is created?

   A. `sessionDidActivate(HttpSessionEvent)`

   B. You check with `sessionIsAlive()`.

   C. You only know when it is killed.

   D. When the `SESSIONID` becomes null.

APPLY YOUR KNOWLEDGE

9. How do you know when a session is destroyed?

   A. `sessionBound(HttpSessionEvent)`

   B. `sessionFinalize(HttpSessionEvent)`

   C. `sessionWillPassivate(HttpSessionEvent)`

   D. `valueBound(HttpSessionEvent)`

10. Given that URL-rewriting must be used for session management, identify the query string attribute used when URL-rewriting.

    A. `sessionid`

    B. `servletid`

    C. `jsessionid`

    D. `containerid`

11. Where are cookies stored?

    A. On the server.

    B. In web.xml.

    C. On the client.

    D. In HTML.

12. Where are session IDs stored?

    A. In cookies.

    B. In HTML form fields.

    C. In query strings.

    D. Session IDs are not stored.

13. Which two technique can be used by a Web container to manage session IDs?

    A. `deleteAttribute(String)`

    B. `attributeRemove(String)`

    C. `removeAttribute(String)`

    D. `setAttribute(null)`

14. How do you get the date stamp of the session's creation?

    A. `getCreationTime()`

    B. `sessionDate()`

    C. `getSession(Date)`

    D. From the response object.

Answers to Review Questions

1. The following are the four most frequently used methods of persisting data between views: Field-field value persistence, placing data in the HTML in a hidden form field, appending data to the query string or a hyperlink in the HTML, and using cookies. See "Sharing State Information Between Requests," earlier in this chapter.

2. The servlet container uses the `HttpSession` interface to create a session between an HTTP client and an HTTP server. You use it to create a session that lasts for a specified time period, across page requests from a single user. This interface allows you to view and manipulate information about a session and bind objects to sessions, too. See "Using Session Objects," earlier in this chapter.

3. Cookies are still important. While we don't normally store data in cookies, we still need them to store the session ID, without which it is hard to maintain state. See "Sharing State Information Between Requests," earlier in this chapter.

4. The listener interface allows an object to be notified when a session attribute changes within a given Web application. You would use these methods when monitoring attributes within a session.

APPLY YOUR KNOWLEDGE

There are also methods that are triggered when a servlet is coded to explicitly unbind an attribute from a session, due to a session being invalidated, or due to a session timeout. See "Event Listeners," earlier in this chapter.

5. The primary events defined for sessions are session creation and destruction, and when an attribute is added, changed, or removed from a session. The listener interface monitors these events and calls associated methods. See "Event Listeners."

Answers to Exam Questions

1. **A** and **D**. You append the session ID in URLs by calling the response's `encodeURL(URL)` (or `encodeRedirectURL()`) method on all URLs returned by a servlet. This method includes the session ID in the URL only if cookies are disabled; otherwise, it returns the URL unchanged. See "Session Tracking Through a URL Rather Than a Cookie," earlier in this chapter.

2. **D**. To get the current session in a servlet, you call the `getSession()` method of `HttpServletRequest`. You have one parameter to think about. If you don't provide a boolean, this method will create a session if one doesn't exist. The same behavior occurs when you provide a true boolean. However, the container will not create a new session if it doesn't already exist when you use a false argument. See "Storing and Retrieving Session Objects," earlier in this chapter.

3. **C**. This is the same question as #2, but stated differently. You call the `getSession()` method of `HttpServletRequest` to create a session. See "Storing and Retrieving Session Objects," earlier in this chapter.

4. **B**. You use the `setAttribute(java.lang.String name, java.lang.Object value)` method to add objects to a session. The other methods listed are fake. See "Storing and Retrieving Session Objects," earlier in this chapter.

5. **B**. This is somewhat difficult. You use `getSession(false)` method and test for a null result.

```
        HttpSession session = request.
➥getSession(false);
        if (session = null) {
            //do something about lacking a
➥session
        }
```

If you get a null then the session is alive. You can also check for the session ID with `getId()`, which returns the id of the session as a String representing the unique identifier assigned to this session. If the session is dead, it will return a null. See "Storing and Retrieving Session Objects," earlier in this chapter.

6. **C**. Only the `invalidate()` method can destroy a session. Notice that the session can't be referenced after this method has been called. A and D are fake and B isn't used properly. See "Storing and Retrieving Session Objects," earlier in this chapter.

7. **D**. The `attributeAdded(HttpSessionBindingEvent se)` method gets called as the notification that an attribute has been added to a session. The other options are fake. See "Storing and Retrieving Session Objects," earlier in this chapter.

8. **A**. The `sessionDidActivate(HttpSessionEvent)` method is called when the session has just been activated. The other options are fake. See "Invalidating Sessions," earlier in this chapter.

APPLY YOUR KNOWLEDGE

9. **C.** The `sessionWillPassivate(HttpSessionEvent)` method is called as the notification that the session is about to be passivated. This is strange language so don't feel bad. They should have used another term such as alive or destroy. A and B are fake. D (`valueBound(HttpSessionBindingEvent)`) is the notification to the object that it is being bound to a session, but doesn't tell you about the session being destroyed. See "Invalidating Sessions," earlier in this chapter.

10. **C.** The `jsessionid` is the parameter that is appended to URLs by the `encodeURL()` method when cookies are not available to maintain state. The other options are fake. See "Session Tracking Through a URL Rather Than a Cookie," earlier in this chapter.

11. **C.** Cookies are stored on the client only. See "Sharing State Information Between Requests," earlier in this chapter.

12. **A** and **C.** Session IDs are stored in cookies on the client machine. If cookies are turned off, session IDs can be stored in query strings. See "Sharing State Information Between Requests," earlier in this chapter.

13. **C.** The `removeAttribute(java.lang.String name)` method removes an attribute. It deletes it from the session object. The other options are fake. See "Using Session Objects," earlier in this chapter.

14. **A.** The `getCreationTime()` method returns a long containing the date stamp of creation. The other options are incorrect. See "Using Session Objects," earlier in this chapter.

Suggested Readings and Resources

1. Sun's excellent J2EE Tutorial—`java.sun.com/j2ee/tutorial/1_3-fcs/doc/J2eeTutorialTOC.html`.

2. The Java Language Specification—`java.sun.com/docs/books/jls/second_edition/html/j.title.doc.html`.

3. Exam objectives for the Sun Certified Web Component Developer for J2EE Platform—`http://suned.sun.com/US/certification/java/exam_objectives.html`.

4. The Java Servlet 2.3 Specification—`http://jcp.org/aboutJava/communityprocess/first/jsr053/index.html`.

5. Sun's official Servlet page—`http://java.sun.com/products/servlet/`.

6. Sun's J2EE API—`http://java.sun.com/j2ee/sdk_1.3/techdocs/api/index.html`.

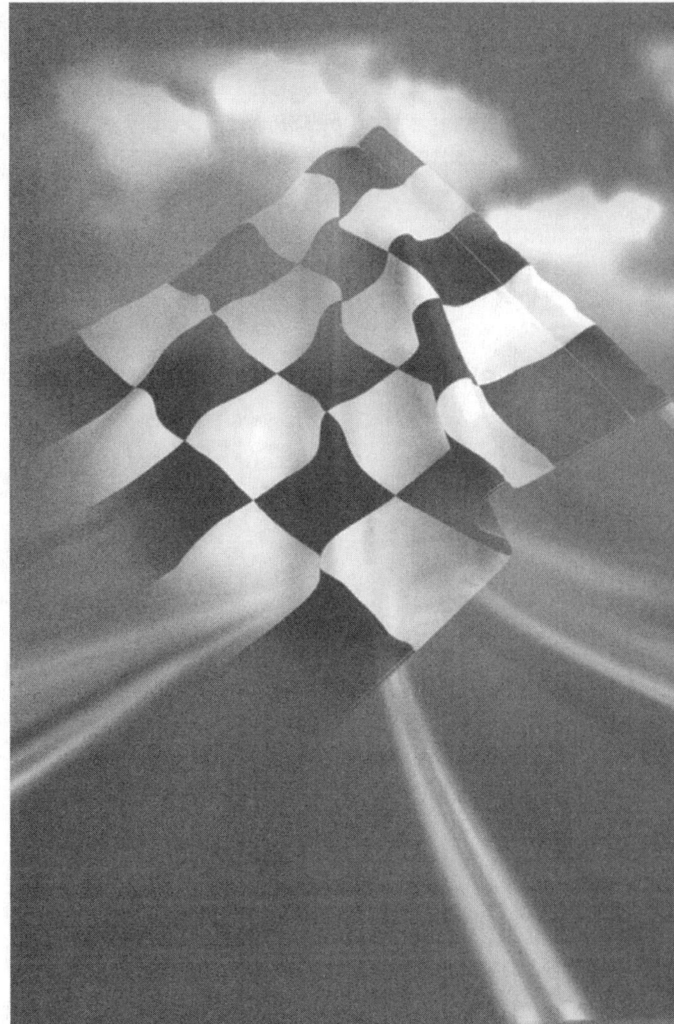

CHAPTER 7

JavaServer Pages (JSP) Technology Model

OBJECTIVES

This chapter covers the following Sun-specified objectives for Section 8—The JavaServer Pages (JSP) Technology Model of the Sun Certified Web Component Developer for J2EE Platform exam:

8.1 Write the opening and closing tags for the standard JSP tag types.

- **Directive**
- **Declaration**
- **Scriptlet**
- **Expression**

- JSP elements let you insert Java code into an otherwise standard Web page. The server will use the opening and closing JSP tags (similar to, but not exactly XML) to generate, and compile, a servlet. This servlet is a small application like any other except that it waits for a call by the Web server and its output is returned to the same server.

- The first time a JSP is invoked, the server translates the JSP page into servlet code and then compiles it into a servlet, which is then loaded into memory. If the JSP file is changed then the container repeats the translation and compilation. The JSP tags tell the server which parts of the page contain Java code and which parts contain HTML or other markup that should simply be passed through to the browser. The plain text is compiled as quoted strings. This section of the chapter focuses on the syntax rather then the details of each element type, which are covered later in the chapter.

OBJECTIVES

8.2 Given a type of JSP tag, identify correct statements about its purpose or use.

- There are several distinct types of JSP tags. You will learn the purpose of each. This section of the exam will test your understanding of what each type of tag is used for.

8.3 Given a JSP tag type, identify the equivalent XML-based tags.

- The JSP technology has matured to read JSP tags in two forms. The syntax for a scriptlet is `<% yourCode %>`, very similar to Microsoft's ASP. However, another, I think better, form is XML-like, but not exactly. You can also use the XML equivalent (real XML) such as `<jsp:scriptlet>yourCode </jsp:scriptlet>`. This part of the exam focuses on these XML equivalencies.

8.4 Identify the page directive attribute, and its values that:

- **Import a Java class into the JSP page**
- **Declare that a JSP page exists within a session**
- **Declare that a JSP page uses an error page**
- **Declare that a JSP page is an error page**

- The page directive is how you tell the servlet engine to treat the entire JSP page. The scope of this directive's attributes are page-wide, thus its name. It defines attributes that apply to the entire JSP page. You use this tag to do things like import classes, define buffer size, and identify an error page. Although there are only four specific page directives named in the test objective, we recommend you study all of them.

8.5 Identify and put in sequence the elements of the JSP page lifecycle.

- **Page translation**
- **JSP page compilation**
- **Load class**
- **Create instance**
- **Call jspInit**
- **Call jspService**
- **Call jspDestroy**

- Each page has a lifecycle within the servlet engine. You will be required to understand each step of the cycle and know the order of the steps.

8.6 Match correct descriptions about purpose, function, or use with any of the following implicit objects.

- `request`
- `response`
- `out`
- `session`
- `config`
- `application`
- `page`
- `pageContext`
- `exception`

- The JSP implicit objects give the programmer a shortcut to functionality. These objects are a direct link to the Servlet Container. They are used in scriptlets just like other objects except you do not explicitly declare them; this is done for you automatically.

Objectives

8.7 Distinguish correct and incorrect scriptlet code for Java statements.

- **A conditional statement**
- **An iteration statement**

▶ This section of the exam tests your ability to understand Java syntax. It is less about JSP and more about Java syntax. This objective is about how to properly delimit template text with complex scriptlet code, such as iterations and conditionals. It is a common error to place the curly-braces in the wrong place or to leave them out completely.

9.1 Given a description of required functionality, identify the JSP page directive or standard tag in the correct format with the correct attributes required to specify the inclusion of a Web component into the JSP page.

▶ This section of the exam covers how to perform a server-side include in a JSP page. Please see the section on the `include` directive below. It discusses both the `include` directive (`<%@ include...>` represents a static include) and the include action (`<jsp:include...>` represents a dynamic include).

Outline

Outline

Study Strategies

- The key to this section of the exam is understanding the JSP syntax (plain Java inside tags) and the lifecycle (JSP is compiled into a servlet). Don't be thrown by servlets: They are classes that satisfy a specific functional interface for operating on a Web server.
- There are several tags to know. Make sure you learn the basic tags and their XML equivalents. The XML is easy, as the tag names make sense, like `<jsp:scriptlet>` for scriptlets. Scriptlets are Java code sections delimited in JSP so that the container knows to treat the section as Java code rather than plain text.
- If you know Java, JSP is easy. The difference between the two has to do with making Java play nicely within a Web page. The interface between Java and the Web server is the tag set.

INTRODUCTION

JSP and servlets have greatly enhanced the way in which you can create and manage Web pages with Java. The difficulty level of JSP is between HTML and pure Java. For simple tasks like displaying the current date, you write a normal HTML page and add only a small amount of Java as a scriptlet. For big tasks like processing a shopping cart, you use JSP as the mediator between the Web form and a component (bean or servlet) that has all the horsepower.

CGI had its day. Almost immediately after HTML became the Web's lingua franca, programmers were meddling. CGI, Perl, and their cousins gave Web content dynamic capability, an obvious evolution. However, using them to go beyond text processing and simple database queries involves error-prone complexities. Microsoft Active Server Pages (ASP) was the first Web server scripting champion. Tightly integrated with the Windows operating system, ASP is the most widely used Web server language, and to great effect. The Achilles' heel is its Windows-only attitude. A few vendors have stepped in, providing ASP engines for the major non-Windows platforms. I like ASP, but it isn't portable, object-oriented, or designed for building enterprise class server applications. Notice, while porting the scripting part of ASP to other platforms is easy, porting the COM/COM+ objects is almost impossible. This is a big advantage of JSP: Not only does JSP run on all major platforms, but the JavaBeans used by these JSPs run on all major platforms as well.

JSP competes directly with ASP. In fact, you would be forgiven if you thought it was a copy. Sun took the same approach to JSP as it did with Java. Sun borrowed the syntax of its best competitor (ASP for JSP and C++ for Java) with tweaks, but built everything under the hood from scratch. Java syntax comes from C++, but it works on all platforms with no portability migraines for the developer. JSP structure comes from ASP (for example, ASP was the first popular scripting platform to use `<% %>` to mark code and now JSP does, too). The look and feel, and some syntax, is the same. However, ASP primarily uses Microsoft's versatile VBScript, while JSP uses the more powerful and portable Java.

The designers of JSP modeled the architecture on a certain pattern. A pattern is a blueprint for how to solve a problem within a given context. It is a way to standardize an approach to solving a recurring need.

JSP is based on the Model-View-Controller design pattern, which provides centralized dispatching of requests via a controller servlet. The exam is likely to ask a pattern question. See Chapter 11, "Design Patterns," which discusses Section 13, "Design Patterns," of the exam objectives for more information on this fascinating subject.

While it helps to know JSP's history, I won't say more about it. Let's focus on the exam objectives. Let us start with a sample JSP page as follows:

LISTING 7.1

RANDOM NUMBER GENERATOR

```
<html>
<head>
<title>Que Java Training Guide - JSP Example</title>
</head>
<body>
<center>
<h1><a href="http://www.que.com">Que</a>
<br>Random Number Generator</h1>
<b>Guess the random numbers:</b>
<hr></hr>
  <%
  StringBuffer html = new StringBuffer();
  html.append("<ol type=\"I\">");
  java.util.Random randomInt = new java.util.Random();
  int limit = 10;
  for (int count=0; count<limit; count++)
  {
    html.append("<li>" + randomInt.nextInt() + "</li>");
  }
  html.append("</ol>");
  out.println( html.toString() );
  %>
</center>
</body>
</html>
```

The previous code listing shows you an example of JSP. See Figure 7.1 for the output. The bulk of the code is ordinary HMTL. The code between the `<% %>` delimiters is Java. This is a scriptlet where you can access the full Java API, enabling you to create very powerful Web applications. Figure 7.1 shows the result of running Listing 7.1 in a JSP-enabled Web server (here, Apache Tomcat/4.0.1).

The JavaServer Pages specification defines a JSP container as a system-level entity that provides life-cycle management and runtime support for JSP pages and servlet components. The container manages the Java application service typically used by the Web server (for example, Tomcat is configured such that Apache Web server handles requests for JSP pages to the container).

IN THE FIELD

HOW DOES JSP WORK?

The JSP container parses the JSP source and converts the entire JSP page (HTML becomes strings and Java source code embedded in a JSP page gets copied into methods) into a Java servlet class. The HTML text is converted into a bunch of `out.println` statements in the order encountered. Finally, the container compiles this class into Java bytecodes.

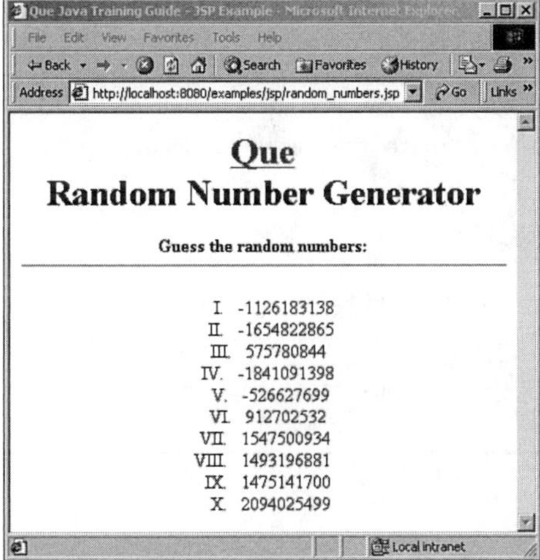

FIGURE 7.1
You can create dynamic content using JSP.

It is often helpful to look at a snapshot of the syntax before exploring the topics of a language. Shown in Table 7.1 is a snapshot of JSP syntax used in this chapter and on the exam:

TABLE 7.1

JSP SYNTAX SNAPSHOT

Element	*Syntax*	*Example*
HTML Comment	<!-- comment -->	<!-- This HTML comment is passed through to the client -->
JSP Comment	<%-- comment --%>	<%-- This comment is ignored by the server --%>
Page Directive	<%@ page [key]="[value]" %>	<%@ page import="java.util.*" %>
Declaration	<%! Declaration %>	<%! String name = new String ("Patricia"); %>
Expression	<%= expression %>	Your shopping cart total is: <b><%= shoppingCart.getTotal() %></b>.

Scriptlet	<% code %>	<% String password =request.getParameter("password");
		if (password == null)
		{
		%>
		Password is required, thank you.
		<%
		} else
		{
		%>
		Welcome to the member's area.
		<%
		}
		%>

Static include, parsed at compile-time	<%@ include file="file" %>	<%@ include file="welcome.jsp>
Dynamic include, request-time and not parsed	<jsp:include page="file" />	<jsp:include page="welcome.html" />

OPENING AND CLOSING JSP TAGS

8.1 Write the opening and closing tags for the standard JSP tag types.

- **Directive**
- **Declaration**
- **Scriptlet**
- **Expression**

The intent behind this objective is making sure you are familiar with the syntax of opening and closing the primary tags in JSP. The following discussion demonstrates all the syntax you need to know for the exam.

One type of code that is not mentioned in the objectives, but for which examples appear on the exam, is comments. Just so you don't get confused by them, please review the two ways of commenting code.

This is a JSP comment.

```
<%-- comment --%>
```

The compiler ignores everything embedded in it, including elements, directives, and actions.

This is an HTML comment.

```
<!-- comment -->
```

The compiler treats the HTML comment as text, so it passes it through to the output stream unaltered. The text that results from any JSP, including HTML comments, is then passed on to the browser, which doesn't display it. However, JSP comments are ignored during translation. For example

```
<!-- page visited on:
     <%=(new java.util.Date()).toLocaleString()%>
-->
```

displays in the page source as

```
<!-- page visited on March 21, 2002 -->
```

IN THE FIELD

COMMENTS IN JSP

A JSP comment is ignored by the JSP engine: It is skipped by the compiler, as are comments in all Java source files. On the other hand, an HTML comment is added to the output stream because it is treated as pure text, which the servlet container simply passes through to the output stream. If there is a scriptlet embedded in an HTML comment, it will be processed normally. The JSP engine recognizes Java in an HTML comment, but the HTML viewer will not display it.

Directive

Directives are a communication link between the JSP page and the JSP container. Directives have this syntax:

```
<%@ directive { attr="value" }* %>
```

Directives are not used to display text; they don't contribute anything into the current output stream. There are three directives: include, page, and taglib. Each directive has several attributes that affect how the container processes the page.

include Directive

> **9.1 Given a description of required functionality, identify the JSP page directive or standard tag in the correct format with the correct attributes required to specify the inclusion of a Web component into the JSP page.**

The basic syntax of the `include` directive is as follows:

```
<%@ include file="relativeURLspec" %>
```

The `include` directive is a placeholder that lets you include the text in another file. The text that is included by this directive is part of the translation into a servlet. It is good practice to decompose complex pages into several files. Doing so doesn't impact performance, but does make your code more manageable. Header (for example, company logo and quip) and footer (for example, legal and navigation) information is a good candidate for includes. If you want to include the results from another servlet or JSP then use the XML equivalent, because that way the JSP simply invokes the resource and takes the results. The include action instead of directive is sometimes the better choice, because that would include an outside file without recompilation (thus less overhead involved).

IN THE FIELD

INCLUDING EXTERNAL DATA

To simply add text from another file, but not parse it, use the XML equivalent `<jsp:directive.include file="url"\>`. This tag includes a file at request time instead of translation time. Therefore content is not parsed, but rather included in place. The `jsp:directive.include` tag is the XML equivalent to the `<%@include%>` directive which is performed at translation-time.

The first code listing could have been constructed as follows with the same result:

```
<html>
<head>
<title>QueQue Java Training Guide - JSP Example</title>
</head>
<body>
<center>
<h1><a href="http://www.que.com">QUE</a>
<br>Random Number Generator</h1>
<b>Que presents the following random numbers:</b>
<hr></hr>
<!--the code for generating and listing random numbers-->
<%@ include file="random_number_java.inc" %>
</center>
</body>
</html>
```

The random_number_java.inc file would look like this:

```
<!--text from random_number_java.inc-->
<%
StringBuffer html = new StringBuffer();
html.append("<ol type=\"I\">");
java.util.Random randomInt = new java.util.Random();
int limit = 10;
for (int count=0; count<limit; count++)
{
  html.append("<li>" + randomInt.nextInt() + "</li>");
}
html.append("</ol>");
out.println( html.toString() );
%>
```

`taglib` Directive

The basic syntax of the `taglib` directive is as follows:

```
<%@ taglib uri="tagLibraryURI" prefix="tagPrefix" %>
```

JSP technology makes it easy to embed Java code and functionality into HTML documents. However, the author has to know Java to use scriptlets. This is true for JavaBeans as well. You can use custom tags through the tag library facility. You can embed functionality into JSP pages with easy-to-use custom tags that look like XML or HTML. With custom tags, you are better able to separate presentation from business logic.

Chapter 8, "Extend JSP with JavaBeans," discusses the tag library feature of JSP at length. A taglib is a mechanism that enables you to specify your own custom tags. JSP custom tags are merely Java classes with a special interface that makes it easy to access them from a JSP page.

You start by writing a class that implements the Tag interface like so:

```
public class MyTag implements Tag { }
```

You code the methods of the Tag interface, including `setPageContext`, `doStartTag` and `doEndTag`. The JSP container knows how to map the tag in the JSP to your custom `MyTag` class, where you encapsulate your functionality. Then you create a Tag Library Descriptor (TLD) that tells the JSP container about your tag library. Finally, you use your tags in the JSP page by first including the `taglib` directive, then using the actual tags like so:

```
<%@ taglib uri="/WEB-INF/jsp/myTaglib.tld" prefix="myTag"
%>
...
<body>
myTag produces: <myTag:myMethod/>
```

page Directive

The `page` directive gives directions to the servlet engine about the general setup of the page. This directive is covered in detail later in this chapter.

Declaration

In Java you must declare a variable before you use it. Largely, you type Java the same in a JSP page, except for the delimiters. The syntax is nearly identical except for delimeters and the expression (`<%=someCodeThatCreatesOutput%>`). A declaration declares one or more variables or methods. Once declared, you can use them later in the JSP page. Also, the scope of these declarations can be either local (for example, inside a block) or instance declaration (apply to the entire JSP page).

The syntax inside the delimiters is the same as Java, so you can declare any number of variables or methods within one declaration and you end each statement with a semicolon. Why would you want to use this when it seems that a standard scriptlet opening/closing will do just the same? You would because it makes your intentions more explicit.

The following are examples:

```
<%! int j = 0; %>
<%! int customerLimit, total, cashSum; %>
<%! MyClass teamScores = new MyClass(); %>
```

IN THE FIELD

AVOID DUPLICATE VARIABLE DECLARATIONS

You can use variables or methods that are declared in an imported package (using the `page` directive) or included page (using `include`) without declaring them directly in the current JSP page.

Scriptlet

The scriptlet is a way to include Java code directly in the page. Aside from the requirement for the delimiters (which tells the JSP engine where to separate Java from HTML), it is regular Java. The following is a trivial example (assume `java.util.*` has been imported):

```
<% if (Calendar.getInstance()
               .get(Calendar.AM_PM) == Calendar.AM)
   {%>
      Time for breakfast!
<% } else
   { %>
      Time for dinner!
<% } %>
```

Scriptlets have access to the entire Java API. They are very powerful. The test questions about these will require you to know Java syntax.

Expression

The basic syntax of the expression element is as follows:

```
<%= your_expression %>
```

An expression element contains Java code that is evaluated, converted to a string, and inserted into the output stream. Expressions are never terminated with a semicolon, a break with normal Java convention. Notice that an expression must be converted to a String. Internally, JSP replaces the expression element with a String to append to the output stream. During translation, the expression text is placed in a *out.print(<expr>);* statement when the container transforms the JSP page into a servlet. Therefore, you can treat it as text, such as place it in the middle of an HTML tag, or anywhere for that matter. For example, the following is how you could dynamically set the color of a font with an expression:

```
<font color="<%= Color.getCurrentColor() %>">
                                        Colored Text</font>
```

As another example, you could display the current date like so:

```
<%= (new java.util.Date()).toLocaleString() %>
```

The Purpose of JSP Tags

8.2 Given a type of JSP tag, identify correct statements about its purpose or use.

This objective is intended to get you to shift your focus from just syntax to purpose. This section does not address the objective, per se. To be able to identify the correct use of the tags, you must understand them in broader context. If you read this chapter thoroughly, you will understand all the tags that appear on the test in terms of why and when to use them, not just how to use them.

JSP Tags as XML

8.3 Given a JSP tag type, identify the equivalent XML-based tags.

JSP enables you to use two forms of certain tag types. Table 7.2 offers a quick review of the XML equivalents you need to know.

TABLE 7.2

XML EQUIVALENTS FOR CERTAIN JSP TAG TYPES

JSP Tag Type	*Syntax*	*XML*

Expression	`<%=expression%>`	`<jsp:expression>`
		`expression`
		`</jsp:expression>`

Scriptlet	`<% yourCode %>`	`<jsp:scriptlet>`
		`yourCode`
		`</jsp:scriptlet>`

Declaration	`<%! yourCode %>`	`<jsp:declaration>`
		`yourCode`
		`</jsp:declaration>`

`page` Directive	`<%@ page att="val" %>`	`<jsp:directive.page att="val"/>`
`include` Directive	`<%@ include file="url" %>`	`<jsp:directive.include` `file="url"/>`

Actions	`None (XML only)`	`<jsp:useBean>`
		`<jsp:setProperty>`
		`<jsp:getProperty>`
		`<jsp:include>`
		`<jsp:forward>`
		`<jsp:plugin>`

Tag Library	`<%@ taglib uri="URIForLibrary" prefix="tagPrefix" %>`	No equivalent

Table 7.3 provides a list of examples for the XML actions you can take in JSP using the XML equivalents.

TABLE 7.3

XML EQUIVALENT ACTIONS

JSP Tag Type	*Syntax*	*XML*
Bean	`<jsp:useBean>`	`<jsp:useBean id="calc" scope="page" class="session.Calc" />`
Bean property	`<jsp:setProperty>`	`<jsp:setProperty name="amount" property="56.90" />`
Bean property	`<jsp:getProperty>`	`<jsp:getProperty name="calc" property="amount" />`
Dispatch	`<jsp:forward>`	`<jsp:forward page="welcome.html">`
Include	`<jsp:include>`	`<jsp:include page="copyright.html" />`

continues

TABLE 7.3 *continued*

XML EQUIVALENT ACTIONS

JSP Tag Type	*Syntax*	*XML*
Plugin	`<jsp:plugin>`	`<jsp:plugin type=applet code="Customer.class" codebase="/html"> <jsp:params> <jsp:param name="debt" value="large" /> </jsp:params> <jsp:fallback> <p>Unable to load applet</p> </jsp:fallback> </jsp:plugin>`

Let's contrast two code snippets that result in the same output. The first is regular JSP syntax:

```
<%@ page language="java" %>
<%=customerCount%>
```

The second snippet generates the same results as the previous snippet using the XML equivalent:

```
<jsp:directive.page language="java"/>
<jsp:expression>customerCount</jsp:expression>
```

THE PAGE DIRECTIVE

8.4 Identify the page directive attribute, and its values.

- **Import a Java class into the JSP page.**
- **Declare that a JSP page exists within a session.**
- **Declare that a JSP page uses an error page.**
- **Declare that a JSP page is an error page.**

The page directive defines a page-dependent property (such as buffer size, location of an error page) used by the JSP container. For example

```
<%@ page page_directive_attr_list %>
<%@ page info="Customer Support Page" %>
```

A JSP page, and any files included via the include directive, can contain one or more page directives but no duplicates (the same attribute appearing more than once on a page). The JSP container will apply all the attributes to the page. The position of these page directives is irrelevant, but it is good practice to keep them together at the top of the page.

While you can't duplicate any of the other attributes (which would result in a fatal translation error), you can make multiple uses of the import attribute, the only exception to the no-duplicate rule.

The following is the page directive syntax:

```
<%@ page
    [ language="java" ]
    [ extends="package.class" ]
    [ import="{package.class | package.*}, ..." ]
    [ session="true|false" ]
    [ buffer="none|8kb|sizekb" ]
    [ autoFlush="true|false" ]
    [ isThreadSafe="true|false" ]
    [ info="text" ]
    [ errorPage="relativeURL" ]
    [ contentType="mimeType [ ; charset=characterSet ]" |
      "text/html ; charset=ISO-8859-1" ]
    [ isErrorPage="true|false" ]
    [ pageEncoding="characterSet | ISO-8859-1" ]
%>
```

While we cover all page directive attributes for completeness, the test objectives specifically name the import, session, isErrorPage, and errorPage attributes, so these are given more thorough discussion.

Importing Classes

Like in normal Java, you import classes to gain access to them. These imports are cumulative, both in Java and JSP. The import attribute of the page directive is how you import Java classes into a JSP page. The following is an example of how you would import several packages:

```
<%@ page import="java.io.*,java.util.*,com.myCompany.*" %>
```

You can use many page directives or just one with a comma separated list of packages or classes as the value of the import attribute. Like an import declaration in the Java programming language, the value is either a fully qualified type name or a package name followed by the ".*" string, denoting all the public types declared in that package.

IN THE FIELD

AUTOMATICALLY IMPORTED CLASSES

In JSP, you do not have to use the `page` directive for the default import list of `java.lang.*`, `javax.servlet.*`, `javax.servlet.jsp.*`, and `javax.servlet.http.*`. These are automatically available to you.

Declare That a JSP Page Exists Within a Session

The session attribute indicates that the page is part of a session, like so:

```
<%@ page session="true" %>
```

The JSP container does all the work for you. The Web server tracks sessions by storing a session identifier in a cookie. When this attribute is set to `"true"` (default), the implicit variable named "session" (`javax.servlet.http.HttpSession`) references the current session for the page. If it is set to `"false"` then the session object is not available (this is different from being null) and any reference to it within the body of the JSP page throws a fatal error. One reason why you'd want to set it to false is to save a little memory and gain some performance.

WARNING

Using `autoFlush` If `autoFlush="true"` and the contents of the initial JspWriter have been flushed to the `ServletResponse` output stream, any subsequent attempt to dispatch an uncaught exception from the offending page to an `errorPage` may fail. When an error page is also indicated in the `web.xml` descriptor, the JSP error page applies first, then the `web.xml` page.

Declare That a JSP Page Uses an Error Page

The `errorPage` attribute defines a URL that is processed when any throwable object is thrown but not caught by a try-catch block in the page, like so:

```
<%@ page errorPage="formError.jsp" %>
```

The throwable object is transferred from the JSP page that generates it to the error page. Internally, it does this by saving the object reference on the common `ServletRequest` object using the `setAttribute()` method, with a name of "`javax.servlet.jsp.jspException`".

Declare That a JSP Page Is an Error Page

The `isErrorPage` attribute tells the container if that page is available to be an error page for another JSP page (the current page is the URL in another page's `errorPage` attribute) like so:

```
<%@ page isErrorPage="true" %>
```

If this attribute is set to `"true"` then the variable "`exception`" is available to you. Otherwise (default is `"false"`), if you try to reference the exception, you will get a fatal error.

language

The `language` attribute defines the scripting language to be used in the scriptlets, expression scriptlets, and declarations. It looks like this:

```
<%@ page language="java" %>
```

Notice that this declaration also applies to any files included using the `include` directive. In JSP 1.2, the value for this attribute is `"java"` and cannot be anything else. The idea is that Servlet Container vendors will one day allow other languages such as JavaScript, VBScript, Perl (Practical Extraction and Report Language), or C++.

extends

The `extends` attribute works just like it does in regular Java. It allows you to inherit a class by naming the superclass of the class created by runtime compiling this JSP page. It looks like this:

```
<%@ page extends="package.class" %>
```

Be careful about using this attribute. Use this one sparingly because it allows the developer to circumvent the JSP engine.

buffer

This attribute tells the JSP container how much space to allocate for the initial buffer (`"out"`, which is the JspWriter). The syntax is

```
<%@ page buffer="16kb" %>
```

You should note that when the buffer is full, it writes the content in the buffer to the output stream. If this attribute is set to `"none"`, all output is written directly to the output stream (`ServletResponse PrintWriter`). The size is set in kilobytes (the suffix "KB" is required). If this attribute is not explicitly set, the page starts with a default size of 8KB.

autoFlush

The `autoFlush` attribute tells the JSP container whether the buffered output should be flushed. It is used thusly:

```
<%@ page autoFlush="true" %>
```

When it is set to `"true"`, the container automatically sends the contents of the buffer to the output stream when the buffer becomes full.

The default setting is `"true"`. You would want to set this to `"false"` if you wanted to raise an exception to indicate a buffer overflow condition.

WARNING

Do Not Set `autoFlush` to `"false"` When the Buffer Is Set to None!
It is illegal to set `autoFlush` to `"false"` when the buffer is set to none. Also, if `autoFlush` is `"true"` and the buffer gets flushed, any subsequent uncaught exception will likely fail to return the specified errorPage reference.

isThreadSafe

The syntax for the `isThreadSafe` attribute is as follows:

```
<%@ page isThreadSafe="true" %>
```

The JSP container uses this attribute to handle a page's level of thread safety. If this is set to `"false"`, then the JSP container will service multiple client requests one at a time. Otherwise it will allow simultaneous access to the same page. The `"true"` (default) setting assumes you have synchronized the page elements.

info

The `info` attribute stores an arbitrary string that can subsequently be retrieved with the `Servlet.getServletInfo()` method. It is used like so:

```
<%@ page info="myPageInfo" %>
```

contentType

The `contentType` attribute tells the browser what kind of page it is. This attribute specifies the MIME type of the page's output. The output type is included in the HTTP header prior to data being printed to the client. The syntax is

```
<%@ page contentType="text/html; charset=ISO-8859-1" %>
```

The default is text (`"text/html"`), but you can specify many other types. Table 7.4 is a short list of common page types:

TABLE 7.4

PAGE TYPES AS SET BY THE contentType ATTRIBUTE

Value	*Description*
application/msword	MS Word document
application/pdf	Acrobat (.pdf) file
application/vnd.ms-excel	MS Excel spreadsheet

You cannot use MIME types that are binary format (like GZIP) as these cannot be constructed in a JSP file. For a full list of MIME types, please see `http://www.oac.uci.edu/indiv/ehood/MIME/MIME.html`. Also, look at the web.xml file in `CATALINA_HOME/conf/web.xml` for the MIME types that all Web applications will use. The following is a snippet declaring two MIME types for the jpeg image file:

```
<mime-mapping>
  <extension>jpeg</extension>
  <mime-type>image/jpeg</mime-type>
</mime-mapping>
<mime-mapping>
  <extension>jpg</extension>
  <mime-type>image/jpeg</mime-type>
</mime-mapping>
```

The `charset` defines the character encoding. The JSP container applies this encoding for the JSP page and for the response of the JSP page.

NOTE

Notice! If you use Tomcat as recommended in this book, notice that Tomcat's JspCServletContext (`org.apache.jasper.servlet.JspCServletContext`) is a simple `ServletContext` implementation without HTTP-specific methods. In this class, you can call `getMimeType()` to return the MIME type for the specified filename. Also, you can add MIME types to Tomcat through the `<mime-mapping>` tag in the web.xml configuration file as explained in the Tomcat documentation. The `getMimeType` method is part of the `SerlvetContext` interface; therefore, it is a generic mechanism; it is *not* unique to Tomcat.

JSP Page Lifecycle

8.5 Identify and put in sequence the elements of the JSP page lifecycle.

- **Page translation**
- **JSP page compilation**
- **Load class**
- **Create instance**
- **Call `jspInit`**
- **Call `jspService`**
- **Call `jspDestroy`**

The JSP page lifecycle is on the exam. A JSP's life starts when it is first requested. The Servlet Container (which does double duty by handling both JSP and servlets) parses the JSP, creates a servlet, runs the servlet, handles responding to the request, and manages servlet persistence. Smart containers place the servlet in memory only once upon the first request to speed up processing. Table 7.5 offers a quick review of the JSP page lifecycle you need to know.

TABLE 7.5

JSP Page Lifecycle

JSP Process Step	*Explanation*
Page translation	`<%=expression%>` Translates this to a string. It is equivalent to `out.print(expression);`.
Page compilation	`<% yourCode %>` Compiles this.
Load class	Loads the JSP page's servlet class upon first request.
Create instance	Instantiates an instance of the servlet class.
Call `jspInit`	Initializes the servlet instance by calling the `jspInit` method.
Call `_jspService`	Invokes the `_jspService` method, passing a request and a response object.
Call `jspDestroy`	If the container needs to remove the JSP page's servlet, it calls the `jspDestroy` method.

A JSP page is always converted to a servlet. Therefore the lifecycle of a JSP page is largely determined by how the JSP container handles Java servlets.

Each JSP page is eventually converted to a servlet class and then compiled. Each time a request is sent to a JSP page, the container compares the file dates. If the JSP is younger than the servlet, the container recompiles it and then sends the request to the servlet. The compiling process is performed automatically when the server receives a request for that page.

There are two phases of a JSP page's life: translation and execution. In the translation phase, the container starts building the final page, adding contents from any includes and skipping JSP comments (but retaining HTML comments). The container interprets all the Java code, such as directives, actions, and the custom actions referencing tag libraries that occur in the page. Once this is done, the container compiles the result into a servlet class. This completes the translation phase and the servlet is ready to receive requests.

The execution phase involves instantiating request and response objects and invoking the correct servlet based on the request. After the servlet finishes its work, it hands the response object to the container. The container then sends the response back to the client.

> **WARNING**
>
> **The JSP Remains a Static Page Until Requested!** The translation and compilation phases can yield errors that are seen only when the page is requested for the first time.

There are many types of elements in a JSP page, and each is processed differently. The plain text (non-Java) is called template data and is simply passed through by adding it to the output stream for the client. The directives and scripting elements are inserted into the eventual servlet class.

JSP Implicit Objects

8.6 Match correct descriptions about purpose, function, or use with any of JSP implicit objects.

- `request`
- `response`
- `out`
- `session`
- `config`

- **application**
- **page**
- **pageContext**
- **exception**

To simplify code in JSP expressions and scriptlets, you are supplied with eight automatically defined variables, sometimes called implicit objects. The available variables are `request`, `response`, `out`, `session`, `application`, `config`, `pageContext`, and `page`. Details for each are given in the following sections.

request

This is the `HttpServletRequest` class instance associated with the client request. The client sends a request message to the Web server. This object enables you to inspect that request message. There is a surprising amount of information stored in it. For example, you get the request type (`GET`, `POST`, and `HEAD`) and the associated cookies. You can extract information from the request object and act on that data. The following code listing shows you the various methods of the request object:

```
<html>
<body>
<h1> Inspecting the Request Object </h1>
<font size="4">
Request Method: <%= request.getMethod() %><br>
Request URI: <%= request.getRequestURI() %><br>
Request Protocol: <%= request.getProtocol() %><br>
Servlet path: <%= request.getServletPath() %><br>
Path info: <%= request.getPathInfo() %><br>
Path translated: <%= request.getPathTranslated() %><br>
Query string: <%= request.getQueryString() %><br>
Content length: <%= request.getContentLength() %><br>
Content type: <%= request.getContentType() %><br>
Server name: <%= request.getServerName() %><br>
Server port: <%= request.getServerPort() %><br>
Remote user: <%= request.getRemoteUser() %><br>
Remote address: <%= request.getRemoteAddr() %><br>
Remote host: <%= request.getRemoteHost() %><br>
Authorization type: <%= request.getAuthType() %><br>
Browser type: <%= request.getHeader("User-Agent") %>
</font>
</body>
</html>
```

Figure 7.2 shows the result of running the previous listing.

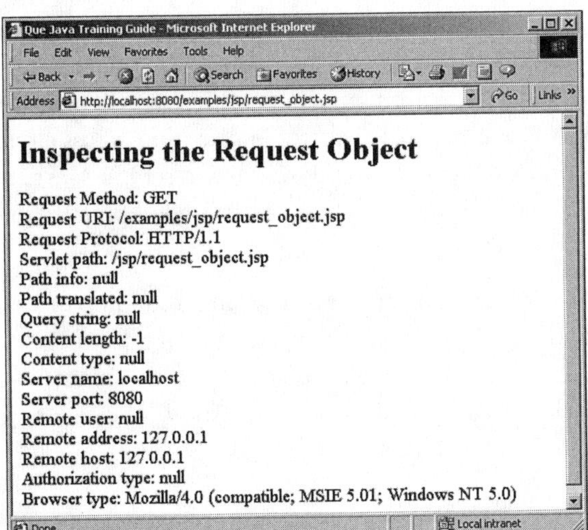

FIGURE 7.2
Walking through the `request` objects parameters dynamically.

response

```
response.setContentType("text/html")
```

This is the `HttpServletResponse` class that manages the response to the client. You use this object to send data back to the client. For example, among other things, you can add cookies (`addCookie`), add a specified header (`addHeader`), and return an error that includes a status and a default message (`sendError`). You can redirect a browser to another URL with `sendRedirect`. You can set the content type and the HTTP status (`setStatus`) as well.

The response object doesn't do much. Besides manipulating the output buffer (such as, `setBufferSize()`, `flushBuffer()`, and `getBufferSize()`), Sun's public interface `ServletResponse` defines only the following methods: `getLocale()`, `getOutputStream()`, `getWriter()`, `isCommitted()`, `setContentLength()`, `setContentType()`, and `setLocale()`.

session

This is the `HttpSession` object associated with the request. The JSP container handles (creates, tracks, and destroys) sessions automatically. You can use the `session` attribute of the `page` directive to turn sessions off. When off, there is no session state for a given JSP page, and any reference to the session variable causes a fatal error.

The primary use of the session variable is to store state information between pages for a given user. A session applies to a single user where you can share information across JSP pages. This differs from the application object, which shares information across all users. The session is on by default, so you don't have to set the `"session=true"` attribute in the JSP page directive, but it is good practice to make your intentions clear.

The exam objectives only address your understanding of what a session is and how to turn on session tracking for a JSP page. Still, you should at least review the methods and properties of the `session` object, as they might appear in a test question. They are as follows (deprecated ones have been removed):

- `getAttribute`
- `getAttributeNames`
- `getCreationTime`
- `getId`
- `getLastAccessedTime`
- `getMaxInactiveInterval`
- `invalidate`
- `isNew`
- `putValue`
- `removeAttribute`
- `setAttribute`
- `setMaxInactiveInterval`

The following is an example of using the session object:

```
<%@page errorPage="incompleteForm.jsp" import="java.io.*"
➥%>
<html>

<%
  String firstname = request.getParameter("firstname");
  String lastname = request.getParameter("lastname");
  String address = request.getParameter("address");
  String city = request.getParameter("city");
  String state = request.getParameter("state");
  String zip = request.getParameter("zip");
```

```
  if (firstname == null || firstname.length() == 0)
        firstname="Not Provided";
  if (lastname == null || lastname.length() == 0)
        lastname="Not Provided";
  if (address == null || address.length() == 0)
        address="Not Provided";
  if (city == null || city.length() == 0)
        city="Not Provided";
  if (state == null || state.length() == 0)
        state="Not Provided";
  if (zip == null || zip.length() == 0)
        zip="Not Provided";

  session.setAttribute("firstname", firstname);
  session.setAttribute("lastname", lastname);
  session.setAttribute("address", address);
  session.setAttribute("city", city);
  session.setAttribute("state", state);
  session.setAttribute("zip", zip);
%>


<%--@include file="companyBanner.html" --%>
<TITLE>Providing Address Information</TITLE>
<H1>Please provide your address:</h2>
  <form action="session.jsp" method=post>
    <table>
    <td>
      <table>
      <tr><td>first name:</td>
        <td><input type=text size=20 name="firstname"
           value="<%=session.getAttribute("firstname")%>">
           </td></tr>
      <tr><td>last name:</td>
        <td><input type=text size=20 name="lastname"
           value="<%=session.getAttribute("lastname")%>">
           </td></tr>
      <tr><td>street address:</td>
        <td><input type=text size=20 name="address"
           value="<%=session.getAttribute("address")%>">
           </td></tr>
      <tr><td>city:</td>
        <td><input type=text size=20 name="city"
           value="<%=session.getAttribute("city")%>">
           </td></tr>
      <tr><td>province/state:</td>
        <td><input type=text size=20 name="state"
           value="<%=session.getAttribute("state")%>">
           </td></tr>
      <tr><td>postal code</td>
        <td><input type=text size=20 name="zip"
           value="<%=session.getAttribute("zip")%>">
           </td></tr>
      <tr><td colspan=2 align="center">
        <input type=submit value="submit address">
           </td></tr>
```

```
      </table>
    </form>

</body>
</html>
```

IN THE FIELD

SESSION AUTOMATICALLY MANAGED

Each new session gets its own unique id number. That is how the JSP container keeps track of browsers. The number has to be long enough to eliminate the possibility of session id collision. Please see Chapter 6, "Session Management," for more on this.

config

The `config` implicit object is an instance of the class `javax.servlet.ServletConfig`. It is usually used in servlets rather than JSP pages. The methods of this object return initialization parameters for the page which are declared in the web.xml file. You define initialization parameters by setting the property when you register a servlet in the web.xml file, the deployment descriptor. The most used methods of this object are `getInitParameter` and `getInitParameterNames`. The following snippet demonstrates how to use this object:

```
<%
String DEFAULT_PARAMETER_ONE = "first parameter";
String DEFAULT_PARAMETER_TWO = "second parameter";
String parameter_one =
                config.getInitParameter("first_parameter");
if (parameter_one == null)
{
     parameter_one = DEFAULT_PARAMETER_ONE;
}
String parameter_two =
               config.getInitParameter("second_parameter");
if (parameter_two == null)
{
     parameter_two = DEFAULT_PARAMETER_TWO;
}
%>
<%="parameter_one: " + parameter_one %>
<%="<P>" %>
<%="parameter_two: " + parameter_two %>
<%="<P>"%>
```

application

While a session object shares information between JSP pages for a given user, an application object shares information among all users of a currently active JSP application. You can also use this object to communicate with the Servlet Container running the current JSP page. Normally, there is one application object per Java Virtual Machine. So, every JSP page on a Web server shares the same application object.

When we need to store information for use throughout an application, we can store it in the Servlet context, which is used to store the state for an entire Web application. This is sometimes referred to as the application object. In JavaServer pages, the implicit application object represents the Servlet context. Notice that unlike a session object, the Servlet context is not invalidated by any updates or recompiling of a given JSP page, or servlet for that matter. Whatever information you store in the Servlet context will remain until the Web application itself is invalidated.

Be careful when you use the application or session objects. When your JSP page is translated, depending on the vendor's implementation, the resulting servlet declares certain objects internally. It is easy to cause an error. For example, Tomcat translates most JSP pages into a servlet and places the code into the _jspService method. The following objects are declared in that process:

```
//in public void _jspService(...
{
//...
        HttpSession session = null;
        ServletContext application = null;
        ServletConfig config = null;
        JspWriter out = null;
//...
        application = pageContext.getServletContext();
        config = pageContext.getServletConfig();
        session = pageContext.getSession();
        out = pageContext.getOut();
//...
```

Therefore, you shouldn't, and don't need to, declare a session object. Use session. If you do declare your own, you can't use the names shown previously or you'll get an error. If you write a servlet, and want to get the Servlet context, call the getServletContext() method from inside the doGet() or doPost() method. This method returns the javax.servlet.http.ServletContext instance that is associated with this Web application.

Beyond sharing information among client requests, the `application` object provides information about the environment of the JSP page. It also has methods for writing messages to the server log.

A few of the methods and properties for the application are very similar to those of the `session` object. The primary difference is scope, whether the objects are shared only between pages being viewed by a single user (session) or all users (application). The methods and properties include the following:

- `getAttribute`
- `getAttributeNames`
- `getMajorVersion/getMinorVersion`
- `getMimeType`
- `getRealPath`
- `getResource`
- `getServerInfo`
- `log`
- `removeAttribute`
- `setAttribute`

The following code listing demonstrates how to use the `application` object:

```
<html>
<head>
<title>Que Java Training Guide - JSP Example</title>
</head>
<body>
<center>
<h1><a href="http://www.quepublishing.com\">QUE</a>
<br>Application Object</h1>
<b>The application object has the following attributes:</b>
<hr></hr>
 <%
 String requestedURI = request.getRequestURI() ;
 String filePath = application.getRealPath(requestedURI) ;
 String serverInfo = application.getServerInfo() ;
 int majorVersion = application.getMajorVersion() ;
 int minorVersion = application.getMinorVersion() ;
```

```
 StringBuffer html = new StringBuffer();
 html.append("<ol type=\"A\">");
 html.append("<li>" + requestedURI + "</li>");
 html.append("<li>" + filePath + "</li>");
 html.append("<li>" + serverInfo + "</li>");
 html.append("<li>Major Version = "+ majorVersion
+"</li>");
 html.append("<li>Minor Version = "+ minorVersion
+"</li>");
 html.append("</ol>");
 out.println( html.toString() );
 %>
</center>
</body>
</html>
```

The above code listing produces the screen in Figure 7.3 on the author's machine.

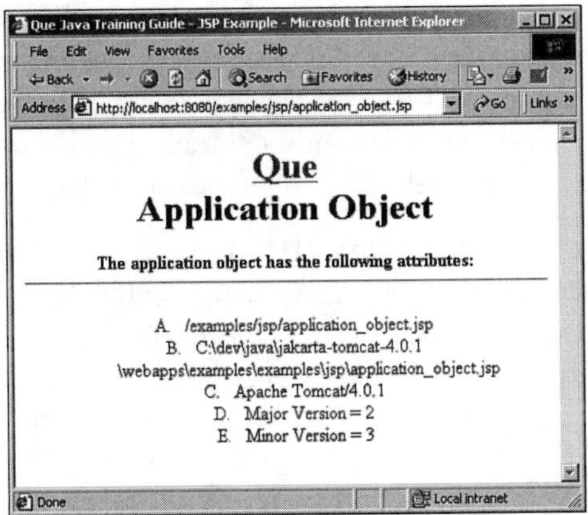

FIGURE 7.3
You can use the `application` object to share data between users and to get information about the JSP container.

pageContext

JSP has a class called `pageContext`. This is used in servlets to encapsulate server-specific features. The following is a sample use:

```
HttpSession session = pageContext.getSession();
JspWriter   out     = pageContext.getOut();
```

The advantage is portability. The main goal of the `pageContext` is to encapsulate the complete state of a single request-execution of a single JSP page. This object is passed to custom actions so that these Java objects have access to anything that the JSP page has access to.

page

In standard Java, the `this` keyword is a reference to the object for which the instance method was invoked, or to the object being constructed (that is, using `this` in a constructor). `page` is JSP's version of Java's `this`, but it isn't useful in JSP. The JSP designers created it to address JSP's support for other scripting languages beside Java. We recommend that you use the Java `this` keyword instead.

out

> **WARNING**
>
> **The `clear` method deletes all the content of the current buffer** You have to be very careful when using this method. Once the buffer has been flushed, automatically or through code, calling clear throws an IOException error. Once data is written to the client response stream, it is illegal to call the `clear` method.

This is what the `PrintWriter` used to send output to the client. However, in order to make the `response` object (see the "`response`" section earlier in this chapter) useful, this is a buffered version of `PrintWriter` called `JspWriter`. Note that you can adjust the buffer size, or even turn buffering off, through use of the buffer attribute of the `page` directive. Also note that `out` is used almost exclusively in scriptlets, since JSP expressions automatically get placed in the output stream, and thus rarely need to refer to `out` explicitly.

The `out` variable is a Java `PrintWriter` you can use to write HTML to the browser page from inside JSP tags. The following is an example of using the `out` object:

```
<%
out.clear(); //clears all output to the browser
out.print(out.getBufferSize()); //bytes available in Buffer
out.print("Hello Reader");
out.print( out.getRemaining() ); //bytes left in Buffer
out.newLine(); //prints a line return
out.flush(); //flushes the buffer
%>
```

JSP SCRIPTLETS

8.7 Distinguish correct and incorrect scriptlet code for Java statements.

- **A conditional statement**
- **An iteration statement**

A JSP scriptlet is used to contain Java code fragments in a page. The following is an example:

```
<html>
<body>
  <%
  java.util.Random randomInt = new java.util.Random();
  int limit = 10;
  %>
<ol type='i'>
  <% for (int count=0; count<limit; count++) { %>
 <li> <%=randomInt.nextInt()%> </li>
  <% } %>
</ol>
</body>
</html>
```

In this example, the iteration construct begins on line 8 and ends on line 10. However, if the developer left out line 10, then the iteration statement would not be correctly structured.

The scripting language is normally Java. The point of this objective is to determine whether the candidate understands how to structure scriptlet code *around* template text (and other JSP code). This piece of code embedded in a page is transformed into a Java programming language statement fragment by the compiler. It is then inserted into the service method of the JSP page's servlet.

> NOTE
>
> **Notice!** Notice how all variables created within a scriptlet are accessible from the appropriate scope, including anywhere within the JSP page if declared outside any block.

```
<html>
<body>
  <%
  java.util.Random randomInt = new java.util.Random();
  int limit = 10;
  %>
<ol type='i'>
  <% for (int count=0; count<limit; count++) { %>
 <li> <%=randomInt.nextInt()%> </li>
  <% } %>
</ol>
</body>
</html>
```

CHAPTER SUMMARY

KEY TERMS

- JSP
- servlet
- directive
- expression
- scriptlet
- implicit object
- JSP container
- JSP page lifecycle
- tag library
- Web application

JSP is Java's way of making servlets easy to code while not losing any of the power of server-side processing. JSP is a direct competitor to technologies like CGI, ASP, ColdFusion, and PHP. A JSP page is comprised of several elements. This chapter discusses all JSP elements and shows you what you need to know to answer the exam questions about them.

APPLY YOUR KNOWLEDGE

Review Questions

1. What is JavaServer Pages?
2. What is the difference between JSP and servlets?
3. What is a Web application?

Exam Questions

1. Assume the custom tag is GLOOP and the prefix is TWONG. Which of the following is the syntax for an empty custom tag?

   A. <TWONG:GLOOP/>

   B. <GLOOP:TWONG/>

   C. <GLOOP:TWONG></GLOOP:TWONG>

   D. <TWONG:GLOOP></TWONG:GLOOP>

2. Which design pattern did the designers of JSP use to provide centralized dispatching of requests via a controller servlet?

   A. Model-View-Controller

   B. Facade

   C. Server-Client

   D. Publish-Subscribe

3. Which of the following options is a valid declaration?

   A. <%! String name="Patricia" %>

   B. <%! String name="Patricia"; %>

   C. <% String name="Devyn" %>

   D. <% public String name="Devyn"; %>

4. The following are the contents of comment.jsp:

```
1 <html>
2 <head><title>Two Comments</title></head>
3 <body>
4 <%-- JSP Comment --%>
5 <!-- HTML Comment -->
6 </body>
7 </html>
```

   Which option best describes what happens upon executing comment.jsp?

   A. A fatal error occurs because the body is empty.

   B. Line 5 (but not 4) gets added to the output stream.

   C. 4 (but not 5) gets added to the output stream.

   D. All seven lines get added to the output stream.

5. The following are the contents of request_parameter.jsp:

```
<html>
<head>
  <title>Retrieve Request Parameter</title>
</head>
<body>
<% String customerName =
        request.getParameter("customer"); %>
<p>
The customer is <%=customerName %>
</body>
</html>
```

   Assuming the www.que.com server is responding correctly and the page path is valid, what displays in the browser if the user types http://www.quepublishing.com/customer/request_parameter.jsp?customer=Devyn?

   A. The customer is

   B. A blank page.

   C. The customer is Devyn

   D. An error page.

APPLY YOUR KNOWLEDGE

6. The following are the contents of welcomeHeader.inc:

```
<h1>Welcome to our drive through
Java coding service!</h1>
```

The following are the contents of index.jsp:

```
<html>
<head><title>Java Quick Code</title></head>
<body>
<% String file="welcomeHeader.inc"; %>
<%@ include file="file" %><p>
We are the most convenient
Java coders on the planet.
</body>
</html>
```

Which option best describes what happens upon executing index.jsp?

A. An error occurs.

B. The page displays including the welcome header.

C. The page displays excluding the welcome header.

D. The page displays, but replaces the welcome header with the words welcomeHeader.inc.

7. Which of the following options is a JSP implicit object?

A. `objRequest`

B. `Request.send`

C. `request`

D. `servlet`

8. Which of the following options is not a JSP implicit object?

A. `out`

B. `in`

C. `response`

D. `page`

9. Which of the following will not compile (assume <x:tag> is a valid custom tag that is declared for the current JSP file)?

A. `<% String employees = "Patricia"+"Devyn"; %>`

B. `<x:tag value='<%= "5" %>' />`

C. `<x:tag value="<%= "hi!" %>" />`

D. `<x:tag value='<%="Joe said \\"" +statement+ "\\"."%>'/>`

10. Which among the following objects is the best choice to share information between users?

A. `application`

B. `page`

C. `request`

D. `session`

11. Which among the following objects is the best choice to share information between pages for a single user?

A. `application`

B. `page`

C. `request`

D. `session`

12. Which of the following objects is used to share information between pages using the `setAttribute` and `getAttribute` methods?

A. `application`

B. `page`

APPLY YOUR KNOWLEDGE

C. request

D. session

13. Which option is a valid page directive?

A. <%@ page language="java" import="com.myco.*" buffer="16kb" %>

B. <%@ page import="com.myco.class" buffer="16" %>

C. <%@page language="javaScript" buffer= "16" %>

D. <%@page import='com.myco.*' buffer= '16' %>

14. Which option indicates whether the current JSP page is intended to be the URL target of another JSP page's error page?

A. <%@ page isErrorPage="true" %>

B. <%@ page isErrorPage="/messages/ errorPage.jsp" %>

C. <%@ page errorPage="true" %>

D. <%@ page errorPage="/messages/ errorPage.jsp" %>

15. Which option defines a URL to a resource to which any Java programming language Throwable object(s) thrown but not caught by the page implementation are forwarded for error processing?

A. <%@ page isErrorPage="true" %>

B. <%@ page isErrorPage="/messages/ errorPage.jsp" %>

C. <%@ page errorPage="true" %>

D. <%@ page errorPage="/messages/ errorPage.jsp" %>

16. Which of the following options is a valid expression?

A. <%! String name="Patricia" %>

B. <%! String name="Patricia"; %>

C. <%= (new java.util.Date()). toLocaleString() %>

D. <% public String name="Devyn"; %>

17. Which of the following options is a valid XML equivalent to the include directive?

A. <jsp:directive.include file= "relativeURLspec" />

B. <jsp:page.include file= "relativeURLspec" />

C. <include file="relativeURLspec" />

D. <jsp.directive.include "relativeURLspec" />

18. What is Template Data?

A. The JSP blueprint or pattern.

B. The data that is defined as default for a given page.

C. The plain text (such as HTML) outside JSP tags (non Java) in a JSP page.

D. The taglib XML namespace.

19. Put in sequence the following elements of the JSP page lifecycle:

A. Page translation, JSP page compilation, Load class, Create instance, Call jspInit, Call jspDestroy, Call _jspService

B. Page translation, JSP page compilation, Load class, Create instance, Call jspInit, Call _jspService, Call jspDestroy

APPLY YOUR KNOWLEDGE

C. JSP page compilation, Page translation, Load class, Create instance, Call `jspInit`, Call `_jspService`, Call `jspDestroy`

D. Page translation, JSP page compilation, Create instance, Load class, Call `jspInit`, Call `_jspService`, Call `jspDestroy`

Answers to Review Questions

1. JavaServer Pages is the Java 2 Platform, Enterprise Edition (J2EE) technology for building applications for generating dynamic Web content, such as HTML, DHTML, XHTML, and XML. The JavaServer Pages technology enables the easy authoring of Web pages that create dynamic content with maximum power and flexibility. See "Introduction."

2. JSP is the text page that provides a simple, yet powerful, way to add dynamic data. The JSP is never run as-is when requested. It is compiled into a servlet. A servlet is a special class with hooks for running on a Web server. See "Introduction."

3. A Web application is based on servlets. The specification defines a Web application as being composed from

    - Java Runtime Environment(s) running in the server (required)
    - JSP page(s) that handle requests and generate dynamic content
    - Servlet(s) that handle requests and generate dynamic content
    - Server-side JavaBeans components that encapsulate behavior and state
    - Static HTML, DHTML, XHTML, XML, and similar pages
    - Client-side Java applets, JavaBeans components, and arbitrary Java class files
    - Java Runtime Environment(s) running in client(s) (downloadable via the Plugin and Java Web Start technology)

    See "Introduction."

Answers to Exam Questions

1. **A, D.** These use the correct syntax for an empty custom tag of GLOOP having the prefix TWONG. See "Opening and Closing JSP Tags."

2. **A.** The Model-View-Controller design pattern is the one the designers of JSP use to provide centralized dispatching of requests via a controller servlet. See "Introduction."

3. **B.** This is a valid declaration. Be careful about the semicolon, which is required in a declaration. See "Declaration."

4. **B.** Remember that the JSP Comment is ignored by the compiler. However, the HTML Comment is passed through. Even though the browser doesn't display content in response to it, the JSP container does add it to the output stream. See "Introduction."

5. **C.** The declaration is correct. The `customer is <%=customerName %>` fragment becomes `The customer is Devyn`. See "Declaration."

6. **A.** The following is wrong: `<%@ include file="file" %>`. It should have been `<%@ include file="welcomeHeader.inc" %>`. Note that `"file"` in quotes literally means you were asking the system to include a file whose filename is "file." See "`include` Directive."

APPLY YOUR KNOWLEDGE

7. **C.** Option C is correct if the request is the only implicit object. See "JSP Implicit Objects."

8. **B.** All of these are JSP implicit objects except the fictitious `in`. See "JSP Implicit Objects."

9. **C.** All of these will compile except C, because there are quotes within quotes. It should have been `<x:tag value="<%= \"hi!\" %>" />`. See "Introduction."

10. **A.** The same `application` object is accessible by all users. See "JSP Implicit Objects."

11. **D.** The `session` object is the best choice for sharing information between pages for a single user. Users can see their own `session` object, but can't see others' `session` objects. See "JSP Implicit Objects."

12. **A, C,** and **D.** Both the `application` and the `session` objects can be used to share information between pages with the `setAttribute` and `setAttribute` methods. Either A or D is correct. Option C is also valid because you can share attributes from a "master" page to an "included" page. See "JSP Implicit Objects."

13. **A.** Only A is correct. All the others are syntactically wrong. Notice the `kb` requirement on the `buffer` attribute. See "The Page Directive."

14. **A.** This is the `isErrorPage` attribute of the `page` directive. Another page can now, but doesn't have to, use this page as an error page. See "The Page Directive."

15. **D.** The `errorPage` attribute of the `page` directive defines a URL to a resource to which any Java programming language Throwable object(s) thrown but not caught by the page implementation are forwarded for error processing. See "The Page Directive."

16. **C.** This is the only expression in the group. See "Expression."

17. **A.** JSP elements have XML equivalents (except for `taglib`). A question like this is very likely to appear on the exam. See "JSP Tags as XML."

18. **C.** Don't let the fancy label throw you. It is simply the plain text (that is, HTML) outside JSP tags (non Java) in a JSP page. See "Introduction."

19. **B.** All the others have the correct steps, but they are in the wrong order. See "JSP Page Lifecycle."

APPLY YOUR KNOWLEDGE

Suggested Readings and Resources

1. JSP Downloads & Specifications (`http://java.sun.com/products/jsp/download.html`).
2. JavaServer Pages Technology (`http://java.sun.com/products/jsp/`).
3. Sun's excellent J2EE Tutorial (`java.sun.com/j2ee/tutorial/1_3-fcs/doc/J2eeTutorialTOC.html`).
4. The Java Language Specification (`java.sun.com/docs/books/jls/second_edition/html/j.title.doc.html`).
5. XML in the Java Platform (`java.sun.com/xml`).
6. XML home page at W3C (`www.w3.org/XML`).
7. HTML home page at W3C (`www.w3.org/MarkUp`).
8. XML.org home page (`www.xml.org`).
9. Registry of content types (`ftp://ftp.isi.edu/in-notes/iana/assignments/media-types/`).

OBJECTIVES

This chapter covers the following Sun-specified objectives for Section 10, "Designing and Developing JSP pages Using JavaBean Components," of the Sun Certified Web Component Developer For J2EE Platform exam:

10.1 For any of the following tag functions, match the correctly constructed tag, with attributes and values as appropriate, with the corresponding description of the tag's functionality:

- **Declare the use of a JavaBean component within the page.**
- **Specify, for `JSP:USEBEAN` or `JSP:GETPROPERTY` tags, the name of an attribute.**
- **Specify, for a `JSP:USEBEAN` tag, the class of the attribute.**
- **Specify, for a `JSP:USEBEAN` tag, the scope of the attribute.**
- **Access or mutate a property from a declared JavaBean.**
- **Specify, for a `JSP:GETPROPERTY` tag, the property of the attribute.**
- **Specify, for a `JSP:SETPROPERTY` tag, the property of the attribute to mutate, and the new value.**

▶ The `useBean`, `getProperty`, and `setProperty` standard tags are the bulk of what you need to know for the exam regarding JavaBeans. These elements are how you instantiate a Bean and get and set the Bean's properties.

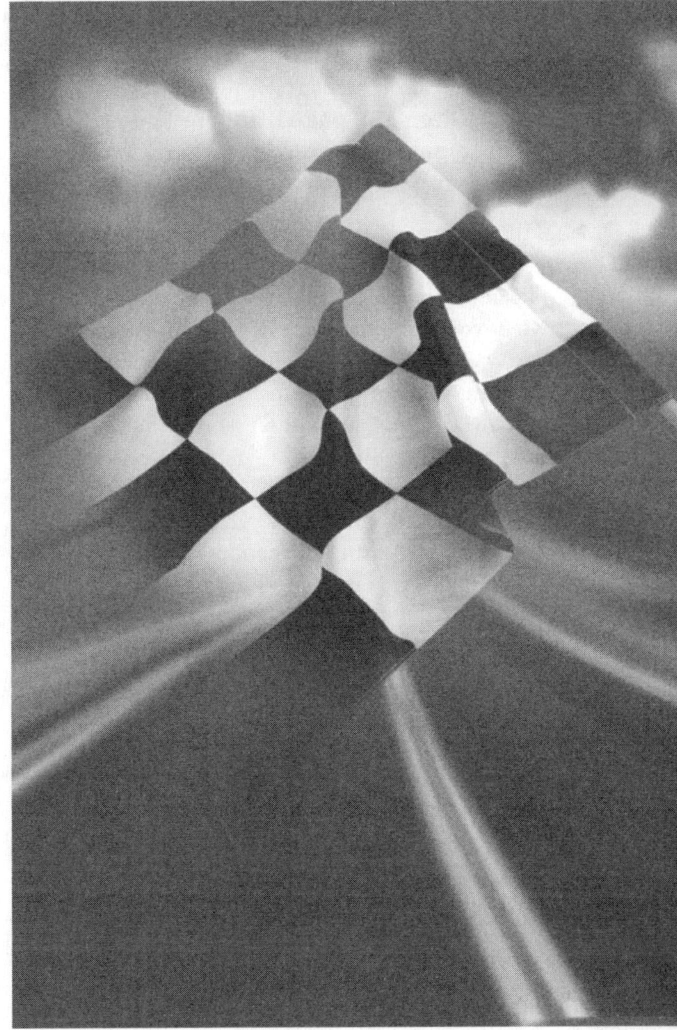

CHAPTER 8

Extend JSP with JavaBeans

OBJECTIVES

10.2 Given JSP page attribute scopes: request, session, and application, identify the equivalent servlet code.

- This objective is poorly worded. What Sun wants you to understand is that the Bean has scope, just like all variables. What does the code look like when you instantiate a Bean within a given scope, and then later refer to it in scriptlet code? The practical value of JavaBeans is the capacity to use prebuilt components and reusability. Sun's implementation also provides programmers an elegant way to copy request form parameters directly into bean properties without manual code. The essence of this chapter is an explanation of how JavaBeans is a standard way to snap in modular functionality.

10.3 Identify techniques that access a declared JavaBean component.

- How do you use a declared Bean in JSP code? This objective reflects the fact that you need to be able to access Beans with both standard actions and scriptlets.

OUTLINE

STUDY STRATEGIES

- The key to this section of the exam is understanding how JSP uses JavaBeans. You need to know how to call JavaBeans from JSP. While writing JavaBeans is not on the exam, knowing how to create them really helps you understand this technology.
- There are few methods to know regarding JavaBeans on the exam, but you do need to know the XML syntax for calling and using JavaBeans.
- While I will show you how to create JavaBeans, they are not on the exam directly; only in terms of calling them from JSP. However, it is important to know how that Sun defines them as a Java class that satisfies the following requirements: a) the class contains a no-argument constructor, b) the class uses standardized method names for property accessors and mutators, and c) there are no public instance variables.

INTRODUCTION

Visual Basic became a sensation because of its plug-and-play development capabilities. Visual Basic is a language, but Microsoft also used the same name to refer to the IDE. The language itself was, and is, neither fast nor elegant. However, Bill Gates knew that if he made it easy to use, programmers would adopt it as their development tool, so he came up with a visual IDE that took the development industry by storm. Microsoft combined QuickBasic with Alan Cooper's drag-and-drop shell, resulting in the first tool that allowed programmers to quickly create Windows applications. Thousands of programmers and newbies loved the visual drag-and-drop programming model. VB attracted an unprecedented number of newbies. The old guard was offended by all the new faces who knew nothing about the intricacies of sophisticated software techniques. No matter, a flood of good and bad software flowed from the VB community, which had a major impact on the whole software industry. Mr. Gates' intuition about a plug-and-play IDE was proven right.

Sun's attempt at plug-and-play development is JavaBeans. These are reusable components. The core idea behind JavaBeans is the component architecture. This architecture exposes a component's (JavaBean's) properties and methods, has events and listeners, and has a standard way for containers to manipulate them. Some IDEs allow you to build and manipulate JavaBeans visually, which makes it much easier. Even without an IDE, JavaBeans are Java components that can be easily accessed from JSPs using just three tags. They are to Java what COM objects are to Microsoft Active Server Pages (Windows's server-side scripting language).

The original focus of JavaBeans was visual componentry. Like the original Visual Basic IDE (now Visual Studio), you can drag and drop buttons and the like in an Integrated Development Environment (such as JBuilder, VisualAge, and Café). These IDEs use components that are JavaBeans. Don't confuse JavaBeans that are used for visual components like buttons and textboxes (for stand-alone executable development) with JavaBeans that used for JSP (for Web applications). Sun provides a BeanBox which makes it easy to construct visual-type JavaBeans components. Presently, Sun has the Bean Builder (`java.sun.com/products/javabeans/beanbuilder/index.html`), which helps you construct applications using JavaBeans.

The Bean Builder extends the capabilities of the original BeanBox. These JavaBeans are not part of the exam. The JavaBeans that are used with JSP are invisible to the user and are meant to act as state machines.

While it is not part of the exam, you might look at the JavaBeans Development Kit (BDK), which can help you develop JavaBeans components. The BDK has a Bean container called the "BeanBox," a variety of sample Beans, and a tutorial explaining the main JavaBeans 1.0 concepts using the BeanBox (`java.sun.com/products/javabeans/software/bdk_download.html`). The BeanBox is not designed to help you build JavaBeans for JSP. It is a visual component builder for GUI work. However, it is a decent tool otherwise.

Programmers often confuse Web application JavaBeans with Enterprise JavaBeans. JavaBeans and Enterprise JavaBeans are two entirely different things sharing the same name due to their use for similar purposes. EJBs are also not on the exam. However, here is a little explanation; then we drop them altogether. EJBs are either session beans or entity beans. An enterprise bean is a server-side component just like a JavaBean in JSP. They both encapsulate the business logic of an application. However, an EJB such as a session bean class, like any session bean, must meet requirements that a JavaBean for JSP doesn't. For example, the session bean must implement the SessionBean interface and one or more ejbCreate methods. Furthermore, Enterprise JavaBeans run inside an EJB container, while a JSP JavaBean runs inside a servlet container. In both cases, a client cannot directly instantiate the bean. In the case of EJB, the container instantiates an enterprise bean by invoking the appropriate ejbCreate method in the bean. An EJB entity bean represents a business object in a persistent storage mechanism. In the J2EE SDK, entity beans are stored in a relational database (each bean has an underlying table and each instance of the bean corresponds to a row in that table). Entity beans differ from session beans in that Entity beans are persistent, allow shared access, have primary keys, and may participate in relationships with other entity beans. EJBs are sophisticated technology due to container-managed persistence and remote interfaces. While they are implemented differently, EJBs encapsulate business logic and properties in the same manner as JavaBeans for JSP.

Let me give you one example of how you could use EJB. Imagine you have a database of marketing data that different departments in your company need access to. Rather than allow these departments to write their own code that talks to the database (which would have security implications and would cause problems anytime you changed the database schema), you decide to give the departments JavaBeans to use for the integration. The JavaBeans handle the business logic and the departments write their own JSPs to handle the presentation logic. Here's the gotcha: If you hand out the JavaBeans to 15 departments and later discover a bug with them or change the database schema, you have to fix the beans and redistribute updated beans to each department, where they must be installed successfully. With EJB, the actual "bean" can live on your server. The departments interface with the EJB through the remote and home interfaces, not with the EJB directly. If you ever have to update the internal application logic of the EJB, or the database schema changes, you won't have any problem unless a change in the remote or home interface is necessitated.

JavaBeans and EJBs encapsulate the business logic of an application. Just remember that the exam doesn't include EJBs, but does focus on JavaBeans.

The way Sun has designed JavaBeans for use in a JSP environment ignores much of JavaBeans' original GUI focus. While it *is* possible to have a JSP IDE which represents beans graphically, making visual components for presentation, the original JavaBeans motivation is left out completely. The name indicates reusable components, so they kept it along with the read/write (get/set method convention) properties and some of the plumbing underneath. In JSP, we have a stripped down version of JavaBeans (no GUI): This is what you'll see on the exam. However, JSP code can get unwieldy. When the number of scriptlet lines exceeds 100, a JSP gets ugly and hard to maintain. Of course, you could always use servlets. However, using beans is even better because beans separate display and logic, whereas servlets tend to mix the two. Sometimes, though, it is best to use a component that is good not only for JSP but for many situations, such as for the GUI portion of a standalone application. Each JavaBean component has the expected class structure, but follows a convention that includes get and set methods. This convention is what transforms a regular class into a JavaBean.

A JavaBean itself is ordinary. JavaBeans do not extend any specific class. Rather, the container allows JSP to access classes, and this access, along with the JavaBean convention of set/get methods, are the interesting features. A class becomes a JavaBean if it is public, has a public constructor with no arguments, follows the set/get paradigm, and is placed where the container can access it. Once you meet these criteria you can take advantage of the JavaBean, sometimes called simply Bean, by writing the XML tags in JSP that bring that Bean into play. It is more a matter of how you use the class that makes a Bean rather than syntax or inheriting a special class.

Before we dive into details, look at Figure 8.1, which illustrates how the container processes a request to a JSP page that employs a JavaBean. This is a high-level process diagram, but it gives a nice framework to see what is going on.

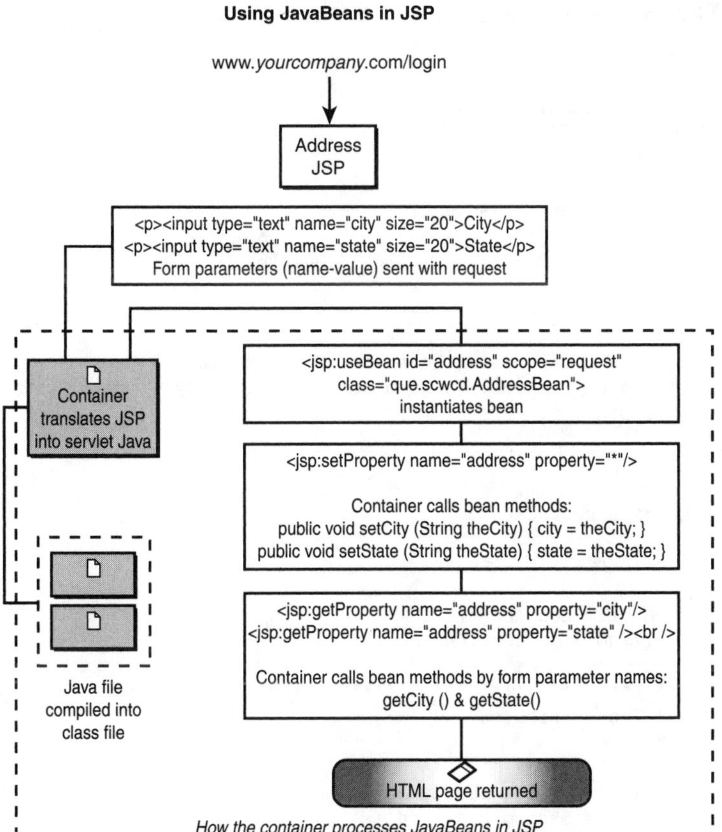

FIGURE 8.1
How the container processes JavaBeans in JSP.

CREATING JAVABEANS

10.1 For any of the following tag functions, match the correctly constructed tag, with attributes and values as appropriate, with the corresponding description of the tag's functionality.

Let us start with a quick example. Listing 8.1 presents a small JavaBean. You can see that there is nothing in the code itself to indicate that it is a Bean. What makes it a Bean is how it is used by the application, not any keyword. Notice that there isn't anything special about making a bean *except* the no-arg constructor and set/get method nomenclature. Listing 8.1 demonstrates a JavaBean class.

LISTING 8.1

THE SOURCE CODE FOR A SMALL JAVABEAN

```
/**
 *
 * que.scwcd.SmallBean.java
 *
 * Called by jsp:useBean.
 *
 * ==============================================
 *
 * Que: SCWCD Training Guide Sample Bean
 *
 * ==============================================
 *
 * This is a trivial bean that demonstrates
 * two attributes. It is used in the book by
 * login.jsp.
 *
 */

package que.scwcd;

public class LoginBean
{
   public LoginBean()
   {//no args constructor }

  /**********************************************
   * The attributes
   *
   */
  private String username = "";
  private String password = "";
```

```
/***********************************************
 * Get methods for the attributes
 *
 */
 public String getUsername()
 {
   return(username);
 }
 public String getPassword()
 {
   return(password);
 }

/***********************************************
 * Set methods for the attributes
 *
 */
 public void setUsername(String value)
 {
   username = value;
 }
 public void setPassword(String value)
 {
   password = value;
 }

/***********************************************
 * The validate method.
 * Of course, you would implement something
 * better, but this suffices to show
 * you how the bean and JSP interact.
 */
 public boolean confirmLogin()
 {
     boolean valid = true;
     if (username.length() == 0 ||
         password.length() == 0)
     {
         valid = false;
     }

     return(valid);
 }
}

<%-- login.jsp example includes a JavaBean --%>

<%@ page session="false"%>
<jsp:useBean id="security" class="com.myCom.LoginBean"/>
<jsp:setProperty name="security" property="*"/>

<%
   if (security.confirmLogin())
   {
```

continues

LISTING 8.1 *continued*

THE SOURCE CODE FOR A SMALL JAVABEAN

```
  %>
      <jsp:forward page="welcome.jsp"/>
  <%
     }
  %>

  <html>
  <head>
  <title>JavaBean Example</title>
  </head>
  <body bgcolor="#FFFFFF">
  <p />
  <h1>JavaBean Example</h1>
  <form method="POST" action="login.jsp">
  <table>
    <tr>
        <td>
            User name
        </td>
        <td>
             <input name="username"
                 size=15 value="<%=security.getName()%>">
        </td>
    </tr>
    <tr>
        <td>
            Password
        </td>
        <td>
                <input type=password name="password" size=15>
        </td>
    </tr>
    <tr>
        <td colspan="2" align="center">
          <input type="submit" value=" Login ">
        </td>
    </tr>
  </table>
  </form>
  </center>
  </body>
</html>
```

Listing 8.1 shows a JavaBean and JSP combination with only two attributes. The username and password attributes are really private variables with class scope. You also see the attributes' get and set methods. Lastly, you read a no args constructor. These three things are all you need to have a JavaBean.

When you use `jsp:useBean` and specify the class, it must be in the correct class path. This can be confusing. I've read various bogus pieces of advice on this. In Tomcat on Windows, the servlets directory has the default path of `CATALINA_HOME\webapps\examples\WEB-INF\classes`. You access servlets in this directory with `http://localhost:8080/examples/servlet/` (`CATALINA_HOME` refers to the directory into which you have installed Tomcat). On my Windows machine, I placed the class in `CATALINA_HOME\webapps\examples\WEB-INF\classes\que\scwcd\SmallBean.class`. Notice that the package is que.scwcd. To compile it you need to start in the classes directory with the command `javac que\scwcd\SmallBean.java`. A bean class (like any other Java class in a Web app) can be placed in either the `WEB-INF/classes/` directory or in the `WEB-INF/lib/` directory (if the class exists in a JAR file).

> **WARNING**
>
> **Beans must belong to a Java package!** Be careful about how the JSP compiler places the generated servlet code into a package which reflects the source's directory structure. The JSP translator puts the JSP page into its own package. If the class/type attribute of a useBean refers to a class in the "default" package, the compiler will try to find that class in the package of the JSP servlet classes. However, the JavaBeans in your JSP can't be referenced by the generated servlet code unless you place them in a package (a directory beneath the default class folder). You *MUST* place your JavaBeans in a package or the servlet engine (such as Tomcat) will throw an exception because it won't be able to find the JavaBean.

Let us now look at the JSP page that will use the JavaBean in Listing 8.1. Listing 8.2 uses the `jsp:useBean` element to declare a JavaBean. It then sets a property, of which there is only one in this JavaBean. Finally, it gets the value of the same property and adds that value to the output stream.

LISTING 8.2

THE SOURCE CODE FOR JSP THAT USES JSP:USEBEAN (SMALLBEAN)

```
<!DOCTYPE HTML PUBLIC
            "-//W3C//DTD HTML 4.0 Transitional//EN">
<HTML>
<HEAD>
<TITLE>Using JavaBeans in JSP</TITLE>
</HEAD>

<BODY>

<CENTER>
<h1>Using JavaBeans in JSP</h1>
</CENTER>
<P>
<!--load your bean with useBean-->
<jsp:useBean id="lilFella" class="que.scwcd.SmallBean" />
<jsp:setProperty name="lilFella"
       property="message"
       value="Congratulations! You will pass the exam." />

<h3>Bean Attribute</h3>
<b>
```

continues

LISTING 8.2 *continued*

THE SOURCE CODE FOR JSP THAT USES JSP:USEBEAN (SMALLBEAN)

```
   <!--JSP engine replaces this next line with
       the value of attribute in the bean
       which has been set to "Congratulations..."
       with the jsp:setProperty element above.-->
   <jsp:getProperty name="lilFella" property="message" />
   </b>

   </BODY>
</HTML>
```

Listing 8.2 shows a JSP page that uses the `jsp:useBean` element. There is little magic going on, with only one attribute set, then retrieved and displayed. That is all you need to have a JavaBean. This file is called BeanInJSP.jsp and is in the directory `CATALINA_HOME\webapps\examples\jsp\que\scwcd\BeanInJSP.jsp`. I called it using: `http://localhost:8080/examples/jsp/que/scwcd/BeanInJSP.jsp`. Now, let us see what HTML was generated.

Listing 8.3 shows the HTML generated by Listing 8.2. Again, this is all trivial code, but you can easily follow the flow of what is going on that way.

LISTING 8.3

THE SOURCE CODE FOR JSP THAT USES JSP:USEBEAN (SMALLBEAN)

```
<!DOCTYPE HTML PUBLIC
          "-//W3C//DTD HTML 4.0 Transitional//EN">
<html>
<head>
<title>Using JavaBeans in JSP</title>
</head>

<body>

<center>
<h1>Using JavaBeans in JSP</h1>
</center>
<p />
<!--load your bean with useBean-->
```

```
  <h3>Bean Attribute</h3>
  <b>
  <!--JSP engine replaces this next line with
      the value of attribute in the bean
      which has been set to the "Congratulations..."
      with the jsp:setProperty element above.
  -->
  Congratulations! You are closer to passing the exam.
  </b>

  </body>
</html>
```

Listing 8.3 shows the HTML produced by the previous listings. Notice that `CATALINA_HOME` will be something like `jakarta-tomcat-4.0\work\standalone\localhost`. The HTML in Listing 8.3 is rendered by a browser, where it looks like Figure 8.2.

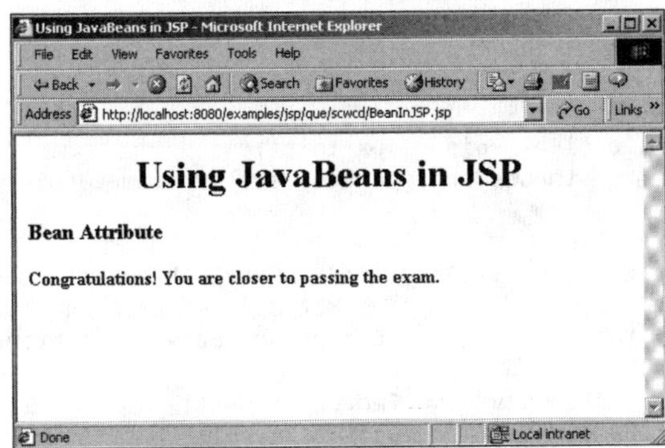

FIGURE 8.2
You can create dynamic content using a JavaBeans.

It is helpful to look at how Tomcat converted the JSP page in Listing 8.2 into a servlet. Using JavaBeans is easy because the container is doing a lot of work for you. You can see the file if you go to `CATALINA_HOME\work\localhost\examples\jsp\que\scwcd\BeanInJSP$jsp.java`. Of course, while each vendor's container will handle this somewhat differently, they will all follow the specification concerning JavaBeans. Listing 8.4 shows you the code Tomcat generated when it converted BeanInJSP.jsp into a servlet. Notice what it did about the `jsp:useBean` element.

LISTING 8.4

THE SOURCE CODE PRODUCED AFTER CONVERTING JSP WITH JSP:USEBEAN (SMALLBEAN)

```
package org.apache.jsp;

import javax.servlet.*;
import javax.servlet.http.*;
import javax.servlet.jsp.*;
import org.apache.jasper.runtime.*;


public class BeanInJSP$jsp extends HttpJspBase {

    // begin [file="/jsp/que/scwcd/BeanInJSP.jsp"...
    // end

    static {
    }
    public BeanInJSP$jsp( ) {
    }

    private static boolean _jspx_inited = false;

    public final void _jspx_init()
            throws org.apache.jasper.runtime.JspException {
    }

    public void _jspService(HttpServletRequest request,
                            HttpServletResponse  response)
        throws java.io.IOException, ServletException {

        JspFactory _jspxFactory = null;
        PageContext pageContext = null;
        HttpSession session = null;
        ServletContext application = null;
        ServletConfig config = null;
        JspWriter out = null;
        Object page = this;
        String  _value = null;
        try {

            if (_jspx_inited == false) {
                synchronized (this) {
                    if (_jspx_inited == false) {
                        _jspx_init();
                        _jspx_inited = true;
                    }
                }
            }
            _jspxFactory = JspFactory.getDefaultFactory();
            response.setContentType(
                            "text/html;charset=ISO-8859-1");
            pageContext = _jspxFactory.getPageContext(this,
                                        request, response,
                            "", true, 8192, true);
```

```
application = pageContext.getServletContext();
config = pageContext.getServletConfig();
session = pageContext.getSession();
out = pageContext.getOut();

// HTML // begin [file="/jsp/que/scwcd/BeanI...
    out.write("<!DOCTYPE HTML PUBLIC \"-//W3C"+
    "//DTD HTML 4.0 Transitional//EN\">\r\n"+
    "<HTML>\r\n<HEAD>\r\n<TITLE>Using "+
    "JavaBeans in JSP</TITLE>\r\n</HEAD>\r\n"+
    "\r\n<BODY>\r\n\r\n<CENTER>\r\n<h1>Using"+
    " JavaBeans in JSP</h1>\r\n</CENTER>\r\n"+
    "<P>\r\n<!--load your bean with useBean"+
    "-->\r\n");

// end
// begin [file="/jsp/que/scwcd/BeanInJSP...
    que.scwcd.SmallBean lilFella = null;
    boolean _jspx_speciallilFella  = false;
     synchronized (pageContext) {
        lilFella= (que.scwcd.SmallBean)
        pageContext.getAttribute("lilFella",
                       PageContext.PAGE_SCOPE);
        if ( lilFella == null ) {
            _jspx_speciallilFella = true;
            try {
               lilFella = (que.scwcd.SmallBean)
                  java.beans.Beans.instantiate(
                  this.getClass()
                  .getClassLoader(),
                   "que.scwcd.SmallBean");
           } catch (ClassNotFoundException exc)
           {
             throw new InstantiationException(
                         exc.getMessage());
            } catch (Exception exc) {
                throw new ServletException (
               "Cannot create bean of class "+
                "que.scwcd.SmallBean", exc);
            }
           pageContext.setAttribute("lilFella",
           lilFella, PageContext.PAGE_SCOPE);
        }
     }
     if(_jspx_speciallilFella == true) {
 // end
 // begin [file="/jsp/que/scwcd/BeanInJSP.jsp...
     }
 // end
 // HTML // begin [file="/jsp/que/scwcd/BeanI...
     out.write("\r\n");

 // end
```

continues

LISTING 8.4 *continued*

THE SOURCE CODE PRODUCED AFTER CONVERTING JSP WITH JSP:USEBEAN (SMALLBEAN)

```
                // begin [file="/jsp/que/scwcd/BeanInJSP.jsp...
                    JspRuntimeLibrary.introspecthelper(
                       pageContext.findAttribute("lilFella"),
                        "attribute","Congratulations! You will"+
                        " pass the exam.",null,null, false);
                // end
                // HTML // begin [file="/jsp/que/scwcd/BeanI...
                    out.write("\r\n             \r\n<h3>Bean"+
                    " Attribute</h3> \r\n<b>\r\n<!--JSP engi"+
                    "ne replaces this next line with \r\n   "+
                    " the value of attribute in the bean\r\n"+
                    "     which has been set to the \"Congrat"+
                    "ulations...\" \r\n     with the jsp:setP"+
                    "roperty element above.-->\r\n");

                // end
                // begin [file="/jsp/que/scwcd/BeanInJSP.jsp...
                    out.print(JspRuntimeLibrary.toString((((
                      que.scwcd.SmallBean)pageContext
                       .findAttribute("lilFella"))
                      .getAttribute())));
                // end
                // HTML // begin [file="/jsp/que/scwcd/BeanI...
                    out.write("\r\n</b>\r\n               "+
                    " \r\n</BODY>\r\n</HTML>\r\n");

                // end

            } catch (Throwable t) {
                if (out != null && out.getBufferSize() != 0)
                    out.clearBuffer();
                if (pageContext != null)
                     pageContext.handlePageException(t);
            } finally {
                if (_jspxFactory != null)
                  _jspxFactory.releasePageContext(pageContext);
            }
        }
}
```

Clearly, a lot is happening. I apologize for the appearance; the code was edited to fit on the page. Focus on the code that handles the `jsp:useBean` element. The first line of interest is this:

```
pageContext.getAttribute("lilFella",PageContext.PAGE_SCOPE)
➥;
```

The above line creates an attribute with page scope. Then it instantiates the class with this:

```
lilFella = (que.scwcd.SmallBean) java.beans.Beans.
instantiate(this.getClass().getClassLoader(), "que.scwcd.
SmallBean");
```

This is the key line that shows you what the container does with the `jsp:useBean` element. The container loads the class you specified with the class attribute. Below that, the code shows how the container uses the `JspRuntimeLibrary` class to add the value given in the `setProperty` element, and then later still how it gets the value named in the `getProperty` element.

Next, the servlet replaces the `jsp:getProperty` action in JSP with the following code:

```
out.print(JspRuntimeLibrary.toString((((que.scwcd.
SmallBean)pageContext.findAttribute("lilFella")).getAt-
tribute())));
```

Now that we have walked through the entire process of using a JavaBean in JSP, we need to discuss the specifics of the syntax which will be on the exam.

jsp:useBean

The `jsp:useBean` JSP element declares that a bean is stored within and accessible from the specified scope (application, session, request, or page). It boils down to creating an object which has get and set methods that are easy to use in JSP. Even if you need only a simple object to hold values, and especially if you have to do more than that (such as compute tax), I recommend you write a JavaBean.

When you use `jsp:useBean`, the container performs several actions. Basically, it instantiates the object in memory and provides a variable name for you to use within the scope you set in the tag. If the bean class hasn't been loaded, the container will try to locate it and load it. The container creates the bean and stores it as an attribute of the scope object. The value of the `id` attribute determines the name of the bean within the object scope. Also, you use that name to refer to the object in other JSP elements and scriptlets.

The syntax is

```
<jsp:useBean id="name"
      scope="page|request|session|application" typeSpec />
typeSpec ::= class="className" |
class="className" type="typeName" |
type="typeName" class="className" |
beanName="beanName" type="typeName" |
type="typeName" beanName="beanName" |
type="typeName"
```

The `id` and `scope` are easy. The confusion arises over the `typeSpec`. The container will always look for the Bean. However, if the `typeSpec` is used one way, the container will throw an exception if it can't find that Bean (not already instantiated). If it is used another way, it will create a new instance of the Bean if one hasn't been created already.

The typical use of the `jsp:useBean` element is this:

```
<jsp:useBean ...>
    Body
</jsp:useBean>
```

This is a way to instantiate a bean. Table 8.1 explains the syntax. The body is executed upon instantiation but not after the bean is loaded, so be careful about this. So, there are two behaviors of `useBean`: to instantiate an object or to retrieve an object as a Webapp attribute.

To get you started, Table 8.1 offers a quick overview of the useBean attributes.

WARNING

If the bean has been instantiated already, the body is not executed! The Body portion of the `jsp:useBean` element is executed only when the bean is first instantiated. If the bean instance has already been loaded into memory from a previous `jsp:useBean` (for example, in the previous page with session scope) the body of the `jsp:useBean` element will not be executed. Since beans can be shared, `jsp:useBean` doesn't always newly instantiate a bean. The body is executed only once for a given bean, regardless of how many `jsp:useBean` elements refer to it. Also, you'll get an exception if more than one `jsp:useBean` refers to the same ID.

TABLE 8.1

USEBEAN ATTRIBUTES

Attribute	*Definition*
`id`	The case sensitive name used to identify the object instance in the specified scope. This name doubles as the scripting variable name declared and initialized with that object reference.
`scope`	The scope within which the reference is available. The default value is page. The options are page, request, session, and application.
`class`	The fully qualified name of the class. If the `class` and `beanName` attributes are not specified the object must be present in the given scope. The class must not be abstract (or an interface) and must have a public, no-argument constructor, but the implicit no args constructor will suffice.

Attribute	*Definition*
`beanName`	The name of a Bean, as expected by the `instantiate()` method of the `java.beans.Beans` class. This name can be set dynamically by an expression as a value.
`type`	If specified, it defines the type of the variable defined. The type is required to be the class itself, a superclass of the class, or an interface implemented by the class specified. If unspecified, the value is the same as the value of the class attribute.

Let's study an example. The following is a more complete JavaBean example. Listing 8.5 represents an address JavaBean. The combination of attribute and associated set and get methods is here. Get and set methods are not required in JavaBeans. `setProperty` and `getProperty` expect proper JavaBean mutator and accessor method names. If you don't have these methods, you can still call other methods the bean might have, but you can't use the setProperty and getProperty elements.

LISTING 8.5

THE SOURCE CODE FOR A FULL JAVABEAN

```
/**
 * AddressBean.java
 *
 * represents an address object including attributes
 * and operations to encapsulate all the information
 * necessary to contact an individual. You could make
 * a contact object by extending this object and adding
 * things like company, department, jobTitle...
 *
 * @version 1.0
 * @author Alain Trottier
 */
package que.scwcd;

public class AddressBean
{

    /*  CLASS ATTRIBUTES  */
     String fullName;
     String firstName;
     String lastName;
     String street;
     String city;
     String state;
```

continues

LISTING 8.5 *continued*

THE SOURCE CODE FOR A FULL JAVABEAN

```
 String zip;
 String country;
 String phone;
 String cell;
 String pager;
 String email;
 String webPage;
 String note;

/*  CLASS METHOD  */

public boolean isValid () {

 if (firstName == null || firstName.length()==0 ||
     lastName == null || lastName.length()==0 ||
     street == null || street.length()==0 ||
     city == null || city.length()==0 ||
     state == null || state.length()==0 ||
     zip == null || zip.length()==0 ||
     country == null || country.length()==0 ||
     email == null || email.length()==0)
  {   return false;   }

 return true;

}


/*  GET METHODS  */

/**
 * Returns the fullName
 * @return A String that represents the fullName.
 */
public String getFullName () {
   return fullName;
}

/**
 * Returns the firstName
 * @return A String that represents the firstName.
 */
public String getFirstName () {
   return firstName;
}

/**
 * Returns the lastName
 * @return A String that represents the lastName.
 */
public String getLastName () {
```

```
        return lastName;
    }

    /**
     * Returns the street
     * @return A String that represents the street.
     */
    public String getStreet () {
        return street;
    }

    /**
     * Returns the city
     * @return A String that represents the city.
     */
    public String getCity () {
        return city;
    }

    /**
     * Returns the state
     * @return A String that represents the state.
     */
    public String getState () {
        return state;
    }

    /**
     * Returns the zip
     * @return A String that represents the zip.
     */
    public String getZip () {
        return zip;
    }

    /**
     * Returns the country
     * @return A String that represents the country.
     */
    public String getCountry () {
        return country;
    }

    /*  SET METHODS  */

    /**
     * Sets the value of fullName.
     * @param fullName String
     */
    public void setFullName (String theFullName) {
        fullName = theFullName;
    }

    /**
     * Sets the value of fullName.
```

continues

LISTING 8.5 *continued*

THE SOURCE CODE FOR A FULL JAVABEAN

```
     * @param fullName String
     */
    public void setFullName () {
       fullName = firstName + " " + lastName;
    }

    /**
     * Sets the value of firstName.
     * @param firstName String
     */
    public void setFirstName (String theFirstName) {
       firstName = theFirstName;
    }

    /**
     * Sets the value of lastName.
     * @param lastName String
     */
    public void setLastName (String theLastName) {
       lastName = theLastName;
    }

    /**
     * Sets the value of street.
     * @param street String
     */
    public void setStreet (String theStreet) {
       street = theStreet;
    }

    /**
     * Sets the value of city.
     * @param city String
     */
    public void setCity (String theCity) {
       city = theCity;
    }

    /**
     * Sets the value of state.
     * @param state String
     */
    public void setState (String theState) {
       state = theState;
    }

    /**
     * Sets the value of zip.
     * @param zip String
     */
    public void setZip (String theZip) {
```

```
        zip = theZip;
    }

    /**
     * Sets the value of country.
     * @param country String
     */
    public void setCountry (String theCountry) {
        country = theCountry;
    }

    /**
     * the get/set methods for phone, cell, pager,
     * email, webpage and note have been
     * omitted for space. They are present
     * in the full source on the CD and Web site.
     */
}
```

Listing 8.5 showed you an example of a more useful JavaBean. Once the bean is compiled, you can use it in a JSP-based Web page with this:

```
<jsp:useBean id="addressBean" scope="request"
class="que.scwcd.AddressBean">
```

This XML snippet is how you create an instance of the `AddressBean` class in the container. Once you do that, the Bean is in memory, but the attributes are initially null. To change these attributes, you can use scriptlets or XML. Generally, XML is better than scriptlets, so try to stay with XML.

When you use `jsp:useBean`, the container performs several actions. Basically, it instantiates the object in memory and provides a variable name for you to use within the scope you specified in the tag. If this JavaBean doesn't actually exist, the container will try to create it. The following actions are paraphrased from the specification:

- An attempt is made to locate an object based on the attribute values id and scope.
- Container declares a variable for the class with the same name as the id. It has the same scope as declared in the tag.
- If the object is found, the variable's value is initialized with a reference to the located object, cast to the specified type. If the cast fails, a `java.lang.ClassCastException` shall occur. This ends the processing of this `jsp:useBean` action.

- If the `jsp:useBean` element had a non-empty body, it is ignored. This ends the processing of this `jsp:useBean` action.
- If the object is not found in the specified scope and neither class nor beanName are given, a java.lang.InstantiationException shall occur. This ends the processing of this `jsp:useBean` action.
- If the object is not found in the specified scope, and the class specified names a non-abstract class that defines a public no-args constructor, the class is instantiated. The new object reference is associated with the scripting variable using the scope specified (see PageContext). After this, the last step listed below is performed.
- If the object is not found, and the class is abstract, an interface, or no public no-args constructor is defined, then a java.lang.InstantiationException shall occur. This ends the processing of this `jsp:useBean` action.
- If the object is not found in the specified scope and beanName is given, then the container attempts to create the bean. If it succeeds, the new object reference is associated with the scripting variable in the specified scope.
- If the `jsp:useBean` element has a non-empty body, the body is processed. The variable is initialized and available within the scope of the body. The text of the body is treated as elsewhere. Any template text will be passed through to the out stream. Scriptlets and action tags will be evaluated. Usually, you use `jsp:setProperty` in here.

You can see that the container does a lot of work for you so that you only need a few tags to perform helpful work.

Ideally, the entire JSP page is in XML; that would be best. Presently, we will use `<jsp:setProperty>` to change the attributes to the values from a set of fields from an HTML form. There is less coding to do when the form field names match the JavaBean property names. This is one of the main purposes of Beans, to make life easier for the programmer. At least it makes certain steps more concise and less prone to mistakes. Listing 8.6 shows the JSP that uses the AddressBean.

LISTING 8.6

THE SOURCE CODE FOR JSP THAT USES JSP:USEBEAN (ADDRESSBEAN)

```
<jsp:useBean id="addressBean" scope="request"
                      class="que.scwcd.AddressBean">
<!-- Set all the attributes at once with property="*".
     Values come from the request object, previous post.
     You could add attributes with jsp:setProperty setting:
     property="attributeName" value="yourValue"
-->
        <jsp:setProperty name="addressBean" property="*"/>
</jsp:useBean>

<!--
     Demonstrates how to use Bean in scriptlet.
     Make sure to use semicolon.
-->
<% addressBean.setFullName(); %>

<html>

<head>
<title>Provide Address Information</title>
</head>

<body>
<center>
<h1>Provide Address Information</h1>

<form method="POST" action="address.jsp">
  <!--
      Keep simple for space. Make pretty with a table.
      You can persist values with
      value="<%=addressBean.getFirstName() %> for each.
      Notice there is no statement terminating semicolon.
  -->
  <p><input type="text" name="firstName" size="20">
                                              First Name</p>
  <p><input type="text" name="lastName" size="20">
                                               Last Name</p>
  <p><input type="text" name="street" size="20">Street</p>
  <p><input type="text" name="city" size="20">City</p>
  <p><input type="text" name="state" size="20">State</p>
  <p><input type="text" name="zip" size="20">Zip Code</p>
  <p><input type="text" name="country"
➥size="20">Country</p>
  <p><input type="text" name="phone" size="20">Phone</p>
  <p><input type="text" name="pager" size="20">Pager</p>
  <p><input type="text" name="cell" size="20">Cell</p>
  <p><input type="text" name="email" size="20">Email</p>
  <p><input type="text" name="webPage" size="20">Web
➥Page</p>
```

continues

LISTING 8.6 *continued*

THE SOURCE CODE FOR JSP THAT USES JSP:USEBEAN (ADDRESSBEAN)

```
    <p><input type="text" name="note" size="20">Note</p>
    <p> </p>
    <p>
      <input type="submit" value="Submit">
      <input type="reset" value="Reset">
    </p>
  </form>

  <hr />

  <!--
     This is a silly thing to do, but it shows you how
     to get values back out of a bean.
  -->
  First Name:<jsp:getProperty name="addressBean"
                              property="firstName" /><br />
  Last Name:<jsp:getProperty name="addressBean"
                              property="lastName" /><br />
  Full Name:<jsp:getProperty name="addressBean"
                              property="fullName" /><br />
  Street:<jsp:getProperty name="addressBean"
                              property="street" /><br />
  City:<jsp:getProperty name="addressBean"
                              property="city" /><br />
  State:<jsp:getProperty name="addressBean"
                              property="state" /><br />
  Zip Code:<jsp:getProperty name="addressBean"
                              property="zip" /><br />
  Country:<jsp:getProperty name="addressBean"
                              property="country" /><br />
  Phone:<jsp:getProperty name="addressBean"
                              property="phone" /><br />
  Pager:<jsp:getProperty name="addressBean"
                              property="pager" /><br />
  Cell:<jsp:getProperty name="addressBean"
                              property="cell" /><br />
  Email:<jsp:getProperty name="addressBean"
                              property="email" /><br />
  Web Page:<jsp:getProperty name="addressBean"
                              property="webPage" /><br />
  Note:<jsp:getProperty name="addressBean"
                              property="note" />

  </body>
</html>
```

Listing 8.6 shows you how to use the AddressBean in a JSP page. It produces ugly HTML, but it serves as an instructive example.

IN THE FIELD

HOW DO JAVABEANS IN JSP WORK?

You write a JavaBean like you would any normal class. The class must meet a few criteria in order to be a JavaBean, including the following: It must be a public class, it must have a public constructor with no arguments, and it must have get and set methods for any properties you want accessed or mutated. The container handles the communication between the JSP page and the JavaBean. All you have to do is use the useBean, getProperty, and setProperty actions to get and set the attributes of the bean. Also, you can refer to the bean like any other class in scriptlets by the name specified in the ID attribute of the useBean element.

Getting and Setting Properties

You have used get and set methods before, so this is not new. The following snippet is the convention required for the container to match the XML elements in JSP to the actual methods in the JavaBean:

```
public void setName(String name);
public String getName( );
```

In Listing 8.5, you see the get and set methods for the JavaBean properties like phone, email, and first name. In the case of setting the city property, the JavaBean method is `public void setCity (String theCity)`. You could set this property with a scriptlet such as `<% myAddress.setCity("Dover"); %>`. You could then retrieve this value with `<%=myAddress.getCity()%>`. While the JavaBean is valid without these set and get methods, they are usually part of each JavaBean. The preferred way to set and get properties is to use the `jsp:setProperty` element to set a property and the `jsp:getProperty` to get the value of a property.

If you place `jsp:setProperty` after, but outside of, a `jsp:useBean` element, it is always executed. However, if the `jsp:setProperty` is inside the `jsp:useBean` element body then `jsp:setProperty` is executed only if the `jsp:useBean` element instantiates the JavaBean. Remember that the body of the `jsp:useBean` element is not executed if it finds a JavaBean loaded already.

jsp:setProperty Action

You use `jsp:setProperty` to set the properties values of beans that have been referenced earlier in the JSP page. In Listing 8.5 you see several setProperty actions for setting the JavaBean properties.

In the following case, the `jsp:setProperty` is executed regardless of whether a new bean was instantiated or an existing bean already exists in memory, because it is not inside the body of the `jsp:useBean` tag.

```
<jsp:useBean id="beanName" ... />
<jsp:setProperty name="beanName"
                 property="propertyName" ... />
```

However, in the next case, the `jsp:setProperty` is executed only the first time the JavaBean is instantiated. It is ignored if the JavaBean has already been loaded in memory, as would happen if the JavaBean was loaded on a previous page with application scope, or session scope by the same person.

```
<jsp:useBean id="beanName" ... >
<jsp:setProperty name="beanName"
                 property="propertyName" ... />
</jsp:useBean>
```

There are three ways to assign values to JavaBean properties using the `jsp:setProperty` element. The first is a simply giving a value. The following element sets a property from a value:

```
<jsp:setProperty name="addressBean" property="phone"
value="<%= "714-" + phone %>" />
```

The container assigns the value from the JSP page to the JavaBean attribute variable.

The next way to do this is a shortcut between the request object parameter and the JavaBean property. You tell the container which parameter to take the value from and which JavaBean property to assign that value to. The parameter name in the request object doesn't have to match the property name in the JavaBean, but making them the same makes your code cleaner. When using the `jsp:setProperty` element, the container will take the parameter value and assign it to the JavaBean property variable. You do that like so:

```
<jsp:setProperty name="addressBean" property="state"
param="state" />
```

The property is the name of the attribute in the JavaBean, while the param is the name of the parameter in the request object. Notice how the param attribute is optional if it is the same as the property attribute. There is yet another shortcut. If you look in Listing 8.5, you'll find the following element:

```
<jsp:setProperty name="addressBean" property="*"/>
```

You'll notice that the property is set to the wildcard star. That tells the container to match as many request parameters with JavaBean properties as possible. With each match, the container takes the value from the request object and places it in the JavaBean property variable. Due to how the HTML form and JavaBean were designed, only one tag was needed to accomplish transferring all the form field values in Listing 8.5 to the JavaBean properties. Notice that the HTML field names have to match exactly (that is, case-sensitively) with the JavaBean properties for this elegant trick to work.

Table 8.2 offers a quick overview of the setProperty attributes. The definitions are slightly edited from the specification.

TABLE 8.2

SETPROPERTY ATTRIBUTES

Attribute	*Definition*
`name`	The case sensitive name of a Bean instance defined by a `<jsp:useBean>` element. The Bean instance must contain the property you want to set. The defining element must appear before the `<jsp:setProperty>` element in the same file.
`property`	The name of the Bean `property` whose value you want to set. If you set `propertyName` to `*`, the tag will iterate over the current ServletRequest parameters, matching parameter names and value type(s) to property names and setter method type(s), setting each matched property to the value of the matching parameter. If a parameter has a value of "", the corresponding property is not modified.
`param`	The name of the request parameter (Web form or query string) whose value you want to give to a Bean property. If you omit `param`, the request parameter name is assumed to be the same as the Bean property name. If the `param` is not set in the Request object, or if it has the value of "", the `jsp:setProperty` element has no effect. An action may not have both `param` and `value` attributes.
`value`	The value to assign to the given property. This attribute can accept a request-time attribute expression as a value. An action may not have both `param` and `value` attributes.

jsp:getProperty Action

A <jsp:getProperty> action places the value of a Bean instance property into the implicit out object. The String representation is sent to the HTTP response stream. Unlike a scriptlet, which can get a value and assign it to a variable, the getProperty action converts the Bean property value to a String and immediately adds that String to the output stream. You cannot assign the value from this tag to a variable in most containers.

You use jsp:getProperty to get the property values of beans that have been referenced earlier in the JSP page. In Listing 8.5, you see several getProperty actions for getting the JavaBean properties.

Regarding when this action takes place, in the following case, the jsp:getProperty is executed regardless of whether a new bean was instantiated or an existing bean already exists in memory.

```
<jsp:useBean id="beanName" ... />
<jsp:getProperty name="beanName"
                 property="propertyName" ... />
```

However, in the next case, the jsp:getProperty is executed only the first time the JavaBean is instantiated. It is ignored if the JavaBean has already been loaded in memory.

```
<jsp:useBean id="beanName" ... >
<jsp:getProperty name="beanName"
                 property="propertyName" ... />
</jsp:useBean>
```

Table 8.3 offers a quick overview of the getProperty attributes. There are only two, less than the more complicated setProperty element.

TABLE 8.3

GETPROPERTY ATTRIBUTES

Attribute	*Definition*
name	The case-sensitive name of a Bean instance defined by a <jsp:useBean> element. The Bean instance must contain the property you want to set. The defining element must appear before the <jsp:setProperty> element in the same file.
property	The name of the Bean property whose value you want to get. If you get a propertyName that doesn't exist, you will generate an error.

SCOPE OF JAVABEANS IN JSP

10.2 Given JSP page attribute scopes: request, session, and application, identify the equivalent servlet code.

JavaBeans have scope, just like all variables. You declare this in the `jsp:useBean` element. If you declare the Bean in session scope, all JSP pages within that session have access to the same JavaBean. Figure 8.3 illustrates object scope. The Page scope is least visible. These objects are accessible only on the page where they were created. Request scope means objects are accessible during the processing of the request (that is, they can be transferred between pages as in a forward). The session scope means objects are accessible throughout the life of the session. Finally, an object with application scope can be accessed anywhere within the application. Given the chart Page-->Request-->Session-->Application, objects on the left can see objects on the right, but not the other way. So, objects with Page scope can see objects with any other scope, but objects with Application scope can not see objects with any other scope.

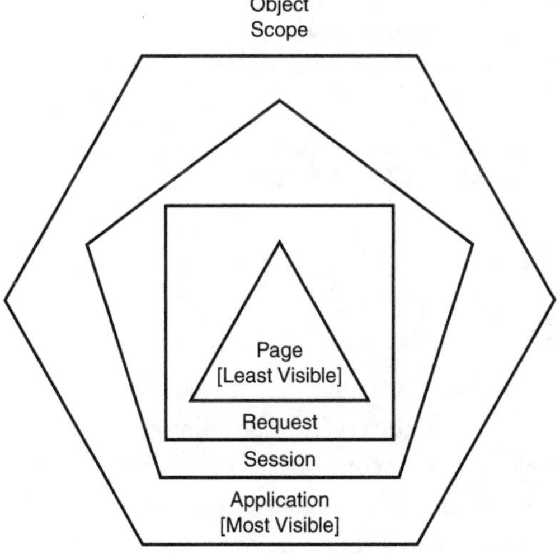

FIGURE 8.3
Object scope.

The following list describes the four scopes including Page, Request, Session, and Application. There is an example snippet for each of the four types of scope that Beans can have. I'd like to acknowledge and commend Alex Chaffee at jGuru for an excellent set of examples in his FAQ (`www.jguru.com/faq/view.jsp?EID=53309`).

Page

The address bean is instantiated as a local variable. Since its scope is page, the reference disappears once the JSP page is processed. It can't be referenced by another JSP or servlet, even if a forward or include is used. The syntax is `<jsp:useBean id="address" class="que.scwcd.AddressBean" scope="page" />`. The following snippet demonstrates how to use it:

```
que.scwcd.AddressBean address =
                new que.scwcd.AddressBean();
```

Request

The address bean is instantiated into the current request object. It can be accessed by any JSP or servlet within the same request. This reference remains alive in any other servlets/JSPs called by `jsp:include` and `jsp:forward`, or in ones called via a `RequestDispatcher` object. The syntax is `<jsp:useBean id="address" class="que.scwcd.AddressBean" scope="request" />`. The following snippet demonstrates how to use it:

```
que.scwcd.AddressBean address =
    (que.scwcd.AddressBean)request.getAttribute("address");
if (address == null)
{
  address = new que.scwcd.AddressBean();
  request.setAttribute("address", address);
}
```

Session

The address bean is instantiated into the current session. It can then be accessed by any JSP or servlet responding to requests by the current user. The syntax is `<jsp:useBean id="address" class="que.scwcd.AddressBean" scope="session" />`. The following snippet demonstrates how to use it:

```
HttpSession session = request.getSession(true);
que.scwcd.AddressBean address =
    (que.scwcd.AddressBean)session.getAttribute("address");
if (address == null)
{
  address = new que.scwcd.AddressBean();
  session.setAttribute("address", address);
}
```

Application

The AddressBean bean is instantiated within the servlet context. It can be accessed by any JSP or servlet within the servlet context, thus by any user. The syntax is `<jsp:useBean class="que.scwcd.AddressBean" scope="application" />`. The following snippet demonstrates how to use it:

```
que.scwcd.AddressBean address = (que.scwcd.AddressBean)
                                getServletContext()
                                .getAttribute("address");
if (address == null)
{
  address = new que.scwcd.AddressBean();
  getServletContext().setAttribute("address", address);
}
```

How to Access JavaBeans in JSP

10.3 Identify techniques that access a declared JavaBean component.

How do you use a declared Bean in JSP code? This objective wants you to be able to access Beans with both XML elements and scriptlets. A declared JavaBean can be accessed by the name specified in the id attribute of `<jsp:useBean>` by using Scriptlets, Expressions, and XML elements. This chapter has already demonstrated all three.

Table 8.5 gives you a list of three examples representing the three ways to access Beans.

TABLE 8.5

GETPROPERTY ATTRIBUTES

Access	*Example*
XML	`<jsp:getProperty name="addressBean" property="city" ... />`
Scriptlet	`<% String city = myAddress.getCity()%>`
Expression	`<%= myAddress.getCity()%>`

EXAM TIP

What are the three ways to reference a bean in JSP? A JavaBean can be referenced in three ways: through an expression, scriptlet, or XML tag.

KEY TERMS

- JavaBean
- Bean properties
- XML
- Bean scope and attributes
- get/set method pairs
- JavaBeans Development Kit (BDK)

CHAPTER SUMMARY

The JavaBeans are components for use in JSP (at least as far as this exam is concerned; they are used elsewhere, too). JavaBeans components are Java classes that are easy to access from JSP. The JavaBeans are intended to be reused, so it is a good idea to collect business logic in them, which takes the equivalent amount of code out of JSP, a very good thing. There are no special classes to extend. A class becomes a JavaBean if you follow certain design conventions, including a public class, public constructor with no arguments, and get/set methods.

The JavaServer Pages specification supports JavaBeans with specific JSP language elements. These elements include useBean, setProperty, and getProperty. With these elements, you can easily initialize a JavaBean and get/set the values of its properties. This chapter discussed all the exam objectives covering JavaBeans and their use in JSP. For more information about using JavaBeans in JSP, please see `java.sun.com/products/javabeans`.

APPLY YOUR KNOWLEDGE

Review Questions

1. What is the purpose of JavaBeans?
2. Why would you clutter JSP with JavaBeans code?
3. What are the advantages of using JavaBeans?
4. What makes a class a JavaBean?
5. What was the original purpose for JavaBeans?

Exam Questions

1. Which one of the following interfaces is implemented when declaring a JavaBean?

   A. `JavaBean`

   B. `ServiceBean`

   C. `HttpJavaBean`

   D. `ServletBean`

   E. None of the above.

2. Which one of the following objects is passed to a JavaBean when one of its properties is set via a JSP action?

   A. `ServletRequest`

   B. `HttpServletRequest`

   C. `ServletResponse`

   D. `HttpServletResponse`

   E. None of the above.

3. By default, how many instances of a JavaBean will be created by a servlet container when there are five `useBean` elements with the same ID on the same JSP page?

   A. One

   B. Five

   C. One per session

   D. None of the above

4. Which of the following cannot be used as the scope when using a JavaBean with JSP?

   A. response

   B. request

   C. session

   D. application

   E. page

5. Which of the following are used by servlet containers to set JavaBean properties?

   A. cookies

   B. form fields

   C. memory

   D. disk

6. Which of the following scopes best fits with this description: "An object inside this scope is accessible from all pages processing the request during which the object was created?"

   A. page

   B. session

   C. application

   D. request

7. Is it impossible to share a page scope variable with another JSP or servlet?

   A. Yes

   B. No

   C. Sometimes

   D. Configurable

APPLY YOUR KNOWLEDGE

8. Given a form field named lastName, what is the get method for the associatedJavaBean property?

   A.
   ```
   public String getFirstName ()
                     {
                          return firstName;
                     }
   ```

   B.
   ```
   public String getFirstName (boolean
   returnValue)
                     {
                          if (returnValue)
                               return
   firstName;
                     }
   ```

   C.
   ```
   public String getFirstname ()
                     {
                          return Firstname;
                     }
   ```

   D.
   ```
   public String get("FirstName")
                     {
                          return FirstName;
                     }
   ```

Answers to Review Questions

1. JavaBeans are intended to act as reusable components. You can encapsulate business logic and properties in them. You can access the functionality and properties from JSP. See "Introduction," in this chapter.

2. Using JavaBeans doesn't clutter JSP; it has the opposite effect of cleaning up the appearance of code within JSP. Since potentially many lines of scriptlet code are transferred into a JavaBean, using Beans removes clutter from JSP code. Using JavaBeans separates presentation and business logic (which also allows the designers and the programmers to be separated, at least in theory). See "Introduction," in this chapter.

3. JavaBeans make JSP code easier to read and maintain. Also, the JavaBean itself becomes a self-contained component so it also is easier to maintain. Lastly, JavaBeans are easy to reuse and share among developers. See "Introduction," in this chapter.

4. There are four things that make a class a JavaBean in JSP. They are a public class, a public constructor with no arguments, public set and get methods to simulate properties, and declaring a JavaBean within a JSP page. See "Creating JavaBeans," earlier in this chapter.

5. The original purpose for JavaBeans was for visual component reuse. Inspired by Visual Basic's amazing success, the designers of Java wrote a specification that defined reusable components which were easy for IDEs to manipulate and present to developers in a plug-and-play environment. See "Introduction," in this chapter.

Answers to Exam Questions

1. **E.** None of the interfaces mentioned in the answers is implemented when declaring a JavaBean. It isn't an interface that makes a class a JavaBean; it's the way it is used with a public class, public constructor without arguments, and the get/set paradigm. Notice that neither "none of the above" nor "all of the above" answers are allowed on the actual exam. I made an exception here and for question 2 to test your high-level understanding of JavaBeans. See "Creating JavaBeans," earlier in this chapter.

APPLY YOUR KNOWLEDGE

2. **E**. None of the objects mentioned in the answers is passed to a JavaBean when a property is changed from JSP. Rather, it is simply a method call transferred from the JSP page to the Bean with either the setProperty element or with a direct call within a scriptlet. See "Creating JavaBeans," earlier in this chapter.
3. **D**. There will only be one instance of a JavaBean with the same ID created by a servlet container, even when there are five useBean actions on the same JSP page. If you have more than one useBean action with the same ID, you will get a CompileException for the duplicate bean name. See "Creating JavaBeans," earlier in this chapter.
4. **A**. The response object cannot be used as the scope when using a JavaBean with JSP. See "Scope of JavaBeans in JSP," earlier in this chapter.
5. **B**. The JavaBean attributes are set when the container captures the form field name-value pairs, and then calls the setter methods in the bean for the attributes which have the same name as the form fields. See "Getting and Setting Properties," earlier in this chapter.
6. **D**. The request scope best fits the description given by the question. See "Scope of JavaBeans in JSP," earlier in this chapter.
7. **A**. This is true that it is impossible to share a page scoped variable with another JSP or Servlet. See "Scope of JavaBeans in JSP," earlier in this chapter.
8. **B**. When you write a get method for a JavaBean property, use *set* or *get* followed by the first letter of the property name capitalized. See "Getting and Setting Properties," earlier in this chapter.

APPLY YOUR KNOWLEDGE

Suggested Readings and Resources

1. JavaBeans homepage—http://java.sun.com/beans.
2. JavaBeans Component Architecture FAQ—http://java.sun.com/products/javabeans/FAQ.html.
3. JavaBeans specification—http://java.sun.com/products/javabeans/docs/spec.html.
4. JavaBeans API Definitions (javadoc generated)—http://java.sun.com/j2se/1.3/docs/api/java/beans/package-summary.html.
5. Guidelines for Bean development—http://java.sun.com/products/javabeans/docs/initial.html.
6. Sun's JavaBeans Tutorial—http://java.sun.com/docs/books/tutorial/javabeans/.
7. Java Software FAQ Index—http://java.sun.com/docs/faqindex.html.
8. Tomcat—an implementation of the Java Servlet 2.2 and JavaServer Pages 1.1 Specifications—http://jakarta.apache.org/tomcat/index.html.
9. Java Training by the MageLang Institute—http://www.magelang.com/.
10. Glossary of Java Technology-Related Terms—http://java.sun.com/docs/glossary.html.
11. jGuru FAQ on JSP—http://www.jguru.com/faq/subtopic.jsp?topicID=364.

OBJECTIVES

This chapter covers the following Sun-specified objectives for Section 11, Designing and Developing JSP Pages Using Custom Tags, and Section 12, Designing and Developing a Custom Tag Library, of the exam:

11. 2 Identify properly formatted TAGLIB directives in a JSP page.

- The `taglib` directives in a JSP page define the `taglib` prefix for your JSP page. The prefix is the namespace of tags; it's how you refer to the given tag library throughout the JSP page. The `taglib` directive creates a reference to the prefix. The prefix tells the container which library you want. Once that is done, you can use a custom tag, so called because it is your tag, not a standard one that came shipped with the container. See "Taglib Directive."

11.3 Given a custom tag library, identify properly formatted custom tag use in a JSP page. Uses include:

- **An empty custom tag**
- **A custom tag with attributes**
- **A custom tag that surrounds other JSP code**
- **Nested custom tags**

- A custom tag is simply a clean XML syntax that gives you easy access to the tag handler methods. There are several ways to use these tags in a JSP page. You can have an empty tag, use attributes, embed JSP code, and nest them. This makes custom tags versatile. They are an elegant way to add functionality to a JSP page without a lot of code.

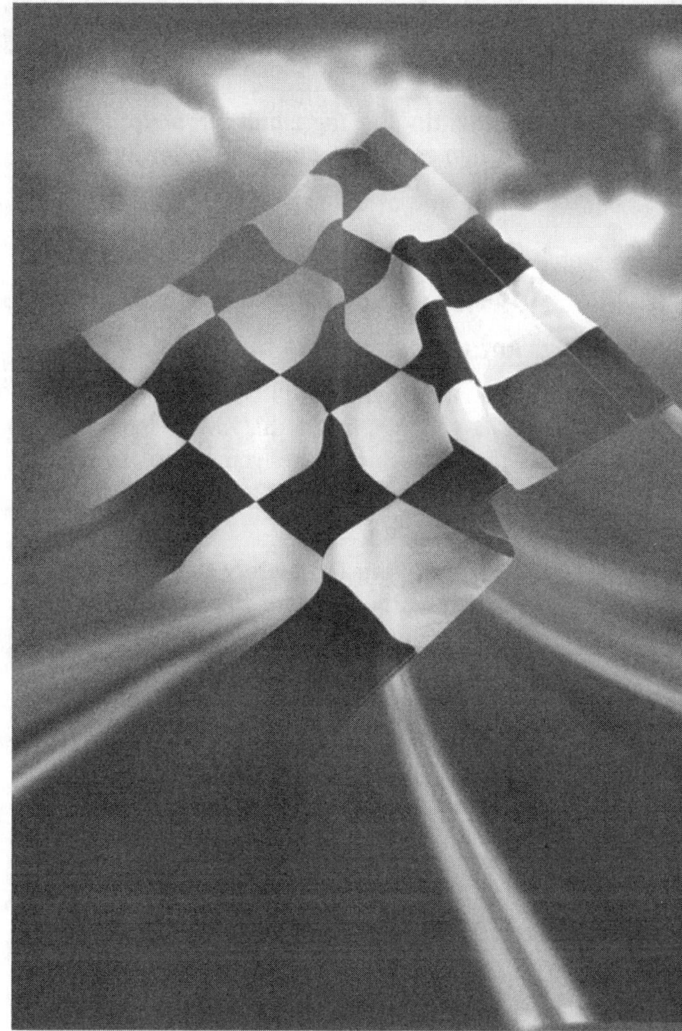

CHAPTER 9

Customize JSP with Tag Libraries

OBJECTIVES

12.1 Identify the Tag Library Descriptor element names that declare the following:

- **The name of the tag**
- **The class of the tag handler**
- **The type of content that the tag accepts**
- **Any attributes of the tag**

▶ Tag Library Descriptor (TLD) is how you define your custom tags. It is in this XML file that you tell the container which classes you will be using as tag handlers and how you plan to use them.

12.2 Identify the Tag Library Descriptor element names that declare the following:

- **The name of a tag attribute**
- **Whether a tag attribute is required**
- **Whether the attribute's value can be dynamically specified**

▶ The Tag Library Descriptor also takes attribute definitions for custom tags. This is where you tell the container which attributes the tag handler expects and whether it is required in the custom tags.

12.3 Given a custom tag, identify the necessary value for the `BODYCONTENT` TLD element for any of the following tag types:

- **Empty tag**
- **Custom tag that surrounds other JSP code**
- **Custom tag that surrounds content that is used only by the tag handler**

▶ Custom tags, like all XML tags, can have a body. There are certain elements in the Tag Library Descriptor that tell the container how you may use the custom tag in a JSP page. A custom tag may be empty, have JSP in it, or have content that is special to the tag handler.

12.4 Given a tag event method (`DOSTARTTAG()`, `DOAFTERBODY()`, and `DOENDTAG()`), identify the correct description of the method's trigger.

▶ The JSP specification allows container builders to employ an event model for processing custom tags. When a container encounters a custom tag, it triggers an event (`doStartTag()`). These events occur during processing of a request of a JSP page. You write a class that becomes the tag handler, a class that extends the `TagSupport` abstract class (`doStartTag()`, `doEndTag()`...). This section addresses what these event methods are and when they are invoked.

12.5 Identify valid return values for the following methods:

- **`DOSTARTTAG()`**
- **`DOAFTERBODY()`**
- **`DOENDTAG()`**
- **`PAGECONTEXT.GETOUT()`**

▶ Each of the event methods has return values. These return values affect how the container proceeds. For example, the `SKIP_BODY` value tells the container to ignore the body of the tag, if any exists. You can tell the container to stop processing the actual JSP page, too, and more.

Objectives

12.6 Given a "BODY" or "PAGE" constant, identify a correct description of the constant's use in the following methods:

- **DOSTARTTAG()**
- **DOAFTERBODY()**
- **DOENDTAG()**

▶ These constants tell the container what to do with either the body of the custom tag or the entire JSP page. For example, you may want to repeat the tag processing in an iteration situation. You can also stop the repetition with another constant.

12.7 Identify the method in the custom tag handler that accesses:

- **A given JSP page's implicit variable**
- **The JSP page's attributes**

▶ Remember the implicit variables in JSP? They are available to your custom tag handler. This section covers the syntax and the methods that you use to manipulate implicit variables such as the `Request`, `Response`, and `Session` objects.

12.8 Identify methods that return an outer tag handler from within an inner tag handler.

▶ The JSP specification allows you to nest tags. That is a very powerful architecture. However, because of the ability to nest there will be times when you need to access one of the outer tags from the inner one. This section covers this capability.

Outline

Study Strategies

- Tag libraries are very powerful. There is a lot to them. Be sure to build a tag library as described in this chapter because the exam will expect you to understand how they work and how the various pieces relate to one another.
- Make sure you know the basic syntax of the tag library directive and the Tag Library Descriptor.
- Take some time to play with a few free tag libraries. Doing so will provide you with a shortcut to understanding how JSP implements tag libraries, without requiring you to write tag libraries from scratch.

INTRODUCTION

You'll recall how JavaBeans provided a way to encapsulate functionality in classes accessible via tags in JSP pages using XML notation. Although the reference to such a JavaBean allows you to access attributes and methods via scriptlets, the XML notation itself is limited to getting and setting properties in the JavaBean. Once you have the reference, as mentioned, you can treat the JavaBean like any object in scriptlets by calling its methods and getting/setting its properties. However, in many cases, you may prefer to use an XML-based syntax for invoking these methods rather than having to invoke them via a scriptlet. Sun's answer is called a *tag library*.

A tag library is similar to JavaBeans in that you can reference a class from JSP using XML notation. However, unlike JavaBeans, tag libraries have a specific lifecycle protocol. So, whenever you use a tag library tag, the container calls the lifecycle event methods in your tag handler (`doStart`, `doStartTag`, `doAfterBody`). Typically, you use these methods to return a string, which the container places inline where the tag is located in the JSP page.

A tag library maps XML tags to underlying class methods in a Tag Library Descriptor (.tld) file. This file defines the custom tags that you can use in JSP to access the associated Java class. Your container (that is, Tomcat) uses the TLD to convert the XML in your JSP page into Java code. TLD files are written in XML notation. For example, Listing 9.1 is an example of how you can define a tag.

LISTING 9.1

THE SOURCE CODE FOR DEFINING A TAG IN A TAG LIBRARY DESCRIPTOR

```
<tag>
     <name>whatColorIsIt</name>
     <tagclass>examples.ColorTagHandler</tagclass>
     <info>Simply echos back some text</info>
     <attribute>
         <name>color</name>
         <required>true</required>
         <rtexprvalue>false</rtexprvalue>
     </attribute>
</tag>
```

The following section explains how the container uses a Tag Library Descriptor file to expand the functionality of a JSP page utilizing custom tags.

Creating a Tag Library Example

> **WARNING**
>
> **Be careful about refreshing files!** There is a little weirdness in some containers when it comes to refreshing files. If you update the tag handler (by changing code and then recompiling), Tomcat will see the new class and its changes after a few seconds. If you change the web.xml file, Tomcat will ignore the changes. You have to recycle Tomcat because this file is part of its initialization. Also, if you change your Tag Library Descriptor (*.tld), your changes will not take effect at first. Notice that the container converts your custom tags into Java calls during the JSP page translation, so any change to the tag library itself won't take effect until the next translation of the JSP pages that refer to that library. When the container translates and recompiles a JSP page, the changes to the tag library will finally take effect. So, the custom tag is converted to Java during the translation step. Therefore, if you want to change the tag library, you must force Tomcat to recompile the JSP page that refers to it.

In Chapter 8, you learned about JavaBeans and how to use them in JSP pages. The idea behind this is to allow the developer to replace Java code in the JSP page with XML notation. This is cleaner and reduces errors. JavaBeans allow you to separate your applications into presentation code (contained in the JSP) and business logic (contained in the beans). JavaBeans is a good start, but doesn't go far enough. We want to access more functionality through custom tags, beyond getting and setting attributes that we were limited to with JavaBeans. Because this need made its way into Sun's Java wish list, we now have custom tags, which are tags of your design backed up with tag libraries.

Before discussing the details, let's review a simple example. This example will provide you with a nice overview of how tag libraries work. Our example here involves four files. The tag handler is an object invoked by a Web container. It processes the calls based on the custom tag in the JSP page. This is where the bulk of the work happens. It is a class that extends the `TagSupport` abstract class (`doStartTag()`, `doEndTag()`...). The tag handler can retrieve all the other implicit objects (request, session, and application) accessible from a JSP page through the page context object (`javax.servlet.jsp.PageContext`). The next file is the Tag Library Descriptor (TLD). A TLD is an XML document that describes a library as a whole and each tag contained in the library. TLDs are used by a Web container to validate the tags. JSP page development tools also peek at this. The web.xml file tells the container where the tag library is located. When the JSP page references the tag library with a URI, the container maps that URI (which could be anything and doesn't have to be real) to a file path. Lastly, the JSP page itself uses special XML tags to reference the supporting class called a tag handler so you can access attributes and methods using a clean XML convention.

Table 9.1 describes the four files involved in this simple example.

TABLE 9.1

FILES COMPRISING THE TAG LIBRARY EXAMPLE

File	*Description*
`YourTagHandler.java`	The *tag handler* class that does the work, similar to a JavaBean.
`YourTagLibraryDefinition.tld`	The actual tag library that defines the tag names and associates them with classes.
`web.xml`	The container's configuration file that tells the container where the tag libraries are located and what each one's URI is.
`yourJSP.jsp`	The JSP page that uses XML (custom tags) to access classes defined in the tag library.

Defining a Tag Library in web.xml

This tag library example includes code snippets from the four files. Let's start with the web.xml file, which is the container's configuration file.

The web.xml file is used as the deployment descriptor (see Chapter 10, "Deploying Web Applications and Components"). The deployment descriptor defines the elements and configuration information of a Web application. In it, you define elements to support the Web application within a servlet container, including `ServletContext init` parameters, session configuration, and servlet declarations. The specification defines an optional `taglib` element that has become standard for the latest containers. The `taglib` element is used to describe a JSP tag library. The syntax for the `taglib` element in the web.xml file is `<!ELEMENT taglib (taglib-uri, taglib-location)>`. The required `taglib`-location element contains the location (as a resource relative to the root of the Web application) of the Tag Library Descriptor file for the tag library. The `taglib-uri` element describes a URI, relative to the location of the web.xml document, that identifies a tag library used in the Web application. You use the URI to give a tag library a unique address or namespace.

The `taglib` element is simply a mapping of a URI to a tag library file. The `taglib`-location element is a file path relative to the Web application directory root. It goes in the web.xml file so that upon startup, the container is aware of the URI and the library it points to. When you use an XML tag that has this URI in it, the container will know that you are really pointing to a specific file. In the web.xml file (`TOMCAT_HOME\webapps\examples\WEB-INF`), you tell the container where to find your tag library, as shown in Listing 9.2.

LISTING 9.2

THE SOURCE CODE FOR A WEB DEPLOYMENT DESCRIPTOR

```
  <web-app>
  <!-- XML removed for space -->
      <taglib>
          <taglib-uri>
                 http://www.yourcompany.com/yourTagLibrary
          </taglib-uri>
          <taglib-location>
             /WEB-INF/yourTagLibrary.tld
          </taglib-location>
      </taglib>
  <!-- XML removed for space -->
</web-app>
```

The container maps the URI to the tag library file upon startup. The following JSP page (`TOMCAT_HOME\webapps\examples\jsp\yourTagLibrary.jsp`) tells the container to use the library to store the color red and then print it again. The `taglib` directive here takes two parameters. First is the URI, which matches the same URI in the web.xml initialization file. The second is the prefix, which is the name you use within the JSP page. A JSP page that uses a tag library can be as simple as this:

```
<html>
<head>
<%@ taglib uri=http://www.yourcompany.com/yourTagLibrary
        prefix="yourLibrary" %>
</head>

<body>
<yourLibrary:whatColorIsIt color="red"/>.
<br />
Your first tag library is functioning.
You are closer to passing the exam.
```

```
</body>
</html>
```

The `taglib` directive creates a reference to the prefix, `yourLibrary` in this case. The prefix tells the container which library you want. Once that is done, you can use a custom tag, so called because it is your tag, not a standard one that came shipped with the container. Within that library can be many tags. You must specify which tag handler to use, in this case `whatColorIsIt`. This class has an attribute called color. We are setting it to red in the previous custom tag. The main point here is not the functionality itself; you must use the tag name to which the tag handler class is mapped. Using custom tags cleans up the JSP code considerably. In the extreme case, we can write the entire JSP page in XML, making it easier to use tools that could check the validity of the page and build the page. Even if you only replace a few scriptlet-JavaBeans portions with custom tags, you are ahead.

When this JSP page is called, the container will then find the library and insert the appropriate Java into the servlet as part of the translation step.

The library (`TOMCAT_HOME\webapps\examples\WEB-INF\yourTagLibrary.tld`) for this example looks like Listing 9.3.

LISTING 9.3

THE SOURCE CODE FOR A TAG LIBRARY DESCRIPTOR

```
<?xml version="1.0" encoding="ISO-8859-1" ?>
<!DOCTYPE taglib PUBLIC
"-//Sun Microsystems, Inc.//DTD JSP Tag Library 1.2//EN"
http://java.sun.com/j2ee/dtd/web-jsptaglibrary_1_2.dtd">

<taglib>
    <tlibversion>1.0</tlibversion>
    <jspversion>1.1</jspversion>
    <shortname>yourLibrary</shortname>
    <uri>http://www.yourcompany.com/yourTagLibrary</uri>
    <info>Your first tag library</info>

    <tag>
        <name>whatColorIsIt</name>
        <tagclass>examples.ColorTagHandler</tagclass>
        <info>Simply echos back some text</info>
        <attribute>
            <name>color</name>
```

continues

LISTING 9.3 *continued*

THE SOURCE CODE FOR A TAG LIBRARY DESCRIPTOR

```
                <required>true</required>
                <rtexprvalue>false</rtexprvalue>
            </attribute>
        </tag>
</taglib>
```

The "tag library" is not merged into the servlet-file for the JSP page; rather, custom tags in the JSP file are translated into Java code that executes the lifecycle method for the tags used in the JSP page. Although each vendor will do this somewhat differently, let's look at how Tomcat does it, because its approach is typical. The following is a slightly edited snippet from `yourTagLibrary$jsp`, which Tomcat generated in the `TOMCAT_HOME\work\localhost\examples\jsp` folder:

```
jspxFactory = JspFactory.getDefaultFactory();
response.setContentType("text/html;charset=ISO-8859-1");
pageContext = _jspxFactory.getPageContext(this, request,
response, "", true, 8192, true);

application = pageContext.getServletContext();
config = pageContext.getServletConfig();
session = pageContext.getSession();
out = pageContext.getOut();

out.write("<html>\r\n<head>\r\n");
out.write("\r\n</head>\r\n\r\n<body>\r\n");

/* ----  yourLibrary:whatColorIsIt ---- */
examples.ColorTagHandler
        _jspx_th_yourLibrary_whatColorIsIt_0 =
        new examples.ColorTagHandler();
//code removed for clarity
     try {
      int _jspx_eval_yourLibrary_whatColorIsIt_0 =
      _jspx_th_yourLibrary_whatColorIsIt_0.doStartTag();

      if (_jspx_eval_yourLibrary_whatColorIsIt_0 ==
           javax.servlet.jsp.tagext
           .BodyTag.EVAL_BODY_BUFFERED)
   throw new JspTagException("Since tag handler class"+
   " examples.ColorTagHandler does not implement "+
   "BodyTag, it can't return BodyTag.EVAL_BODY_TAG");
      if (_jspx_eval_yourLibrary_whatColorIsIt_0 !=
           javax.servlet.jsp.tagext.Tag.SKIP_BODY) {
   do {
   } while (_jspx_th_yourLibrary_whatColorIsIt_0
             .doAfterBody() == javax.servlet.jsp.tagext
```

```
                              .BodyTag.EVAL_BODY_AGAIN);
      }
      if (_jspx_th_yourLibrary_whatColorIsIt_0.doEndTag()
          == javax.servlet.jsp.tagext.Tag.SKIP_PAGE)
    return;
     } finally {
      _jspx_th_yourLibrary_whatColorIsIt_0.release();
     }
     out.write(".\r\n<br />\r\nYour first tag library "+
     "is functioning. You are closer to passing the "+
     "exam.\r\n</body>\r\n</html>\r\n\r\n\r\n");
```

As you can see, the container sets the color attribute specified in the JSP page custom tag with `_jspx_th_yourLibrary_whatColorIsIt_0.setColor("red")`. Then it invokes the `doStartTag()` method automatically. The `setColor()` and `doStartTag()` methods are in the tag handler.

The tag handler is a class that implements an interface, which makes it a tag handler. Usually a tag handler class extends `TagSupport` (which implements `IteratorTag` interface). The tag handler overrides the tag processing event methods of the `TagSupport` class to process the tag. Like you saw in JavaBeans (see Chapter 8, "Extend JSP with JavaBeans"), the container converts attribute tags in XML to get/set calls. The tag handler (`TOMCAT_HOME\webapps\examples\WEB-INF\classes\examples\ColorTagHandler.java`) used in this example looks like Listing 9.4.

LISTING 9.4

THE SOURCE CODE FOR A TAG HANDLER

```
//must be in a package or Tomcat won't find it
package examples;

import java.io.*;
import javax.servlet.jsp.*;
import javax.servlet.jsp.tagext.*;

/**
* Given a color, simply send back the value.
*
* @author      QUE reader
*/
public class ColorTagHandler
   extends javax.servlet.jsp.tagext.TagSupport
{   //       makes this a tag handler^^^^^^^^^^
```

continues

LISTING 9.4 *continued*

THE SOURCE CODE FOR A TAG HANDLER

```
        /** color attribute */
        private String color;
        //              ^^^^^ attribute available to JSP
        //                    through get/set methods

        /**
         * Processes this tag.
         */
        public int doStartTag() throws JspException
        {//        ^^^^^^^^^^ is called automatically as
         //                   part of tag library feature

            // build up some HTML
            String html = "The current color is: ";

            // add to output stream
            try {
                pageContext.getOut().write( html + color);
            } catch (IOException ioe) {
                throw new JspException(ioe.getMessage());
            }

            return EVAL_BODY_INCLUDE;
        }

        /**
         * JavaBeans-style property setter for color.
         *
         * @param s        a String representing the color
         */
        public void setColor(String s)
        //            ^^^^^^^^ is called like a JavaBean
        //                     setter method
        {
            this.color = s;
        }
}
```

All together, this trivial example produces the following HTML when you browse to `http://localhost:8080/examples/jsp/yourTagLibrary.jsp`:

```
<html>
<head>

</head>
```

```
<body>
The current color is: red.
<br />
Your first tag library is functioning.
You are closer to passing the exam.
</body>
</html>
```

As the warning mentions, be careful about refreshing files. The following list will help you know when changes to the given file will take effect. From slowest to take effect to quickest, they are: web.xml, YourTagLibraryDefinition.tld, YourTagHanlder.java, and yourJSP.jsp. Remember, the container converts your custom tags into Java calls during the JSP page translation. That is why changes to the tag library itself won't take effect until the next translation of the JSP pages that refer to that library.

With JSP 1.2, you no longer have to pack your pages with scriptlets. Web authors also don't have to know Java to create sophisticated Web applications. Making functionality available to Web authors is no problem, as Step by Step 9.1 proves.

STEP BY STEP

9.1 Creating a New Tag Library

1. Write and compile a simple tag handler similar to the `ColorTagHandler` example that services the custom tag in your JSP (JSP custom tag attribute invokes a setter method in tag handler). Place the tag handler Java class files for your tags in the WEB-INF/classes directory of your Web application.
2. Write the tag library descriptor (TLD), which defines the tag library including the name of the tag handler class and attributes. Place it in its directory, which you declare in the deployment descriptor (`CATALINA_HOME/webapps/examples/WEB-INF/veltag.tld`). An example is given earlier in this chapter.

continues

continued

3. Declare the Tag Library Descriptor in the Web application deployment descriptor (`CATALINA_HOME/webapps/examples/WEB-INF/web.xml`):

```
<taglib>
    <taglib-uri>
  http://jakarta.apache.org/tomcat/debug-taglib
    </taglib-uri>
    <taglib-location>
       /WEB-INF/jsp/debug-taglib.tld
    </taglib-location>
</taglib>
```

4. Declare the tag library in your JSP source using the JSP `<taglib>` directive.
5. Use the custom tag in your JSP page.
6. Restart your container and test your tag library.

The previous steps showed you how to create a new tag library and use it in a Web page. As you may remember, JavaBeans came close to serving the same purpose, but didn't go far enough. For functionality beyond getting and setting properties, you had to use scriptlets. Now, tag libraries allow you to use any custom tag in place of scriptlets as noted in the previous steps.

The following goals represent the hope Sun has for tag libraries:

- **Portable.** The functionality of a tag library must be usable in any JSP container.
- **Simple.** People who have less geek in them should be able to understand and use them.
- **Expressive.** This technology will support nested actions, scripting elements inside action bodies, and creation, use, and updating of scripting variables.
- **Flexible.** Although the JSP specification currently only allows Java scripts, the architecture is designed to add other scripting languages.
- **Reusable.** Once you write a tag handler, like a JavaBean, you can use it easily in many projects.

All these goals reflect the same hope for Java in general. I feel tag libraries are the gem of the current JSP specification, above even JavaBeans. The more tag libraries you include in your project, the better the design.

As you can see, creating a tag library is not as daunting as you might have expected. Now that you have a solid overview of this portion of Web component development, let's look at the details that the exam will expect you to know.

Taglib DIRECTIVE

11. 2 Identify properly formatted `TAGLIB` directives in a JSP page.

In Chapter 7 where we covered JSP, you'll remember how I said directives are a communication link between the JSP page and the JSP container. That is, they don't contribute anything into the current output stream. There are three directives: include, page, and `taglib`. The `taglib` directive has the following syntax:

```
<%@ taglib uri="tagLibraryURI" prefix="tagPrefix" %>
```

Tag libraries make it easy to embed functionality into JSP documents. Instead of writing messy scriptlets, you can use custom XML tags that make your intentions more explicit. You are better able to separate presentation from business logic with custom tags.

You add the methods defined in the Tag interface such as `setPageContext()`, `doStartTag()`, and `doEndTag()`. Once you have written your tag handler, you can take advantage of the new functionality in your JSP page. Start by including the `taglib` directive at the top of the page like so:

```
<%@ taglib uri="/WEB-INF/jsp/myTaglib.tld"
                             prefix="myTag" %>
...
<body>
The custom tag returns: <myTag:myMethod/>
...
```

The `taglib` directive only has two attributes. They are the `uri` and the `prefix`. Remember that the `uri` names the tag library with the same namespace as you used in the web.xml deployment descriptor. The `prefix` is any legal identifier. Notice how you can use many `taglib` directives in a single page, but the `prefix` defined in each must be unique.

CUSTOM TAG

11.3 Given a custom tag library, identify properly formatted custom tag use in a JSP page. Uses include:

- **An empty custom tag**
- **A custom tag with attributes**
- **A custom tag that surrounds other JSP code**
- **Nested custom tags**

The custom tag is a convention that allows you to have the container call the tag library life cycle event methods (for example, `doStartTag`), including the attribute get/set calls automatically invoked when attributes are declared in the custom tag. `doStartTag` and `doEndTag` methods are called when the JSP page request is processed. The following is an example of an empty custom tag (no body):

```
<tagHandlerPrefix:customTagName />
```

Table 9.2 lists the four ways to use a custom tag.

TABLE 9.2

WAYS TO USE CUSTOM TAGS

Tag	*Description*
`<libraryPrefix:handlerName />`	The custom tag with no body, said to be an empty custom tag.
`<libraryPrefix:handlerName parameterName="value">`	This tag causes the container to call the `setParameterName` method and pass the "value" to it.

`<libraryPrefix:handlerName parameterName="value">`
`<%= 23 * counter %>`
`<b>Congratulations!</b>`
`</libraryPrefix:handlerName>`
	A custom tag with a body. The body can contain core tags, scripting elements, HTML text, and tag-dependent body content between the start and end tags.

`<library:outerTag>`
`<library:innerTag>`
`</library:innerTag></library:outerTag>`
	This syntax is how you nest custom tags. The XML is easy, but the handler is more involved. Note that the following is wrong: `<X><Y></X></Y>`.

TAG LIBRARY DESCRIPTOR

12.1 Identify the Tag Library Descriptor element names that declare the following:

- **The name of the tag**
- **The class of the tag handler**
- **The type of content that the tag accepts**
- **Any attributes of the tag**

12.2 Identify the Tag Library Descriptor element names that declare the following:

- **The name of a tag attribute**
- **Whether a tag attribute is required**
- **Whether the attribute's value can be dynamically specified**

This section of the exam covers the Tag Library Descriptor. The Descriptor is the file that defines a custom tag in JSP. In the Descriptor, you use a separate element to define each new tag in the tag library. More simply stated, it's how you define a tag. Table 9.3 lists the elements named in the previous objectives.

TABLE 9.3

WAYS TO USE CUSTOM TAGS

Element	*Description*
`<name>`*`tagName`*`</name>`	This required element is the name of the tag and is referred to after the colon in a JSP file (`<libraryName:`*`tagName`*`>`).
`<tagclass>`*`packageName.className`*`</tagclass>`	This required element points to the tag handler class using the fully qualified package name of the class, as if you were using it in a class without the import statement. The package name is the directory structure under the WEB-INF/classes directory.
`<bodycontent>tagdependent | JSP | empty</bodycontent>`	The `tagdependent` option means the tag will regard the contents of the body as non-JSP. The body is passed verbatim to the tag handler itself. The body of the action may be empty. The JSP option means the body will be interpreted before being made available to the tag handler. The body is considered JSP if the `<bodycontent>` element is missing. The empty option means the tag can have no body.

While Table 9.3 lists the basic elements you should use to define a custom tag, Table 9.4 continues with the definition of the attribute portion of a custom tag.

TABLE 9.4

ATTRIBUTE ELEMENT OF A CUSTOM TAG

Element	*Description*
`<name>attributeName</name>`	This required element is the name of the attribute in a tag.
`<required>true | false</required>`	This optional element within the attribute element tells the container whether you must specify a value for this attribute when you use the custom tag in JSP.
`<rtexprvalue>true | false</rtexprvalue>`	This element tells the container whether the attribute can take a scriptlet expression as a value (dynamically assigned).

An example of the tag element with attributes is this:

```
<tag>
  <name>myTag</name>
  <tagclass>examples.MyTag</tagclass>
  <bodycontent>tagdependent</bodycontent>
  <attribute>
      <name>firstName</name>
      <required>true</required>
      <rtexprvalue>false</rtexprvalue>
  </attribute>
  <attribute>
      <name>lastName</name>
      <required>true</required>
      <rtexprvalue>false</rtexprvalue>
  </attribute>
  <attribute>
      <name>middleName</name>
      <required>false</required>
      <rtexprvalue>false</rtexprvalue>
  </attribute>
</tag>
```

CUSTOM TAG BODY

12.3 Given a custom tag, identify the necessary value of the BODYCONTENT TLD element for any of the following tag types:

- **Empty tag**
- **Custom tag that surrounds other JSP code**
- **Custom tag that surrounds content that is used only by the tag handler**

This objective tells us that Sun includes questions on the exam regarding custom tags. You then have to determine what the Tag Library Descriptor looks like.

As shown in Table 9.3, there are three ways to use the body of a custom tag. Table 9.5 matches exam examples with the appropriate Descriptor bodycontent element.

TABLE 9.5

BODYCONTENT ELEMENT OF A CUSTOM TAG

Element	*Associated bodycontent Tag*
<tagLibrary:myTag firstName="Patricia" lastName="Trottier" ... />	<bodycontent>empty</bodycontent>
<tagLibrary:myTag> <%= 23 * counter %> </tagLibrary:myTag>	<bodycontent>JSP</bodycontent>
<tagLibrary:myTag> SELECT * FROM CUSTOMER </tagLibrary:myTag>	<bodycontent>tagdependent </bodycontent>

The `empty` (tag has no body) and `JSP` options (default and interpreted if present) are straightforward. The `tagdependent` option is the strange one. This means the text is sent to the tag handler, but the text is not sent to the output stream, unless the tag prints it to the stream.

TAG EVENT METHOD

12.4 Given a tag event method (DOSTARTTAG(), DOAFTERBODY(), and DOENDTAG()), identify the correct description of the method's trigger.

12.5 Identify valid return values for the following methods:

- **DOSTARTTAG()**
- **DOAFTERBODY()**
- **DOENDTAG()**
- **PAGECONTEXT.GETOUT()**

12.6 Given a "BODY" or "PAGE" constant, identify a correct description of the constant's use in the following methods:

- **DOSTARTTAG()**
- **DOAFTERBODY()**
- **DOENDTAG()**

These objectives are closely related. That is why I cover them together here. Basically, this part of the exam covers the event methods that the container triggers when processing your custom tags along with these method return constants. There are only four methods that you have to study and a few constants.

Table 9.6 lists the return values possible for the custom tag event methods. They are described in more detail immediately after the discussion about these fields. These return constants tell the container what to do after processing the triggered method.

TABLE 9.6

EVENT METHODS OF A CUSTOM TAG

Element	*Associated bodycontent Tag*
EVAL_BODY_INCLUDE	Evaluate body into existing output stream (doStartTag()).
EVAL_BODY_AGAIN	Evaluate body again. Used for iterations (doAfterBody()).
EVAL_PAGE	Continue evaluating the page (doEndTag()).

Element	*Associated bodycontent Tag*
SKIP_BODY	Skip body evaluation. Stop processing the JSP after the current custom tag (doStartTag(), doAfterBody()).
SKIP_PAGE	Stop processing the JSP after the current custom tag (doEndTag()).

Table 9.7 lists the methods that are triggered when the container processes custom tags.

TABLE 9.7

EVENT METHODS OF A CUSTOM TAG

Element	*Associated bodycontent Tag*
doStartTag()	This method is called when the container first starts to process the tag. Notice that when this method is invoked, the body has not yet been evaluated. It can return either the EVAL_BODY_INCLUDE or SKIP_BODY field.
doEndTag()	This method is called after the container completes the doStartTag() method. Notice that the body of your custom tag may not have been evaluated, depending on the return value of doStartTag(). It can return either the EVAL_PAGE or SKIP_PAGE field.
doAfterBody()	This method is used for iterations (IterationTag). It is called after every body evaluation to control whether the body will be reevaluated or not. If this method returns EVAL_BODY_AGAIN, the body will be reevaluated. If it returns SKIP_BODY, the body will be skipped and doEndTag() will be invoked next.
PageConext.getOut()	This is how you add the output stream directly. This method returns javax.servlet.jsp.JspWriter.

Listing 9.5 illustrates a very simple example, as an abstract class, of an example tag handler that shipped with Tomcat.

LISTING 9.5

THE SOURCE CODE FOR AN ABSTRACT TAG HANDLER

```
package examples;

import javax.servlet.jsp.*;
import javax.servlet.jsp.tagext.*;

public abstract class ExampleTagBase
              extends BodyTagSupport
{
    public void setParent(Tag parent)
    {
        this.parent = parent;
    }

    public void setBodyContent(BodyContent bodyOut)
    {
        this.bodyOut = bodyOut;
    }

    public void setPageContext(PageContext pageContext)
    {
        this.pageContext = pageContext;
    }

    public Tag getParent()
    {
        return this.parent;
    }

    public int doStartTag() throws JspException
    {
        return SKIP_BODY;
    }

    public int doEndTag() throws JspException
    {
        return EVAL_PAGE;
    }


    // Default implementations for BodyTag methods,
    // just in case a tag decides to implement BodyTag.
    public void doInitBody() throws JspException
    {
    }

    public int doAfterBody() throws JspException
    {
        return SKIP_BODY;
    }

    public void release()
    {
```

```
        bodyOut = null;
        pageContext = null;
        parent = null;
    }

    protected BodyContent bodyOut;
    protected PageContext pageContext;
    protected Tag parent;
}
```

CUSTOM TAG HANDLER

12.7 Identify the method in the custom tag handler that accesses:

- **A given JSP page's implicit variable**
- **The JSP page's attributes**

The key to answering questions about a JSP page's implicit variables and attributes is to use the `PageContext` object. An instance of this object provides access to all the namespaces and most attributes for a JSP page. You can grab the implicit objects with the following methods:

- **`getOut()`.** This method returns the current JspWriter stream being used for the client response.
- **`getException()`.** This method returns any exception passed to this as an error page.
- **`getPage()`.** This method returns the page implementation class instance (Servlet) associated with this JSP page request. Notice that the PageContext object encapsulates that state of a request upon a JSP page.
- **`getRequest()`.** This method returns the ServletRequest for this JSP page request.
- **`getResponse()`.** This method returns the ServletResponse for this JSP page request.
- **`getSession()`.** This method returns the HttpSession for this JSP page request or null.

- **`getServletConfig()`.** This method returns the ServletConfig for this JSP page request.
- **`getServletContext()`.** This method returns the ServletContext for this JSP page request.

There is nothing special about using these methods in a tag handler. The point is that you are very likely to use one or more of them when writing a tag handler.

Similar to the previous list of methods, the following methods are used to access the attributes in your tag handler for a given JSP page:

- **`setAttribute()`.** This method registers the name and object specified with appropriate scope semantics.
- **`getAttribute()`.** This method returns the object associated with the name in the page scope or null if not found.
- **`findAttribute()`.** This method searches for the named attribute in the page, request, session (if valid), and application scope(s) respectively and returns the associated value or null.
- **`removeAttribute()`.** This method removes the object reference associated with the given name by looking in all scopes in the scope order.

The following methods provide support for forwarding, inclusion, and error:

- **`forward()`.** This method is used to redirect, or "forward" the current ServletRequest and ServletResponse to another active component in the application. The URL is assumed to be a relative URL; however, if the path begins with a `/`,the URL specified is calculated relative to the DOCROOT of the ServletContext for this JSP. Be careful, as once this method has been called successfully, it is illegal for the calling thread to attempt to modify the ServletResponse object. You cannot generate further output to the browser once the `forward()` method has been called.
- **`include()`.** This method causes the specified resource to be processed as part of the current ServletRequest and ServletResponse being processed by the calling thread.

The output of the target resource's processing of the request is written directly to the ServletResponse output stream. Notice that the current JspWriter (out) for this JSP is flushed as a side effect of this call, prior to processing the `include`.

USING OUTER-INNER CUSTOM TAGS

12.8 Identify methods that return an outer tag handler from within an inner tag handler.

The following methods are most helpful when trying to reach another tag from an inner tag:

- **`getParent()`.** This method finds the parent (closest enclosing tag handler) for this tag handler. You might do this to navigate the nested tag handler structure at runtime.
- **`findAncestorWithClass()`.**This method finds the instance of a given class type. This method uses the `getParent()` method from the tag interface.

CHAPTER SUMMARY

Tag libraries and JavaBeans are closely related. JavaBeans provide a way to encapsulate functionality in classes accessible via tags in JSP pages, as well as by using XML notation. Tag libraries also provide this capability. JavaBeans provide easy access only to get/set methods, but tag libraries have more robust functionality to allow you to respond to events that are triggered by the start, body, and end of a custom tag.

Tag libraries are really an extension of JavaBeans in JSP. Although they get and set like JavaBeans, they do much more if you want them to. You can access this extra functionality with XML tags in JSP. You define these XML tags. That is why they are called custom tags.

There are many commercial and free tag libraries available on the market. I recommend you peruse a few to see how they are being used. Although tag libraries are a deep enough topic to deserve a whole book alone, the exam is restricted to the main aspects of this technology, which this chapter is careful to observe.

KEY TERMS

- Custom tags
- Tag libraries
- Tag Library Descriptor
- Web Deployment Descriptor
- Nested tags
- Tag attributes and bodies
- Taglib directive
- `doStartTag()`
- `doEndTag()`

APPLY YOUR KNOWLEDGE

Review Questions

1. How are tag libraries and JavaBeans related?
2. How is XML used in tag libraries?
3. What is the main point of using tag libraries?
4. What should a developer be concerned about when refreshing files associated with tag libraries?

Exam Questions

1. Which three of the following is part of the Tag Library Descriptor element?

   A. namespace

   B. name

   C. tag handler class

   D. tag attributes

2. Which two of the following attributes are not part of the `taglib` directive?

   A. `url`

   B. `uri`

   C. `prefix`

   D. `name`

3. Which file does the following DTD element definition apply to: `<!ELEMENT taglib (taglib-uri, taglib-location)>`?

   A. web.init

   B. YourTagHandler.java

   C. YourTagLibraryDefinition.tld

   D. web.xml

4. Which of the following is the Web Deployment Descriptor, the purpose of which is to configure a Web application?

   A. web.xml

   B. web.init

   C. YourTagLibraryDefinition.tld

   D. YourTagHandler.java

5. Which three of the following files is part of a simple tag library?

   A. web.xml

   B. web.init

   C. YourTagLibraryDefinition.tld

   D. YourTagHandler.java

6. How do you declare a tag library within a JSP page?

   A. You use a declare scriptlet.

   B. You use a taglib directive.

   C. You use a unique variable.

   D. You use the path to the tag handler.

7. Which two of the following options apply to an empty custom tag?

   A. Specified in the web.xml Web component descriptor.

   B. Specified in the tag library handler.

   C. `<libraryPrefix:handlerName />`

   D. A custom tag with no body.

APPLY YOUR KNOWLEDGE

8. What does the container use to validate a custom tag in a JSP page?

   A. web.xml

   B. Xerces

   C. Xmlspy

   D. Tag Library Descriptor

9. Which interface does the `doStartTag()` belong to?

   A. `TagSupport`

   B. `TagProcess`

   C. `Tag`

   D. `TagStart`

10. What does the container do during translation when it encounters a custom tag in a JSP page?

    A. It converts the XML notation into Java calls, inserted into the Java that resulted from the page translation.

    B. It passes it to the tag handler.

    C. It converts it to scriptlets.

    D. It adds the code to the output stream.

11. Which one of the following is a correctly formatted `taglib` directive?

    A. `<%@ taglib url="tagLibraryURL" prefix="tagPrefix" %>`

    B. `<%! taglib url="tagLibraryURL" prefix="tagPrefix" %>`

    C. `<%@ taglib uri="tagLibraryURI" prefix="tagPrefix" %>`

    D. `<%! taglib uri="tagLibraryURI" prefix="tagPrefix" %>`

12. What is the purpose of a URI in a taglib directive?

    A. This is how the client finds the JSP page.

    B. This is the unique namespace of a tag.

    C. This is the unique namespace of a tag library.

    D. This is the relative path to a tag handler.

13. Regarding a custom tag, how is the `tagdependent` element used?

    A. It is part of the `bodycontent` element.

    B. It tells the container to validate the custom tag.

    C. It is part of the `name` element.

    D. It is in the web.xml file.

Answers to Review Questions

1. You'll recall how JavaBeans provided a way to encapsulate functionality in classes accessible via tags into JSP pages using XML notation. Although the reference to such a JavaBean allows you to access attributes and methods via scriptlets, the XML notation is limited to getting and setting properties in the JavaBean. Tag libraries are similar to JavaBeans in that you can reference a class from JSP using XML notation. However, unlike JavaBeans, which allow you to only get/set with XML, tag libraries allow you to call any method in the class via XML. You basically define XML tags and map those to methods and attributes in the class: JavaBeans on steroids. The primary difference is that tag handlers implement a special set of lifecycle methods. See "Introduction."

APPLY YOUR KNOWLEDGE

2. A tag library maps XML tags to underlying class methods in a Tag Library Descriptor (TLD) file. This file defines the XML tags that you can use in JSP to access the associated Java class. Your container (i.e., Tomcat) uses the TLD to convert the XML in your JSP page into Java code as you've seen. The tags you add to JSP page, the TLD files themselves, and the Web Deployment Descriptor are all written in XML notation. See "Introduction."

3. In Chapter 8, you learned about JavaBeans and how to use them in JSP pages. The idea behind this is to allow the developer to replace Java code in the JSP page with XML notation. This is cleaner and reduces errors. JavaBeans is a good start, but doesn't go far enough. We want to access more functionality with XML tags, beyond getting and setting attributes. Tag libraries allow you to design custom tags, which are tags of your design backed up with tag libraries. This gives us a powerful implementation of a wide range of functionality, using clean XML notation within JSP. See "Creating a Tag Library Example."

4. If you update the tag handler (change code and then recompile), the container will see the new class and its changes after a few seconds. However, if you change the web.xml file, Tomcat will ignore the changes. You have to stop and restart Tomcat because this file is part of its initialization. Also, if you change your Tag Library Descriptor (*.tld), your changes will not take effect at first. Notice that the container converts your custom tags into java calls during the JSP page translation, so any change to the tag library itself won't take effect until the next translation of the JSP pages that refer to that library. See "Creating a Tag Library Example."

Answers to Exam Questions

1. **B, C,** and **D.** All of these are part of the Tag Library Descriptor element except option A. Also, you need a JSP file such as yourJSP.jsp. See "Tag Library Descriptor."

2. **A** and **D.** The `taglib` directive only takes two attributes, `uri` and `prefix`. See "Taglib Directive."

3. **D.** The `taglib` element is used to describe a JSP tag library. The syntax for the `taglib` element in the web.xml file is `<!ELEMENT taglib (taglib-uri, taglib-location)>`. The required `taglib-location` element contains the location and the `taglib-uri` element describes a URI identifying a Tag Library used in the Web application. You use the URI to give a tag library a unique address or namespace. See "Taglib Directive."

4. **A.** The web.xml file is used as the deployment descriptor (see Chapter 10, "Deploying Web Applications and Descriptors"). The deployment descriptor defines the elements and configuration information of a Web application. In it you define elements to support the Web application within a servlet container, including `ServletContext` init parameters, session configuration, and servlet declarations. See "Taglib Directive."

5. **A, C,** and **D.** All of these files could be used as part of your tag library except option B because web.init is not a file defined by the specification. Also, you need a JSP file such as yourJSP.jsp. See "Creating a Tag Library Example."

6. **B.** The `taglib` directive creates a reference to the prefix. The prefix tells the container which library you want. Once that is done, you can use a custom tag, so called because it is your tag, not a standard one that came shipped with the container. See "Taglib Directive."

APPLY YOUR KNOWLEDGE

7. **C** and **D.** C uses correct XML notation to refer to an empty tag. By convention, we call a custom tag in a JSP page without a body an empty custom tag. See "Custom Tag."

8. **D.** The Tag Library Descriptor (TLD) is used by a Web container to validate the tags in a JSP page. See "Creating a Tag Library Example."

9. **A.** Your tag handler is a class that extends the `TagSupport` abstract class if it has `doStartTag()` and `doEndTag()` methods. See "Creating a Tag Library Example."

10. **A.** The container will combine the JSP code and tag library into one Java source file. The container converts your custom tags into Java calls during the JSP page translation. See "Taglib Directive."

11. **C.** Option C uses correct syntax, but the other options will cause an error. Notice that the `uri` and `prefix` are based on the information in the TLD file. See "Taglib Directive."

12. **C.** The URI in the JSP directive maps to `<taglib-uri>mytags</taglib-uri>` in the Web descriptor file (web.xml). The web.xml file tells the container where the tag library is located with a URI. When the JSP page references the tag library with a URI, the container maps that URI (which could be anything and doesn't have to be real) to a file path. See "Creating a Tag Library Example."

13. **A.** It is part of the `bodycontent` element. The `tagdependent` option means the tag will regard the contents of the body as non-JSP. The body is passed verbatim to the tag handler. See "Custom Tag."

APPLY YOUR KNOWLEDGE

Suggested Readings and Resources

1. A nice tutorial by Magnus Rydin: `http://www.orionserver.com/taglibtut/lesson1/`.
2. Another nice tutorial by Wrox: `http://tutorials.findtutorials.com/read/category/82/id/233` and `http://tutorials.findtutorials.com/read/category/82/id/234`.
3. A small but helpful introduction to tag libraries by Stardeveloper.com: `http://www.stardeveloper.com:8080/articles/081301-1.shtml`.
4. A good overview of tag libraries from BEA. This is helpful because they use their own excellent product, WebLogic, which will differ somewhat from Tomcat (which is used in this book): `http://edocs.bea.com/wls/docs61/taglib/overview.html#362351`.
5. *Servlets and JavaServer Pages* by Marty Hall is just exceptional. An expert who is highly regarded: `http://www.coreservlets.com/`.
6. *More Servlets and JavaServer Pages* by Marty Hall. This is also very good: `http://www.moreservlets.com/`.
7. *Designing JSP Custom Tag Libraries* by Sue Spielman is a very short, but excellent snapshot of tag libraries: `http://www.onjava.com/pub/a/onjava/2000/12/15/jsp_custom_tags.html`.
8. Sun's reference page has many good links for tag libraries: `http://java.sun.com/products/jsp/taglibraries.html`.

OBJECTIVES

A Web application is made up of all the servlets, HTML pages, classes, and other resources that act as a single application on a Web server. That it is called a Web application is not surprising, but one facet that is interesting is that a Web application can be bundled and run on multiple containers from multiple vendors. In other words you can zip the whole thing up into one Web Archive (WAR) file and give it to the others to install.

The main focus of this chapter is defining what a Web application is, the many parts of one, and how it physically resides on a file system. We will cover these ideas by addressing the following Sun-specified objectives for the Web application section of the Sun Certified Web Component Developer exam:

2.1 Identify the structure of a Web Application and Web Archive file, the name of the WebApp deployment descriptor, and the name of the directories where you place the following:

- **The WebApp deployment descriptor**
- **The WebApp class files**
- **Any auxiliary JAR files**

▶ There is a defined hierarchical structure to be used for deployment and packaging of all Web applications. The servlet specification defines this structure, but the servlet containers are not required to adopt this structure. The primary file is the deployment descriptor (web.xml) configuration file that contains this definition for a given Web application.

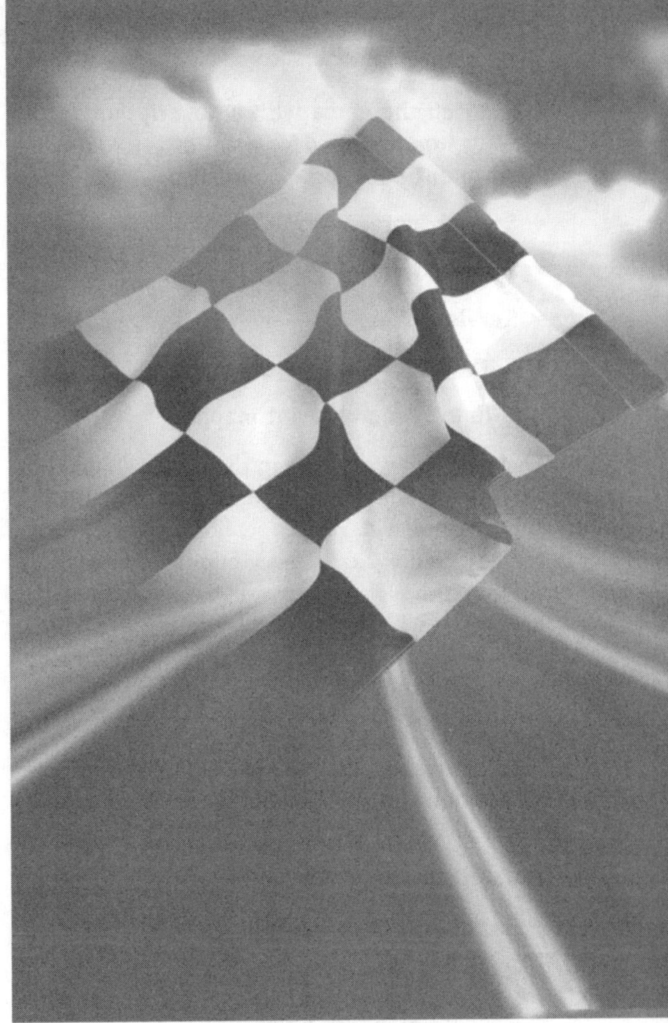

CHAPTER 10

Deploying Web Applications and Components

2.2 Match the name with a description of purpose or functionality, for each of the following deployment descriptor elements:

- **Servlet instance**
- **Servlet name**
- **Servlet class**
- **Initialization parameters**
- **URL to named servlet mapping**

▶ There are many elements in the web.xml descriptor file. This section, and a few more like it, wants you to be familiar with the purpose of these elements and how to use them. This grouping concerns servlets. Although you can add servlets to your Web application without listing them in the deployment descriptor, it makes sense to add the most important ones.

3.2 Identify the WebApp deployment descriptor element name that declares the following features:

- **Servlet context init. parameters**
- **Servlet context listener**
- **Servlet context attribute listener**
- **Session attribute listeners**

▶ The purpose of this objective is to familiarize yourself with the listener element that defines the deployment properties for a Web application listener bean. Also, you will need to know about the context initialization parameters, which apply to the entire application, unlike servlet initialization parameters, which apply only to a given servlet.

4.2 Given a set of business logic exceptions, identify the following:

- **The configuration that the deployment descriptor uses to handle each exception.**
- **How to use a `REQUESTDISPATCHER` to forward the request to an error page.**
- **Specify the handling declaratively in the deployment descriptor.**

▶ The purpose of this objective is to teach you how to configure the deployment descriptor to handle exceptions. Because your Web application may have errors, this section concerns the servlet specification where it addresses how the deployment descriptor configures the Web container to handle exceptions.

6.1 Identify correct descriptions or statements about these security issues:

- **Authentication, authorization**
- **Data integrity**
- **Auditing**
- **Malicious code**
- **Web site attacks**

▶ As developers, we should be very paranoid about security. It gets even more serious with Web applications because some strangers lurking on the Internet have nothing better to do than invade your system. The good news is Sun has added many security features to Java in general and Web applications in particular. You have several ways to authenticate clients and authorize users.

OBJECTIVES

6.2 Identify the deployment descriptor element names, and their structure, that declare the following:

- **A security constraint**
- **A Web resource**
- **The login configuration**
- **A security role**

▶ The purpose of this objective is to teach you about the security elements in the deployment descriptor. These elements are what you use to add security constraints with one or more Web resource collections such as a security role and user roles that should be permitted access to this resource collection.

6.3 Given an authentication type: BASIC, DIGEST, FORM, and CLIENT-CERT, identify the correct definition of its mechanism.

▶ Authentication has been a big part of security from the beginning. Web applications are designed with four types of authentication out of the box. You can always add more types, but these are a good start.

11.1 Identify properly formatted tag library declarations in the Web application deployment descriptor.

▶ Chapter 9, "Customize JSP with Tag Libraries," covers the subject of tag libraries in detail. It tells you that they are similar to JavaBeans in that you can reference a class from JSP using XML notation. The objective covered in this chapter is intended to ensure that you understand how to specify tag libraries (URI and location) within a given Web application.

OUTLINE

Outline

Study Strategies

- The Web application descriptor is just an XML document. Rather than trying to memorize the DTD, write a few descriptors and recycle the servlet container to see the effect it has. Also, notice that most of the elements make sense in context, so study the examples in this chapter.
- Make sure you know the basic Web application directory structure of an application.
- There isn't much syntax to study for this part of the exam. You can still practice with the examples by making changes and recycling the server (for example, Tomcat).

INTRODUCTION

Unlike simple standalone applications, a Web application has built-in complexity. The code you write won't take effect unless it is compiled and placed into the proper directory. Also, you should be mindful of how the server is configured. What if the session timeout is only 20 minutes? Is that appropriate for your application? What do you give a customer when you deploy your Web application? It is difficult to write an installation script for a Web application. The target installation machine may have a non-standard configuration. For example, it may be a Web farm.

The Web application is an extension of the Web server. Therefore, you have to plug your files into the server's directory structure. The servlet standard does tell how to make your directories for a default installation. The exam will assume this default configuration.

The good news is that most of what you need to know involves XML. There is little syntax to memorize. This part of the exam is about being familiar with the web.xml DTD and where to put your files. The DTD itself isn't difficult if you study the purposes of the main elements. Actually, it is a nice architecture to have this web.xml document instead of using initialization text files with non-standard definitions that have been the normal practice for so long.

WEB APPLICATION AND WEB ARCHIVE STRUCTURE

2.1 Identify the structure of a Web application and Web Archive file, the name of the WebApp deployment descriptor, and the name of the directories where you place the following:

- **The WebApp deployment descriptor**
- **The WebApp class files**
- **Any auxiliary JAR files**

The specification defines a hierarchical structure used for deployment and packaging of your Web applications. Although the servlet containers are not required to adopt this structure, most do and the exam definitely follows it. You will have two ways to package your application. You can use an open file system (not wrapped up in a jar) or an archive file.

The application needs a reference point within the hierarchical structure. Here, let's call it TOMCAT_HOME. This represents the root of your server (Tomcat) installation, not your Web application root. In this book, I used Tomcat on a Windows machine (Dell Inspiron). Except for using a forward slash instead of a backward one, and the drive letter, it is the same for Unix installations.

When we talk of a Web application's *context*, we are referring to that Web application's root directory or path within a particular server. A special directory exists within the application hierarchy named WEB-INF. This directory contains all things related to the application that aren't in the document root of the application. It is this WEB-INF directory that is the Web application's root directory, also referred to as the context. The most important file here is web.xml, the name of the WebApp deployment descriptor.

Within a generic context, there are three directories in focus here. The installation directory will vary wildly between installations. This directory is not on the exam. There is a structure for how the container is supposed to be used once you get deep enough into the Web application deployment. Whatever the installation directory, there are predefined subdirectories, one each for the WebApp deployment descriptor, the class files, and the auxiliary JAR files. The Web application structure you'll be questioned about is shown in Table 10.1.

TABLE 10.1

WEB APPLICATION STRUCTURE

Name	*Files*	*Location*
Deployment descriptor	web.xml	`/WEB-INF/web.xml`
class files	MyServlet.class	`/WEB-INF/classes/MyServlet.class`
jar files (servlets, beans, utility classes)	myApp.jar	`/WEB-INF/lib/myApp.jar`
Other files (HTML, JSP)	index.html	`/`

The following is the Web application structure for a small sample Web application:

```
/index.html
/welcome.jsp
/store.jsp
/images/logo.gif
/images/background.gif
/WEB-INF/web.xml
/WEB-INF/taglib.tld
/WEB-INF/lib/shoppingBean.jar
/WEB-INF/classes/com/myCompany/servlets/Shopping.class
/WEB-INF/classes/com/ myCompany/util/CurrencyFormat.class
```

Although the actual paths are not on the exam, seeing where the files actually go illustrates what is going on. For example, I installed Tomcat at `C:\dev\java\jakarta-tomcat-4.0.1` on my machine. I would then refer to this directory as TOMCAT_HOME, or something similar. Tomcat knows to look into the `C:\dev\java\jakarta-tomcat-4.0.1\webapps` directory for Web applications. From here you will configure Tomcat, or another container, with XML files. For example, Tomcat installs with an example application. In the `C:\dev\java\jakarta-tomcat-4.0.1\conf` or just `TOMCAT_HOME\conf` directory there is a server.xml file. Tomcat uses this to configure itself upon starting. There is a context element that you use to map your application's URL to the actual directory path. The following is how you get an examples application:

```
<!-- Tomcat Examples Context -->
<Context path="/examples" docBase="examples" debug="0"
         reloadable="true">
```

So, now that you have an examples Web application, the actual root directory is this: `TOMCAT_HOME\webapps\examples`. If you had the file `TOMCAT_HOME\webapps\examples\hello.jsp` you would call this file with `http://localhost:8080/examples/hello.jsp` (just change the port to whatever one you have your server listening to). Notice how Tomcat converts the URL into a path. Table 10.2 shows you how Tomcat converts several URLs into paths.

TABLE 10.2

WEB APPLICATION PATH

Description	*URL*	*Directory*
installation root		`C:\dev\java\jakarta-tomcat-4.0.1` This is TOMCAT_HOME.
Server root	`http://localhost`	`TOMCAT_HOME\webapps`
Web application	`http://localhost:8080/examples`	`TOMCAT_HOME\webapps\examples`
Static resource	`http://localhost:8080/examples/index.html`	`TOMCAT_HOME\webapps\examples\index.html`
JSP	`http://localhost:8080/examples/hello.jsp`	`TOMCAT_HOME\webapps\examples\hello.jsp`
JSP	`http://localhost:8080/examples/jsp/dates/date.jsp`	`TOMCAT_HOME\webapps\examples\jsp\dates\date.jsp`
Servlet	`http://localhost:8080/examples/servlet/HelloWorldExample`	`TOMCAT_HOME\webapps\examples\WEB-INF\classes\HelloWorldExample.class`

Now that you understand the structure of a Web application, can you just zip it all up and install it somewhere else? Yes, you can use a Web ARchive format (WAR) file. You might recall that JAR files are just ZIP files with a jar extension. You use them for lossless data compression, archiving, decompression, archive unpacking, and electronic signing. To manipulate JAR files, you use the Java Archive Tool provided as part of the Java Development Kit. The Java Archive tool is invoked by using the `jar` command. You can use JAR capability for Web applications by packaging them into a Web ARchive format (WAR) file using the same Java Archive tool. You could package your Web application into an archive file called myWebApplication.war. So, let's discuss where you might place this file and other Web application files.

NOTE

Mapping URLs to Paths! There are many ways to map a URL to an actual path. The server.xml maps a Web application name to a directory under the `TOMCAT_HOME\webapps` directory. The web.xml maps servlet names to paths, too. On top of all this, the server can have other virtual maps and configurations.

Let's create a WAR file. After you have created your application directory, and sub-directories including the WEB-INF directory, you can create a WAR file. You use the "jar" utility from the Java Development Kit to create the WAR file. Follow these steps:

1. Go to the `%TOMCAT_HOME%/webapps/myApplication` directory.
2. Type **jar cvf myApplication.war** *

That is how you create it. Where does the myApplication.war file go? To test your new WAR file, copy it to the webapps directory and then rename the myApplication directory to, say, `myApplicationTemp`. Now, recycle the server and point your browser to one of your old servlets or JSP pages.

DEPLOYMENT DESCRIPTOR ELEMENTS

2.2 Match the name with a description of purpose or functionality, for each of the following deployment descriptor elements:

- **Servlet instance**
- **Servlet name**
- **Servlet class**
- **Initialization parameters**
- **URL to named servlet mapping**

3.2 Identify the WebApp deployment descriptor element name that declares the following features:

- **Servlet context init. parameters**
- **Servlet context listener**
- **Servlet context attribute listener**
- **Session attribute listeners**

6.2 Identify the deployment descriptor element names, and their structure, that declare the following:

- **A security constraint**
- **A Web resource**
- **The login configuration**
- **A security role**

11.1 Identify properly formatted tag library declarations in the Web application deployment descriptor.

This section of the exam is primarily a test of your familiarity with the XML DTD for the Servlet 2.3 deployment descriptor. Remember that the deployment descriptor of a Web application is the web.xml file. This file is located in the WEB-INF directory whether in the file system or in a WAR file. You don't have to memorize the whole XML DTD (see `http://www.w3.org/TR/REC-xml#dt-element` for an element definition). There are 77 elements total, but you don't have to know all of them and many are trivial like `name` and `description`. This isn't painful if you use a little shortcut for the task. Some folks use a mnemonic from the first letter of the tags listed in the exam objectives. The following is the root element for the descriptor:

```
<!ELEMENT web-app (icon?, display-name?, description?,
distributable?, context-param*, filter*, filter-mapping*,
listener*, servlet*, servlet-mapping*, session-config?,
mime-mapping*, welcome-file-list?, error-page*, taglib*,
resource-env-ref*, resource-ref*, security-constraint*,
login-config?, security-role*, env-entry*, ejb-ref*,
 ejb-local-ref*)>
```

The main elements are defined in Table 10.3.

TABLE 10.3

WEB-APP ELEMENTS

Element	*DTD*
context-param	<!ELEMENT context-param (param-name, param-value, description?)>
listener	<!ELEMENT listener (listener-class)> <!ELEMENT listener-class (#PCDATA)>
Servlet	<!ELEMENT servlet (icon?, servlet-name, display-name?, description?, (servlet-class|jsp-file), init-param*, load-on-startup?, run-as?, security-role-ref*)> <!ELEMENT servlet-name (#PCDATA)> <!ELEMENT servlet-class (#PCDATA)> <!ELEMENT load-on-startup (#PCDATA)> <!ELEMENT run-as (description?, role-name)> <!ELEMENT security-role-ref (description?, role-name, role-link?)>
servlet-mapping	<!ELEMENT servlet-mapping (servlet-name, url-pattern)>
session-config	<!ELEMENT session-config (session-timeout?)> <!ELEMENT session-timeout (#PCDATA)>
welcome-file-list	<!ELEMENT welcome-file (#PCDATA)>

Element	*DTD*
error-page	`<!ELEMENT error-page ((error-code | exception-type), location)>` `<!ELEMENT error-code (#PCDATA)>` `<!ELEMENT exception-type (#PCDATA)>`
Taglib	`<!ELEMENT taglib (taglib-uri, taglib-location)>` `<!ELEMENT taglib-location (#PCDATA)>` `<!ELEMENT taglib-uri (#PCDATA)>`
security-constraint	`<!ELEMENT security-constraint (display-name?, web-resource-collection+, auth-constraint?, user-data-constraint?)>` `<!ELEMENT auth-constraint (description?, role-name*)>` `<!ELEMENT web-resource-collection (web-resource-name, description?, url-pattern*, http-method*)>` `<!ELEMENT user-data-constraint (description?, transport-guarantee)>`
login-config	`<!ELEMENT login-config (auth-method?, realm-name?, form-login-config?)>`
security-role	`<!ELEMENT security-role (description?, role-name)>`

As previously stated, you don't have to know the entire DTD. Out of the root element you should focus on these:

C = `<context-param>`

L = `<listener>`

S = `<servlet>`

S = `<servlet-mapping>`

S = `<session-config>`

W = `<welcome-file-list>`

E = `<error-page>`

T = `<taglib>`

S = `<security-constraint>`

L = `<login-config>`

S = `<security-role>`

One shortcut comes from Ricardo Cortes and Kevin Postlewaite whose posts on JavaRanch were very helpful (`http://saloon.javaranch.com/cgi-bin/ubb/ultimatebb.cgi?ubb=get_topic&f=18&t=001389`). Mr. Postlewaite's unforgettable phrase is CLaSSSic WET SeaLS. Perhaps you can also remember mine, which is CLaSS SWEaTS LotS.

We need to go through each element individually including a description, the XML syntax, and an example.

context-param

The `context-param` element declares the Web application's servlet context-initialization parameters.

Element

```
<!ELEMENT context-param (param-name, param-value,
                                     description?)>
```

Example

```
<web-app>
    ...
    <context-param>
        <param-name>TOMCAT_ROOT</param-name>
        <param-value>C:\dev\java\jakarta-tomcat-4.0.1
        </param-value>
    </context-param>
    <context-param>
        <param-name>Support</param-name>
        <param-value>helpdesk@mycompany.com</param-value>
    </context-param>
    ...
</web-app>
```

listener

The `listener` element defines the deployment properties for a Web application listener bean.

Element

```
<!ELEMENT listener (listener-class)>
  <!ELEMENT listener-class (#PCDATA)>
```

Example

```
<web-app>
    ...
<listener>
   <listener-class>listeners.MyListener</listener-class>
</listener>    ...
</web-app>
```

servlet

The servlet element is how you define a servlet in a Web application. The servlet element establishes a mapping between a servlet name and the fully qualified name of the servlet class. Of course, you don't have to name all your servlets in the web.xml file. However, there are servlets that you may need defined here so the container can load them upon starting (load-on-startup element), for example.

Element

```
<!ELEMENT servlet (icon?, servlet-name, display-name?,
description?, (servlet-class|jsp-file), init-param*,
load-on-startup?, run-as?, security-role-ref*)>
  <!ELEMENT servlet-name (#PCDATA)>
  <!ELEMENT servlet-class (#PCDATA)>
  <!ELEMENT load-on-startup (#PCDATA)>
  <!ELEMENT run-as (description?, role-name)>
  <!ELEMENT security-role-ref (description?, role-name,
                                             role-link?)>
```

Example

```
<web-app>
    ...
        <servlet>
        <servlet-name>
            MyTestServlet
        </servlet-name>
        <servlet-class>
            MyTestServlet
        </servlet-class>
    </servlet>
    ...
</web-app>
```

servlet-mapping

The servlet-mapping element defines a mapping between a servlet and a URL pattern. When a request is received by the container it must determine which servlet should handle it. Using the deployment descriptor, you can map certain paths (aliases) to a specific servlet. You define this mapping with the servlet-mapping element. The alias is appended after the context root in an HTTP request URL.

Element

```
<!ELEMENT servlet-mapping (servlet-name, url-pattern)>
```

Example

```
<web-app>
    ...
    <servlet-mapping>
        <servlet-name>
            MyTestServlet
        </servlet-name>
        <url-pattern>
            /testServlet
        </url-pattern>
    </servlet-mapping>
    ...
</web-app>
```

session-config

The `session-config` element defines the session parameters for this Web application such as the session timeout, which defines the default session timeout interval for all sessions created in this Web application.

Element

```
<!ELEMENT session-config (session-timeout?)>
  <!ELEMENT session-timeout (#PCDATA)>
```

Example

```
<web-app>
    ...
  <session-config>
    <session-timeout>30</session-timeout>
  </session-config>
    ...
</web-app>
```

welcome-file

The `welcome-file` element contains a filename to use as a default file, such as index.html.

Element

```
<!ELEMENT welcome-file (#PCDATA)>
```

Example

```
<web-app>
    ...
  <welcome-file-list>
    <welcome-file>index.jsp</welcome-file>
    <welcome-file>index.html</welcome-file>
    <welcome-file>index.htm</welcome-file>
  </welcome-file-list>
    ...
</web-app>
```

error-page

The error-page element contains a mapping between an error code or exception type to the path of a resource in the Web application.

Element

```
<!ELEMENT error-page ((error-code | exception-type),
                                         location)>
  <!ELEMENT error-code (#PCDATA)>
  <!ELEMENT exception-type (#PCDATA)>
```

Example

```
<web-app>
    ...
    <error-page>
        <error-code>404</error-code>
        <location>/NotFoundErrorPage</location>
    </error-page>
    ...
</web-app>
```

taglib

The `taglib` element is used to describe a JSP tag library, including the tag library location (Tag Library Description file) and the URI for it which is a unique namespace identifying a tag library used in the Web application.

Element

```
<!ELEMENT taglib (taglib-uri, taglib-location)>
  <!ELEMENT taglib-location (#PCDATA)>
  <!ELEMENT taglib-uri (#PCDATA)>
```

Example

```
<web-app>
    ...
    <taglib>
        <taglib-uri>
                http://www.yourcompany.com/yourTagLibrary
        </taglib-uri>
        <taglib-location>
           /WEB-INF/yourTagLibrary.tld
        </taglib-location>
    </taglib>
    ...
</web-app>
```

security-constraint

The `security-constraint` element is used to associate security constraints with one or more Web resource collections such as a security role and user roles that should be permitted access to this resource collection.

Element

```
<!ELEMENT security-constraint (display-name?,
web-resource-collection+, auth-constraint?,
user-data-constraint?)>
  <!ELEMENT auth-constraint (description?, role-name*)>
  <!ELEMENT web-resource-collection (web-resource-name,
   description?, url-pattern*, http-method*)>
  <!ELEMENT user-data-constraint (description?,
                                   transport-guarantee)>
```

Example

```
<web-app>
    ...
    <security-constraint>
        <web-resource-collection>
            <web-resource-name>All Users Allowed Area
            </web-resource-name>
            <url-pattern>/allowed/*</url-pattern>
        </web-resource-collection>
        <auth-constraint>
```

```
            <role-name>*</role-name>
        </auth-constraint>
    </security-constraint>
    ...
</web-app>
```

login-config

The `login-config` element is used to configure the authentication method that should be used, the realm name that should be used for this application, and the attributes that are needed by the form login mechanism.

Element

```
<!ELEMENT login-config (auth-method?, realm-name?,
                                   form-login-config?)>
```

Example

```
<web-app>
    ...
    <login-config>
        <auth-method>BASIC</auth-method>
        <realm-name>Authentication Servlet</realm-name>
    </login-config>
    ...
</web-app>
```

security-role

The `security-role` element contains the definition of a security role. The definition consists of an optional description of the security role, and the security role name.

Element

```
<!ELEMENT security-role (description?, role-name)>
```

Example

```
<web-app>
    ...
  <security-role>
  <description>
```

```
      This role includes all customers who have a credit
      line with us based on at least one previous purchase.
   </description>
     <role-name>customer</role-name>
   </security-role>
     ...
</web-app>
```

Web Application Descriptor Example

Now that we have reviewed all the elements individually, let's look at a complete example. The following web.xml file includes all the previously listed elements. The majority of this descriptor comes by way of snippets from many samples that shipped with Tomcat. Listing 10.1 is the source for web.xml.

LISTING 10.1

THE SOURCE CODE FOR A WEB APPLICATION DEPLOYMENT DESCRIPTOR

```
<?xml version="1.0" encoding="ISO-8859-1"?>

<!DOCTYPE web-app PUBLIC
"-//Sun Microsystems, Inc.//DTD Web Application 2.3//EN"
    "http://java.sun.com/j2ee/dtds/web-app_2_3.dtd">

<!-- Deployment Descriptor for your Web Application -->
<!-- Some elements come from Tomcat examples. -->

<web-app>

    <!-- General description of your web application -->
    <!-- You won't be tested on these two tags,
         but you might see them -->

    <display-name>My Web Application</display-name>
    <description>
      This is version X.X of an application to perform
      a wild and wonderful task, based on servlets and
      JSP pages.  It was written by Dave Developer
      (dave@mycompany.com), who should be contacted for
      more information.
    </description>

<!-- ======= Filter Definitions not on exam====== -->

<!-- ======= Context Initialization ============ -->
<!-- Context initialization parameters that define shared
    String constants used within your application, which
```

```
can be customized by the system administrator who is
installing your application.  The values actually
assigned to these parameters can be retrieved in a
servlet or JSP page by calling:

String value =
    getServletContext().getInitParameter("name");

where "name" matches the <param-name> element of
one of these initialization parameters.

You can define any number of context initialization
parameters, including zero.
-->

<context-param>
  <param-name>webmaster</param-name>
  <param-value>myaddress@mycompany.com</param-value>
  <description>
    The EMAIL address of the administrator to whom
    questions and comments about this application
    should be addressed.
  </description>
</context-param>

<!--=== Listener Definitions =================== -->

<listener>
    <listener-class>yourPackage.YourListener
    </listener-class>
</listener>

<!-- ==== Servlet Definitions ================= -->

<!-- Servlet definitions for the servlets that make up
     your web application, including initialization
     parameters.  With Tomcat, you can also send
     requests to servlets not listed here with a
     request like this:

http://localhost:8080/{context-path}/servlet/{classname}

     but this usage is not guaranteed to be portable.
     It also makes relative references to images and
     other resources required by your servlet more
     complicated, so defining all of your servlets
     (and defining a mapping to them with
     a servlet-mapping element) is recommended.

     Servlet initialization parameters can be retrieved
     in a servlet or JSP page by calling:

         String value =
          getServletConfig().getInitParameter("name");
```

continues

LISTING 10.1 *continued*

THE SOURCE CODE FOR A WEB APPLICATION DEPLOYMENT DESCRIPTOR

```
         where "name" matches the <param-name> element of
         one of these initialization parameters.

         You can define any number of servlets, even zero.
    -->

    <servlet>
        <servlet-name>CustomerSupport</servlet-name>
        <servlet-class>yourPackage.CustomerSupport
        </servlet-class>
    </servlet>

    <servlet>
        <servlet-name>Authentication</servlet-name>
        <servlet-class>yourPackage.Authentication
        </servlet-class>
        <security-role-ref>
            <role-name>alias</role-name>
            <role-link>tomcat</role-link>
        </security-role-ref>
    </servlet>

  <servlet>
    <servlet-name>Store</servlet-name>
    <servlet-class>yourPackage.Store</servlet-class>
    <init-param>
      <param-name>itemCount</param-name>
      <param-value>0</param-value>
    </init-param>
    <init-param>
      <param-name>listings</param-name>
      <param-value>true</param-value>
    </init-param>
    <load-on-startup>1</load-on-startup>
  </servlet>

<!-- ===== Servlet Mappings ===== -->

    <!--
Define mappings that are used by the servlet container to
translate a particular request URI (context-relative) to a
particular servlet.  The examples below correspond to the
servlet descriptions above.  Thus, a request URI like:

           http://localhost:8080/{contextpath}/graph

will be mapped to the "graph" servlet, while a request
like:
```

```
http://localhost:8080/{contextpath}/saveCustomer.do

will be mapped to the "controller" servlet.

You may define any number of servlet mappings, including
zero. It is also legal to define more than one mapping
for the same servlet, if you wish to.
    -->

    <servlet-mapping>
        <servlet-name>CustomerSupport</servlet-name>
        <url-pattern>/CustomerSupport</url-pattern>
    </servlet-mapping>

    <servlet-mapping>
        <servlet-name>Authentication</servlet-name>
        <url-pattern>/Authentication</url-pattern>
    </servlet-mapping>

    <servlet-mapping>
        <servlet-name>Store</servlet-name>
        <url-pattern>/commerce/store</url-pattern>
    </servlet-mapping>

  <!-- === Default Session Configuration === -->

  <!-- You can set the default session timeout
       (in minutes) for all newly
       created sessions by modifying the value
       below.                       -->

  <session-config>
    <session-timeout>30</session-timeout>
  </session-config>

    <!-- === Error Page Mappings === -->

    <error-page><!-- SC_PRECONDITION_FAILED -->
        <error-code>412</error-code>
        <location>/ErrorPage02</location>
    </error-page>

    <error-page>
        <exception-type>java.lang.ArithmeticException
        </exception-type>
        <location>/ErrorPage06</location>
    </error-page>

  <!-- === Tag Libraries Configuration === -->
    <taglib>
        <taglib-uri>
     http://jakarta.apache.org/tomcat/examples-taglib
        </taglib-uri>
        <taglib-location>
```

continues

LISTING 10.1 *continued*

THE SOURCE CODE FOR A WEB APPLICATION DEPLOYMENT DESCRIPTOR

```
            /WEB-INF/jsp/example-taglib.tld
        </taglib-location>
    </taglib>
    <taglib>
        <taglib-uri>
            http://www.mycompany.com/taglib
        </taglib-uri>
        <taglib-location>
            /WEB-INF/taglib.tld
        </taglib-location>
    </taglib>

    <taglib>
        <taglib-uri>
                http://www.yourcompany.com/yourTagLibrary
        </taglib-uri>
        <taglib-location>
            /WEB-INF/yourTagLibrary.tld
        </taglib-location>
    </taglib>



    <!-- === Security Constraints === -->

    <security-constraint>
      <display-name>Example Security Constraint
      </display-name>
      <web-resource-collection>
         <web-resource-name>Protected Area
         </web-resource-name>
   <!-- Define the context-relative URL(s)
                          to be protected -->
         <url-pattern>/jsp/security/protected/*
         </url-pattern>
   <!-- If you list http methods,
            only those methods are protected -->
   <http-method>DELETE</http-method>
         <http-method>GET</http-method>
         <http-method>POST</http-method>
   <http-method>PUT</http-method>
      </web-resource-collection>
      <auth-constraint>
         <!-- Anyone with one of the listed roles
                           may access this area -->
         <role-name>tomcat</role-name>
   <role-name>role1</role-name>
      </auth-constraint>
    </security-constraint>
    <login-config>
        <auth-method>BASIC</auth-method>
```

```
        <realm-name>Authentication Servlet</realm-name>
    </login-config>

    <security-role>
        <description>Security role we are testing for
         </description>
        <role-name>tomcat</role-name>
    </security-role>

<!-- === Environment Entries - not on exam === -->


  <!-- === Default Welcome File List === -->

  <!-- When a request URI refers to a directory, the
       default servlet looks for a "welcome file" within
       that directory and, if present, to the
       corresponding resource URI for display.
       If no welcome file is present, the default servlet
       either serves a directory listing, or returns a
       404 status, depending on how it is configured.-->

  <welcome-file-list>
    <welcome-file>index.html</welcome-file>
    <welcome-file>index.htm</welcome-file>
    <welcome-file>index.jsp</welcome-file>
  </welcome-file-list>

  <!-- === Session Configuration === -->

    <!-- Define the default session timeout for your
         application, in minutes.  From a servlet or
         JSP page, you can modify the timeout for a
         particular session dynamically by using
         HttpSession.getMaxInactiveInterval().
    -->
</web-app>
```

WEB APPLICATION EXCEPTIONS

4.2 Given a set of business logic exceptions, identify the following:

- **The configuration that the deployment descriptor uses to handle each exception.**
- **How to use a `REQUESTDISPATCHER` to forward the request to an error page.**
- **Specify the handling declaratively in the deployment descriptor.**

Your Web application will have errors; all software does. The servlet specification addresses the need to handle errors. The first part of this objective addresses how the deployment descriptor handles exceptions. The following snippet shows you how to use the error-page element, which defines which resource the container should use for a given exception.

```
<web-app>
        <error-page>
                <error-code>404</ error-code>
                <location> /404.html </location>
        </error-page>
</web-app>
```

With this definition, the client will get the 404.html page if it requests a page that the container decides isn't available.

You can accomplish the same thing a little more dynamically with the `RequestDispatcher`. You can forward a request to an error page easily like so:

```
ServletContext context = getServletContext();
dispatcher = context.getRequestDispatcher(
                              "/errors/error.jsp");
dispatcher.forward(request,response);
```

Although this is more dynamic, it ignores all kinds of rules for good practice. It would be better to use the error-page element most of the time but forward to an error page with the `RequestDispatcher` on occasion.

You can also specify the exception handling declaratively in the deployment descriptor. You do this with the `error-page` element and the `exception-type` subelement like so:

```
<web-app>
  <error-page>
    <exception-type> javax.servlet.ServletException
    </exception-type>
    <location>/servlet/ErrorDisplay</location>
  </error-page>
</web-app>
```

This is a good practice as it makes the intention explicit for your Web application as opposed to relying on defaults.

WEB APPLICATION SECURITY

6.1 Identify correct descriptions or statements about the security issues:

- **Authentication, authorization**
- **Data integrity**
- **Auditing**
- **Malicious code**
- **Web site attacks**

The security issues are ever present in software, and more so for Web applications because you are exposing part of your machinery to the wild wild Internet. Sun made a big effort to make Java secure, whether as a standalone or Web application.

This objective is really just a matter of a few definitions. The following list defines each of the items in the objective:

- **Authentication.** The means by which communicating entities prove to one another that they are acting on behalf of specific identities. Are you really you?
- **Authorization.** This is access control where interactions with resources are limited to collections of users or programs for the purpose of enforcing integrity, confidentiality, or availability constraints. You have permission to use a given page.
- **Data integrity.** The means used to prove that information has not been modified by a third party while in transit. The data is really what was sent.
- **Auditing.** Maintain a record of Web application activity. For example, you can log resource accesses including times and requester IP and ID. This usually involves a log somewhere.
- **Malicious code.** Code that deliberately behaves in a way other than advertised, especially to compromise your server.
- **Web site attacks.** An overt attempt to compromise your Web site. The most popular attack is the denial-of-service attack where the attacker floods the server with requests, reducing its capacity to service legitimate requests.

There is no end to the imagination of those who can't compete within society's rules. You should design your Web application to withstand at least a minimum level of attack, which is sometimes just an accident, or so we like to hope.

AUTHENTICATION TYPES

6.3 Given an authentication type: BASIC, DIGEST, FORM, and CLIENT-CERT, identify the correct definition of its mechanism.

As mentioned previously, authentication is the mechanism that makes sure you are really you. Somehow, the Web client has to prove to your Web application its identity. There are four ways to do that including HTTP Basic, HTTP Digest, HTTPS Client, and Form Based authentication.

The following list defines each of the authentication types in the objective:

- **HTTP Basic Authentication.** Authentication based on a username and password. It is the authentication mechanism defined in the HTTP/1.0 specification. A Web server requests a Web client to authenticate the user. The Web client obtains the username and the password from the user and transmits them to the Web server. The Web server then authenticates the user. This is the lowest level security of the four here.
- **HTTP Digest Authentication.** The password is encrypted. Like HTTP Basic Authentication, HTTP Digest Authentication authenticates a user based on a username and a password. However, the authentication is performed by transmitting the password in an encrypted form.
- **HTTPS Client Authentication.** This is end user authentication using HTTPS (HTTP over SSL). This mechanism uses public key encryption, which requires the user to possess a Public Key Certificate (PKC). This is the highest level security of the four here.

- **Form Based Authentication.** This is similar to Basic except that a form is used with predefined fields. These fields must be named `j_username` and `j_password`, respectively and the form method and action must be named `POST` and `j_security_check`, respectively. An example is this:

```
<form method="POST" action="j_security_check">
        <input type="text" name="j_username">
        <input type="password" name="j_password">
</form>
```

All four of the security mechanisms can be used singly; you can only select one authentication mechanism for a single WebApp. However, if you need real security, do it with SSL.

CHAPTER SUMMARY

There are many aspects to deploying an application. The two major concerns are what directories to use and what pieces comprise the application. The deployment descriptor gives you a way to clearly define these aspects of your Web application. This chapter described all the objectives associated with the deployment descriptor on the SCWCD exam.

KEY TERMS

- Web application
- Web archive file
- WebApp deployment descriptor
- Authentication, authorization
- Security constraint
- Tag library

APPLY YOUR KNOWLEDGE

Review Questions

1. What is a Web application?
2. How is the WebApp deployment descriptor used?
3. What types of client authentications are there?
4. Why would you use a WAR file?
5. How can you handle exceptions in a Web application?

Exam Questions

1. Which two statements apply to the following code snippet? (Choose two.)

```
<servlet>
<servlet-name>
    testServlet
</servlet-name>
<servlet-class>
    myPackage.MyTestServlet
</servlet-class>
</servlet>
```

   A. It is a mapping between a servlet name and the fully-qualified name of the servlet class.

   B. It is a map between a URL and a servlet.

   C. This code belongs in the WebApp deployment descriptor.

   D. It tells the container where to install the servlet.

2. Which two of the following statements most closely relate to HTTPS Client Authentication?

   A. It uses a Status-Code element (three-digit integer).

   B. It uses predefined form fields.

   C. It is the most secure form of authentication.

   D. It uses SSL.

3. Which directory is the location for myApp.jar?

   A. `/WEB-INF/`

   B. `/WEB-INF/classes/`

   C. `/WEB-INF/lib/`

   D. `/`

4. In which two elements can you define initialization parameters?

   A. `servlet`

   B. `context-param`

   C. `welcome-file`

   D. `login-config`

5. Which three of the following are elements of the Web Application Descriptor?

   A. `servlet`

   B. `context-param`

   C. `listener`

   D. `error`

6. What is the configuration that the deployment descriptor uses to handle each exception?

   A. `error-page`

   B. `exception`

   C. `error`

   D. `exception-page`

APPLY YOUR KNOWLEDGE

7. What is the deployment descriptor file named?

   A. server.conf

   B. server.xml

   C. web.xml

   D. web.conf

8. Which directory is the location for Web application class files?

   A. `/WEB-INF/`

   B. `/WEB-INF/classes/`

   C. `/WEB-INF/classpath/`

   D. `/META-INF/classes`

9. What does the security-role element do?

   A. It configures the authentication method that should be used by the form login mechanism.

   B. It defines the status codes for security breaches.

   C. It contains a mapping between an error code or exception type to the path of a resource in the Web application.

   D. It describes and names the security role.

10. Which directory is the location for the deployment descriptor?

    A. `/WEB-INF/`

    B. `/WEB-INF/classes/`

    C. `/WEB-INF/lib/`

    D. `/`

11. Which of the following best defines authentication?

    A. The means used to prove that information has not been modified by a third party while in transit.

    B. This is access control where interactions with resources are limited to collections of users or programs for the purpose of enforcing integrity, confidentiality, or availability constraints.

    C. You have permission to use a given page.

    D. The means by which communicating entities prove to one another that they are acting on behalf of specific identities.

12. What is the best definition for auditing?

    A. This is access control where it defines who can interact with what resources.

    B. Maintaining a record of Web application activity.

    C. This is a check of the Web application when it is used for commercial transactions.

    D. This prevents Web site attacks.

13. What two statements are true regarding the following code snippet?

```
<servlet-mapping>
  <servlet-name>CustomerSupport</servlet-
➥name>
  <url-pattern>/CustomerSupport</url-
➥pattern>
</servlet-mapping>
```

    A. It defines how you refer to a given servlet in code.

    B. It is a subelement of `<servlet>`.

    C. It defines how you refer to a given servlet from a client.

    D. It is a subelement of `<webapp>`.

APPLY YOUR KNOWLEDGE

Answers to Review Questions

1. A Web application is a collection of servlets, HTML pages, classes, and other resources that make up a complete application on a Web server. It can be bundled and run on multiple containers from multiple vendors. See "Introduction."
2. Remember that the deployment descriptor of a Web application is the web.xml file. It defines many aspects of the Web application. See "Web Application and Web Archive Structure."
3. There are four types of authentication, namely, BASIC, DIGEST, FORM, and CLIENT-CERT. See "Authentication Types."
4. You use a WAR file because Web applications can be packaged and signed into a Web ARchive format (WAR) file using the standard Java Archive tools. When packaged into such a form, a META-INF directory will be present that contains information useful to Java Archive tools. See "Web Application and Web Archive Structure."
5. Given a set of business logic exceptions, you can configure the deployment descriptor to handle each exception, you can use a `RequestDispatcher` to forward the request to an error page, and you can specify the handling declaratively in the deployment descriptor. See "Web Application Exceptions."

Answers to Exam Questions

1. **A** and **C.** The servlet element establishes a mapping between a servlet name and the fully-qualified name of the servlet class. You would place this code in the WebApp deployment descriptor. See "Web Application and Web Archive Structure."
2. **C** and **D.** This is end user authentication using HTTPS (HTTP over SSL). This mechanism uses public key encryption that requires the user to possess a Public Key Certificate (PKC). This is the highest level security of the four here. See "Authentication Types."
3. **C.** The jar files go in the `/WEB-INF/lib/` directory. See "Web Application and Web Archive Structure."
4. **A** and **B.** The initialization parameters are defined in both the `context-param` and the `servlet` elements of the Web deployment descriptor. See "Deployment Descriptor Elements."
5. **A**, **B**, and **C.** All of these are elements except there is no `error` element. It should have been error-page. See "Deployment Descriptor Elements."
6. **A.** The error-page element, which defines what resource the container should use for a given exception.

```
<web-app>
   <error-page>
       <error-code>404</ error-code>
       <location> /404.html </location>
   </error-page>
</web-app>
```

   See "Web Application Exceptions."

7. **C.** web.xml is the deployment descriptor file. See "Web Application and Web Archive Structure."
8. **B.** You place your servlets and utility classes in `/WEB-INF/classes/`. See "Web Application and Web Archive Structure."

APPLY YOUR KNOWLEDGE

9. **D.** The security-role element contains the definition of a security role. The definition consists of an optional description of the security role, and the security role name. See "Deployment Descriptor Elements."

10. **A.** web.xml is the deployment descriptor file in `/WEB-INF/web.xml`. See "Web Application and Web Archive Structure."

11. **D.** Authentication is the means by which communicating entities prove to one another that they are acting on behalf of specific identities. In other words, it is the attempt to prove that you are really you. See "Authentication Types."

12. **B.** Maintain a record of Web application activity. For example, you can log resource accesses including times and requester IP and ID. This usually involves a log somewhere. See "Web Application Security."

13. **C** and **D.** When a request is received by the container it must determine which servlet should handle it. Using the deployment descriptor you can map certain paths (aliases) to a specific servlet. You define this mapping with the servlet-mapping element. The alias is appended after the context root in an HTTP requesst URL. See "Deployment Descriptor Elements."

Suggested Readings and Resources

1. Tomcat's deployment descriptor at `http://jakarta.apache.org/tomcat/tomcat-4.0-doc/appdev/deployment.html`.
2. The Java Web Applications Tutorial at `http://java.sun.com/webservices/docs/ea1/tutorial/doc/WebApp.html`.
3. O'Reilly's OnJava article Deploying Web Applications to Tomcat at `http://www.onjava.com/pub/a/onjava/2001/04/19/tomcat.html`.
4. Sun's excellent J2EE Tutorial at `java.sun.com/j2ee/tutorial/1_3-fcs/doc/J2eeTutorialTOC.html`.
5. BEA's WebLogic Deployment Descriptor at `http://edocs.bea.com/wls/docs61/programming/index.html`.
6. Deployment on JBoss at `http://www.jboss.org/online-manual/HTML/ch13s72.html`.
7. Servlet 2.3 Specifications and JavaDoc at `http://java.sun.com/products/servlet/download.html`.
8. J2EE DTDs at `http://java.sun.com/dtd/`.
9. Introduction to Web Applications in WebSphere Studio Application Developer at `http://www7b.boulder.ibm.com/wsdd/techjournal/0110_deboer/deboer.html`.

OBJECTIVES

This chapter covers the following Sun-specified objectives for the "Design Patterns" section of the "Sun Certified Web Component Developer For J2EE Platform" exam:

13.1 Given a scenario description with a list of issues, select the design pattern (Value Object, MVC, Data Access Object, or Business Delegate) that would best solve those issues.

- This objective wants you to understand how to apply patterns to problems. You are given a description of a problem and then asked to choose the pattern that would best solve that problem. For example, if told that you need to build an object to manage database queries, you would select the Data Access Object pattern.

13.2 Match design patterns with statements describing potential benefits that accrue from the use of the pattern, for any of the following patterns:

- **Value Object**
- **MVC (Model-View-Controller)**
- **Data Access Object**
- **Business Delegate**
- **Front Controller**

- This objective encompasses the definition of each pattern. Each pattern is defined at length, so you won't have difficulty answering these correctly. The idea is to know the patterns well enough to correctly match definition statements.

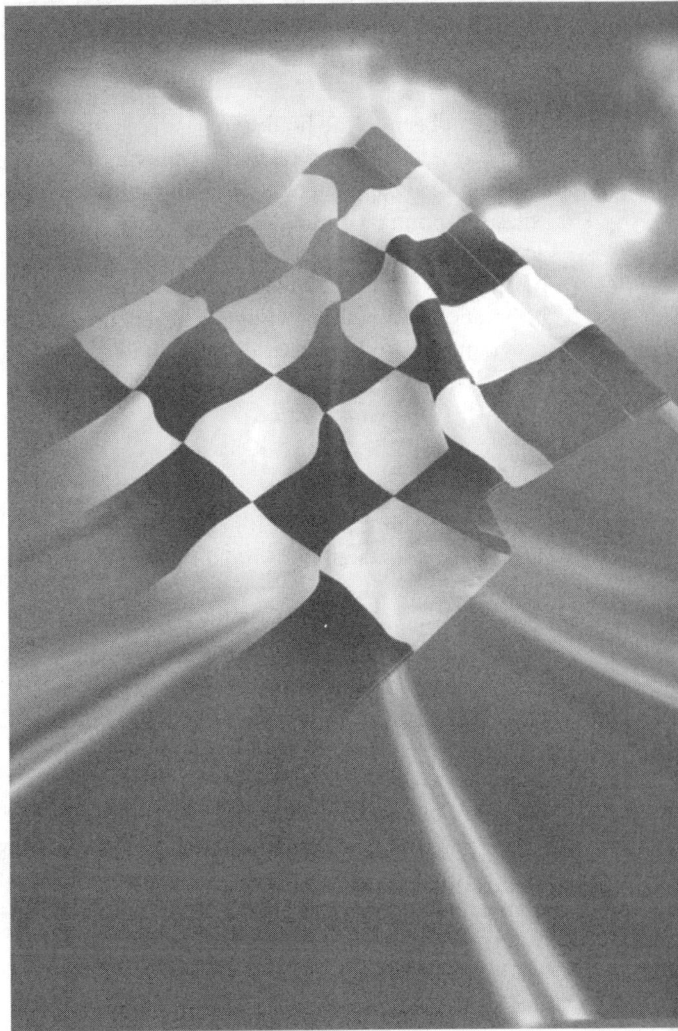

CHAPTER 11

Design Patterns

OBJECTIVES

- Have you been to the bookstore lately? New books on *patterns* are added weekly. The growing interest is about a new approach to designing software that is fast becoming a darling of the industry. I like the academic nature of the topic (this should come first), but some of the books on this subject are impractical. After all, most of the buyers now are programmers, so they need direct help with code. This chapter endeavors to demonstrate how to apply the theory to practice.

- Although there is a never-ending demand for software applications, underneath the new GUIs are largely just a few well known requirements such as how to access, filter, and view the data in a repository. These requirements have been met so many times that it is now known that there are good ways to do this and bad. In other words, there are patterns to the solutions, often referred to as *best practices*. Erich Gamma, Richard Helm, Ralph Johnson, and John Vlissides are affectionately known as the Gang of Four or simply GoF. They established design patterns as the preferred way to describe these best practices, an important aspect of software architecture and design. From GoF to now, industry experts have sifted through these so-called best practices, stripped them of non-essential details, and produced definitions for these common solutions, called *design patterns*. This chapter explains the four design patterns that you will encounter on the exam. It also goes a little beyond these four for those of you who want to understand them better.

OUTLINE

OUTLINE

Study Strategies

- As you read through this chapter, you should concentrate on the following key items:
  - What design patterns are
  - Which design patterns are used in servlets and JSP
  - How design patterns can make better software
- The best way to study these items is to read through the chapter and work each of the examples. Then answer the review and exam questions. If you get an answer wrong, study your answer and the correct answer and make sure that you understand the differences between them.

INTRODUCTION

In this chapter you'll learn about *design patterns*, a new approach to designing software that Sun is advocating engineers use for Java, especially J2EE. There is no API to know for this exam area. Instead, you'll learn the basics of design patterns so that you can use this knowledge to complete this section of the exam. Hopefully, this chapter will be so useful you'll apply it to your development assignments as well.

Whether you are a software manager, designer, engineer, or student, design patterns are the new foundation upon which to design and build software projects. This chapter helps you bridge the gap between the highly abstract GoF presentation, including the many books based on it, and the real-world challenges of writing code. If used as Sun suggests, and this chapter echoes, patterns become a core asset of any software shop. Patterns show the developer how to solve problems created by market and technology forces in a systematic way.

This chapter assumes you've read the previous chapters first and that you are very familiar with object-oriented programming, including the popular UML diagramming notation. This chapter describes the four pattern solutions named in the objectives. It also discusses patterns beyond the four. This bonus section is optional, but will probably help you understand the first four better. Certainly, you will encounter many more throughout your career as you address enterprise design needs.

DESIGN PATTERNS DEFINED

The term "pattern" comes from the architect Christopher Alexander who wrote several books on the topic, especially *A Pattern Language: Towns, Buildings, Construction* (Oxford University Press, 1977). Although he was interested in urban planning and building architecture, his notions were clearly useful in many areas. Alexander, a building architect, was the first to "codify" patterns for architecture. Then GoF applied them to software design. Alexander didn't invent the idea of patterns nor was he the first to see them in designs.

Of course, they were there before him, but his work on urban planning and building architecture isolated the idea better than anyone before him. Alexander was an architect extraordinaire. He is one of those rare people who take a step back and question why people do things the way they do. He gave the result of his inquiry the name *Pattern Language* and defined it at length in his seminal book by the same name.

While Alexander was thinking buildings and foundations, it became clear to many that his design patterns were abstract enough to be useful elsewhere. That is when the Gang of Four, as Erich Gamma, Richard Helm, Ralph Johnson, and John Vlissides are now known, applied his patterns to software in their classic *Design Patterns: Elements of Reusable Object-Oriented Software* (1995, Addison-Wesley). It took a while, but the GoF have started a ground swell. There are now dozens of books, and many more on the way, about design patterns.

Design patterns are often defined as "a solution to a problem in a context." This falls short of the abstract definition that experts prefer. Suppose you have an object that makes copies of files. What is the design pattern? We don't know yet, so let's throw in an object that copies the content of one text box to another. There is something about the copying that is the same between the two objects. Neither the files nor the text boxes differ, but the copying is the same. So, the sameness is copying. By itself this isn't a pattern, but we are on the way to finding one.

What are design patterns? Sun defines them in the following way: "A design pattern describes a proven solution to a recurring design problem, placing particular emphasis on the context and forces surrounding the problem, and the consequences and impact of the solution." It is like the old guy who doesn't say much. There is commotion in the car design room over how they can fit the chromed company logo on the back of the trunk lid as close to the key hole as possible. They are trying just above, below, then perhaps they go wild and go vertical… The old guy grows weary so he comes over to the young guns and, without a word, drills a hole in the logo and places the logo hole exactly centered over the key hole so that you can just stick a key into it. It doesn't look bad, either. They stare, and then nod in unison. From years of experience of doing back ends of cars, he knows that is the best way to handle it. It's a pattern the old guy knows, and now the kids just learned it.

Design Pattern Elements

There are many ways to define a pattern, but the classical way is to describe its elements, or the aspects of a pattern. There are several lists of elements in the literature today. I will use a dolled-up version of the GoF's approach.

All of them center on three base elements, namely, *context*, *problem*, and *solution*. The following are their definitions:

- *Context* is the recurring situation in which a problem to be solved is found.
- Problems are the so-called forces, such as marketing and technological forces, that occur in this context.
- Solution is the defined design that reorganizes or manipulates, some say resolves, the problem forces into a desired outcome within that context.

The design pattern is not only these three, but the relationship between the three and the formal language that describes the whole business. That is a lot of heady language that doesn't seem to touch earth and is certainly not on the exam. I'll say more on this at the end of the chapter if you care to regress to some intriguing musings. Presently, I'll list the elements.

Remember that context, problem, and solution are at the core. The remainder is my way of expanding these three in the hope of providing a few more handles to grab as a way to understand the essence of a given pattern. The purist will gawk, but so what, they aren't taking the exam. The pattern elements used in this book are as follows:

- Is—A direct explanation of what the pattern is, without jargon.
- Is Not—An attempt at contrasting the concept because it is often helpful to understand what something is by looking at what it isn't.
- Analogy—This provides a comparison based on general aspects. Analogies, hopefully, give you a way to connect what you already know to these patterns which may be new to you.
- Problem—A statement of the problem that describes the patterns raison d'etre and intent.

- Responsibility—This describes what the pattern is accountable for; the primary things it accomplishes.
- Intent [or goals and constraints]—These are the goals and objectives the pattern should reach within the given context.
- Primary Activity—Okay, a pattern is wonderful and all, but it has one thing it has to get done.
- Context—The conditions and environment in which the problem and its solution recur. In other words, where should you consider and apply this pattern?
- Motivation or Forces—Why bother? These are the forces that affect the context and the reason why you would use a pattern. This tells you about the advantages the pattern offers.
- Applicability—Which kinds of situations are good candidates for this pattern.
- Solution
    - Strategy—How you should go about applying this pattern.
    - Pseudo Code—This is pseudo-code to help you see how you might actually implement the pattern, to reduce the concept to practice.
- Consequences—This describes the result of using the pattern, the final state of the system. There are good and bad consequences of applying the pattern. It may solve one problem, but give rise to a new one.
- Known Uses—This tells you one or more examples of how this pattern is being used.
- Related Patterns—This names other patterns that are related by context, solution, or consequences. The related pattern may solve the same problem in another way or share the same context, but resolve different forces.
- Reference—This points you to a resource that will provide more material on the pattern.

PATTERNS ON THE EXAM

As mentioned, there are five patterns that you must know for the exam. They are Value Object, Data Access Object, Business Delegate, Front Controller, and MVC. If you see any other pattern name, ignore it unless the question is one of those about which one is not a pattern.

The following five definitions list more than you need to know about each one. However, it's hard to understand these patterns without this kind of detailed explanation. The end of the chapter questions represent what you can expect on the exam, but read these five definitions to get a feel for what patterns are in general and to understand these five in particular.

Value Object

This pattern provides the best way to exchange data across tiers or system boundaries, especially when there is network communication involved. This is a pattern that solves performance issues around network latency.

Is

This pattern is an object that encapsulates a set of values (namesake) that is moved across the boundary so that attempts to get the values of those attributes are local calls.

Is Not

This pattern is not a concrete object. You wouldn't use it to create, say, a car object. You could use it to hold values about a car though, such as the color and model of the car.

Analogy

This would be like placing several letters in a box to be mailed once a week instead of mailing the letters separately. The box is mailed once. When the box arrives, the mail carrier can just reach in the box for the next letter; she doesn't have to go back to the origin, which would take a long time. The problem is she doesn't know if the sender is still at the originating address anymore since the box has been delivered for some time.

Problem

In J2EE, server-resident business applications often use session beans and entity beans. The session beans are responsible for functionality that is involved in one-to-one transactions with the client. Contrast that with the entity beans, which are intended to handle persistent data. So, the client will make many calls to the session bean to get data. That represents a lot of traffic, potentially, to and from a remote location because the bean may be at a server there. Likewise, the session bean may make many calls to the entity bean getting and setting attributes. The Value Object pattern encapsulates the data fields of an entity bean; VO has nothing to do with session beans (except that it is usually a `session` method call that returns a VO, instead of a remote entity reference). By the way, this is EJB terminology, which is not on the exam—this is just an example.

This activity is inefficient. We need a way to eliminate all these potential network calls reducing overhead and providing a more direct access approach.

Responsibility

This pattern provides a mechanism to exchange many remote calls to local, direct calls.

Intent [or Goals and Constraints]

This pattern attempts to reduce the network overhead by minimizing the number of network calls to get data from the business tier.

Primary Activity

Used to collect remote data into an object that is sent to the client, so now the client makes local calls to get values rather than remote ones.

Context

Multi-tier applications that need to exchange sets of data between the client and server often.

Motivation or Forces

- J2EE applications often use enterprise beans. All calls to these beans are performed via remote interfaces to the bean due to Java's architecture. This introduces overhead.
- The frequency of reads is greater than updates because the client gets the data from the business tier for presentation.
- The client usually needs a set of data, not just one attribute.
- Client calls to enterprise beans accessed over the network affects WebApp performance because of the sum of network latency of multiple attribute access to the entity bean.
- Regardless of Java's bean architecture, it would be better to collect attributes into one object and get them from it rather than make invoking remote methods for the same information.

Applicability

This pattern is useful when you need a collection of data from a remote source or, more likely, when a client has to make several calls for data from entity beans.

Solution

- Strategy—Use a Value Object to encapsulate a collection of data so that it takes only one call to get or set the collection.
- Pseudo-code—Listing 11.1 is an example code snippet for this pattern.

LISTING 11.1

THE VALUE OBJECT PATTERN SKELETON PROGRAM

```
public class CustomerOrder implements java.io.Serializable
{

        // public members
    public int customerID;
    public int accountNumber;
    public int OrderNumber;
    public float OrderAmount;
```

continues

LISTING 11.1 *continued*

THE VALUE OBJECT PATTERN SKELETON PROGRAM

```
    // default constructor
    public CustomerOrder() {}

    // constructor accepting data values
    public CustomerOrder(int customerID,
    int accountNumber, int OrderNumber, float OrderAmount)
    {
       init(customerID, accountNumber,
            OrderNumber, OrderAmount);
    }

    // constructor to create a new VO based
    // using an existing VO instance
    public ContactVO(ContactVO contact)
    {
        init (contact.firstName,
        contact.lastName, contact.address);
    }
    // method to set all the values
    public void init(int customerID,
    int accountNumber, int OrderNumber, float OrderAmount)
    {
        this.firstName = firstName;
        this.customerID = customerID;
        this.accountNumber = accountNumber;
        this.OrderNumber = OrderNumber;
        this.OrderAmount = OrderAmount;
    }

    // create a new value object
    public CustomerOrder getData()
    {
        return new CustomerOrder(this);
    }
    // create a new value object
    public boolean setData()
    {
           boolean success = false;
           //get data from database
           //which sets the success flag

            return success;
    }
}
```

Consequences

- Simplifies Entity Bean and Remote Interface—Sun suggests using `getData()` and `setData()` methods on certain entity beans as a way to get and set a value object containing the set of attribute values. Calling the `getData()` method once replaces multiple calls to get methods. Likewise, the `setData()` method replaces many set calls.
- Using this pattern transfers a set of values in one method call improving overall performance, especially over the network. It represents coarse versus fine-grained interfaces.
- The client can update, delete, and read the values that are now local at will. When done, it can update the data source in one call. However, there may be a problem with synchronization as the other clients won't know about the changes until the update call. In the case of updates, there can be two conflicting update calls by two clients, so this must be synchronized somehow.

Known Uses

The `ResultSet` of JDBC is a collection of data returned from the data source resulting from a query. The data is now local in the `ResultSet` object so all calls to it are local rather than many calls to the data source directly.

Related Patterns

- Aggregate Entity that uses Value Object to get data across tiers.
- Session Façade, which is the business interface for clients of J2EE applications. This pattern often uses value objects as an exchange mechanism with participating entity beans.
- Value List Handler is another pattern that provides lists of value objects constructed dynamically by accessing the persistent store at request time.
- Value Object Assembler builds composite value objects from different data sources. The data sources are usually session beans or entity beans that may be requested to provide their data as value objects.

References

`http://developer.java.sun.com/developer/restricted/patterns/ValueObject.html`. This page is only available to registered members of the Java Developer connection.

Data Access Object

The pattern provides the connection between the business logic tier and the resource (usually database or file) tier. The Data Access Object represents a general interface to the resources layer: It handles all calls to it. JDBC is an example of this.

Is

This pattern is an object that encapsulates a set of behaviors for accessing databases, files, and other resources. This way you have only one API to deal with rather than a different one for every type of resource.

Is Not

This is not a pattern for a resource itself. It isn't a way to build a database or file manager, in other words.

Analogy

This is like using an ATM machine. The same interface will fetch the information requested from the back end, even though the bank changed database products the previous week so, of course, it reports a negative balance.

Problem

Applications often need to use persistent data. This data persists in many forms such as files, relational databases, XML storage, and other types of repositories. All these stores have different APIs. Interfacing with so many APIs presents a problem when designing clients.

Responsibility

This pattern provides a uniform API to any persistent data storage.

Intent [or Goals and Constraints]

This pattern attempts to consolidate the accessing of data from a complex source or set of sources to one object. This will reduce the network overhead by minimizing the number of network calls to get data, but the reduction of network traffic is not the primary intent.

Primary Activity

Getting and setting data from and to a permanent data source.

Context

Access methods to data vary between types of storage and vendor.

Motivation or Forces

Various parts of an application require access to persistent stores like databases and files. The APIs are inconsistent between types of stores and even between different vendors of the same type of storage. There needs to be a layer that has a uniform API to access these disparate data sources.

Applicability

Any application that requires access to several data source types or even an application that accesses only one, but may switch in the future. The SQL is encapsulated in the method. That way if the SQL or datasource change, the layers above won't because the API remains constant.

Solution

- Strategy—Use this pattern to design a Data Access Object that abstracts the access API to various data sources.

- Pseudo-code—The example shown in Listing 11.2 is small. The real class would likely have more SQL, but it does represent an interface that defines the API DAO for a single entity and uses an Abstract Factory to create the necessary implementation objects at runtime. Listing 11.2 is an example of this pattern.

LISTING 11.2

THE DATA ACCESS OBJECT PATTERN SKELETON PROGRAM

```
import java.sql.Connection;
import java.sql.ResultSet;
import java.sql.SQLException;
import java.sql.Statement;
import java.util.Collection;

/**
 * This class is an example of DAO because
 * it encapsulates the SQL calls made by other objects.
 * This layer maps the relational data stored in the
 * database to the objects needed by another layer.
 */
public class CustomerDAO
{
    private Connection con;

    public CustomerDAO(Connection con)
    {
        this.con = con;
    }

    public Customer getCustomer(String customerId)
                             throws SQLException
    {
    String sql = "select customerid, firstName, " +
    "lastName, from " +
    DatabaseNames.Customer_TABLE +
    " where customerid = '" + CustomerId + "'";
    Statement stmt = con.createStatement();
    ResultSet rs = stmt.executeQuery(sql);
    Customer cus = null;
    while (rs.next()) {
        int i = 1;
        String customerid = rs.getString(i++).trim();
        String name = rs.getString(i++);
        String descn = rs.getString(i++);
        cus = new Customer(customerid, firstName,
                                    lastName);
    }
    rs.close();
    stmt.close();
```

```
        return cat;
    }

    public Order getOrder(String OrderId) throws SQLException
    {

        Order order = new Order(Orderid);
        String sql =
            "select itemid, listprice, unitcost, " +
            "name, descn " +
            "from " + DatabaseNames.ITEM_TABLE +
            "from " + DatabaseNames.Order_TABLE + " where " +
            "Orderid = '" + OrderId + "'";

        Statement stmt = con.createStatement();
        ResultSet rs = stmt.executeQuery(sql);
        Order Order = null;
        while (rs.next()) {
            int i = 1;
            String itemid = rs.getString(i++).trim();
            double listprice = rs.getDouble(i++);
            double unitcost = rs.getDouble(i++);
            String attr1 = rs.getString(i++);
            String Orderid = rs.getString(i++).trim();
            String name = rs.getString(i++);
            String descn = rs.getString(i++);
            order.add(itemid, listprice, unitcost,
                                         name, descn);

        }
        rs.close();
        stmt.close();
        return order;
        }
}
```

Consequences

- Clients and components can now access data with the same API, which makes the variety of sources transparent and reduces complexity.
- This makes changing data sources easy and reduces errors.

Known Uses

At one level, JDBC uses an Abstract Factory technique to provide one API to many databases and types of files; the very essence of this pattern. However, the emphasis Sun places on this pattern is that of encapsulating the SQL so the implementation of actually querying the database is hidden from the next layer.

Related Patterns

- Abstract Factory [GoF]: Sun uses this factory for data access object strategy. They base it on the abstract factory method.

References

`http://java.sun.com/blueprints/patterns/DAO.html`

Business Delegate

This pattern reduces the dependency between tiers. It is an attempt to make tiers interchangeable so one can access the services of any other.

Is

This pattern is a proxy that hides the complexity of remote service lookup and error recovery. It makes it easier to communicate requests and results from one layer to another.

Is Not

This is not a pattern for a layer itself. It isn't a way for you to create a business logic component or structure. Rather, it is an interface to a tier so that you can change the underlying components and not disturb the presentation tier.

Analogy

This pattern is like an ambassador. Like all good ambassadors, it can relay a message from the host country to any other.

Problem

Whenever there is a dependency on a remote service, the likelihood of change between the caller and called increases. How can you reduce the chances of the layer depending on the remote service breaking should the remote service change? This pattern helps protect the local layer from changes made to the remote service. Perhaps the presentation tier interacts directly with a remote business logic layer.

What if the business services change and the old API becomes invalid? If this happens the presentation tier will break.

Responsibility

This delegate is the proxy between the local layer and the remote service layer. It is responsible for reliably allowing the front layer to access the remote service.

Intent [or Goals and Constraints]

This pattern isolates the presentation layer from changes in the business tier API.

Primary Activity

This pattern matches presentation component calls to the correct business tier methods.

Context

The current approach to multi-tier systems is to couple the presentation tier directly to the entire business service API; sometimes this coupling is made across a network.

Motivation or Forces

- Presentation-tier clients (including devices) need access to business services.
- The business tier API may change.
- The industry trend for large systems is to minimize coupling between presentation-tier clients and the business service API. This isolates the two so that a change in either side can be managed by the middle layer.
- There is a need for a cache between tiers.
- This pattern adds more work to building a system. Is this extra layer really necessary?

Applicability

Large systems change components often. There is often a change in the business tier that breaks the access portion of clients.

Solution

- Strategy—Sun says, "Use a Business Delegate to reduce coupling between presentation-tier clients and business services. The Business Delegate hides the underlying implementation details of the business service, such as lookup and access details of the EJB architecture."
- Sample code—Look up Java API for XML Messaging ("JAXM") and its use of XML messaging using SOAP. This reference will show you a very good example of JAXM using SOAP, which acts like a Business Delegate pattern (`http://java.sun.com/webservices/docs/ea2/tutorial/doc/JAXM.ws.html`).

Consequences

- Caching is always good between parts that exchange a lot of data.
- This pattern changes the interface with the intent of making the API more stable from the presentation tier perspective.
- This pattern will now handle any exceptions, whether from the business tier itself or from the plumbing between it and the requester.
- This pattern isolates the presentation and the business tiers from each other by adding a director between the two, making it is easier to manage changes on either side.

Known Uses

- B2B systems usually employ an XML exchange for communicating between disparate systems.
- Proxy services represent this pattern.
- Look up services usually represent this pattern, too.

- This pattern can be thought of as an underlying design feature of Java's overloading capability such as the `System.out.print()` group of methods. Using the same method name, you can print almost anything to the console, because the printing service handles the different data types. This pattern is bigger than that, but overloading illustrates the idea.

Related Patterns

- Service Locator Pattern—This pattern provides a common API for any business service lookup and access code.
- Proxy Pattern—Provides a stand-in for objects in the business tier.
- Adapter Pattern—You can use the Adapter pattern to provide coupling for disparate systems.

References

`java.sun.com/blueprints/patterns/BusinessDelegate.html`

Model-View-Controller (MVC)

The Model-View-Controller architecture compartmentalizes the data and business logic (model) from the presentation (view) from the user action interpreter (controller). This pattern is the hardest on the exam. The idea is closely related to the recent move from two-tier to three-tier architectures. This arrangement allows multiple views to share the same enterprise data model.

Is

This pattern is a clear functional separation of roles. It is a formalization of the data-business-presentation movement that dominated three-tier architectures over the last decade.

Is Not

This pattern is very abstract. It is not simply a front end to a datasource.

Analogy

This would be like an automobile. The speed of a car is affected by the accelerator pedal (Controller), the speed is shown by the speedometer (View), and the speed is manifested by the engine (Model).

Problem

Different views of the same data are a common need. Conversely, the same client needs access to different models.

Responsibility

This pattern carefully manages communication between the client and model data and functionality. It must allow changing the client or changing the model with minimal impact on the system.

Intent [or Goals and Constraints]

The main goal is separation of concerns. This pattern attempts to minimize the impact of changing any of the three pieces.

Primary Activity

This pattern decouples views from data and business logic; MVC interjects a controller between them, which interprets user actions into operations on the business logic and the selection of the next view to send to the user.

Context

An application is expected to support varying client and business logic tiers.

Motivation or Forces

- Various clients and data models are being developed. These two tiers need to talk to each other.
- Non-interface-specific code is duplicated in many applications.
- The same enterprise data will be accessed by different views: for example, HTML, WML, JFC/Swing, and XML.

- The same enterprise data will be accessed (requested, modified, and deleted) from various actions (HTML links, JFC/Swing events, SOAP XML calls).

Applicability

Although the primary purpose of MVC is for building UIs, it can be used to establish an analogous notification protocol between non-visual objects. The Observer/Observable objects in java.util were designed with this pattern in mind.

Solution

- Strategy—Use the Model-View-Controller architecture to decouple presentation from core data access functionality. Also, this pattern allows you to control the communication between them so that multiple views can see the same enterprise data model, or multiple data models can present to the same view. So, the types of Web components used in the WebMVC pattern are these: servlet as Controller/Dispatcher, JSP pages as Views, and Java classes (or EJBs) as Model.
- Pseudo-code—MVC is used for many things. For example, it has been used for Swing to build user interfaces where Sun uses the model as the underlying logical representation, the view as the visual representation, and the controller as the part that handles user input. When a model changes (the user modifies text in a text field), it notifies all views that depend on it (listeners). This allows you to present a single set of data in list, table, or simple text presentations. As you update the data model, the model notifies both views and gives each an opportunity to update itself. In this architecture, the controller determines which action to take when the user alters the model (types text into field). Please see: `http://developer.java.sun.com/developer/onlineTraining/GUI/Swing2/shortcourse.html#JFCMVC`.

Consequences

- Clients access a controller that accesses the model instead of the data directly.

- Another layer has to be built which adds work.
- It is easier to break a project into pieces because both the view and model developers are targeting the controller API.

Known Uses

Java uses MVC for JFC/Swing. Also, Struts and Velocity use this pattern as their underlying framework.

Related Patterns

- A very high-level pattern, whereas the others on the exam are lower-level. This one has few related patterns.

References

```
http://java.sun.com/blueprints/patterns/j2ee_patterns
/model_view_controller/index.html
```

Front Controller

This pattern presents one entry point to a Web site or service. It provides a centralized entry point that controls and manages Web request handling. It eliminates the dependency of the user on a direct resource. Suppose you wanted to get the latest version of the servlet specification. You would be better off going to a central page that presents options that change over time than bookmarking the servlet specification directly as that will break quickly.

Is

This pattern is a presentation controller that allows the resources to change without breaking all the bookmarks to a given resource. Many sites use this. For example, Microsoft often changes the content in its excellent developer's MSDN library. However, there is front end for it that rarely changes. This way, you can bookmark that front-end URL and not worry about what they do behind it.

Is Not

This is not a pattern for a data storage viewer. It isn't a way for you to control data retrieval. Rather, it is a steady interface to the underlying Web resources that behave as the presentation tier.

Analogy

This pattern is like a travel agent. On every trip you start by stopping at the agency. You tell the agent where you want to go and she will take care of the arrangements. The actual flight, train, bus, and hotel details change between trips, but she always gets there.

Problem

When the user accesses resources directly without going through a centralized mechanism, the resource may have moved. Also, each view is on its own and required to provide its own system services. Lastly, each view has to provide navigation, but this is a problem as it doesn't know about the context or the global site.

Responsibility

This controller must delegate the request to the proper resource and view.

Intent [or Goals and Constraints]

This pattern isolates the actual resources from direct access by the user.

Primary Activity

This pattern matches the correct resource to the request.

Context

Simplified Web sites expose all its resources directly. As a site grows, there comes a time when it is better to decouple the navigation from the resources. There needs to be a controller that manages the requests and decides which resource best satisfies the request.

Motivation or Forces

- It is better to have a central controller allocate shared resources rather than have individual resources fend for themselves independently.
- The location of resources may change.
- This pattern adds only a little more work to building a Web site at first.
- Multiple resources share common needs such as security (that is, authentication and authorization).

Applicability

Large Web sites especially benefit from a front controller.

Solution

- Strategy—Sun says, "Use a Controller as the initial point of contact for handling a request. The Controller manages the handling of the request, including invoking security services such as authentication and authorization, delegating business processing, managing the choice of an appropriate view, handling errors, and managing the selection of content-creation strategies."
- Sample code—This pattern can be used to centralize request processing and view selection. For example, the class `MainServlet` is the front controller for Sun's Java Pet Store sample application Web site. All requests that end with *.do are sent through the `MainServlet` for processing. Please see `http://java.sun.com/blueprints/code/jps11/src/com/sun/j2ee/blueprints/petstore/control/web/MainServlet.java.html`.

Consequences

- Caching is always good between parts that exchange a lot of data.
- This pattern changes the interface with the intent of making the API more stable from the presentation tier perspective.

- This pattern will now handle any exceptions, whether from the business tier itself or from the plumbing between it and the requester.
- This pattern isolates the presentation and the business tiers by adding a mediator between the two, making it easier to manage changes on either side.

Known Uses

- Servlet Front Strategy—This pattern is implemented as a servlet, which manages the aspects of request handling that are related to business processing and control flow. Because this strategy is not specifically related to display formatting, it is a bad idea to implement this component as a JSP page.
- Command and Controller Strategy—This strategy provides a generic interface to the helper components. The controller delegates responsibility to the helper components, which minimizes the coupling among these components.
- Logical Resource Mapping Strategy—In this case users request logical names rather than physical locations. This way the physical location can be mapped to the logical names dynamically, say, in a database or XML document.

Related Patterns

- View Helper Pattern—The Front Controller is combined with the View Helper pattern to provide containers for factoring business logic out of the view and to provide a central point of control and dispatch. Logic is factored forward into the front controller and back into the Helpers.
- Service to Worker—The Service to Worker pattern is the result of combining the View Helper Pattern with a Dispatcher, in coordination with the Front Controller pattern.
- Dispatcher View—The Dispatcher View pattern is the result of combining the View Helper Pattern with a Dispatcher, in coordination with the Front Controller pattern.

References

http://java.sun.com/blueprints/corej2eepatterns/Patterns/FrontController.html

PATTERNS BEYOND THE EXAM

The information presented in this section does not apply directly to the exam. The topic of patterns is deep so I thought it appropriate to provide a little more discussion, hoping that it will help you understand them better.

I hope this extra section will help you understand and apply Design Patterns to your software projects, whether you are a software manager, designer, engineer, or student. It bridges the gap between the highly abstract GoF presentation, including the many books based on it, and the real-world challenges of writing code. If used as this chapter suggests, patterns become a core asset of any software shop. This section of the chapter shows you how to solve problems created by market and technology forces in a systematic way.

One field of study precedes and is more mature than patterns. You can look to it for help with patterns. That field is *topology*. It says a donut and coffee cup are the same even though I eat a donut, but not a coffee cup (drunk friends don't count). Topologists ignore this difference. What you consider and what you don't determines how you think about something. Topology is an excellent place to turn to if patterns are still foggy. Don't worry, topology is worse so you'll forget your pattern headaches.

Overlooking the context and forces aspects of patterns, how are they like topology? More to the point, how do we define a pattern at all? One way is to use the concept of invariance. A pattern is something that doesn't vary when something else changes. Take an algebraic formula `A * B = C`. This formula rigorously defines a relationship between variables (elements and forces in patterns). The values of A, B, and C vary, but the relationship between them is fixed. The defined relationship is the pattern.

Back to topology, the donut and coffee cup have a hole. No matter how much you sit on your donut it still has a hole. Topology doesn't care if you stretch and twist, but you can't tear.

If your cup was made of plastic then you could warm it gently and, with a little effort, form it into a donut where the handle now becomes the center hole. Likewise, before you cook it, you could take a donut shaped dough ring and shape it like a cup where the center hole becomes the handle. Then cook it. So, the hole is invariant and makes the two equal topologically.

In software, what is invariant? The rules for making an interface that consistently accesses resources (that is, the database) should be invariant. These rules, and their explicit description, represent a pattern. So far, no one has determined how to rigorously define aspects of software so that we could declare a formal language to describe patterns. UML is a recent improvement toward this end.

I would like to define patterns as a named design strategy and model outlining solutions that address a set of responsibilities in a popular context. It's a guide that should survive functional changes handled at the implementation level. The set of responsibilities recurs; it is not a rare situation and addresses many circumstances at once. The context is popular, not an obscure one, which insures that it is worth the effort. Patterns give a rationale for their context of applicability.

Good design starts with requirements (wish list), moves to responsibilities (a set of objects that fulfill requirements), and ends with functionality (behavior within objects that meets responsibilities). The requirements are given to the designer while the functionality is in the details of an implementation. Between these are the responsibilities—the focus of patterns.

A pattern canonizes a design approach for a set of responsibilities. We could propose Screen as a pattern where it defines how to design user interfaces. Indeed, computers could use better interfaces, but Screen is so broad and encompasses so many responsibilities that it loses utility. At the other extreme we could propose a pattern named Choice where it defines how to write code that makes decisions (that is, switch). It would provide some guidance beyond using a `switch` statement, but Choice is too close to implementation, too narrow in scope, and tries to address a responsibility that occurs in too many contexts. Another bad candidate would be `MyCompany` Customer Manager, which addresses the need to manage one particular company's flat file database that stores customer information. Although it is complex, too few programmers would use it because it deals with a proprietary situation.

Real patterns are between all these. For example, the Façade Pattern tells you how to design one interface that acts as a mediator for many others. It reduces to one the number of interfaces a client faces, rather than many. The Façade defines a parent interface, making a subsystem easier to use. The Façade has fewer responsibilities than Windows and `MyCompany` Customer Manager. It has a context encountered by more programmers than `MyCompany` Customer Manager. It is bigger than Choice. Finally, it is useful because it is easily applied to many programming assignments.

Sample Pattern

The following pattern is of my own definition. I have many of them, but they are not proven, so be careful before you try to use this one. However, I offer it to you as an example of how approaching software design through patterns can make sharing ideas more efficient, clearer, and easier to test.

Name

`Transcoder`

Summary

Defines how to convert a message in one code to another (HTML to WML, ASCII into XML, XML-XSL-HTML).

The need to change how we encapsulate messages, change how they are encoded, occurs often in software engineering. We want a clear plan on how to achieve these conversions to avoid problems later. Also, we want to canonize what is common between converting HTML to WML and XML-HTML, indeed most code-to-code conversions. Transcoding is a complicated process that can involve both mapping tables and algorithmic mapping, so we need a concise blueprint.

Although translation is older (Sumerians needed to talk to the Acadians and later Babylonians to Egyptians), transcoding is old also. From ancient times governments needed a way to convert between number systems or accounting standards within their own language. The most likely situation will involve XML where the input XML has one schema and the output requires a different schema. Also, many scenarios require conversion between XML and other encodings like ASCII and HTML.

Is

This pattern is simply a translator for code.

Is Not

Its focus is not formatting, although it may include formatting.

Analogy

Telegraph operator converts English into Morse Code.

Problem

Describes the design issues faced by the developer when translating a message encoded one way into another code. One current problem is how to convert a message in ASCII or XML to HTML.

Responsibility

Ensure meaning encoded one way completely transfers when encoded another way and is recoverable.

Intent [or Goals and Constraints]

Code-neutral mechanism for converting between codes.

Primary Activity

Code-to-code translation.

Context

Application clients need to exchange data with enterprise systems and with each other.

Motivation or Forces

- Message consumers vary in their interpretation capabilities.
- What consumers do with delimiters varies (HTML presents them).
- Some consumers mingle processing with parsing.

- The business service API may change as business requirements evolve.
- Need to decouple code details from message handling, thus hiding the underlying implementation details of the service, such as lookup and access. SOAP and Web services are examples.

Applicability

Exchanges, message store and forward services, viewers.

Solution

- Structure. The structure is described in Figure 11.1.

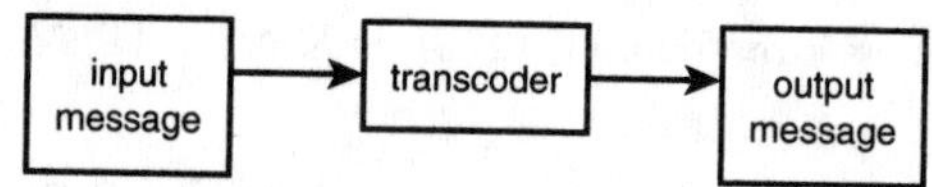

FIGURE 11.1
The structure of the Transcoder pattern.

- Strategy—To codify the translation of an input in one schema to an output in another schema.
- Implementation— Have the class that manages the transcoding contain an abstract class that has abstract methods specifying how to obtain the input source, perform the conversion, and make available the resultant output source. Each derived class implements the appropriate conversion algorithm.
- Pseudo-code—This controller receives a code document, the type of code it is, and the type of code it expects. In Listing 11.3, the sample converts between three commerce XML standards. You could more easily take XML documents (`mathML`, `musicML`, and so on) and convert them to HTML using XSL. This scenario is far more popular. However, to avoid muddying the waters with a code to a presentation code (Hey! That is presentation, not code.) objection, we will do a simple code-to-code translation. Also, notice that the conversions are within a specific category. You certainly could convert between, say, `mathML` and `voiceML`, where you could describe the formulas. Our math friends might like that, but it would be hard to do.

LISTING 11.3

The Transcoder Pattern Skeleton Program

```
/**
 * Translates one code to another. Meaning is not altered.
 */
public class Transcoder {

    private int sourceSchema;
    private int outputSchema;
    private String source;
    private String output;
    private Reader reader;

    /*
     * set of XML business documents and their
     * components by Commerce One Inc.
     * http://www.xcbl.org/
     */
    private static final int xCBL = 1;

    /*
     * ediML ANSI 4010 850 XML Message
     * components by GE Global Exchange Services
     * http://www.xml.org/xml/schema/90a9a94b/AN4850.DTD
     */
    private static final int ediML = 2;

    /*
     * FedEx Trade Networks is XML mark-up to encapsulate
     * all the information contained in EDI.
     */
    private static final int FedEx = 3;

    /*
     * ebXML is a framework, not a spec for, say, invoices
     * shown for interest. You could do ebXML to SOAP.
     */
    //private static final int ebXML = 4;

    /**
     * Default constructor.
     */
    public Transcoder() {}

    /**
     * Sets the source schema.
     *
     * @param sourceSchema Schema of source code.
     */
    public void setSourceSchema(int originSchema)
    {
        this.sourceSchema = originSchema;
    }
```

continues

LISTING 11.3 *continued*

THE TRANSCODER PATTERN SKELETON PROGRAM

```
/**
 * Sets the source code.
 *
 * @param source code to be translated.
 */
public void setSource(String origin)
{
  //perhaps preprocess source
  switch (sourceSchema)
  {
     case xCBL:
        //do something with xCBL
        break;
     case ediML:
        //do something with ediML
        break;
     case FedEx:
        //do something with FedEx
        break;
     case ebXML:
        //do something with ebXML
        break;
     default:
        //do something else
        break;
  }

    this.source = origin;
}

/**
 * Sets the output code.
 *
 * @param outputSchema The schema to translate into.
 */
public void setOutputSchema (int outputSchema)
{
    this.outputSchema = outputSchema;
}

/**
 * Sets the output code.
 *
 * @param output The code string that was translated.
 * This would be used internally by the reader.
 */
public void setOutput(String output)
{
```

```
        //perhaps postprocess output
        switch (outputSchema)
        {
           case xCBL:
              //do something with xCBL
              break;
           case ediML:
              //do something with ediML
              break;
           case FedEx:
              //do something with FedEx
              break;
           case ebXML:
              //do something with ebXML
              break;
           default:
              //do something else
              break;
        }

          this.output = output;
      }

      /**
       * Set the Reader to be used for the Source.
       *
       * @param reader A valid Reader or the code.
       */
      public void setReader(Reader reader)
      {
          this.reader = reader;
      }


      /**
       * get the Reader to be used for the Source.
       */
      public boolean translate()
      {
          //process source with reader, the real work
          boolean successfullyRead Source = reader(source,
                                 inputSchema, outputSchema);
          if (successfullyRead)
          {
              output = reader.getTranslation();
          } else
          {
              output = null;
          }

          return successfullyRead;
      }
}
```

Consequences

- This pattern defines a family of transcoding algorithms.
- You must invoke all conversions the same way.
- Should it handle converting one DB schema to the schema of another DB? It is not intended to handle crossing mediums on it own (as it needs to be combined with another pattern for that).

Known Uses

The best example of this pattern is XSL. Its whole purpose in life is to convert one XML schema into another.

Synonyms

translator, transcripter

Glossary

- Coupling—High probability that a change in one module will require change in other modules.
- Code—Delimiting a message in a way that enables the definition, transmission, validation, and interpretation of data among applications, systems, and organizations.
- XML—Extensible Markup Language, a specification developed by the W3C.

Related Patterns

Strategy pattern. You could also have a factory of translators.

References

None.

CHAPTER SUMMARY

In this chapter, you were introduced to *Design Patterns*, a fundamentally sound approach to designing applications. For example, Swing GUIs are built with the Model-View-Controller pattern. You learned how to think about patterns, the problems they solve, and how they work. Finally, your familiarity with the four patterns listed in the objectives will help you answer the related questions on the exam.

KEY TERMS

- JFC/Swing architecture
- Design Patterns
- Model-View-Controller
- Value Object
- Data Access Object
- Front Controller
- Business Delegate

APPLY YOUR KNOWLEDGE

Review Questions

1. What is a design pattern?
2. Give an example of a pattern used in Java.
3. Where did patterns come from and who invented them?
4. Why should you use patterns?
5. What is the primary benefit of patterns?

Exam Questions

1. Which design pattern has as its primary responsibility to decouple presentation and service tiers, and a central director?

    A. Value Object

    B. Composite View

    C. Business Delegate

    D. Model-View-Controller

2. Which design pattern has as its primary responsibility to exchange data between tiers?

    A. Value Object

    B. Composite View

    C. Business Delegate

    D. Model-View-Controller

3. Which design pattern has as its primary responsibility to abstract data sources and provide transparent access to the data in these sources?

    A. Value Object

    B. Data Access Object

    C. Business Delegate

    D. Model-View-Controller

    E. None of the above

4. Which design pattern has as its primary responsibility to isolate the presentation and the business tiers from each other by adding a director between the two, making it is easier to manage changes on either side?

    A. Session Facade

    B. Data Access Object

    C. Business Delegate

    D. Model-View-Controller

    E. Aggregate Entity

5. Which one of the following is most likely used for cache?

    A. Value Object

    B. Data Access Object

    C. Business Delegate

    D. Cache Object

    E. Aggregate Entity

6. Which design pattern acts as a switchboard, dispatching incoming requests to the correct resource?

    A. Value Object

    B. Data Access Object

    C. Business Delegate

    D. Front Controller

APPLY YOUR KNOWLEDGE

7. Which design pattern is most likely to care about RDBMS, OODBMS, and flat files?

   A. Value Object

   B. Data Access Object

   C. Business Delegate

   D. Cache Object

   E. Aggregate Entity

8. Which design pattern does the following force most affect?

   Persistent storage APIs vary between vendors, which causes a lack of uniform APIs to address the requirements for accessing storages.

   A. Value Object

   B. Data Access Object

   C. Business Delegate

   D. Cache Object

   E. Aggregate Entity

9. Which design pattern has as its primary role to provide control and protection for the business service?

   A. Value Object

   B. Data Access Object

   C. Business Delegate

   D. Cache Object

   E. Aggregate Entity

10. Which design pattern is most likely to be used as a proxy?

    A. Business Delegate

    B. Data Access Object

    C. Model-View-Controller

    D. Value Object

11. Which design pattern reduces the number of remote network method calls required to obtain the attribute values from the entity beans?

    A. Business Delegate

    B. Data Access Object

    C. Model-View-Controller

    D. Value Object

12. Which design pattern that usually is a good candidate to work with entity beans becomes less useful when a cache is used to persist data?

    A. Business Delegate

    B. Data Access Object

    C. Model-View-Controller

    D. Value Object

Answers to Review Questions

1. Sun says, "A design pattern describes a proven solution to a recurring design problem, placing particular emphasis on the context and forces surrounding the problem, and the consequences and impact of the solution." See "Design Patterns Defined."

2. Design patterns abound in Java as Sun has made a point of using them in the architecture of Java. For example, the Swing architecture uses MVC. `javax.swing.JComponent`, which extends `java.awt.Container`, and uses the Model-View-Controller pattern. See "Design Patterns Defined."

APPLY YOUR KNOWLEDGE

3. Alexander, a building architect, invented patterns and then GoF applied them to software design. We have been refining the idea ever since. See "Introduction."

4. Patterns formalize design strategy, which benefits from the knowledge and experience of other people who understanding contexts, forces, and solutions and the relationship among the three. See "Introduction."

5. Good patterns are more reusable than code. See "Introduction."

Answers to Exam Questions

1. **D**. The Model-View-Controller pattern has as its primary responsibility to decouple presentation and data/business logic tiers, by using a director or switchboard between them. See "Model-View-Controller (MVC)."

2. **A**. The Value Object pattern has as its primary responsibility to exchange data between tiers. Although the Business Delegate and Model-View-Controller also do this, it isn't their primary responsibility. See "Value Object."

3. **B**. The Data Access Object pattern has as its primary responsibility to abstract data sources and provide transparent access to the data in these sources. The Business Delegate and Model-View-Controller may do so, but the Data Access Object always does this. See "Data Access Object."

4. **D**. The Model-View-Controller pattern has as its primary responsibility to minimize the impact of changing the client or business tier. Remember that this is a very high-level pattern, so it often uses other patterns. See "Model-View-Controller."

5. **A**. The Value Object pattern is most likely used for cache. Notice that its whole purpose is to collect data from somewhere far and bring it close in a neat package. The Data Access Object and Business Delegate often actually use a Value Object underneath. The Cache Object is fiction and the Aggregate Entity is not one of the four that you might see on the exam. See "Value Object."

6. **D**. The front controller pattern acts as a switchboard, dispatching incoming requests to the correct resource. See "Front Controller."

7. **B**. The Data Access Object design pattern is one that deals with RDBMS, OODBMS, excel, flat files, and more. This is pattern you use to isolate the access API from the actual data repository implementation. Value Object and Business Delegate don't do this. The other two patterns mentioned are distracters. See "Data Access Object."

8. **B**. The Data Access Object design pattern is affected most by varying persistent storage APIs due to different vendors and non-uniform APIs to address the requirements to access storages. Whenever you see the word *persistent,* think Data Access Object design pattern. See "Data Access Object."

9. **C**. The Business Delegate design pattern has as its primary role to provide control and protection for the business service. Although you can't just ignore the rest of the question, normally when a question focuses on the business service, think Business Delegate design pattern. See "Business Delegate."

APPLY YOUR KNOWLEDGE

10. **A.** The Business Delegate design pattern is most likely to be used as a proxy. Its whole purpose is being the mediator between a business service and the rest of the world, especially, but not limited to, clients. This is what proxies do, too. See "Business Delegate."

11. **D.** The Value Object design pattern reduces the number of remote network method calls required to obtain the attribute values from the entity beans. Although the four patterns in the answers do this, it's the main reason for using a Value Object. See "Value Object."

12. **B.** The Data Access Object design pattern is usually a good candidate to work with data that is remote or and costly to query often, but becomes a bad choice with container-managed persistence. This is tricky because the container often, but not always, will persist data as a primary function. See "Data Access Object."

Suggested Readings and Resources

1. J2EE Design Patterns home page (`http://java.sun.com/blueprints/patterns/j2ee_patterns/index.html`).
2. Sun Java Center J2EE Pattern article (`http://developer.java.sun.com/developer/technicalArticles/J2EE/patterns/`).J2EE Patterns Catalog (`http://developer.java.sun.com/developer/restricted/patterns/J2EEPatternsAtAGlance.html`).
3. Sun's Catalog of 15 J2EE Patterns (`http://java.sun.com/blueprints/corej2eepatterns/Patterns/index.html`).
4. Sun's MVC definition (`http://java.sun.com/blueprints/patterns/j2ee_patterns/model_view_controller/index.html`).
5. A good Patterns home page (`http://hillside.net/patterns/`).
6. "Designing Enterprise Applications with the J2EETM Platform." An excellent book available free online at `java.sun.com/blueprints/guidelines/designing_enterprise_applications_2e/app-arch/app-arch2.html#1106026`.

PART II

FINAL REVIEW

Becoming a Sun Certified Web Component Developer

The Fast Facts listed in this chapter provide the means to quickly review facts that are relevant to the Java 2 Programmer exam. Review these facts to identify any potential gaps in your understanding of the points covered in Chapters 3 through 11. (Chapter 1 is a study plan for the exam and Chapter 2 is an overview. Neither chapter presents any technical information.) You can also use these facts as a last-minute refresher before taking the exam.

These facts provide a rapid review of the material presented in Chapters 3 through 11. However, this information is no substitute for the actual material that is covered in these chapters.

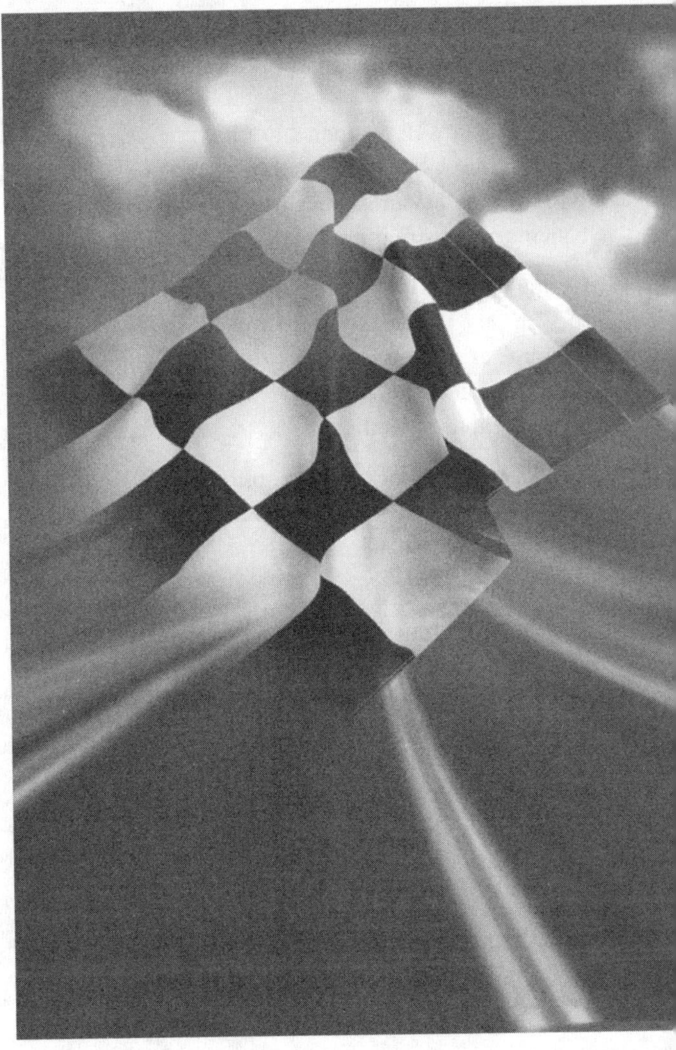

Fast Facts

310-080

Chapter 3, "JSP and Servlet Overview"

The Internet primarily uses the TCP/IP protocol.

We use Hypertext Transfer Protocol (HTTP) to shuttle HTML documents back and forth over the Internet. With HTML running over HTTP, an end-user can browse files housed on a distant server.

The HTTP protocol is a request/response scheme where a client sends a request to the server (in this case, a servlet container). There are four major portions of this request, namely, a request method (`GET`, `POST`...), URI (`www.que.com`), and protocol version (HTTP/1.1), and finally a MIME-like message.

According to the standard, HTTP/1.1 (HTTP uses a `"<major>.<minor>"` numbering scheme) is "an application-level protocol for distributed, collaborative, hypermedia information systems." These error codes have been used by the World Wide Web since 1990.

A servlet is a Web component written in Java that runs in a container. It generates content for HTML clients (HTML, images and so forth). It is pure Java, so the benefits and restrictions of regular Java classes apply.

Containers (servlet engines) are plug-ins or extensions to Web servers that run inside the JVM. Servlets look the same as static Web pages (just a URL to the browser) to the client, but are really complete programs capable of complex operations.

The servlet container is an extension of a Web server. Similarly, JSP is like ASP and PHP. A servlet functions like these, but the language is Java.

The servlet architecture makes the container manage servlets through their lifecycle. The container invokes a servlet upon an HTTP request, exposing to the servlet several objects storing information about the request and the container configuration.

JSP are a mixture of HTML and Java. JSPs are converted to servlets before the container runs them.

CHAPTER 4, "SERVLET CONTAINER MODEL"

The first time a servlet is loaded, the container calls your servlet's `init()` method, if there is one. Notice that it gets called only once. The container will call your `service()` method each time a request is received for your servlet. The `HttpServlet` class, which you must extend in your servlet, already has this method so you don't have to write one. The `service()` method then passes the request to the appropriate method (usually `GET` to retrieve data or `POST` to submit form data) such as the `doGet()` method if it is a `GET` request, or the `doPost()` method if it is a `POST` request.

The `doXXX()` methods are the ones you need to override and where you will spend most of your effort. The servlet processes the request (code you write in `doGet()` or `doPost()`), returning the HTML to the container. The container sends that string back to the browser.

`GET` is the most common type of browser request. The `GET` method retrieves the information identified by the `Request-URI`.

The `POST` type request is most often used by HTML forms. The method that processes it has the following syntax (all `doXXX` methods have this signature):

```
public void doPost(HttpServletRequest request,
            HttpServletResponse response)
        throws IOException, ServletException
       { //your code here}
```

The `PUT` type request is a means of uploading files to the server. It is not used as much as the `GET` or `POST` methods.

The types of events that generate a `GET` type of request are clicking a hyperlink, changing the address directly by typing in the address text box on a browser or application that has HTML functionality, and submitting an HTML form where the method header is set to `GET`, as in `'method=get'`.

The characteristics of the `GET` method are as follows:

- Gets information such as a simple HTML page or the results of a database query.
- Supports query strings. Servers usually limit query strings to about 1000 characters.
- Allows bookmarks.

The characteristics of the `POST` method are as follows:

- Sends information to the server such as form fields, large text bodies, and key-value pairs.
- Hides data because it isn't passed as a query string, but passed instead in the message body.
- Sends unlimited length data as part of its HTTP request body.
- Disallows bookmarks.

The `HEAD` method returns the same header lines that a `GET` method would return; however, no body or content is returned.

The primary benefit of the `HEAD` method is message size. The `HEAD` method receives and returns very small messages.

The interface that defines the form parameter methods is `ServletRequest`.

The four methods associated with getting parameters are as follows:

- `getParameter(String)`. You use this method if you know the particular parameter name. It returns the value of a request parameter as a string, or returns null if the parameter does not exist. Use this method when you are sure the parameter has only one value, otherwise use `getParameterValues()`. Be careful, if you use this method with a multi-valued parameter, you won't get an error. You will get the first value in the array returned by `getParameterValues()`.
- `getParameterMap()`. You use this method to create a map of the form parameters supplied with this request.
- `getParameterNames()`. This one returns an enumeration of `String` objects containing the names of the parameters contained in this request, or an empty enumeration if the request has no parameters.
- `getParameterValues(String)`. This method returns an array of the `String` values corresponding to a given parameter, or null if the parameter does not exist. If the parameter has a single value, the array has a length of 1.

A Web application includes many parts; it rarely is just one class or file. It can be a combination of JSP pages, Servlets, tag libraries, Java beans, and other class files. The Java Virtual Machine creates a memory box for all these called a `ServletContext` object, which maintains information (context) about your Web application.

Context means application scope. The `getInitParameter` and `getInitParameterNames` methods retrieve context-wide or application-wide (Web application) parameters. The `getInitParameter` method returns a string containing the value of the parameter (you provide the name), or returns null if the parameter does not exist.

The `getInitParameterNames` method retrieves the names of the context's initialization parameters as an enumeration of `String` objects.

If you want to open a binary file in a browser from a servlet, you have to write the file to the servlet's output stream, as follows:

```
ServletOutputStream out =
res.getOutputStream();
```

You set the file type in the response object using one of the standard MIME (Multipurpose Internet Mail Extension) protocols such as `response.setContentType("text/html");`.

The `request` object has the `sendRedirect` method, which sends a temporary redirect response to the client and includes a new location URL. You can use relative or absolute URLs because the servlet container translates relative URLs to an absolute URL before sending the response to the client.

When a browser hits a URL with a servlet at the other end, the servlet container creates an `HttpServletRequest` object. It passes this object as an argument to the servlet's service methods (`doPut()`, `doGet()`, and `doPost()`). It also creates the response object; both are passed as arguments.

The session scope includes all hits from a single machine (multiple browser windows if they share cookies). Servlets maintain state with sessions. A session is multiple hits from the same browser across some period of time.

You can get information from the servlet container such as its major and minor version, the path to a given servlet, and more. The following list summarizes the additional methods you might use from the `ServletContext` API:

- `getAttributeNames()`: Returns an `Enumeration` object containing the attribute names available within this servlet context.
- `getContext(String uripath)`: Returns a `ServletContext` object that corresponds to a specified URL on the server.
- `getInitParameter(String name)`: Returns a string containing the value of the named context-wide initialization parameter, or null if the parameter does not exist.
- `getInitParameterNames()`: Returns the names of the context's initialization parameters as an enumeration of `String` objects, or an empty enumeration if the context has no initialization parameters.
- `getNamedDispatcher(String name)`: Returns a `RequestDispatcher` object that acts as a wrapper for the named servlet.
- `getRequestDispatcher(String path)`: Returns a `RequestDispatcher` object that acts as a wrapper for the resource located at the given path.

The servlet lifecycle is not obvious. The container calls three methods, namely, `init()`, `service()`, and `destroy()`, in that order.

Remember, the `init()` method may be called when the server starts (telling web.xml to load the servlet upon startup), it may be called when first requested, and sometimes it is called via the container-management console as part of the server administration.

The `init()` method will only be called once per servlet instance and throws a `ServletException` if anything goes wrong.

The `destroy()` method, like `init()`, is called only once. It is called when the servlet is taken out of service and all pending requests to this specific servlet are done, including timeouts.

`RequestDispatcher` can perform programmatic server-side includes or send the whole request to another servlet or JSP with a forward using `RequestDispatcher.include(url)` and `RequestDispatcher.include(url)`, respectively.

There are three ways to get the `RequestDispatcher`. The first is through the `Context` with `ServletContext.getRequestDispatcher(java.lang.String)`. Another way is with `ServletContext.getNamedDispatcher(java.lang.String)`. This returns a `RequestDispatcher` object that acts as a wrapper for the named servlet (in web.xml, the Web application deployment descriptor). The final way is with `ServletRequest.getRequestDispatcher(java.lang.String)`.

CHAPTER 5, "SERVLET EXCEPTIONS"

Servicing requests from users on the Web means you will sometimes receive bad information. Also, you may make a mistake in your code. How do you handle these conditions in servlets? Chapter 5 discusses error and exception handling.

The main focus of this part of the exam is servlet exceptions and HTTP error codes, how they are used, and the effects they have on servlet behavior.

Internally, the `sendError()` and `setStatus()` methods are closely related. In fact, they both set the error message to be displayed by the client and the status code used by the client. The default status code is `HttpServletResponse.SC_OK` (internally this is `"OK"`); however, there are a few dozen standard codes.

Servlets are just as prone to logic errors and bugs as standalone applications. Java has a smart facility for handling them in both environments. To see an example of this please see Listing 5.1.

The `sendError` method sends an error response to the client using the specified status. Using this method clears the buffer. The server creates an HTML-formatted server error page. This page contains a default, or the message you provide as an argument. It also sets the content type to `"text/html"`, even if you changed this, but leaves cookies and other headers unmodified.

Once the `sendError` method is invoked, all buffered output will be discarded. If data has been written to the response buffer, but not returned to the client (not committed), the data is cleared and replaced with the data sent by the `sendError` method. The `sendError` method will commit the response, if it has not already been committed, and terminate it. Data written to the response afterward is ignored. However, if you write data to the response buffer and try to commit it *after* `sendError` has been invoked, an `IllegalStateException` will be thrown.

The `setStatus` method sets the status code for a given response. Use this method, instead of `sendError`, when there is no exception or serious error (for example, a forbidden page). If there is a serious error, the `sendError` method should be used, otherwise use `setStatus`. Like the `sendError` method, using this method clears the buffer, but leaves cookies and other headers unmodified.

The `log()` method writes a specified message to a servlet log file. This can be used as a debug log or simply an event log. The name and type of the servlet log file is specific to the servlet container. Tomcat allows you to modify this.

When you call the `sendError` method, the server responds with a status line containing the protocol version and a success or error code (this is what `sendError` affects directly). Of course, it also returns a MIME-like message containing server information, entity metainformation, and body content.

Calling `sendError` will throw an `IllegalStateException` exception if the response was already sent (committed). None of the other choices will throw this exception.

CHAPTER 6, "SESSION MANAGEMENT"

This section of the exam covers your familiarity with session objects within servlets.

The container generates a session ID. When you create a session, the server saves the session ID on the client's machine as a cookie. If cookies are turned off, it appends the ID in the URL. On the server, whatever you add to the session object gets placed in server memory. The server associates that object in memory with the session ID. When the user sends a new request, the session ID is sent, too. The server can then match the objects in its memory with that session ID. This is how you maintain client state.

The primary methods associated with sessions belong to the `HttpSession` interface. The following summarizes the session methods you need to know for the exam:

- `getAttribute(java.lang.String name)`: Returns an `Object` associated with that name that was stored in the session object.
- `getAttributeNames()`: Returns an `Enumeration` object that lists the names of the objects stored in the session object.
- `invalidate()`: Destroys a session. The session can't be referenced after this method has been called.
- `removeAttribute(java.lang.String name)`: Removes an attribute. It deletes it from the session object.
- `setAttribute(java.lang.String name, java.lang.Object value)`: You use this method to add objects to a session.

- `setMaxInactiveInterval(int interval)`: Specifies the time, in seconds, between client requests before the servlet container will invalidate this session.

The listener interface that allows an object to monitor changes to the attribute lists of sessions within a given Web application is `HttpSessionAttributeListener` extends java.util.EventListener. The methods that concern us here are as follows:

- `attributeAdded(HttpSessionBindingEvent se)`: This is the notification that an attribute has been added to a session.
- `attributeRemoved(HttpSessionBindingEvent se)`: This is the notification that an attribute has been removed from a session.
- `attributeReplaced(HttpSessionBindingEvent se)`: This is the notification that an attribute has been replaced in a session.

The six most frequent ways to invalidate a session are as follows:

- Calling the `HttpSession.setMaxInactiveInterval(int secs)` method and explicitly setting how many minutes the session will last after the last request from the client.
- The session will automatically be invalid after a certain time of inactivity. This is defined in the web.xml; and the default is vendor-specific.
- The user exits the browser. Although not explicitly sending the message to the server, the session ID is lost so the session dies due to the timeout.
- The session will expire when it is explicitly invalidated by a servlet by calling `invalidate()`.
- The server is stopped or crashes, unless the vendor implements a failover.
- You can set the default timeout in the web.xml file (`<web-app><session-config> <session-timeout>`).

You append the session ID (`JSESSIONID`) in URLs by calling the response's `encodeURL(URL)` (or `encodeRedirectURL()`) method on all URLs returned by a servlet. This method includes the session ID in the URL only if cookies are disabled; otherwise, it returns the URL unchanged.

To get the current session in a servlet, you call the `getSession()` method of `HttpServletRequest`. You have one parameter to think about. If you don't provide a Boolean, this method will return a session object if a session doesn't exists. The `no-arg` method always returns a non-null value (a new session object if it doesn't already exist). `getSession()` is the same as `getSession(true)`. However, if you provide a true Boolean, the container will automatically create a new session if it doesn't already exist.

You use the `setAttribute(java.lang.String name, java.lang.Object value)` method to add or change objects to a session.

Chapter 7, "JavaServer Pages (JSP) Technology Model"

JavaServer Pages is the Java 2 Platform, Enterprise Edition (J2EE) technology for building applications for generating dynamic Web content, such as HTML, DHTML, XHTML, and XML. The JavaServer Pages technology enables the easy authoring of Web pages that create dynamic content with maximum power and flexibility.

The JavaServer Pages Specification defines a JSP container as a system-level entity that provides life-cycle management and runtime support for JSP pages and servlet components.

The JSP container parses the JSP source and converts the entire JSP page (HTML becomes strings and Java source code embedded in a JSP page gets copied into methods) into a Java servlet class. The HTML text is converted to a set of `out.println()` statements in the order encountered. Finally, the container compiles this class into Java byte code. This is how JSPs are converted to servlets.

There are a few general syntax rules to keep in mind:

- All tags are case-sensitive.
- A pair of single quotes is equivalent to a pair of double quotes. This is generally true in HTML tags as well.
- Outside of quotes, spaces don't count, but inside they do. Also, spaces are not allowed between an equals sign and an attribute value.
- You can't mix the XML-version of JSP tags with regular JSP within a page. You don't place JSP inside an XML tag. Likewise, JSP will choke if you place an XML tag inside, say, a scriptlet.

Table FF.1 shows a snapshot of JSP syntax used in this chapter and on the exam.

TABLE FF.1
JSP SYNTAX SNAPSHOT

Element	*Syntax*	*Example*
HTML comment	<!-- comment -->	<!-- This HTML comment is passed through to the client -->
JSP comment	<%-- com ment --%>	<%-- This comment is ignored by the server --%>
Page directive	<%@ page [key]="[value]" %>	<%@ page import="java.util.*" %>
Declaration	<%! Declaration %>	<%! String name = new String ("Patricia"); %>
Expression	<%= expression %>	Your shopping cart total is: <b><%= shoppingCart.getTotal() %></b>.

Scriptlet	<% code %>	<% String password =
		request.getParameter("password");
		if (password == null)
		{
		%>
		Password is required, thank you.
		<%
		} else
		{
		%>
		Welcome to the member's area.
		<%
		}
		%>

Static include, parsed at compile-time	<%@ include file="file" %>	<%@ include file="welcome.jsp">
Dynamic include, request-time and not parsed	<jsp:include page="file" />	<jsp:include page="welcome.html" />

Directives are not used to display text; they don't contribute anything into the current out stream. There are three directives: include, page, and taglib. Each directive has several attributes that affect how the container processes the page.

The include directive is a placeholder that lets you include the text in another file. The text that is included by this directive is part of the translation into a servlet.

To simply add text from another file, but not parse it, use the XML equivalent <jsp:directive.include file="url"\>. This tag includes a file at request time instead of translation time; therefore, content is not parsed, but is included in place.

The page directive gives directions to the servlet engine about general setup of the page.

Scriptlets have access to the entire Java API.

An expression element contains Java code that is evaluated, converted to a string, and inserted into the output stream. Expressions are never terminated with a semicolon, which is a break with normal Java convention.

JSP allows you to use two forms of certain tag types. Table FF.2 offers a quick review of the XML equivalents you need to know.

TABLE FF.2
XML EQUIVALENTS TO CERTAIN JSP TAG TYPES

JSP Tag Type	*Syntax*	*XML*
Expression	<%=expression%>	<jsp:expression> expression </jsp:expression>
Scriptlet	<% yourCode %>	<jsp:scriptlet> yourCode </jsp:scriptlet>
Declaration	<%! yourCode %>	<jsp:declaration> yourCode </jsp:declaration>
page directive	<%@ page att="val" %>	<jsp:directive.page att="val"/>
include directive	<%@ include file="url" %>	<jsp:directive.include file="url"/>
Actions	None (XML only)	<jsp:useBean/> <jsp:setProperty/> <jsp:getProperty/> <jsp:include/> <jsp:forward/> <jsp:plugin/>

The following are the page directive attributes covered on the exam:

```
<%@ page
    [ import="{package.class | package.*},..." ]
    [ session="true|false" ]
    [ errorPage="relativeURL" ]
    [ isErrorPage="true|false" ]
%>
```

The `session` attribute indicates that the page is part of a session.

The `errorPage` attribute defines a URL that is processed when any `Throwable` object is thrown but not caught by a try-catch block in the page.

The `isErrorPage` attribute tells the container if that page is available to be an error page for another JSP page (the current page is referenced by the URL or path in another page's `errorPage` attribute).

In JSP you do not have to use the `page` directive for the default import list of java.lang.*, javax.servlet.*, javax.servlet.jsp.*, and javax.servlet.http.*. These are automatically available to you.

Table FF.3 offers a quick review of the JSP page lifecycle steps you need to know.

TABLE FF.3
JSP PAGE LIFECYCLE

JSP Process Step	*Explanation*
Page translation	`<%=expression%>` Translates the expression to a string. The expression can be any valid Java expression such as `34 + customerCount` or a call to a method that returns a value.
Page compilation	`<% yourCode %>` The source code generated from the scriptlet is compiled.
Load class	Loads the JSP page's servlet class upon first request.
Create instance	Instantiates an instance of the servlet class.
Call `jspInit`	Initializes the servlet instance by calling the `jspInit` method.
Call `_jspService`	Invokes the `_jspService` method, passing a request and response object.
Call `jspDestroy`	If the container needs to remove the JSP page's servlet, it calls the `jspDestroy` method.

A JSP page is always converted to a servlet. Therefore, the life cycle of a JSP page is largely determined by how the JSP container handles Java servlets.

The `HttpServletRequest` is the interface associated with the client request. With this class, you can retrieve things like the request method, query string, and client IP address.

The `HttpServletResponse` is the interface that manages the response to the client. It is with this object that you send data back to the client. You can add cookies (`addCookie`), a specified header (`addHeader`), and return an error that includes a status and a default message (`sendError`). You can even redirect a browser to another URL with `sendRedirect`. You can set the content type and the HTTP status (via `setStatus`) as well.

The `HttpSession` object associated with the request is the session. The JSP container handles (creates, tracks, and destroys) sessions automatically. You can use the `session` attribute of the `page` directive to turn sessions off. When off, there is no session state for a given JSP page and any reference to the `session` variable causes a fatal error.

The primary use of the `session` variable is to store state information between pages for a given user.

The `config` implicit object is the class `javax.servlet.ServletConfig`.

Whereas a session object shares information between JSP pages for a given user, an application object (`ServletContext`) shares information among all users of a currently active JSP application. A few of the methods and properties for the application are very similar to those of the `session` object. The primary difference is *scope*—whether the objects are shared only between pages being viewed by a single user (session) or all users (application).

CHAPTER 8, "EXTEND JSP WITH JAVABEANS"

Sun's attempt at plug-and-play development is JavaBeans. These are reusable components. The core idea behind JavaBeans is the component architecture. This architecture exposes a component's (a JavaBean) properties and methods, defines events and listeners, and has a standard way for containers to manipulate them.

JavaBeans and Enterprise JavaBeans are two entirely different things, although they share the same name due to similar purposes.

A class is considered a JavaBean if it is public, has a public constructor with no arguments, follows the set/get paradigm, and is placed where the container can access it.

When you use `jsp:useBean` and specify the class, it must be in the correct class path. The `jsp:useBean` JSP element declares that a bean is stored within and accessible from the specified scope (application, session, request, or page). It boils down to creating an object having `GET` and `SET` methods that are easy to use in JSP.

When you use `jsp:useBean`, the container instantiates the object in memory and provides *an attribute* name for you to use within the scope you set in the tag. If this bean hasn't been loaded, the container will try to locate it and then load it. The container creates the bean and stores it as an attribute of the session object.

The value of the ID attribute determines the name of the bean in the scope object. Also, you use that name to refer to the object in other JSP elements and scriptlets.

The body portion of the `jsp:useBean` element is executed only when the bean is first instantiated. If the bean has already been loaded into memory from a previous `jsp:useBean` (for example, in the previous page with session scope), the body of the `jsp:useBean` element will not be executed.

Table FF.4 offers a quick overview of the `useBean` attributes.

TABLE FF.4
useBean ATTRIBUTES

Attribute	*Definition*
`id`	The case-sensitive name used to identify the object instance in the specified scope. This name doubles as the scripting variable name declared and initialized with that object reference.
`scope`	The scope within which the reference is available. The default value is page. The options are `page`, `request`, `session`, and `application`.
`class`	The fully qualified name of the class. If the class and `beanName` attributes are not specified, the object must be present in the given scope. The class must not be abstract (or an interface) and must have a public, no-argument constructor.
`beanName`	The name of a bean, as expected by the `instantiate()` method of the `java.beans.Beans` class. This attribute can accept a `request-time` attribute expression as a value.
`type`	If specified, it defines the type of the scripting variable defined. The type is required to be either the class itself, a superclass of the class, or an interface implemented by the class specified. If unspecified, the value is the same as the value of the `class` attribute.

When you use `jsp:useBean`, the container performs several actions. Basically, it instantiates the object in memory and provides a variable name for you to use within the scope you set in the tag. If this JavaBean doesn't actually exist, the container will try to create it. The following actions are edited from the specification:

- An attempt to locate an object based on the attribute value's ID and scope.
- The container declares a variable for the class with the same name as the ID. It has the same scope as declared in the tag.
- If the object is found, the variable's value is initialized with a reference to the located object, cast to the specified type. If the cast fails, a `java.lang.ClassCastException` occurs. This ends the processing of this `jsp:useBean` action.
- If the `jsp:useBean` element had a non-empty body, it is ignored. This ends the processing of this `jsp:useBean` action.
- If the object is not found in the specified scope and neither class nor `beanName` are given, a `java.lang.InstantiationException` occurs. This ends the processing of this `jsp:useBean` action.
- If the object is not found in the specified scope, and the class specified names a non-abstract class that defines a public `no-args` constructor, the class is instantiated. The new object reference is associated with the scripting variable using the scope specified.
- If a `java.lang.InstantiationException` occurs, the processing of this `jsp:useBean` action halts. This might happen if the object is not found or if there is missing a no public no-args constructor.
- If the object is not found in the specified scope and `beanName` is given, the container attempts to newly create the bean. If it succeeds, the new object reference is associated with the scripting variable in the specified scope.
- If the `jsp:useBean` element has a non-empty body, the body is processed. The variable is initialized and available within the scope of the body. The text of the body is treated as elsewhere. Any template text will be passed through to the out stream. Scriptlets and action tags will be evaluated. Usually, you use `jsp:setProperty` in here.

You use `jsp:setProperty` to set the propert values of beans that have been referenced earlier in the JSP page.

The following snippet shows you how to use a JavaBean in JSP:

```
<jsp:useBean id="beanName" ... />
<jsp:setProperty name="beanName"
            property="propertyName" ... />
```

Table FF.5 offers a quick overview of the `setProperty` attributes. The definitions are slightly edited from the specification.

TABLE FF.5
`setProperty` ATTRIBUTES

Attribute	*Definition*
`name`	The case-sensitive name of a `Bean` instance defined by a `<jsp:useBean>` element. The `Bean` instance must contain the property you want to set. The defining element must appear before the `<jsp:setProperty>` element in the same file.
`property`	The name of the `Bean` property whose value you want to set. If you set `propertyName` to `*`, the tag will iterate over the current `ServletRequest` parameters, matching parameter names and value type(s) to property names and setter method type(s), setting each matched property to the value of the matching parameter. If a parameter has a value of `""`, the corresponding property is not modified.

continues

TABLE FF5 *continued*
setProperty ATTRIBUTES

Attribute	*Definition*
`param`	The name of the request parameter (Web form or query string) whose value you want to give to a `Bean` property. If you omit `param`, the request parameter name is assumed to be the same as the `Bean` property name. If the `param` is not set in the `Request` object or if it has a value of `""`, the `jsp:setProperty` element has no effect. An action cannot have both `param` and `value` attributes.
`value`	The value to assign to the given property. This attribute can accept a `request-time` attribute expression as a value. An action cannot have both `param` and `value` attributes.

A `<jsp:getProperty>` action places the value of a `Bean` instance property into the implicit `out` object. Unlike a scriptlet, which can get a value and assign it to a variable, the `getProperty` action converts the `Bean` property value to a string and immediately adds that string to the output stream. You cannot assign the value from this tag to a variable in most containers.

Table FF.6 offers a quick overview of the `getProperty` attributes. There are only two (fewer than the more complicated `setProperty` element).

TABLE FF.6
getProperty ATTRIBUTES

Attribute	*Definition*
`name`	The case-sensitive name of a `Bean` instance defined by a `<jsp:useBean>` element. The `Bean` instance must contain the property you want to set. The defining element must appear before the `<jsp:setProperty>` element in the same file.
`property`	The name of the `Bean` property whose value you want to get. If you get a `propertyName` that doesn't exist, you will generate an error.

Table FF.7 gives you a list of four examples representing the four types of scope that beans can have.

TABLE FF.7
SCOPE SCRIPTLET CODE EXAMPLES

Scope	*Example*
Page	`<jsp:useBean id="address" class="que.scwcd.AddressBean" scope="page" />`
Scriptlet	`Que.scwcd.AddressBean address = new que.scwcd.AddressBean();`
Description	The address bean is instantiated as a local variable. Because its scope is `page` the reference disappears once the JSP page is processed. It can't be reference by another JSP or servlet even if a `forward` or `include` is used.
Request	`<jsp:useBean id="address" class="que.scwcd.AddressBean" scope="request" />`

Scriptlet	`Que.scwcd.AddressBean address = (que.scwcd.AddressBean)request.getAttribute("address");`
	`if (address == null)`
	`{`
	`address = new que.scwcd.AddressBean();`
	`request.setAttribute("address", address);`
	`}`

Scope	*Example*
Description	The address bean is instantiated into the current request object. It can be accessed by any JSP or servlet within the same request. This reference remains alive during the use of `RequestDispatcher`, `<jsp:include>`, and `<jsp:forward>`.
Session	`<jsp:useBean id="address" class="que.scwcd.AddressBean" scope="session" />`

Scriptlet	`HttpSession session = request.getSession(true);`
	`que.scwcd.AddressBean address = (que.scwcd.AddressBean)session.getValue("address");`
	`if (address == null)`
	`{`
	`address = new que.scwcd.AddressBean();`
	`session.putValue("address", address);`
	`}`

Description	The address bean is instantiated into the current session. It can then be accessed by any JSP or servlet responding to requests by the current user.
application	`<jsp:useBean class="que.scwcd.AddressBean" scope="application" />`

Scriptlet	`que.scwcd.AddressBean address =`
	`(que.scwcd.AddressBean)getServletContext().getAttribute("address");`
	`if (address == null)`
	`{`
	`address = new que.scwcd.AddressBean();`
	`getServletContext().setAttribute("address", address);`
	`}`

Description	The `AddressBean` bean is instantiated within the servlet context. It can be accessed by any JSP or servlet within the servlet context.

Table FF.8 gives you a list of three examples representing the three ways to access beans.

TABLE FF.8
`getProperty` ATTRIBUTES

Access	*Example*
XML	`<jsp:getProperty name="beanName"` `property="propertyName" ... />`
Scriptlet	`<% String city = myAddress.getCity()%>`
Expression	`<%= myAddress.getCity()%>`

The advantage of using JavaBeans is that it makes JSP code easier to read and maintain. Also, the JavaBean itself becomes a self-contained component so it also is easier to maintain. Lastly, JavaBeans are easy to reuse and share among developers. Note the importance of JavaBeans for separating presentation and business layers.

CHAPTER 9, "CUSTOMIZE JSP WITH TAG LIBRARIES"

A tag library is similar to JavaBeans in that you can reference a class from JSP using XML notation. You basically define XML tags and map those to methods and attributes in the class.

A tag library defines custom tags in a Tag Library Descriptor (TLD) file so that the appropriate underlying class methods are called when the container processes the custom tags. This file defines the custom tags that you can use in JSP to access the associated Java class. Your container (Tomcat) uses the TLD to convert the XML in your JSP page into Java code as you'll see. TLD files themselves are written in XML notation.

The following is an example of one tag definition within a Tag Library Descriptor.

```
<tag>
      <name>whatColorIsIt</name>
      <tag-class>examples.ColorTagHandler
➥</tag-class>
      <info>Simply echoes back some text</info>
<attribute>
           <name>color</name>
           <required>true</required>
           <rtexprvalue>false</rtexprvalue>
      </attribute>
</tag>
```

Table FF.9 lists the four files and their description that are involved in a typical tag library.

TABLE FF.9
FILES COMPRISING TAG LIBRARY EXAMPLE

File	*Description*
YourTagHandler.java	The 'tag handler' class that does the work, similar to a JavaBean.
YourTagLibraryDefinition.tld	The actual tag library that defines the tag names and associates them with classes.
web.xml	The container's configuration file that tells the container where the tag libraries are located and what each one's URI is.
yourJSP.jsp	The JSP page that uses XML (custom tags) to access classes defined in the tag library.

The following steps show you how to create a new tag library and use it in a Web page.

STEP BY STEP

FF.1 Creating a New Tag Library

1. Open the web.xml file and add a `taglib` element like so:

   ```
   <taglib>
        <taglib-uri>
    http://jakarta.apache.org/tomcat/
    ➥debug-taglib
        </taglib-uri>
        <taglib-location>
           /WEB-INF/jsp/debug-taglib.tld
        </taglib-location>
   </taglib>
   ```

2. Write a Tag Library Descriptor. An example is given above.
3. Write and compile a simple tag handler. Make sure the Tag Library Descriptor has the right class name.
4. Write a JSP page that includes a `taglib` directive and custom tag.
5. Restart your container.
6. Now test your tag library.

The following goals represent the hope Sun has for tag libraries:

- **Portable.** The functionality of a tag library must be usable in any JSP container.
- **Simple.** People who have less geek in them should be able to understand and use tag libraries.

- **Expressive.** This technology will support nested actions, scripting elements inside action bodies, and the creation, use, and updating of scripting variables.
- **Any scripting language.** Although the JSP specification currently only allows Java scripts, the architecture is designed to support other scripting languages.
- **Reusability.** Once you write a tag handler, like a JavaBean, you can use it easily in many projects.

The taglib directive has the following syntax:

```
<%@ taglib uri="tagLibraryURI"
➥prefix="tagPrefix" %>
```

You add the methods defined in the Tag interface such as `doStartTag()` and `doEndTag()`.

The taglib directive only has two attributes. They are `uri` and `prefix`. Remember that the `uri` names the tag library with the same namespace as you use in the web.xml deployment descriptor. The `prefix` is any legal identifier.

Table FF.10 lists the four ways to use a custom tag.

TABLE FF.10
WAYS TO USE CUSTOM TAGS

Tag	*Description*
`<libraryPrefix:handlerName />`	The custom tag with no body, said to be an empty custom tag.
`<libraryPrefix:handlerName parameterName="value">`	This tag causes the container to call the `setParameterName` method passing the `"value"` to it.

`<libraryPrefix:handlerName parameterName="value">`
`<%= 23 * counter %>`
`<b>Congratulations!</b>`
`</libraryPrefix:handlerName>`
	A custom tag with a body. The body can contain core tags, scripting elements, HTML text, and tag-dependent body content between the start and end tag.

`<library:outerTag>`
`<library:innerTag/>`
`</library:outerTag>`
	This syntax is how you nest custom tags. The XML is easy, but the handler is more involved.

Table FF.11 lists the basic elements you will use to define a custom tag.

TABLE FF.11
WAYS TO USE CUSTOM TAGS

Element	*Description*
`<name>tagName</name>`	This required element is the name of the tag and is referred to after the colon in a JSP file (`<libraryName:tagName>`).
`<tag-class>packageName.className</tag-class>`	This required element points to the tag handler class using the fully qualified package name of the class, as if you were using it in a class without the import statement. The package name is the directory structure under the WEB-INF/classes directory.
`<bodycontent>tagdependent | JSP | empty</bodycontent>`	The `tagdependent` option means the tag will regard the contents of the body as non-JSP. The body is passed verbatim to the tag handler. The body of the action may be empty. The JSP option means the body will be interpreted before being made available to the tag handler. The body is considered JSP if the `<bodycontent>` element is missing. The empty option means the tag can have no body.

Table FF.12 continues with the definition of the attribute portion of a custom tag.

TABLE FF.12
ATTRIBUTE ELEMENT OF A CUSTOM TAG

Element	*Description*
`<name>attributeName</name>`	This required element is the name of the attribute in a tag.
`<required>true | false</required>`	This optional element within the attribute element tells the container if you have to specify a value for this attribute when you use the custom tag in JSP.
`<rtexprvalue>true | false</rtexprvalue>`	This element tells the container whether the attribute can take a scriptlet expression as a value (dynamically assigned). This is a request time expression value.

As shown in Table FF.12, there are three ways to use the body of a custom tag. Table FF.13 matches examples that look like what you will encounter on the exam with the appropriate descriptor `bodycontent` element.

TABLE FF.13
bodycontent ELEMENT OF A CUSTOM TAG

Element	*Associated* **bodycontent** *Tag*
`<tagLibrary:myTag firstName="Patricia" lastName="Trottier" ... />`	`<bodycontent>empty</bodycontent>`

`<tagLibrary:myTag>`
`<%= 23 * counter %>`
`</tagLibrary:myTag>`
	`<bodycontent>JSP</bodycontent>`

`<tagLibrary:myTag>`
`SELECT * FROM CUSTOMER`
`</tagLibrary:myTag>`
	`<bodycontent>tagdependent</bodycontent>`

Table FF.14 lists the return values possible for the event methods. These return constants tell the container what to do after processing the triggered method.

TABLE FF.14
EVENT METHODS OF A CUSTOM TAG

Element	*Associated bodycontent Tag*
EVAL_BODY_INCLUDE	Evaluate body into existing out stream (doStartTag()).
EVAL_BODY_AGAIN	Evaluate body again. Used for iterations (doAfterBody()).
EVAL_PAGE	Continue evaluating the page (doEndTag()).
SKIP_BODY	Skip body evaluation. Stop processing the JSP after the current custom tag (doStartTag(), doAfterBody()).
SKIP_PAGE	Stop processing the JSP after the current custom tag (doEndTag()).

Table FF.15 lists the methods that are triggered when the container processes custom tags.

TABLE FF.15
EVENT METHODS OF A CUSTOM TAG

Element	*Associated bodycontent Tag*
doStartTag()	This method is called when the container first starts to process the tag. Notice that when this method is invoked, the body has not yet been evaluated. It can return either the EVAL_BODY_INCLUDE or SKIP_BODY field.
doEndTag()	This method is called after the container completes the doStartTag() method. Notice that the body of your custom tag may not have been evaluated, depending on the return value of doStartTag().It can return either the EVAL_PAGE or SKIP_PAGE field.
doAfterBody()	This method is used for iterations (IterationTag). It is called after every body evaluation to control whether the body will be reevaluated. If this method returns EVAL_BODY_AGAIN, the body will be reevaluated. If it returns SKIP_BODY, the body will be skipped and doEndTag() will be invoked next.
PageContext.getOut()	This is how you add the output stream directly. This method returns an instance of javax.servlet.jsp.JspWriter.

The tag handler is the class a custom tag refers to.

You use a tag handler to access a JSP page's implicit variables and attributes using the `PageContext` object. An instance of this object provides access to all the namespaces and most attributes for a JSP page. You can grab the implicit objects with the following methods:

- **`getOut()`.** Returns the current JspWriter stream being used for client response.
- **`getException()`.** Returns any exceptions passed to this as an `errorpage`.
- **`getPage()`.** Returns the `Page` implementation class instance (Servlet) associated with this `PageContext`.
- **`getRequest()`.** Returns the `ServletRequest` for this `PageContext`.
- **`getResponse()`.** Returns the `ServletResponse` for this `PageContext`.
- **`getSession()`.** Returns the `HttpSession` for this `PageContext` or null.
- **`getServletConfig()`.** Returns the `ServletConfig` for this PageContext.
- **`getServletContext()`.** Returns the `ServletContext` for this `PageContext`.

The following methods are how you access the attributes in your tag handler for a given JSP page using `PageContext`:

- **`setAttribute()`.** Registers the name and object specified with appropriate scope semantics.
- **`getAttribute()`.** Returns the object associated with the name in the page scope, or null if not found.
- **`findAttribute()`.** Searches for the named attribute in the `page`, `request`, `session` (if valid), and `application` scope(s) in order and returns the value associated or null.
- **`removeAttribute()`.** This method removes the object reference associated with the given name by looking in all scopes in the scope order.

The following methods provide support for forwarding, inclusion, and error:

- **`forward()`.** Used to redirect, or "forward," the current `ServletRequest` and `ServletResponse` to another active component in the application. The URL is assumed to be a relative URL; however, if the path begins with a `/`, the URL specified is calculated relative to the `DOCROOT` of the `ServletContext` for this JSP. Be careful, as once this method has been called successfully, it is illegal for the calling thread to attempt to modify the `ServletResponse` object.
- **`include()`.** Causes the resource specified to be processed as part of the current `ServletRequest` and `ServletResponse` being processed by the calling thread. The output of the target resources processing of the request is written directly to the `ServletResponse` output stream. Notice that the current JspWriter "out" for this JSP is flushed as a side-effect of this call, *prior* to processing the include.

CHAPTER 10, "DEPLOYING WEB APPLICATIONS AND COMPONENTS"

A Web application is all the servlets, HTML pages, classes, and other resources that act as a single application on a Web server.

You will have two ways to package your application. You can use an open file system or an archive file.

A Web application is based on servlets. The specification defines a Web application as being composed from (not all of these components have to be present):

- Java Runtime Environment(s) running in the server (required)
- JSP page(s) that handle requests and generate dynamic content
- Servlet(s) that handle requests and generate dynamic content
- Server-side JavaBeans components that encapsulate behavior and state
- Static HTML, DHTML, XHTML, XML, and similar pages
- Client-side Java applets, JavaBeans components, and arbitrary Java class files
- Java Runtime Environment(s) running in client(s) (downloadable via the plug-in and Java Web Start technology)

The specification defines a hierarchical structure used for deployment and packaging your Web applications.

Within a generic context, there are four directories you must know. The installation directory will vary wildly between installations. This directory is not on the exam. Whatever the installation directory, it will contain one subdirectory each for the WebApp deployment descriptor, the class files, and the auxiliary JAR files. The Web application structure you'll be questioned about is shown in Table FF.16.

TABLE FF.16
WEB APPLICATION STRUCTURE

Name	*Files*	*Directory*
Deployment Descriptor	web.xml	`/WEB-INF/web.xml`
class files	MyServlet.class	`/WEB-INF/classes/MyServlet.class`
jar files (servlets, beans, utility classes)	myApp.jar	`/WEB-INF/lib/myApp.jar`
Other files (HTML, JSP)	index.html	`/`

These are the names with a description of purpose or functionality, for each of the primary deployment descriptor elements.

The main elements are defined in Table FF.17.

TABLE FF.17
WEB-APP ELEMENTS

Element	*DTD*
`context-param`	The `context-param` element declares the Web application's servlet context initialization parameters.
`listener`	The `listener` element defines the deployment properties for a Web application listener bean.
`servlet`	The `servlet` element is how you define a servlet in a Web application. Of course, you don't have to name all your servlets in the web.xml file. However, there are servlets that you may need defined here so the container can load them upon starting (`load-on-startup` element), for example. `servlet-mapping` The `servlet-mapping` element defines a mapping between a servlet and a URL pattern.
`session-config`	The `session-config` element defines the session parameters for this Web application, such as the session timeout, which defines the default session timeout interval for all sessions created in this Web application.
`error-page`	The `error-page` element contains a mapping between an error code or exception type to the path of a resource in the Web application.
`taglib`	The taglib element is used to describe a JSP tag library, including the tag library location (Tag Library Description file) and the URI for it, which is a unique namespace identifying a Tag Library used in the Web application.
`security-constraint`	The `security-constraint` element is used to associate security constraints with one or more Web resource collections, such as a security role and user roles that should be permitted access to this resource collection.
`login-config`	The `login-config` element is used to configure the authentication method that should be used, the realm name that should be used for this application, and the attributes that are needed by the form login mechanism.
`security-role`	The `security-role` element contains the definition of a security role. The definition consists of an optional description of the security role and the security role name.

You can use a mnemonic such as *CLaSS SWEaTS LotS* to remember the main elements.

The configuration that the deployment descriptor uses to handle an exception looks like this:

```
<web-app>
        <error-page>
                <error-code>404</ error-code>
                <location> /404.html
➥</location>
        </error-page>
</web-app>
```

This is how to use a `RequestDispatcher` to forward the request to an error page:

```
ServletContext context = getServletContext();
dispatcher = context.getRequestDispatcher
     "/errors/error.jsp");
dispatcher.forward(request,response);
```

This is how to specify the handling declaratively in the deployment descriptor:

```
<web-app>
  <error-page>
      <exception-type>
javax.servlet.ServletException
      </exception-type>
      <location>/servlet/ErrorDisplay</location>
  </error-page>
</web-app>
```

The following will help you identify correct descriptions or statements about Web application security issues:

- **Authentication.** The means by which communicating entities prove to one another that they are acting on behalf of specific identities. It allows you to demonstrate that you are really you.
- **Authorization.** This is access control where interactions with resources are limited to collections of users or programs for the purpose of enforcing integrity, confidentiality, or availability constraints. You have permission to use a given page.
- **Data integrity.** The means used to prove that information has not been modified by a third party while in transit. The data is really what was sent.
- **Auditing.** Maintaining a record of Web application activity. For example, you can log resource accesses including times and requester IP and ID. This usually involves a log somewhere.
- **Malicious code.** Code that deliberately behaves in a way other than advertised, especially to compromise your server.
- **Web site attacks.** At overt attempt to compromise your Web site. The most popular attack is the denial-of-service attack, where the attacker floods the server with requests, reducing its capacity to service legitimate requests.

The following list defines each of the authentication types in the objective:

- **HTTP Basic Authentication.** Authentication based on a username and password. It is the authentication mechanism defined in the HTTP/1.0 specification. A Web server requests a Web client to authenticate the user. The Web client obtains the username and the password from the user and transmits them to the Web server. The Web server then authenticates the user. This is the lowest level security of the four here.
- **HTTP Digest Authentication.** The password is encrypted. Like HTTP Basic Authentication, HTTP Digest Authentication authenticates a user based on a username and a password. However, the authentication is performed by transmitting the password in an encrypted form.
- **HTTPS Client Authentication.** This is end-user authentication using HTTPS (HTTP over SSL). This mechanism uses public key encryption, which requires the user to possess a Public Key Certificate (PKC). This is the highest level security of the four here.
- **Form Based Authentication.** This is similar to Basic except that a form is used with predefined fields. These fields must be named `j_username` and `j_password`, respectively, and the form method and action must be named `POST` and `j_security_check`, respectively.

CHAPTER 11, "DESIGN PATTERNS"

What is a design pattern? Sun defines them as so: "A design pattern describes a proven solution to a recurring design problem, placing particular emphasis on the context and forces surrounding the problem, and the consequences and impact of the solution."

Design patterns center on three basic elements, namely the *context*, the *problem*, and the *solution*. The following are their definitions:

- Context is the recurring situation in which a problem to be solved is found.
- Problems are the so-called forces, such as marketing and technological forces, that occur in this context.
- Solution is the defined design that reorganizes or manipulates, some say resolves, the problem forces into a desired outcome within that context.

There are five patterns that you must know for the exam. They are Value Objects, Data Access Object, Business Delegate, and MVC (Model-View-Controller).

- The Model-View-Controller pattern's main goal is separation of concerns. For example, it is often used to decouple presentation and service tiers, and provides a façade and proxy interface to the services.
- The Value Object pattern provides the best way to exchange data across tiers or system boundaries, especially when there is network communication involved. This is a pattern that solves performance issues around network latency.
- The Data Access Object pattern is primarily responsible for abstracting data sources and providing transparent access to the data in these sources.
- The Business Delegate pattern reduces the dependency between tiers. It is an attempt to make tiers interchangeable so one can access the services of any other. This pattern is a *proxy*—the mediator between services—that hides the complexity of remote service lookup and error recovery. It makes it easier to communicate requests and results from one layer to another.
- The Front Controller pattern presents one entry point to a Web site or service. It provides a centralized entry point that controls and manages Web request handling. It eliminates the dependency of the user on a direct resource.

Patterns formalize the design strategy, which benefits from the knowledge and experience of other people who understand contexts, forces, and solutions, as well as the relationships among the three.

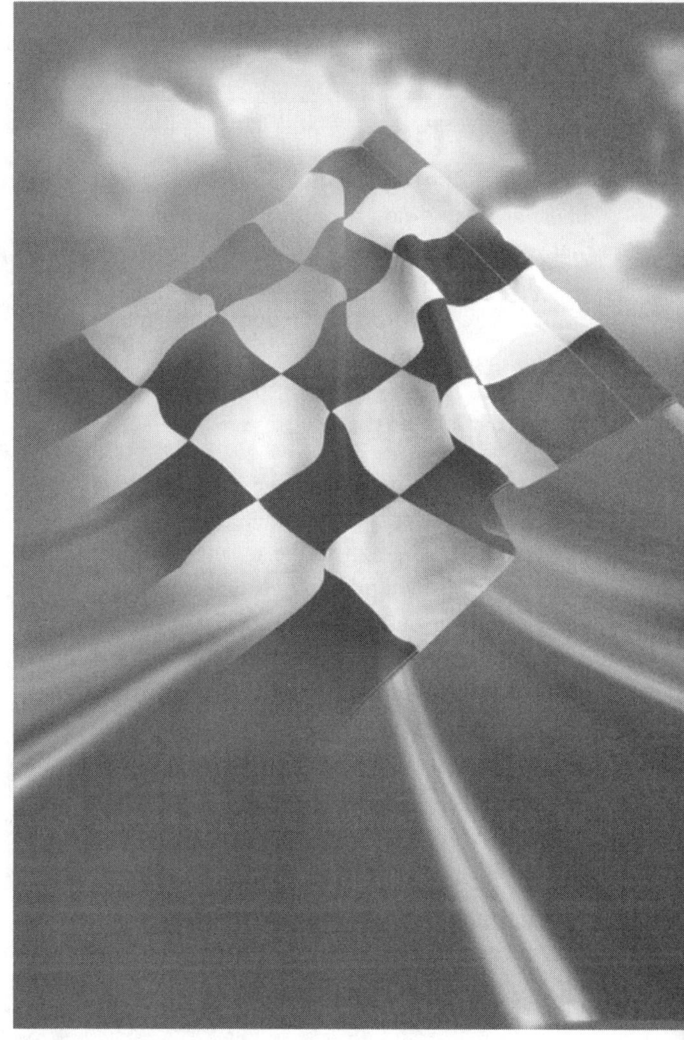

Study and Exam Prep Tips

These study and exam prep tips provide you with some general guidelines to prepare you for the Java 2 certification exams. The information is organized into two sections. The first section addresses your pre-exam preparation activities and covers general study tips. Following this are some tips and hints for the actual test-taking situation. Before tackling those areas, however, think a little bit about how you learn.

Learning as a Process

To better understand the nature of preparation for the exams, it is important to understand learning as a process. You probably are aware of how you best learn new material. You might find that outlining works best for you, or you might need to "see" things as a visual learner. Whatever your learning style, test preparation takes place over time. Obviously, you cannot start studying for this exam the night before you take it; it is very important to understand that learning is a developmental process. And as part of that process, you need to focus on what you know and what you have yet to learn.

Learning takes place when new information is matched to old. You have some previous experience with computers, and now you are preparing for this certification exam. Using this book, software, and supplementary materials will not just add incrementally to what you know; as you study, you will actually change the organization of your knowledge as you integrate this new information into your existing knowledge base. This will lead you to a more comprehensive understanding of the tasks and concepts outlined in the objectives and of computing in general. Again, this happens as a repetitive process rather than a singular event. Keep this model of learning in mind as you prepare for the exam, and you will make better decisions concerning what to study and how much more studying you need to do.

Study Tips

There are many ways to approach studying, just as there are many different types of material to study. The following tips, however, should work well for the type of material covered on the certification exam.

Study Strategies

Although individuals vary in the ways they learn, some basic principles apply to everyone. You should adopt some study strategies that take advantage of these principles. One of these principles is that learning can be broken into various depths. Recognition (of terms, for example) exemplifies a more surface level of learning in which you rely on a prompt of some sort to elicit recall. Comprehension or understanding (of the concepts behind the terms, for example) represents a deeper level of learning. The ability to analyze a concept and apply your understanding of it in a new way represents an even deeper level of learning.

Your learning strategy should enable you to know the material at a level or two deeper than mere recognition. This will help you do well on the exam. You will know the material so thoroughly that you can easily handle the recognition-level types of questions used in multiple-choice testing. You also will be able to apply your knowledge to solve new problems.

Macro and Micro Study Strategies

One strategy that can lead to this deeper learning includes preparing an outline that covers all the objectives for the exam. You should delve a bit further into the material and include a level or two of detail beyond the stated objectives for the exam. Then expand the outline by coming up with a statement of definition or a summary for each point in the outline.

An outline provides two approaches to studying. First, you can study the outline by focusing on the organization of the material. Work your way through the points and subpoints of your outline with the goal of learning how they relate to one another. Be certain, for example, that you understand how each of the objective areas is similar to and different from the others. Next, you can work through the outline, focusing on learning the details. Memorize and understand terms and their definitions, facts, rules and strategies, advantages and disadvantages, and so on. In this pass through the outline, attempt to learn detail rather than the big picture (the organizational information that you worked on during the first pass through the outline).

Research has shown that attempting to assimilate both types of information at the same time seems to interfere with the overall learning process. To better perform on the exam, separate your studying into these two approaches.

Active Study Strategies

Develop and exercise an active study strategy. Write down and define objectives, terms, facts, and definitions. In human information-processing terms, writing forces you to engage in more active encoding of the information. Just reading over it exemplifies more passive processing.

Next, determine whether you can apply the information you have learned by attempting to create examples and scenarios on your own. Think about how or where you could apply the concepts you are learning. Again, write down this information to process the facts and concepts in a more active fashion. An obvious way to do this for the Java exams is to create code and test it.

Common Sense Strategies

Finally, you also should follow common sense practices when studying. Study when you are alert, reduce or eliminate distractions, take breaks when you become fatigued, and so on.

Pre-Testing Yourself

Pre-testing enables you to assess how well you are learning. One of the most important aspects of learning is what has been called *meta-learning*. Meta-learning has to do with realizing when you know something well or when you need to study some more. In other words, you recognize how well or how poorly you have learned the material you are studying.

For most people, this can be difficult to assess objectively on their own. Practice tests are useful in that they reveal more objectively what you have learned and what you have not learned. Use this information to guide review and further study. Developmental learning takes place as you cycle through studying, assessing how well you have learned, reviewing, and assessing again until you think you are ready to take the exam.

You might have noticed the practice exams included in this book. Use them as part of the learning process. The exam software on the CD-ROM also provides a variety of ways to test yourself before you take the actual exam. By using the practice exams, you can take an entire timed practice test quite similar in nature to that of the actual certification exam.

You should set a goal for your pre-testing. A reasonable goal would be to score consistently in the 90% range.

See Appendix E, "What's on the CD-ROM," for a more detailed explanation of the test engine.

Exam Prep Tips

The Java 2 certification exams reflect the knowledge domains established by Sun. The multiple-choice exams are based on a fixed set of exam questions. The individual questions are presented in random order during a test session. If you take the same exam more than once, you will see the same number of questions, but you will not necessarily see the exact same questions.

The multiple-choice and essay certification exams also have a fixed time limit in which you must complete the exam. The test engine on the CD-ROM that accompanies this book provides time-limit exams.

Finally, the score you achieve on the multiple-choice exams is based on the number of questions you answer correctly. If you are in doubt, guess. In addition, do not dwell on any one question for too long. Exam time can be consumed very quickly.

Putting It All Together

Given all these different pieces of information, the task now is to assemble a set of tips that will help you successfully tackle the certification exams.

More Pre-Exam Prep Tips

Generic exam-preparation advice is always useful. Tips include the following:

- Review the current exam-preparation guide on the Sun Web site.
- Memorize foundational technical detail, but remember that you need to be able to think your way through questions as well.
- Take any of the available practice tests. Try the ones included in this book and the ones you can create using the exam software on the CD-ROM.

- Look on the Sun Web site at `http://suned.sun.com/US/certification/guide/index.html` for samples and demonstration items.

During the Exam Session

The following generic exam-taking advice that you have heard for years applies when taking this exam:

- Take a deep breath and try to relax when you first sit down for your exam session. It is important to control the pressure you might (naturally) feel when taking exams.
- You will be provided with scratch paper. Take a moment to write down any factual information and technical detail that you committed to short-term memory.
- Carefully read all information and instruction screens. These displays have been put together to give you information that is relevant to the exam you are taking.
- Read the exam questions carefully. Reread each question to identify all relevant details.
- Tackle the questions in the order they are presented. Skipping around will not build your confidence; the clock is always counting down.
- Do not rush, but also do not linger on difficult questions. The questions vary in degree of difficulty. Do not let yourself be flustered by a particularly difficult or verbose question.
- Note the time allotted and the number of questions appearing on the exam you are taking. Make a rough calculation of how many minutes you can spend on each question and use this to pace yourself through the exam.
- Take advantage of the fact that you can return to and review skipped or previously answered questions. Record the questions you cannot answer confidently, noting the relative difficulty of each question, on the scratch paper provided. After you have made it to the end of the exam, return to the more difficult questions.
- If session time remains after you have completed all questions (and if you are not too fatigued!), review your answers. Pay particular attention to questions that seem to have a lot of detail or that involve code analysis.
- As for changing your answers, the general rule of thumb here is *don't*! If you read the question carefully and completely and you thought that you knew the correct answer, you probably did. Do not second-guess yourself. If, as you check your answers, one clearly stands out as incorrectly marked, then change it. If you are at all unsure, however, go with your first impression.

If you have studied and you follow the preceding suggestions, you should do well. Good luck!

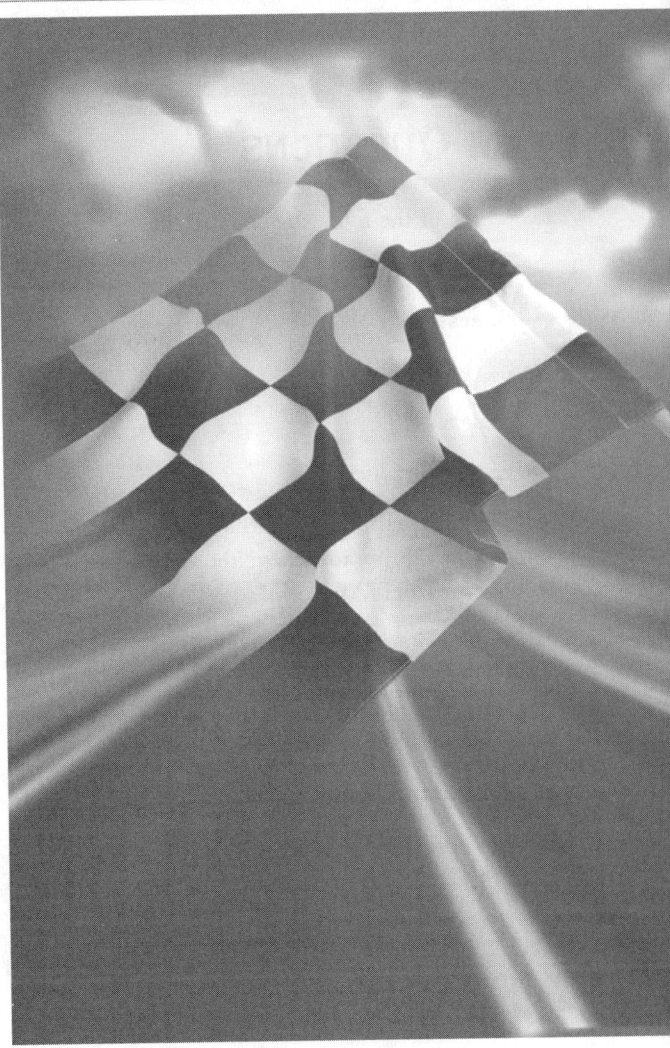

This exam simulates the Sun Certified Web Component Developer for J2EE exam and is representative of what you can expect on the actual exam. It contains 60 questions (the same number as the actual exam). You should spend no more than 90 minutes trying to answer the questions (the same time as allowed for the actual exam). In other words, treat this exam the same as the actual exam. That way, you'll get an idea of how well you'll do on the actual exam.

The content covered is that of the first part of the book, not the whole set of exam objectives. The questions focus on the earlier exam objectives and as such provide a thorough test of your familiarity with that material. I would rate this exam as medium in difficulty. It is easier than the real thing, but you would have a great deal of difficulty passing it without reading the early chapters. Also, in order to provide you additional rigor in your exam preparation, I threw in some questions that were especially hard to figure out due to the similarity between the correct answer and the distracters.

Practice Exam 2 covers the middle of the book, and Practice Exam 3 covers all the objectives. So view the first two Practice Exams as great opportunities to assess your knowledge of the material. Then use Practice Exam 3 as your final tuneup.

Practice Exam 1

EXAM QUESTIONS

1. Which of the following can call the `init` method?

   A. `doPut`

   B. `session`

   C. `service`

   D. `request`

   E. the container

2. Which corresponding method in the `HttpServlet` class do you use to retrieve the value of a text field on an HTML form?

   A. `doPost`

   B. `getParameter(String fieldName)`

   C. `doGet(String fieldName)`

   D. `getHTTP(String fieldName)`

3. Please provide the interface name which you implement to create a context listener.

   ____

4. Which method is used to get a `ServletContext` object?

   A. `getContextServlet`

   B. `getServlet`

   C. `getContext`

   D. `getServletContext`

5. Which two of the following are `HttpServlet` class methods (choose two)?

   A. `doPut`

   B. `getRequest`

   C. `doPost`

   D. `post`

6. Which method does the container call at the end of the servlet lifecycle?

   A. `doDelete`

   B. `end`

   C. `finalize`

   D. `destroy`

7. What type of HTTP request is normally used for simple HTML page requests?

   A. `POST`

   B. `GET`

   C. `DELETE`

   D. `CALL`

8. The `getInitParameterNames` method returns what?

   A. Enumeration of string objects with session-wide parameters.

   B. String array with session-wide parameters.

   C. Enumeration of string objects with application-wide parameters.

   D. String array with application-wide parameters.

9. What types of events trigger a `POST` type request?

   A. When a user clicks a hyperlink.

   B. When a user clicks a button on an HTML form whose method is set to `POST`, as in `method=post`.

   C. This is determined by the browser based on the size of the request.

   D. This is determined by the server based on the size of the request.

10. Read the following code:

```
    protected void
➥service(HttpServletRequest req,
HttpServletResponse resp)
        throws ServletException, IOException
    {
➥response.setContentType("text/plain");
            PrintWriter out =
➥response.getWriter();
            StringBuffer html = new
➥StringBuffer();
            html.append("<html>\n");
html.append("<head><title>Servlet Example" +
➥"</title></head>\n");
            html.append("<body>\n");
            html.append("Servlet Example");
            html.append("</body>");
            html.append("</html>");
            out.print( html.toString() );
    }
```

Which two statements are true regarding this code (choose two)?

A. When a user sends a request to the container (assume servlet has not been loaded), this is the first method it calls.

B. When a user sends a request to the container (assume servlet has not been loaded), this is the second method it calls.

C. The `doGet` method will be called next.

D. The `doGet` method will not be called next.

11. What causes a servlet to load?

A. A Web server start.

B. The container detects that a class file has changed.

C. It is configured to do so periodically.

D. It is loaded upon every request.

12. Which two of the following are benefits of the `POST` method (choose two)?

A. It can send unlimited length data as part of its HTTP request body.

B. It allows bookmarks.

C. It uses simple query strings.

D. It hides data because it isn't passed as a query string, but is passed instead in the message body.

13. Which of the following are application-wide actions?

A.

```
Context.setAttribute(
  "applicationName", "Certification by
Que");
```

B.

```
config.getServletContext  .setAttribute(
  "applicationName", "Certification by
Que");
```

C.

```
config.getServletContext  .getAttribute(
  "applicationName", "Certification by
Que");
```

D.

```
Context  .setAttribute(
  "applicationName", "Certification by
Que");
```

14. What is the benefit of using the `HEAD` HTTP method?

A. It hides the requester identity.

B. It masks the IP address.

C. It can handle any size request.

D. It is the smallest type request.

15. Which interface defines the methods for retrieving form parameters?

    A. `ServletRequest`

    B. `ServletResponse`

    C. `HTTPRequest`

    D. `HTTPResponse`

16. When does the container call `init`?

    A. With each request for a given servlet.

    B. Only on the first request for each user.

    C. It is not called by the container.

    D. Only at the beginning of the servlet lifecycle.

17. Which method do you use to retrieve a single value if you know the particular parameter name?

    A. `getParameterName(String parameterName)`

    B. `getParameterValues(String parameterName)`

    C. `getParameters(String parameterName)`

    D. `getParameter(String parameterName)`

18. Which method returns the URL to the resource that is mapped to a specified path?

    A. `getRealPath(String path)`

    B. `getPath(String path)`

    C. `getPathReal(String path)`

    D. `getResource(String path)`

19. Read the following code:

```
    /**
* Process a GET request for the specified
➥resource.
     *
     * @param request The request we are
➥processing
     * @param response The response we are
➥creating
     *
     * @exception IOException if
➥input/output error
     * @exception ServletException if a
➥servlet
     * error occurs
     */
    protected void doGet(HttpServletRequest
➥request,
➥HttpServletResponse response)
        throws IOException, ServletException
    {
        // Serve the requested resource,
      //  including the data content.
    }
```

Which two statements are true regarding this code (choose two)?

    A. The `doGet()` method is called when the container receives an HTTP `GET` request.

    B. The container always services a request with a `doGet` request as the last method called.

    C. The request object has session scope.

    D. The HTTP `GET` method may include parameters that are retrievable from the request object.

20. How do you perform programmatic server-side includes?

    A. `setForward(String url)`

    B. `RequestDispatcher`

    C. `Request`

    D. `getResource(String url)`

21. Which of the following is true?

    A. `ServletContext.getRequestDispatcher()`— This method uses absolute paths.

    B. `ServletRequest.getRequestDispatcher(String path)`—The path may be relative, but cannot extend outside current servlet context.

C. `ServletRequest.getNamedDispatcher(String path)`—The path may be relative.

D. `ServletContext.getRequestDispatcher()`—This method uses relative paths.

22. Which of the following is correct?

A. `Enumeration names = request.getNames() ;`

B. `String[] names = request.getNames() ;`

C. `Enumeration parameterNames = request.getParameterNames() ;`

D. `String[] parameterNames = request.getParameterNames() ;`

23. Suppose the container received an HTTP `POST` request. How would you process this request in the servlet's `doGet` method?

A. This isn't possible. The `doPost` method will receive the request, not the `doGet` method.

B.

```
    protected void doPost(HttpServletRequest
➥request,
➥HttpServletResponse response)
            throws IOException, ServletException
    {
            //often just throw it at doGet()
            doGet(request, response);
    }
```

C. If there is no form parameters the container will automatically send the request to the `doGet` method.

D.

```
    protected void init(HttpServletRequest
➥request,
➥HttpServletResponse response)
            throws IOException, ServletException
    {
            //often just throw it at doGet()
            doGet(request, response);
    }
```

24. Which method corresponds to the HTTP `GET` method?

A. `get`

B. `httpGet`

C. `doGet`

D. `getHTTP`

25. It happens often that pages move around and a URL becomes invalid. Throwing back a `404` error isn't nice. What could you do that is better?

A. Use the `sendRedirect` method to send viewers to a temporary page.

B. Use the `sendTemporary` method to send viewers to a temporary page.

C. Use the `setTemporary` method to specify a temporary page and set the context parameter to the new URL.

D. Use the `redirect` method to send viewers to a temporary page.

26. Which of the following method lists are in the correct lifecycle order?

A. `request start doPost end`

B. `service start response destroy`

C. `request init getPost`

D. `init service destroy`

27. Which two of the following are called only once during the lifetime of a servlet (choose two)?

A. `destroy`

B. `doPut`

C. `service`

D. `init`

E. `config`

28. Which two of the following HttpServlet class methods receives the response object (choose two)?

    A. get

    B. doPut

    C. getHTTP

    D. doGet

29. What happens if you redirect a request to another URL after some of the response has already been returned?

    A. The container simply discards the partial response and jumps to the new URL.

    B. The container gets confused.

    C. The specification doesn't say what the container is supposed to do. It is up to the vendor to decide.

    D. The container throws IllegalStateException.

30. Read the following code:

```
  public void service(HttpServletRequest
➥request,
                 HttpServletResponse response)
    throws ServletException, IOException
  {
    response.setContentType("text/html");
    PrintWriter out = response.getWriter();
    out.println("<html>");
    out.println("<head><title>Servlet Error
➥Handling " +
                 "Example</title></head>");
    out.println("<body>");
    out.println("A skimpy, but complete
➥servlet.");
    out.println("</body>");
    out.println("</html>");
  }
}
```

Which two statements are true regarding this code (choose two)?

    A. The doGet, doPost, or doPut method is called next depending on the type of request.

    B. This code is invalid because it doesn't call one of the doGet, doPost, or doPut methods.

    C. This code is valid and will handle all three types of HTTP requests including GET, POST, and PUT.

    D. The next method invoked is destroy.

31. How do you set, get, and change application-level (not session-level) attributes and talk to the servlet container?

    A. ServletContext

    B. Context

    C. Response

    D. Request

32. Which three options are events that would trigger a GET type request (choose three)?

    A. A form submission with the METHOD='GET'.

    B. Uploading a file.

    C. A user clicking a hyperlink.

    D. Typing in the address text box on a browser.

    E. Sending email.

33. How do you get application-level initialization parameters?

    A. You use the getParameterValues method.

    B. You use the getInitValues method.

    C. You call the init method, which returns an array of initialization parameters.

    D. You use the getInitParameter and getInitParameterNames methods.

34. You normally write a servlet by overriding the `doPut`, `doGet`, and `doPost` methods. Which class do they come from?

    A. `HttpServletRequest`

    B. `HttpServletResponse`

    C. `HttpServlet`

    D. `HttpSession`

35. Which two of the following options are benefits of the `POST` method (choose two)?

    A. It is used for getting information such as a simple HTML page or the results of a database query.

    B. It is a method that supports query strings of unlimited length.

    C. It hides data because it isn't passed as a query string, but is passed instead in the message body.

    D. It normally saves resources because of the way the request is compressed.

36. Which of the following methods belongs to the `ServletContext` class?

    A. `getInitParameterNames`

    B. `getParameterValues`

    C. `getParameterValues(String)`

    D. `getInitParameter`

37. The session scope includes which two of the following (choose two)?

    A. Requests from several machines.

    B. All hits from a single machine.

    C. Multiple browser windows if they share cookies.

    D. Multiple hits from the same browser across some period of time.

38. Which of the following methods corresponds to the HTTP `PUT` method?

    A. `getPUT`

    B. `putHttp`

    C. `httpPUT`

    D. `doPut`

39. Which method returns an enumeration of `String` objects containing the names of the parameters contained in the request or an empty enumeration if the request has no parameters?

    A. `getParameterNames`

    B. `getMap`

    C. `getParameterMap`

    D. `getParameterValues`

40. Read the following code:

```
<html>
<body>
Devyn likes <b>R/C Buggies</b>. <br>
<%! int count = 100, factor=5; %>
 <%=count * factor%>
</body>
</html>
```

Which two statements are true regarding this code (choose two)?

A. This is a JSP page, but it will not run because it is missing the JSP declaration.

B. The code will display:

```
Devyn likes R/C Buggies.
500
```

C. This JSP page will be translated into servlet code, which will be compiled and invoked as a servlet going forward.

D. You can't declare two integers on the same line in JSP.

41. How do you get the absolute path for a given virtual path?

   A. `getabsolute Path(String path)`

   B. `getPath(String path)`

   C. `getPathabsolute (String path)`

   D. `getPathabsolute ()`

42. Which method do you use to retrieve multiple values for a given parameter?

   A. `getParameterValues`

   B. `getParameterValues(String parameterName)`

   C. `getParameters`

   D. `getParameters(String parameterName)`

43. How would you "print" a text message to the browser?

   A.

```
PrintWriter out = response.getWriter();
out.println(message);
```

   B.

```
response.println(message);
```

   C.

```
ServletOutputStream out =
response.getWriter();
out.println(message);
```

   D.

```
ServletOutputStream out =
response.ServletOutputStream();
out.println(message);
```

44. Which method obtains a resource located at the named path as an `InputStream` object?

   A. `getResourceStream(String path)`

   B. `getResourceAsStream(String path)`

   C. `getResource(String path)`

   D. `getStream(String path)`

45. A browser or application will sometimes send a request to a server just to check the status or get information (such as `'can you handle a file upload?'`) from the server. What method does it use to do this?

   A. `HEAD`

   B. `PING`

   C. `DELETE`

   D. `POST`

46. What does the `getParameter(String)` method do?

   A. It returns the value of a request parameter.

   B. This method is not valid. It really is `getFormParameter`.

   C. It should be `getParameter` without a string parameter of its own.

   D. It can be used to return an integer from a form field.

47. What happens if the container crashes?

   A. The JVM calls `finalize` for all pending servlet requests.

   B. Since it is crashing it doesn't do anything but disappear.

   C. The `destroy` method is called if possible.

   D. The log is noted and then pending requests get simple error returns.

48. The `PUT` type request is for which type of situation?

   A. Uploading files to the server.

   B. Submitting form field values.

   C. Testing for valid URLs.

   D. Using XML for exchanges.

49. Which of the following two options are ways to get a `RequestDispatcher` (choose two)?

    A. `getDispatcher`

    B. `getDispatcherName`

    C. `getNamedDispatcher`

    D. `getRequestDispatcher`

50. Which of the following two options are ways to invoke the `doGet` method (choose two)?

    A. The `init` method calls `doGet`.

    B. The container calls `doGet`.

    C. The request object calls `doGet`.

    D. The service method calls `doGet`.

51. Which method returns the values of a given request parameter as an array of strings, or returns null if the parameter does not exist?

    A. `getParameterMap`

    B. `getParameterValues`

    C. `getParameterValues`

    D. `getParameters`

52. What happens if you set a Web application-wide parameter through `ServletContext`, but don't provide a value?

    A. This cannot happen.

    B. An exception will be thrown.

    C. Retrieving this parameter will return a string containing a servlet container version number.

    D. Retrieving this parameter will return a string containing a servlet container name.

53. What is the most frequently used type of HTTP request?

    A. `POST`

    B. `GET`

    C. `DELETE`

    D. `CALL`

54. How do you get the request header names?

    A. `Enumeration e = request.getHeaderNames ;`

    B. `String[] names = request.getHeaderNames ;`

    C. `Enumeration e = request.getHeaders ;`

    D. `String[] names = request.getHeaders ;`

55. Suppose you want to open a binary file in a browser from a servlet. How would you declare and initialize the output stream?

    A. `ServletContext.getOutStream ;`

    B. `ServletContext.getBinaryStream ;`

    C. `ServletOutputStream out = response.getOutputStream ;`

    D. `PrinterWriter out = response.getPrinterWriter ;`

56. Please provide the interface name that allows you to make your servlet thread-safe.

    ____

57. How do you add the content-type header to the response?

    A. `response.setContentType ;`

    B. `response.setType( contentType );`

    C. `response.setContentType( String );`

    D. `String type = request.getContentType ;`

58. Which of the following two options are features of the GET method (choose two)?

    A. It can handle most request types including file uploading and form submissions.

    B. It is for getting information such as a simple HTML page or the results of a database query.

    C. This method supports query strings. Servers usually limit query strings to about 1,000 characters.

    D. This disallows bookmarks.

59. What happens if, when calling getParameterValues, the parameter has a single value?

    A. It returns an error. You should use the getParameterValue method for single value parameters.

    B. It returns an array with a length of one.

    C. getParameterValues calls getValue for that single value.

    D. It returns a string with that single value.

60. The POST type request is most often used for which of the following situations?

    A. When uploading a file.

    B. With query strings.

    C. The POST request is a combination of a GET and PUT.

    D. When submitting an HTML form.

ANSWERS TO EXAM QUESTIONS

1. **E.** Although all the other answers look promising, they are false. Only the container calls the init, service, and destroy methods. Do not try to call these methods because doing so will generate a servlet exception.

2. **A.** The browser collects the form field names and values in a post. The servlet will access these in the doPost method. The doGet method does not see the form fields, only the query string. The other two methods don't exist.

3. ServletContextListener

4. **C.** The getContext(String uripath) method returns a ServletContext object that corresponds to a specified URL on the server.

5. **A, C.** The methods in the HttpServlet class that correspond to the HTTP GET, POST, and PUT are doGet, doPost, and doPut, respectively. The other answers listed don't exist.

6. **D.** The destroy method, like init, is called only once. It is called when the servlet is taken out of service and all pending requests to this servlet are done, including timeouts.

7. **B.** The GET type request is normally used for simple HTML page requests.

8. **C.** The getInitParameterNames method retrieves the names of the context's initialization parameters as an enumeration of String objects. If there aren't any, it returns an empty enumeration. Be careful, don't confuse this with session-wide parameters.

9. **B**. This occurs when a browser or application submits an HTML form (the user clicks a button) with the method attribute set to `POST`, as in `'method=post'`.

10. **A** and **D**. The servlet lifecycle sequence is `init`, `service`, `destroy`. When a user sends a request to the container the first time, the servlet is loaded and the container calls the `init` method and the `service` method is the second method it calls. Upon subsequent requests, the `service` method is the first method called by the container as the `init` is not called again. If you don't override the `service` method, it will automatically call the `doGet` method next (assuming the request was HTTP `GET`). However, because this code overrides the service method, the `doGet` method will not be called next as there is no explicit call for that method in the code.

11. **A** and **B**. Servlets are loaded in one of two ways. The first way is when the Web server starts. You can set this in the configuration file. Reloads can happen automatically after the container detects its class file (under servlet dir, that is, WEB-INF/classes) has changed.

12. **A** and **D**. `POST` doesn't support bookmarks and it doesn't use query strings. It sends unlimited length data as part of its HTTP request body, and it hides data because it isn't passed as a query string, but in the message body. So, the benefits of the `POST` method are that it is for sending information such as form fields, large text bodies, and key-value pairs to the server. Also it hides data because it isn't passed as a query string, but is passed instead in the message body. This method can send unlimited length data as part of its HTTP request body. Lastly, when creating bookmarks, the data won't be resubmitted when the bookmark is selected.

13. **B** and **C**. To help manage an application, you will sometimes need to set and get information that all of the servlets share, which is called context-wide.

14. **D**. The primary benefit of this method is message size. The `HEAD` method receives and returns very small messages. Therefore, it is fast and lightweight on both ends.

15. **A**. The interface that defines the form parameter methods is `ServletRequest`. The `ServletResponse` interface is for sending information back.

16. **D**. A common question on the exam tests your understanding of when `init` is called. Knowledge of a servlet's lifecycle is crucial to answering these questions successfully. Remember, `init` may be called when the server starts (tell web.xml to load the servlet upon startup) and when first requested. Also, the container management console will allow you to call it as part of the server administration. The exam expects you to know that `init` will only be called once per servlet instance, is not used to send information back to the browser (`HttpServletResponse` is not a parameter), and throws a `ServletException` if anything goes wrong.

17. **D**. You use the `getParameter(String parameterName)` method if you know the particular parameter name. It returns the value of a request parameter as a string, or null if the parameter does not exist.

18. **D**. The `getResource(String path)` method returns a URL to the resource that is mapped to a specified path.

19. **A** and **D**. When the container receives an HTTP `GET` request, it first calls the `init` method and then the `service` method. The `service` method in turn calls the `doGet`. The container always services a request with a call to the `service` method, but whether the `service` method then calls `doGet`, `doPost`, or `doPut` depends on whether the request is `HTTP GET`, `HTTP POST`, or `HTTP PUT`, respectively. The request object has request scope in this code. `HTTP GET` method may include parameters that are retrievable from the request object.

20. **B**. You can perform programmatic server-side includes or send the whole request to another servlet or JSP with a forward. To perform an include, you use `RequestDispatcher.include`.

21. **A** and **B**. The `ServletContext.getRequestDispatcher()` method takes an absolute path, but the `ServletRequest.getRequestDispatcher(String path)` method takes either an absolute or relative path. If it is relative, this path cannot extend outside current servlet context. The `ServletRequest.getNamedDispatcher(String name)` method takes a name declared in the deployment descriptor (web.xml).

22. **C**. The `getParameterNames` method returns an enumeration of `String` objects containing the names of the parameters contained in the request or an empty enumeration if the request has no parameters. The `getNames` method is fake. Answer D is wrong, too, because this method doesn't return a string array.

23. **B**. If the container receives an HTTP `POST` request, the service method will call the `doPost` method. Within this method you can call the `doGet` method as shown in answer B.

24. **C**. The methods in the `HttpServlet` class that correspond to the `HTTP GET`, `POST`, and `PUT` are `doGet`, `doPost`, and `doPut` respectively. The other answers listed don't exist.

25. **A**. The request object has the `sendRedirect` method. This method sends a temporary redirect response to the client, as well as a new location URL. All the other methods are fake.

26. **D**. The servlet lifecycle is `init service destroy`. Typically, the service method calls one of the `doXXX` methods based on the HTTP method request. The `request`, `start`, `end`, `response` methods don't exist.

27. **A** and **D**. The `init` and `destroy` methods are called only once during the lifetime of a servlet. The `service` method is called every time the servlet is requested. The service method calls one of the `doXXX` methods based on the HTTP method request. The `config` method doesn't exist.

28. **B** and **D**. The methods in the `HttpServlet` class that correspond to the `HTTP GET`, `POST`, and `PUT` are `doGet`, `doPost`, and `doPut`, respectively. All three of these are passed to the `Response` object. The following `doPost` shows how all three look, except for the method name:

```
    public void doPost(HttpServletRequest
➥request,
                HttpServletResponse response)
        throws IOException, ServletException
    {
        //process post
    }
```

29. **D**. The two potential problems with this method are sending a bad URL to the client and using this method after the response has already been committed. The bad URL will look bad, but not produce an error. The latter, though, will throw an `IllegalStateException`.

30. **C** and **D**. This code is valid and will handle all three types of HTTP requests including the `GET`, `POST`, and `PUT` context of the request. Notice that this `service` method does not call the `doGet`, `doPost`, or `doPut` methods. Rather, the container calls the `destroy` method, which ends the life of this servlet.

31. **A**. The `ServletContext` object is how you set, get, and change application-level (not session-level) attributes and talk to the servlet container.

32. **A, C**, and **D**. The `GET` type request is normally used for simple HTML page requests. The types of events that generate this type of request are clicking a hyperlink, changing the address directly by typing in the address text box on a browser or application that has HTML functionality, and submitting an HTML form where the `method` header is set to `GET`, as in `'method=get'`. Usually the browser is configured to send a `GET` request even if no method is set explicitly by the HTML. Most browsers allow you to tab through links as well.

33. **D**. Use the `ServletContext.getInitParameter` and `ServletContext.getInitParameterNames` methods to get application-level initialization parameters. The `ServletContext` allows you to get application-level initialization parameters, set and get application attributes, and get `RequestDispatcher` objects to forward requests to other application components.

34. **C**. You must add these methods to your servlet. Answers A and B are passed to these three methods and Answer D is fake.

35. **C**. The `GET` method sends the query string in a way that is easy for the surfer to see. The `POST` method does it differently. It sends along the data in the body of the request, which isn't shown in the address bar of the browser.

36. **A** and **D**. Only A and D are methods belonging to the `ServletContext` class. The `getInitParameter` and `getInitParameterNames` methods retrieve context-wide or application-wide or "Web application" parameters. One way to remember this is to notice that the `ServletContext` class methods have `Init` in their name.

37. **B, C**, and **D**. The session scope includes all hits from a single machine (multiple browser windows if they share cookies). Servlets maintain state with sessions. A session applies to multiple visits to your Web application from the same browser across some period of time. Sharing variables between multiple machines requires application scope. Application variables are available to multiple users running multiple servlets within the same application.

38. **D**. The methods in the `HttpServlet` class that correspond to the `HTTP GET`, `POST`, and `PUT` are `doGet`, `doPost`, and `doPut` respectively. The other answers listed don't exist.

39. **A**. The `getParameterNames` method returns an enumeration of `String` objects containing the names of the parameters contained in the request or an empty enumeration if the request has no parameters.

40. **B** and **C**. This is a JSP page that will run without error. There is no JSP declaration required. It will display option B. As option C states, this JSP page will be translated into servlet code, which will be compiled and invoked as a servlet going forward. Option D is false because you certainly can declare two integers on the same line in JSP, as shown in the code snippet.

41. **A**. The `getRealPath(String path)` method returns a string containing the absolute path for a given virtual path.

42. **B**. `getParameterValues(String parameterName)` retrieves a multivalued parameter. You use this method to get all the values for a particular parameter. Be careful; if you use the `getParameter(String parameterName)` method on a parameter that has several values, you won't get an error. Instead, you will get the first value in the array returned by `getParameterValues`.

43. **A**. You "print" text messages to the client using the `PrintWriter` object. You create a reference to one with `response.getWriter()`. All other options contain incorrect syntax.

44. **B**. Sorry, this was tough, because there is such a small difference between A and B. The `getResourceAsStream(String path)` method returns the resource located at the named path as an `InputStream` object.

45. **A**. A browser or application will sometimes send a request to a server just to check the status or get information (such as, `'can you handle a file upload?'`) from the server. It uses the `HEAD` method to do this. The `HEAD` method returns the same header lines that a `GET` method would return; however, no body or content is returned. This is often accomplished by calling `doGet`, setting the headers, but not setting any output, and then returning the response (without any body) to the requester.

46. **A**. Answers B and C are fake. You use this method if you know the particular parameter name. It returns the value of a `request` parameter as a string (it can't be an integer or anything else), or null if the parameter does not exist. Be careful. Answer D is a trick because this method has a `String` return type.

47. **B**. The container crash is disastrous. The `destroy` method, like `init`, is called only once. It is called when taken out of service and all pending requests to this servlet are done, including timeouts. `destroy` is not called if the container crashes! You should log activity elsewhere when appropriate because the `destroy` method is not called if the servlet container quits abruptly (crashes).

48. **A**. The `PUT` type request is a means of uploading files to the server.

49. **C** and **D**. There are three ways to get the `RequestDispatcher`. The first is through `Context` with `ServletContext.getRequestDispatcher(java.lang.String)`. Another way is with `ServletContext.getNamedDispatcher(java.lang.String)`. This returns a `RequestDispatcher` object that acts as a wrapper for the named servlet (in web.xml, the Web application deployment descriptor). The final way is with `ServletRequest.getRequestDispatcher(java.lang.String)`. Notice that you can use a relative pathname for this method. You must use absolutes with `ServletContext.getRequestDispatcher(java.lang.String)`.

50. **D**. It is the `service` method that calls the `doXXX` methods. Although you normally wouldn't override the `service` method, you could do so. This is not considered good practice by Sun.

51. **C**. The `getParameterValues` method returns an array of values as Strings that the given `request` parameter has, or null if the parameter does not exist.

52. **C** and **D**. Leaving off the method name makes it tougher to figure out. Some parameters have no information, so this method will return a string containing at least the servlet container name and version number. The `getInitParameterNames` method retrieves the names of the context's initialization parameters as an enumeration of `String` objects. If there aren't any, it returns an empty enumeration. Be careful; don't confuse this with session-wide parameters.

53. **B**. `GET` is the most common type of browser request. The `GET` request is defined by the Internet Society's RFC 2616: Hypertext Transfer Protocol—HTTP/1.1. See section 9.3 of RFC 2616 at `ftp://ftp.isi.edu/in-notes/rfc2616.txt`.

54. **A**. The `request` header is where all the details of the request are bundled. This is where the browser specifies the desired file, date, image file support, and more. You use `request.getHeaderNames` to retrieve an enumeration of header names.

55. **C**. The `PrintWriter` handles text only, so if you want to open a binary file in a browser from a servlet you have to write the file to the servlet's output stream. First, you get the servlet's output stream with: `ServletOutputStream out = response.getOutputStream ;`.

56. `SingleThreadModel`

57. **C**. You use an HTTP response header named `content-disposition` to specify information about the file's presentation. You use the `response.setContentType( String )` method to tell the browser what type of content is being returned and the `getContentType` method to determine what type of content is being submitted. Notice that no object is specified in C. This is because the servlet extends the `HttpServlet` class, which has the `getContentType` method. It is not part of the `request` object and obviously it can't be part of the `response` object.

58. **B** and **C**. The benefits of the `GET` method are that it is for getting information such as a simple HTML page or the results of a database query, it supports query strings, and it allows bookmarks. However, it isn't used for file uploading or form submission. `GET` is used to handle form submissions where `method="get"`. In fact, that's the default if you leave the method attribute out of the `<form>` tag.

59. **B**. This method returns an array of values as strings that represent the given request parameter, or null if the parameter does not exist. If the parameter has a single value, the array has a length of one.

60. **D**. The `POST` type request is most often used to submit an HTML form. The `POST` method is more sophisticated than a `GET` request. Normally, this method is used to process a form submitted by a browser. A Web form has fields whose names and values are sent to the server in key-value pairs. `POST` is designed for posting long messages (for example, to bulletin boards, newsgroups, or mailing lists), providing a block of data, such as the result of submitting a form, and submitting long data fields to a database (for example, an email body section from an online email form).

This exam simulates the Sun Certified Web Component Developer for J2EE exam and is representative of what you can expect on the actual exam. It contains 60 questions (the same number as the actual exam) regarding the first two-thirds of the book. You should spend no more than 90 minutes trying to answer the questions (the same time as allowed for the actual exam). As with all three practice exams and the ExamGear on the CD in the back of the book, treat this exam as if it were the actual exam.

The difficulty of questions varies from easy to very hard. This exam, like the real SCWCD exam, has single correct answer multiple-choice questions, multiple correct answer multiple-choice questions, fill-in type questions, and true/false type questions. The answers at the end have detailed explanations. The bulk of each explanation covers the correct choice, but in many cases also discusses the wrong choices to help you understand why a choice is right or wrong.

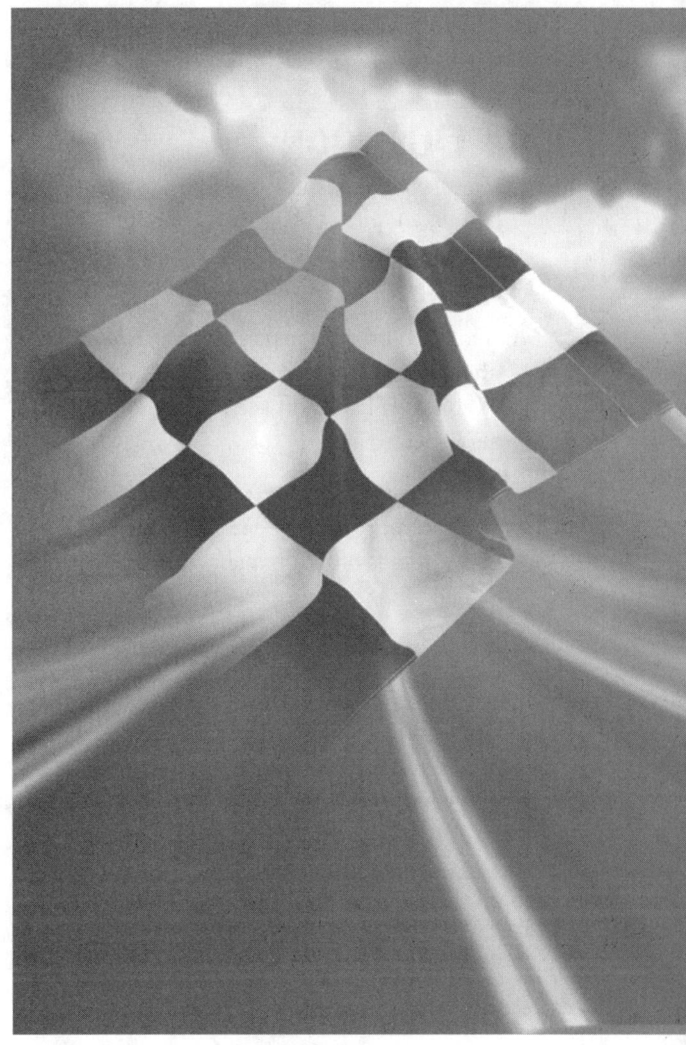

Practice Exam 2

EXAM QUESTIONS

1. Regarding a typical HTTP request/response cycle, which of the following places the described events in their proper order? (Choose two.)

   A. The Web browser makes an HTTP request, the Web server receives the request, and the Web server hands off the request to the servlet container.

   B. A client responds to a servlet validation ping, Web server receives the request, and the Web server hands off the request to the servlet container.

   C. The servlet container receives a request. The container reads the configuration (web.xml), and then calls the appropriate servlet.

   D. The servlet polls the request object to find out what to do, the servlet performs its logic, and then sends data back to the client via the response object.

2. Which of the following are true about JSP comments? (Choose two.)

   A. The JSP syntax is `<%-- comment --%>`

   B. The JSP syntax is `<!-- comment -->`

   C. The XML syntax is `<jsp:comment></jsp:comment>`

   D. They document the JSP page but is not inserted into the response.

3. Servlets are a required API of which Java 2 platform?

   A. J2ME

   B. J2SE

   C. J2EE

   D. J2DE

4. Which of following methods represents the servlet life cycle described in the API? (Choose three.)

   A. `init`

   B. `start`

   C. `service`

   D. `destroy`

   E. `getServletInfo`

5. Which two of the following are true regarding the container initializing a servlet before it can handle requests from clients? (choose two)

   A. The container calls the `init` method.

   B. The container calls the `service` method.

   C. This is how you can keep track of `request` activities.

   D. This is how you set up a `catch/try` block.

6. During initialization, the servlet instance can throw which exceptions? (Choose two.)

   A. `ServletUnavailableException`

   B. `UnavailableException`

   C. `ServletNotFoundException`

   D. `ServletException`

7. Which of the following statements regarding the `forward` method of the `RequestDispatcher` interface are true?

   A. It must be called before the response buffer is full.

   B. It can throw an `IllegalStateException` exception.

   C. It requires an absolute path. A relative path won't work.

   D. The client must have this feature turned on.

8. If during initialization, the servlet instance throws an exception, which of the following statements is true regarding the `destroy()` method?

   A. The method is called `finalize()`.

   B. The container calls the `destroy()` method.

   C. The container invokes the `catch` block.

   D. The container doesn't call the `destroy` method after an exception.

9. Which exceptions can a servlet throw during the service of a request? (Choose two.)

   A. `RequestException`

   B. `ServletException`

   C. `HttpException`

   D. `UnavailableException`

10. Which two of the following are true about page directives in JSP?

    A. They define attributes that apply to an entire JSP page.

    B. If a variable is declared it must appear before it used in the JSP.

    C. You can declare instance variables with them.

    D. There can only be one.

11. Which two statements are true regarding how the servlet container will keep a servlet loaded? (choose two)

    A. A servlet instance may be kept active in a servlet container for the lifetime of the servlet container.

    B. When the session ends, the servlet is unloaded.

    C. The specification defines a session to have a default timeout of 20 minutes.

    D. There is no association between how long a servlet is loaded and the session.

12. Before the servlet container may destroy a servlet, what must be true?

    A. Pending requests are flushed.

    B. `HttpSession` calls `finalize()`.

    C. `ServletContext` calls `finalize()`.

    D. Threads that are currently running in the service method of the servlet must complete execution.

13. Regarding container paths and URL, which of the following equations is always true?

    A. `requestURI = contextPath + servletPath + pathInfo`

    B. `requestURI = contextPath + pathInfo + servletPath`

    C. `contextPath = requestURI + servletPath + pathInfo`

    D. `servletPath = contextPath + pathInfo`

14. How do you include an outside resource into a JSP page?

    A.

```
<jsp:include page="salesTax.jsp">
this works
</jsp:include>
```

    B.

```
<jsp:include uri="salesTax.jsp"/>
```

    C.

```
<jsp:include page="salesTax.jsp">
    <jsp:param name="state" value="CA" />
    <jsp:param name="amount" value="359.92"
➥/>
</jsp:include>
```

    D.

```
<jsp:include uri="salesTax.jsp">
    <jsp:param name="state" value="CA" />
</jsp:include>
```

15. What information does the client send back as part of a cookie?

    A. date, location, name, and value

    B. name and value

    C. location, name, and value

    D. server version, date, and SSL status

16. What is the lifetime of the request object?

    A. Until all threads associated with the session are complete.

    B. This is container vendor specific.

    C. Like garbage collection, exact timing is not specified.

    D. It depends on the scope of a servlet's service method.

17. Which of the following are true about includes in JSP? (Choose two.)

    A. There is no such thing.

    B. The XML syntax is `<jsp:text> </jsp:text>`

    C. The JSP syntax is `<%@ include file="relativeURL" %>`

    D. The JSP syntax is `<% include("string") %>`

    E. The included text is added to the JSP page at translation time, when the JSP page is compiled.

18. What does a servlet container do with buffering? (Choose two.)

    A. It is allowed to buffer output going to the client.

    B. It is not required to buffer output going to the client.

    C. It is required to buffer output going to the client.

    D. The container can be configured to buffer in the buffer.xml configuration file.

19. Which of the following are true about the declarations in JSP? (Choose two.)

    A. The JSP syntax is `<%@ declaration %>`

    B. The JSP syntax is: `<%! declaration %>`

    C. The XML syntax is `<jsp:declare></jsp:declare>`

    D. The JSP syntax is `<% declaration %>`.

20. How do you write a message to the WebApp log?

    A. `Response.log()`

    B. `ServletContext.log(String)`

    C. `Response.errorLog()`

    D. `ServletContext.logger()`

21. Headers may contain data that represents which data types? (Choose two.)

    A. `int`

    B. `String`

    C. `Date`

    D. `Object`

22. Using the `sendError` method has what side effect? (Choose two.)

    A. There is no way to catch errors after calling `sendError`.

    B. It automatically calls the `destroy` method.

    C. It commits the response.

    D. It terminates the response.

23. Which two of the following methods terminate the response so that afterward no more output may be added to the response buffer? (choose two)

   A. The `sendError` method.

   B. The `sendRedirect` method.

   C. The `sendTerminate` method.

   D. The `sendComplete`.

24. Which two of the following are true regarding the Hypertext Transfer Protocol (HTTP)? (choose two)

   A. It is a stateful protocol.

   B. It is a stateless protocol.

   C. Servlets use sockets to make it stateful.

   D. Servlets can only handle real connections so it is the container vendor's responsibility to manage this.

25. Which of the follow are features of URL rewriting?

   A. It converts relative to absolute paths.

   B. It redirects clients to another URL.

   C. It is used for sessions.

   D. It appends to a query string.

26. When is a session considered established?

   A. When a client joins it.

   B. When you create a cookie on the client.

   C. When the client is notified about the session.

   D. When the `request` object is created.

27. Which of the following methods may be used to send error information back to a client? (Choose two.)

   A. `HttpServletError.setError()`

   B. `HttpServletResponse.sendError()`

   C. `HttpServletError.sendStatus()`

   D. `HttpServletResponse.setStatus()`

28. What is the correct syntax for assigning a value to a bean's property?

   A. `<jsp:property name="houseLotBean" property="id" value="33245" />`

   B. `<jsp:useBean name="houseLotBean" property="id" value="33245" />`

   C. `<jsp:setProperty name="houseLotBean" property="id" value="33245" />`

   D. `<jsp:setProperty property="id" value="33245" />`

29. Any object bound into a session is available to which other servlets?

   A. Those servlets that share the same response.

   B. Those servlets that have access to `HttpSession`.

   C. Those servlets in the same container.

   D. Those servlets that belong to the same `ServletContext`.

30. Some objects may require notification when they are placed into, or removed from, a session. This information can be obtained by having the object implement which interface?

   A. `HttpSessionListener`

   B. `ServletContextListener`

   C. `HttpSessionBindingListener`

   D. `HttpServletResponseListener`

31. When will the life of the session expire? (Choose two.)

    A. When you call the `expunge()` method.

    B. When you set the `setMaxInactiveInterval` to -1.

    C. When you call the `invalidate()` method.

    D. When the `service` method completes.

32. What are the methods of the `RequestDispatcher` interface? (Choose two.)

    A. `include`

    B. `getClient`

    C. `forward`

    D. `back`

33. Using XML syntax, how do you add text to the JSP output stream?

    A. `<jsp:page text="your text here" />`

    B.
    ```
    <jsp:text>
    your text
    </jsp:text>
    ```

    C. `<jsp:include param="text" value="your text here"/>`

    D. `<jsp:text value="text here"/>`

34. A servlet being used from within an include has access to which of the following? (Choose two.)

    A. `javax.servlet.include.response_uri`

    B. `javax.servlet.include.context_path`

    C. `javax.servlet.include.servlet_path`

    D. `javax.servlet.include.cookie_info`

35. Which of the following statements is true about how a servlet binds an object attribute into an `HttpSession` implementation by name?

    A. This is determined by the deployment descriptor.

    B. It depends on how you extend a servlet.

    C. It depends on the container.

    D. It binds it to the `HttpServletResponse` object.

36. The `HttpServlet` abstract subclass has which of the following methods beyond the basic Servlet interface? (Choose two.)

    A. `doHead()`

    B. `doGet()`

    C. `doRemove()`

    D. `doCookie()`

37. Which of the following elements are legal in a JSP scriptlet? (Choose two.)

    A. Statements

    B. Variable declarations

    C. `jsp:useBean`

    D. XML action

38. Fill in the name of the method of `HttpServletResponse` used to notify the client of a servlet error (without parentheses and parameters).

    ____

39. Which of the following is true about template data in JSP?

    A. The XML syntax is `<jsp:template> </jsp:template>`

    B. The XML syntax is `<jsp:text> </jsp:text>`

    C. The JSP syntax is `<% expression %>`

    D. It is processed by the JSP engine.

40. Regarding changing the status in the response header, which statement is true?

    A. You use the `addStatus` method.

    B. You use the `setStatus` method.

    C. You use the page directive.

    D. You use an XML action directive.

41. Provide the name of the method that the servlet container calls on every request.

    ____

42. Regarding the `taglib` directive, which of the following two statements are true?

    A. It names the tag library that defines the custom tags and specifies their tag prefix.

    B. It is the tag-library directive, not the `taglib` directive.

    C. It declares that the JSP page uses custom tags.

    D. It declares that the JSP page can use beans as defined in the directive.

43. What happens when the `session` attribute of the page directive is false? (Choose two.)

    A. The `session` attribute doesn't go in the page directive.

    B. You cannot use the `session` object.

    C. Referring to a `session` object in the code causes a translation-time error.

    D. The `session` attribute can only be specified with XML, not JSP syntax.

44. How do you specify that a given JSP page can be used as an error page?

    A. There is no tag for this. It must be done in the web.xml configuration file.

    B. Set the `isErrorPage` attribute of the page directive to true.

    C. Place it in the error directory.

    D. Use the `include` element.

45. Regarding a JSP page that inherits a class, which two of the following are true?

    A. Servlets can inherit a class so JSP pages can too.

    B. It uses the `extends="package.class"` attribute of the page directive.

    C. It can only inherit another JSP page, not a servlet.

    D. It can only inherit a JSP page with the same superclass.

46. Which statement is true about JSP expressions?

    A. You must convert them to strings to append them to the output stream.

    B. The JSP syntax is `<% expression %>`

    C. The JSP syntax is `<%=expression %>`

    D. The JSP syntax is `<% System.out.print(expression) %>`

47. Regarding forwarding a request to a Web resource in JSP, what two of the following are true?

    A. You use the `page` directive. Set the `forward` attribute to true.

    B. You can't do this in JSP. Do it at the servlet level.

    C. `<jsp:forward page="<%= expression %>" />`

    D.
```
<jsp:forward page="relativeURL">
   <jsp:param  name="parameterName"
    value="parameterValue" /> +
</jsp:forward>
```

48. Which of the following are true about the `include` directive and the `jsp:include` element?

    A. The `include` directive is processed when the JSP page is translated into a servlet class. The `jsp:include` element is processed when a JSP page is executed.

    B. The `include` directive is processed when the JSP page is compiled into a servlet class. The `jsp:include` element is processed when a JSP page is translated.

    C. The `include` directive is processed when the JSP page is translated into a servlet class. The `jsp:include` element is processed when a JSP page is translated.

    D. The `include` directive is processed when the JSP page is executed into a servlet class. The `jsp:include` element is processed when a JSP page is executed.

49. How can a servlet set headers of an HTTP response? (Choose two.)

    A. Using a query string.

    B. Using `POST`.

    C. Using `addHeader`.

    D. Using `setHeader`.

50. What kind of scheme is the HTTP protocol?

    A. request/response

    B. store/forward

    C. queuing

    D. search/return

51. If you wanted to use a conditional piece of code, which of the following shows where would you place it?

    A. `<jsp:scriptlet> code goes here </jsp:scriptlet>`

    B. `<jsp:code> code goes here </jsp:code>`

    C. `<jsp:include> code goes here </jsp:include>`

    D. `<jsp:jsp> code goes here </jsp:jsp>`

52. How would you forward a request to another resource?

    A. `<jsp:forward url="page.htm" />`

    B. `<jsp:forward param="page.htm"/>`

    C. `<jsp:forward uri="page.htm" />`

    D. `<jsp:forward page="page.htm" />`

53. What does the `sendError` method do?

    A. It sends an error message to the server.

    B. It sends an error message to the client log.

    C. It logs an error.

    D. It sends an error response to the client using the specified status.

54. Requests are represented by which two of the following objects? (choose two)

    A. `Request`

    B. `Servlet Request`

    C. `HttpServletRequest`

    D. `ContainerRequest`

55. Regarding passing an exception object to the method that writes information to the log file, which statement is true?

    A. You can pass a string but not an exception object to the method that logs a message.

    B. You can pass an exception object to the `ServletContext.errorLog` method that logs a message.

    C. The exception must be converted to a string first.

    D. You can use the `response.log` method to write to the log.

56. Which of the following will include the text of a resource at translation time?

    A. `<%@ include file="relativeURLspec" %>`

    B. `<%! include file="relativeURLspec" %>`

    C. `<%jsp:include file="relativeURLspec" %>`

    D. `<%@ page import="relativeURLspec" %>`

57. Which two of the following are correct uses of the `RequestDispatcher` (assume `req` is a correctly instantiated object of `HttpServletRequest`)? (choose two)

    A. `req.getRequestDispatcher(forwardURL).forward(req, res);`

    B. `req.getRequestDispatcher(includeURL).include(req, res);`

    C. `req.getRequestDispatcher.include(req, res);`

    D. `req.getRequestDispatcher.forward(req, res);`

58. What happens if you send data to the client after `sendError` has been called?

    A. The information is ignored by the server.

    B. The information is ignored by the client.

    C. The method will throw `IllegalStateException`.

    D. The method will throw `IllegalSendException`.

59. Which design pattern acts as a proxy and reduces network traffic?

    A. Value objects

    B. Model-view-controller

    C. Data access objects

    D. Business delegate

60. Regarding the `sendRedirect` method, which two of the following statements are true? (Choose two.)

    A. It is legal to call the `sendRedirect` method with a relative URL path.

    B. It is legal to call the `sendRedirect` method with an absolute URL path.

    C. You must redirect to a servlet that implements the same interface.

    D. You must redirect to a resource that must be defined in the deployment descriptor.

ANSWERS TO EXAM QUESTIONS

1. **A** and **D**. Although A and D are incomplete, the steps outlined in each of these options are in the correct order. The following is a typical sequence of events:

   - A client (for example, a Web browser) accesses a Web server and makes an HTTP request.
   - The request is received by the Web server and handed off to the servlet container.
   - The servlet container determines which servlet to invoke based on the configuration of its servlets, and calls it, passing to it the request and response objects.
   - The servlet uses the `request` object to determine who the remote user is, what HTTP `POST` parameters may have been sent as part of this request, and other relevant data. The servlet performs its logic, and generates data to send back to the client. It sends this data back to the client via the response object.
   - Once the servlet has finished processing the request, the servlet container ensures that the response is properly flushed, and returns control to the host Web server.

2. **A** and **D**. B is an HTML comment that's passed through to the output. C is wrong because there is no XML equivalent.

3. **C**. The Servlet API v2.3 is a required API of the Java 2 Platform, Enterprise Edition, v1.3.1. Servlet containers and servlets deployed into them must meet additional requirements, described in the J2EE specification, for executing in a J2EE environment. They are not mentioned in the specifications for either J2ME or J2SE.

4. **A, C,** and **D**. A servlet is managed through a well-defined life cycle that defines how it is loaded, instantiated, and initialized, handles requests from clients, and how it is taken out of service. This life cycle is expressed in the API by the `init`, `service`, and `destroy` methods of the `javax.servlet.Servlet` interface that all servlets must implement directly or indirectly through the `GenericServlet` or `HttpServlet` abstract classes.

5. **A** and **D**. After the `servlet` object is instantiated, the container must initialize the servlet before it can handle requests from clients. Initialization is provided so that a servlet can read persistent configuration data, initialize costly resources (such as JDBC API based connections), and perform other one-time activities. The container initializes the servlet instance by calling the `init` method of the servlet interface with a unique (per servlet declaration) object implementing the `ServletConfig` interface.

6. **B** and **D**. During initialization, the servlet instance can throw an `UnavailableException` or a `ServletException`.

7. **B**. The `forward` method of the `RequestDispatcher` interface may be called by the calling servlet only when no output has been committed to the client. If output data exists in the response buffer that has not been committed, the content must be cleared before the target servlet's `service` method is called. If the response has been committed, an `IllegalStateException` must be thrown. The path elements of the `request` object exposed to the target servlet must reflect the path used to obtain the `RequestDispatcher`. The only exception to this is if the `RequestDispatcher` was obtained via the `getNamedDispatcher` method. In this case, the path elements of the `request` object must reflect those of the original request. The client has nothing to say about it.

8. **D**. If during initialization, the servlet instance throws an exception, the servlet will be released by the servlet container. The `destroy` method is not called as the servlet initialization is terminated.

9. **B** and **D**. A and C are not real exceptions defined in the API. A servlet may throw either a `ServletException` or an `UnavailableException` during the service of a request. A `ServletException` signals that some error occurred during the processing of the request and that the container should take appropriate measures to clean up the request.

10. **A**. You don't declare variables of any type with page directives. The page directive applies to an entire JSP page and any of its static `include` files, which together are called a *translation unit*. A static `include` file is a file whose content becomes part of the calling JSP page. The page directive does not apply to any dynamic resources. No matter where you position the page directive in a JSP page or included files, it applies to the entire translation unit. However, it is often good programming style to place it at the top of the JSP page.

11. **A** and **D**. There is no association between how long a servlet is loaded and the session. The servlet container is not required to keep a servlet loaded for any particular period of time. A servlet instance may be kept active in a servlet container for a period of milliseconds, for the lifetime of the servlet container (which could be a number of days, months, or years), or any amount of time in between. The specification doesn't define a session's default timeout.

12. **D**. Before the servlet container calls the `destroy` method, it must allow any threads that are currently running in the `service` method of the servlet to complete execution, or exceed a server defined time limit.

13. **A**. It is important to note that, except for URL encoding differences between the request URI and the path parts, the following equation is always true: `requestURI = contextPath + servletPath + pathInfo`.

14. **C**.

```
<jsp:include page="salesTax.jsp">
    <jsp:param name="state" value="CA" />
    <jsp:param name="amount" value="359.92"
➥/>
</jsp:include>
```

The `<jsp:include>` element allows you to include text in a JSP page. There are two kinds. One is static (text is simply inserted as if it were part of the original JSP page) and the other is dynamic (text is processed first and then only the result is inserted into the JSP page). If it is dynamic, you can use a `<jsp:param>` clause to pass the name and value of a parameter to the resource.

15. **B**. Typically, the only information that the client sends back as part of a cookie is the cookie name and the cookie value. Comments are not typically returned. Location is determined by the browser, and the server has no access to this information, or cares. You can set name, value, expires, path, domain, and secure for cookies.

16. **D**. Each request object is valid only within the scope of a servlet's service method, or within the scope of a filter's `doFilter` method (there are no filter questions on the exam though).

17. **C** and **E**. An `include` directive inserts a file of text or code in a JSP page at translation time, when the JSP page is compiled. When you use the `include` directive, the `include` process is static. A static `include` means that the text of the included file is added to the JSP page. The included file can be a JSP page, HTML file, XML document, or text file. If the included file is a JSP page, ts JSP elements are translated and included (along with any other text) in the JSP page.

Once the included file is translated and included, the translation process resumes with the next line of the including JSP page. The included file can be an HTML file, a JSP page, a text file, an XML document, or a code file written in the Java programming language. Be careful that the included file does not contain any `<html>`, `</html>`, `<body>`, or `</body>` tags. Because the entire content of the included file is added to the including JSP page, these tags conflict with the same tags in the including JSP page, causing an error.

18. **A** and **B**. A servlet container is allowed, but not required, to buffer output going to the client for efficiency purposes. Typically servers that do buffering make it the default, but allow servlets to specify buffering parameters with methods in the `ServletResponse` interface such as `getBufferSize`, `setBufferSize`, and `flushBuffer` to be performed on the `ServletOutputStream` or a writer. There is no buffer.xml configuration file.

19. **A** and **B**. A declaration declares one or more variables or methods that you can use in Java code anywhere in the JSP page. In regular Java classes a declaration must precede that variables use, but in JSP the page is translated before it is compiled so you can declare a variable or method anywhere in the JSP page. You can declare any number of variables or methods within one declaration element, as long as you end each declaration with a semicolon. The declaration must be valid in the Java programming language. The XML syntax is `<jsp:declaration></jsp:declaration>`.

20. **B**. You create a string of information and write it to the log file using the built-in logging facility, namely, the `ServletContext.log(String)` method. The server configuration file defines the component elements that comprise the "Server", a singleton element that represents the entire JVM. Two of these elements are the access log and the activity log. These are simple text files to which the container appends messages.

21. **A** and **C**. Headers may contain data that represents an `int` or a `Date` object. The following convenience methods of the `HttpServletResponse` interface allow a servlet to set a header using the correct formatting for the appropriate data type: `setIntHeader`, `setDateHeader`, `addIntHeader`, `addDateHeader`. `Content-Type` (think MIME) has nothing to do with this.

22. **C** and **D**. These methods will have the side-effect of committing the response, if it has not already been committed, and then terminating it. No further output to the client should be made by the servlet after these methods are called. If data is written to the response after these methods are called, the data is ignored. If data has been written to the response buffer, but not returned to the client (that is, the response is not committed), the data in the response buffer must be cleared and replaced with the data set by these methods. If the response is committed, these methods must throw an `IllegalStateException`.

23. **A** and **B**. The `sendError` method terminates the response by committing it. Also, `sendRedirect` sends a temporary redirect response to the client (`SC_MOVED_TEMPORARILY`) using the specified location. The given location must be an absolute URL. Any further attempt to append to the output stream after either of these methods will generate an error.

24. **A**. The Hypertext Transfer Protocol (HTTP) is by design a stateless protocol. To build effective Web applications, it is imperative that requests from a particular client be associated with each other. The servlet specification defines a simple `HttpSession` interface that allows a servlet container to use any of several approaches to track a user's session which is a way to overcome the problem of maintaining client state with a stateless protocol. At a low level, sockets are used, but you won't be concerned with this on the exam. Option D is nonsense.

25. **C** and **D**. URL rewriting is the lowest common denominator of session tracking. When a client will not accept a cookie, URL rewriting may be used by the server as the basis for session tracking. URL rewriting involves adding data, a session ID, to the URL path that is interpreted by the container to associate the request with a session. The session ID must be encoded as a `path` parameter in the URL string. The name of the parameter must be `jsessionid`. Here is an example of a URL containing encoded path information: `http://www.que.com/catalog/books/index.html;jsessionid=33424`.

26. **A**. A session is considered "new" when it is only a prospective session and has not been established. Because HTTP is a request-response based protocol, an HTTP session is considered to be new until a client "joins" it. A client joins a session when session-tracking information has been returned to the server indicating that a session has been established. Until the client joins a session, it cannot be assumed that the next request from the client will be recognized as part of a session. The session is considered to be "new" if either of the following is true: The client does not yet know about the session or the client chooses not to join a session. These conditions define the situation where the servlet container has no mechanism by which to associate a request with a previous request.

27. **B** and **D**. Options A and C don't exist. You use the `sendError` and `setStatus` methods of the `HttpServletResponse` object.

28. **C**. `<jsp:setProperty name="houseLotBean" property="id" value="33245" />`. This element sets the value of one or more properties in a bean, using the bean's setter methods. Of course, the `<jsp:useBean>` tag must be declared first. The most frequent mistake with this tag is to not match the value of name in `<jsp:setProperty>` with the value of ID in `<jsp:useBean>`.

29. **D**. A is wrong because servlets don't normally share the same response, even during a redirect. All servlets have access to `HttpSession`, but this doesn't guarantee that two servlets see the same session. Sharing the same container doesn't address sessions. The only correct answer is D, where servlets belong to the same `ServletContext`.

30. **C**. Some objects may require notification when they are placed into, or removed from, a session. This information can be obtained by having the object implement the `HttpSessionBindingListener` interface.

31. **B** and **C**. The life of the session can be changed by the developer using the `setMaxInactiveInterval` method of the `HttpSession` interface. The timeout periods used by these methods are defined in seconds. By definition, if the timeout period for a session is set to -1, the session will never expire. Also, calling the `invalidate` method kills the session.

32. **A** and **C**. To use a request dispatcher, a servlet calls either the `include` method or the `forward` method of the `RequestDispatcher` interface. The parameters to these methods can be either the `request` and `response` arguments that were passed in via the `service` method of the servlet interface, or instances of subclasses of the `request` or `response` wrapper classes that have been introduced for version 2.3 of the specification. In the latter case, the wrapper instances must wrap the `request` or `response` objects that the container passed into the `service` method.

33. **B**.

```
<jsp:text>
your text
</jsp:text>
```

The `jsp:text` element allows you to add text that you want sent to the client unaltered within the XML tags. The text you place in here is appended literally to the output stream.

34. **B** and **C**. A servlet being used from within an `include` has access to the path by which it was invoked. All of the attributes listed in the question are accessible from the included servlet via the `getAttribute` method on the `request` object. However, if the included servlet was obtained by using the `getNamedDispatcher` method, these attributes are not set.

35. **A**. A servlet can bind an object attribute into an `HttpSession` implementation by name. Any object bound into a session is available to any other servlet that belongs to the same `ServletContext` and handles a request identified as being a part of the same session. It doesn't depend on the container. Answer D names the wrong object.

36. **A** and **B**. The `HttpServlet` abstract subclass has the following methods beyond the basic servlet interface. They are automatically called by the service method in the `HttpServlet` class to aid in processing HTTP-based requests:

    - `doGet` for handling `HTTP GET` requests
    - `doPost` for handling `HTTP POST` requests
    - `doPut` for handling `HTTP PUT` requests

    These methods are also part of the subclass, but you are less likely to see them on the exam:

    - `doDelete` for handling `HTTP DELETE` requests
    - `doHead` for handling `HTTP HEAD` requests
    - `doOptions` for handling `HTTP OPTIONS` requests
    - `doTrace` for handling `HTTP TRACE` requests

37. **A** and **B**. A scriptlet can contain any number of language statements, variable or method declarations, or expressions that are valid in the page scripting language. You cannot embed an XML action such as `jsp:useBean` in a scriptlet.

38. **A**. The method of `HttpServletResponse` used to notify the client of a servlet error is `sendError`.

39. **B**. A `jsp:text` element is used to enclose template data in the XML representation. A `jsp:text` element has no attributes and can appear anywhere that template data can. The interpretation of a `jsp:text` element is to pass its content through and append it to the current value of the `out` stream.

40. **B**. The `setStatus` method sets the status code for a given response. Use this method, instead of `sendError`, when there is no exception or serious error (for example, a forbidden page). If there is a serious error the `sendError` method should be used, otherwise use `setStatus`. Like the `sendError` method, using `setStatus` clears the buffer, but leaves cookies and other headers unmodified.

41. `service`. The servlet lifecycle is the process whereby a servlet is created, processes requests for some duration of time, and is destroyed. `init()` is called when the servlet is created. `service()` is called to process each request. `destroy()` is called when the servlet is shut down.

42. **A** and **C**. The `taglib` directive declares that the JSP page uses custom tags, names the tag library that defines the custom tags, and specifies their tag prefix. You must use a `taglib` directive before you use the custom tag in a JSP page. You can use more than one `taglib` directive in a JSP page, but the prefix defined in each must be unique.

43. **B** and **C**. This one was difficult. If the value is false, you cannot use the session object or a `<jsp:useBean>` element with `scope=session` in the JSP page. Either of these usages would cause a translation time error.

44. **B**. Set the `isErrorPage` attribute of the page directive to true. This attribute determines whether the JSP page displays an error page. If set to true, you can use the exception object in the JSP page. If set to false (the default value), you cannot use the exception object in the JSP page.

45. **A** and **B**. You must use the `extends="package.class"` attribute of the page directive. The fully qualified name of the superclass is used. Use this attribute cautiously, as it can limit the JSP container's ability to provide a specialized superclass that improves the quality of the compiled class.

46. **C**. An expression element contains a scripting language expression that is evaluated, converted to a string, and inserted into the response where the expression appears in the JSP page. Because the value of an expression is converted to a string, you can use an expression within a line of text, whether or not it is tagged with HTML, in a JSP page. The JSP syntax is `<%= expression %>`. Be careful; there is no space between the `<%` and the equals sign. The XML syntax is `<jsp:expression></jsp:expression>`.

47. **C** and **D**. The `<jsp:forward>` element forwards the `request` object containing the client request information from one JSP page to another resource. The target resource can be an HTML file, another JSP page, or a servlet, as long as it is in the same application context as the forwarding JSP page. The lines of code in the JSP page coming after the `<jsp:forward>` element are not processed; they are ignored. The JSP syntax is:

```
<jsp:forward page="{relativeURL | <%=
➥expression %>}" >
   <jsp:param name="parameterName"
      value="{parameterValue | <%=
➥expression %>}" />
</jsp:forward>
```

48. **A**. The `include` directive is processed when the JSP page is translated into a servlet class. The effect of the directive is to insert the text contained in another file, either static content or another JSP page, into the including JSP page. You would probably use the `include` directive to include banner content, copyright information, or any chunk of content that you might want to reuse in another page. The `jsp:include` element is processed when a JSP page is executed. The `include` action allows you to include either a static or dynamic resource in a JSP file. The results of including static and dynamic resources are quite different. If the resource is static, its content is inserted into the calling JSP file. If the resource is dynamic, the request is sent to the included resource, the included page is executed, and then the result is included in the response from the calling JSP page.

49. **C** and **D**. A servlet can set headers of an HTTP response via the `setHeader` and `addHeader` methods of the `HttpServletResponse` interface. The `setHeader` method sets a header with a given name and value. A previous header is replaced by the new header. When a set of header values exist for the name, the values are cleared and replaced with the new value. The `addHeader` method adds a header value to the set with a given name. If there are no headers already associated with the name, a new set is created.

50. **A**. The HTTP protocol is a request/response scheme.

51. **A**. A *conditional* (that is, `if` construction) is Java code that must go between the `jsp:scriplet` action or the scriptlet tags `<% %>`. The other options have incorrect syntax.

52. **D.** `<jsp:forward page="page_moved_page.htm" />`. This element forwards the `request` object (which has all client request information) from one JSP page to another resource. The target can be an HTML file, another JSP page, or a servlet, as long as it is in the same application context as the forwarding JSP page. Notice how the lines in the source JSP page after the `<jsp:forward>` element are not processed.

53. **D.** The `sendError` method sends an error response to the client using the specified status. Using this method clears the buffer. The server creates an HTML-formatted server error page. This page contains a default, or the message you provide as an argument. It also sets the content type to `"text/html"`, even if you changed this, but leaves cookies and other headers unmodified.

54. **B** and **C.** A and D are not real objects defined in the API. After a servlet is properly initialized, the servlet container will use `ServletRequest` to represent client requests. Requests are represented by `request` objects of type `ServletRequest`. The interface `HttpServletRequest` extends `ServletRequest` to provide request information for HTTP servlets. The servlet container creates an `HttpServletRequest` object and passes it as an argument to the servlet's service methods (`doGet`, `doPost`, and so on).

55. **A.** You can pass an exception object to the log method that writes information to the log file. You can write an explanatory message and a stack trace for a given throwable exception to the servlet log file, prepended by the servlet's name with `ServletContext.log(String, Throwable)`.

56. **A.** `<%@ include file="relativeURLspec" %>`. The `include` directive is a placeholder that lets you include the text in another file. The text that is included by this directive is part of the translation into a servlet. It is good practice to decompose complex pages into several files. Doing so doesn't impact performance, but does make your code more manageable. Header (for example, company logo and quip) and footer (for example, legal and navigation) information is a good candidate for includes. If you want to include the results from another servlet or JSP, use the XML equivalent because that way the JSP simply invokes the resource and takes the results. The `include` action instead of directive is sometimes the better choice because it can include an outside file without recompilation (thus less overhead involved).

57. **A** and **B.** The `getRequestDispatcher` returns a `RequestDispatcher` that wraps the resource at the specified path. Then you can forward or include another resource providing a path, which may be interpreted as relative to the current request path.

58. **C.** Output to the client before and after the `sendError` method is invoked will be ignored. The `sendError` method will commit the response, if it has not already been committed, and terminate it. Data written to the response afterward is ignored. If data has been written to the response buffer, but not returned to the client (not committed), the data is cleared and replaced with the data set by these methods. However, if you write data to the response buffer and try to commit it, the method will throw an `IllegalStateException`.

59. **A.** The value object acts as a mediator and reduces network traffic.

60. **A.** The `sendRedirect` method will set the appropriate headers and content body to redirect the client to a different URL. It is legal to call this method with a relative URL path; however, the underlying container must translate the relative path to a fully qualified URL for transmission back to the client. If a partial URL is given and, for whatever reason, cannot be converted into a valid URL, this method must throw an `IllegalArgumentException`.

This exam simulates the Sun Certified Web Component Developer for J2EE exam and is representative of what you can expect on the actual exam. It contains 60 questions (the same number as the actual exam). You should spend no more than 90 minutes trying to answer the questions (the same time as allowed for the actual exam). In other words, treat this exam the same as the actual exam. That way, you'll get an idea of how well you'll do on the actual exam.

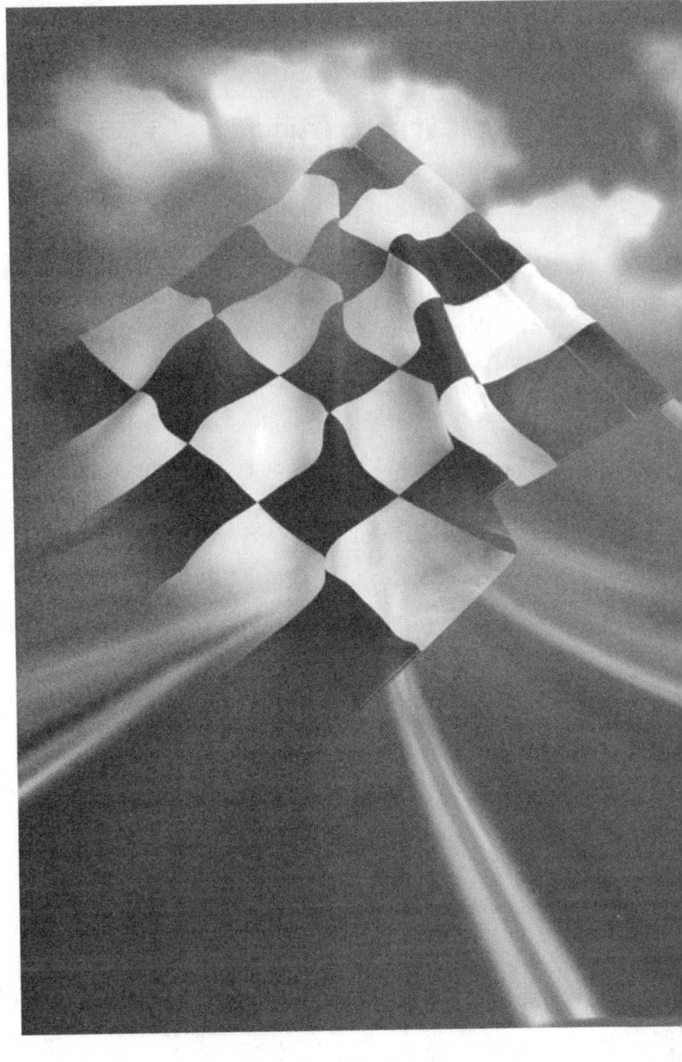

Practice Exam 3

EXAM QUESTIONS

1. Which three of the following are true?

   A. Although servlets can be used for generic request-response services, their main use is in developing Web-based applications.

   B. Servlets are executed via the Common Gateway Interface.

   C. Servlets are server-side components that are written in Java that can be used to extend the capabilities of client-server applications.

   D. Servlets provide capabilities that are similar to those provided by CGI programs.

2. Which of the following HTTP methods are directly handled by the `doGet()` method of `javax.servlet.http.HttpServlet`?

   A. `POST`

   B. `GET`

   C. `DELETE`

   D. `CALL`

3. What is the purpose of the `setContentType()` method of `ServletResponse`?

   A. To set the MIME type associated with the request

   B. To get the MIME type associated with the response

   C. To set the MIME type associated with the response

   D. All of the above

4. What is the purpose of the `getWriter()` method of `ServletResponse`?

   A. To obtain a `ServletWriter` object to send information back to the client.

   B. To obtain a `JspWriter` object to send information back to the client.

   C. To obtain a `PrintWriter` object to send information back to the client.

   D. None of the above.

5. In which of the following circumstances would an HTTP `POST` method typically be used?

   A. Submitting form data.

   B. Requesting an image file.

   C. Determining whether a Web page has been updated.

   D. Deleting a Web resource.

6. Which of the following are used to retrieve HTML form parameters from a request?

   A. `HttpServletRequest.getAttribute()`

   B. `Session.getAttribute()`

   C. `HttpServletRequest.getParameter()`

   D. `ServletRequest.getParameter()`

7. What HTTP method provides an efficient way to determine when a resource has been last modified?

   A. `POST`

   B. `HEAD`

   C. `GET`

   D. `DATE`

8. Given the following deployment descriptor code:

```
<servlet>
  <servlet-name>
      test
  </servlet-name>
  <servlet-class>
      TestServlet
  </servlet-class>
  <init-param>
      <param-name>color</param-name>
      <param-value>green</param-value>
  </init-param>
</servlet>
```

Which two of the following methods can be used to access a servlet initialization parameter color?

A. `Servlet.getInitParameter()`

B. `HttpServletRequest.getParameter()`

C. `ServletContext.getInitParameter()`

D. `ServletConfig.getInitParameter()`

9. Which of the following methods can be used to retrieve HTTP request header information?

A. `ServletRequest.getHeader()`

B. `HttpServletRequest.getHeader()`

C. `Request.getHeader()`

D. `HttpSession.getHeader()`

10. Which interface allows you to set the value of an HTTP response header?

A. `Response`

B. `ServletResponse`

C. `HttpServletRequest`

D. `HttpServletResponse`

11. Which method should be used to obtain a binary stream to send dynamic image information back to a client?

A. `ServletResponse.getWriter()`

B. `ServletResponse.getBinaryWriter()`

C. `ServletResponse.getOutputStream()`

D. `ServletResponse.getInputStream()`

12. Which method should be used to redirect an HTTP request to another URL?

A. `HttpServletResponse.sendRedirect()`

B. `HttpServletResponse.forward()`

C. `HttpServletResponse.redirect()`

D. `HttpServletRequest.redirect()`

13. Which three of the following interfaces support the `getAttribute()` method?

A. `ServletRequest`

B. `ServletResponse`

C. `HttpSession`

D. `ServletContext`

14. Which servlet method is called by the Servlet Container to indicate to a servlet that the servlet is being placed into service?

A. `start()`

B. `service()`

C. `destroy()`

D. `init()`

15. Which servlet method is called by the Servlet Container to allow the servlet to respond to a request?

    A. `start()`

    B. `service()`

    C. `destroy()`

    D. `init()`

16. What is a valid use of the `RequestDispatcher` interface?

    A. Generate test requests to the client.

    B. Receive requests from the client and send them to a resource (such as a servlet, HTML file, or JSP file) on the server.

    C. Redirect responses from one servlet or JSP to another servlet or JSP.

    D. None of the above.

17. Which file or directory may be found directly underneath the application root directory?

    A. web.xml

    B. classes

    C. lib

    D. WEB-INF

18. In which directory are .jar files that are used by a Web application placed?

    A. WEB-INF

    B. lib

    C. jar

    D. web.xml

19. Which two of the following are true about application .war files?

    A. They can be created by the jar tool.

    B. They are placed in the WEB-INF directory.

    C. They can be used to distribute Web applications.

    D. They must be registered with the application's deployment descriptor.

20. Which file or directory is used to specify deployment descriptors?

    A. web.xml

    B. server.xml

    C. WEB-INF

    D. lib

21. Given the following snippet from a deployment descriptor:

```
<servlet>
  <servlet-name>
      test
  </servlet-name>
  <servlet-class>
      TestServlet
  </servlet-class>
  <init-param>
      <param-name>color</param-name>
      <param-value>green</param-value>
  </init-param>
</servlet>
```

    What is the element used to identify the name of a servlet's class?

    A. ________________

22. What deployment descriptor is used to specify servlet initialization parameters?

    A. `web-app/servlet/param`

    B. `web-app/servlet/init`

C. `web-app/servlet/initialization-parameter`

D. `web-app/servlet/init-param`

23. Which event listener interface is used to handle events that occur when an attribute is added or removed from the application's ServletContext?

A. `ServletContextListener`

B. `ServletContextAttributeListener`

C. `HttpSessionListener`

D. `HttpSessionActivationListener`

24. What event listener interface defines the `sessionWillPassivate()` method?

A. `HttpSessionEventListener`

B. `HttpSessionAttributeListener`

C. `HttpSessionListener`

D. `HttpSessionActivationListener`

25. What deployment descriptor is used to specify application event listeners?

A. `web-app/listener/listener-class`

B. `web-app/listener/listener`

C. `web-app/listener/event-listener`

D. `web-app/servlet/listener/listener`

26. Which two of the following are true with respect to distributable applications?

A. Servlet initialization parameters may be individually specified for each servlet container used in the distributable application.

B. `HttpSession` instances are scoped to the machine, across multiple virtual machines if they exist on one machine.

C. Distributed containers are not required to propagate either servlet context events or `HttpSession` events to other virtual machines.

D. Servlet initialization parameters are not individually specified for each servlet container used in the distributable application.

27. Which of the following methods may be used to send error information back to a client?

A. `HttpServletResponse.setError()`

B. `HttpServletResponse.sendError()`

C. `HttpServletResponse.sendStatus()`

D. `HttpServletResponse.setStatus()`

28. Which deployment descriptor is use to specify that an error page is to be used to handle an exception?

A. `web-app/error-page`

B. `web-app/error`

C. `web-app/servlet/error`

D. `web-app/servlet/exception`

29. What method may be used to write to a Web application's log file?

A. `ServletRequest.writeLog()`

B. `HttpSession.log()`

C. `Servlet.writeLog()`

D. `ServletContext.log()`

30. Which method may be used to access a session object?

A. `HttpSession.getSession()`

B. `ServletContext.getSession()`

C. `Servlet.getSession()`

D. `HttpServletRequest.getSession()`

31. Which method of `HttpSession` is used to expunge an existing session object?

A. `expunge()`

B. `terminate()`

C. `invalidate()`

D. `timeout()`

32. Under which two circumstances will an existing session object be invalidated?

A. The object's `setMaxInactiveInterval()` method is invoked with an argument of -1.

B. The object's `invalidate()` method is invoked.

C. The client does not make a request of the server within the session timeout period.

D. None of the above.

33. Which of the following are required to use URL-rewriting for session management?

A. Page URLs must be rewritten to include the `jsessionid` parameter.

B. Cookies must be disabled at the browser.

C. Pages must be served from a path that contains the `jsessionid` value.

D. The `jsessionid` response header must be set to the session ID value.

34. Which of the following best describes data integrity from a security perspective?

A. The means by which communicating entities prove to one another that they are acting on behalf of specific identities that are authorized for access.

B. The means by which interactions with resources are limited to collections of users or programs for the purpose of enforcing integrity, confidentiality, or availability constraints.

C. The means used to prove that information has not been modified by a third party while in transit.

D. The means by which data is protected from disclosure during communication.

35. Which of the following best describes authentication from a security perspective?

A. The means by which communicating entities prove to one another that they are acting on behalf of specific identities that are authorized for access.

B. The means by which interactions with resources are limited to collections of users or programs for the purpose of enforcing integrity, confidentiality, or availability constraints.

C. The means used to prove that information has not been modified by a third party while in transit.

D. The means by which data is protected from disclosure during communication.

36. Which of the following best describes access control or authorization from a security perspective?

A. The means by which communicating entities prove to one another that they are acting on behalf of specific identities that are authorized for access.

B. The means by which interactions with resources are limited to collections of users or programs for the purpose of enforcing integrity, confidentiality, or availability constraints.

C. The means used to prove that information has not been modified by a third party while in transit.

D. The means by which data is protected from disclosure during communication.

37. What deployment descriptor is used to associate security constraints with one or more Web resource collections?

    A. `web-app/constraint`

    B. `web-app/security-constraint`

    C. `web-app/authentication-constraint`

    D. `web-app/user-data-constraint`

38. What deployment descriptor identifies the user roles that should be permitted access to this resource collection?

    A. `web-app/authentication-constraint`

    B. `web-app/auth-constraint`

    C. `web-app/security-constraint/auth-constraint`

    D. `web-app/security-constraint/user-data-constraint`

39. What deployment descriptor identifies how data communicated between the client and container should be protected?

    A. `web-app/security-constraint`

    B. `web-app/login-conf`

    C. `web-app/security-constraint/auth-constraint`

    D. `web-app/security-constraint/user-data-constraint`

40. What deployment descriptor is used to configure the authentication method that should be used to authenticate application users?

    A. `web-app/security-constraint`

    B. `web-app/login-config`

    C. `web-app/security-constraint/auth-constraint`

    D. `web-app/security-constraint/user-data-constraint`

41. Which of the following authentication methods are supported by servlet containers?

    A. BASIC

    B. DIGEST

    C. FORM

    D. CLIENT-CERT

42. Which of the following variable scopes are thread safe?

    A. local variables

    B. request attributes

    C. instance variables

    D. class variables

43. How many instances of a single servlet may access the service method for a servlet that does not implement the `SingleThreadModel` interface?

    A. One.

    B. The number specified by the `web-app/servlet/servlet-instance` deployment descriptor.

    C. The number specified by the `Servlet.setMaxInstances()` method.

    D. There are no restrictions on the number of servlet instances.

44. Can multiple instances of a servlet be created in an application that implements the `SingleThreadModel`?

    A. No.

    B. Yes.

    C. Yes, but only if it is configured in web.xml.

    D. Yes, but only if the application is distributable.

45. What interface is used to declare that a servlet must use the single thread model?

    A. `javax.servlet.SingleThreadModel`

    B. `javax.servlet.http.SingleThreadModel`

    C. `javax.servlet.ServletContext`

    D. `javax.servlet.http.Multithreaded`

46. What are the opening and closing tags of a JSP directive?

    A. `<%` and `%>`

    B. `<%=` and `%>`

    C. `<%!` and `%>`

    D. `<%@` and `%>`

47. What are the opening and closing tags of a JSP declaration?

    A. `<%` and `%>`

    B. `<%=` and `%>`

    C. `<%!` and `%>`

    D. `<%@` and `%>`

48. When a JSP page is written in XML format, what is its top level document element? (Assuming the `jsp:` prefix is used to identify the namespace?)

    A. `jsp:document`

    B. `jsp:root`

    C. `jsp:jsp`

    D. `jsp:page`

49. Which of the following is an example of a JSP declaration written in XML format?

    A. `<jsp:declare>declaration goes here </jsp:declare>`

    B. `<jsp:declare name="value"/>`

    C. `<jsp:declaration>declaration goes here </jsp:declaration>`

    D. `<jsp:declaration-element/>`

50. Which of the following is an example of a JSP scriptlet written in XML format?

    A. `<jsp:scriptlet> code goes here </jsp:scriptlet>`

    B. `<jsp:code> code goes here </jsp:code>`

    C. `<jsp:include> code goes here </jsp:include>`

    D. `<jsp:jsp> code goes here </jsp:jsp>`

51. Which of the following are names of JSP elements?

    A. `jsp:include`

    B. `jsp:forward`

    C. `jsp:plugin`

    D. `jsp:text`

52. Which directive is used to import packages into a JSP?

    A. `import`

    B. `page`

    C. `include`

    D. `taglib`

53. Which of the following objects are available within JSP?

    A. `request`

    B. `response`

    C. `error`

    D. `exception`

54. Which of the following perform a translation-time include?

    A. `<%@include file="file.jsp" %>`

    B. `<jsp:include page="page.jsp" />`

    C. `pageContext.include("file.jsp")`

    D. None of the above.

55. Which deployment descriptor identifies the location (as a resource relative to the root of the Web application) where to find the Tag Library Description file for the tag library?

    A. `web-app/taglib/taglib-uri`

    B. `web-app/taglib/taglib-location`

    C. `web-app/taglib/location`

    D. `web-app/taglib/uri`

56. Which of the following are valid return values for the `doStartTag()` method?

    A. `SKIP_BODY`

    B. `EVAL_BODY_INCLUDE`

    C. `EVAL_BODY_BUFFERED`

    D. `EVAL_BODY_AGAIN`

57. What is the value for the `bodycontent` tag library descriptor element for a custom tag that surrounds content that is used only by the tag handler?

    A. empty

    B. `JSP`

    C. `tagdependent`

    D. `body-content`

58. Which tag library decriptor element identifies whether or not the attribute's value can be dynamically specified?

    A. `taglib/tag/attribute/name`

    B. `taglib/tag/attribute/required`

    C. `taglib/tag/attribute/dynamic`

    D. `taglib/tag/attribute/rtexprvalue`

59. Which tag library descriptor element identifies the class of a tag handler?

    A. `taglib/tag/tag-class`

    B. `taglib/tag/class`

    C. `taglib/tag/name`

    D. `taglib/tag/class-name`

60. Which design pattern decouples presentation and service tiers, and provides a facade and proxy interface to business services?

    A. Value objects

    B. Model-view-controller

    C. Data access objects

    D. Business delegate

ANSWERS TO EXAM QUESTIONS

1. **A, C, and D**. Servlets provide capabilities that are similar to those provided by CGI programs but they are not executed via the CGI.
2. **B**. The `doGet()` method of `javax.servlet.http.HttpServlet` handles the GET HTTP request.
3. **C**. The `setContentType()` method of `ServletResponse` sets the MIME type associated with the response.
4. **C**. The `getWriter()` method of `ServletResponse` returns a `PrintWriter` object.
5. **A**. The HTTP `POST` method is commonly used to submit form data to a server-side program.
6. **D**. The `getParameter()` method is defined in `ServletRequest` and inherited by `HttpServletRequest`.
7. **B**. The `HEAD` method provides an efficient way to determine when a resource has been last modified.
8. **A and D**. Both `Servlet` and `ServletConfig` define the `getInitParameter()` method for retrieving servlet initialization parameters. The `ServletContext` uses parameters for the servlet context (application), not servlet initialization parameters. There are two different sets of init parameters: ones for servlet definitions and ones for the servlet context (the Web app).
9. **B**. The `getHeader()` method is defined by `HttpServletRequest`.
10. **D**. The `HttpServletResponse.setHeader()` method is used to set the value of an HTTP response header.
11. **C**. The `ServletResponse.getOutputStream()` method can be used to obtain a binary stream to send information back to a client.
12. **A**. The `HttpServletResponse.sendRedirect()` method can be used to redirect an HTTP request to another URL.
13. **A, C, and D**. The `ServletResponse` interface does not support the `getAttribute()` method.
14. **D**. The `init()` method is called by the servlet container one time to indicate to a servlet that it is being placed into service.
15. **B**. The `service()` method is called by the servlet container to allow the servlet to respond to a request.
16. **B**. The `RequestDispatcher` interface can be used to receive requests from the client and send them to a servlet, HTML file, or JSP file.
17. **D**. The WEB-INF directory is placed in the application root directory. The web.xml file, classes directory, and lib directory are found underneath the WEB-INF directory.
18. **B**. JAR files are placed in the lib directory.
19. **A and C**. The jar tool can be used to create .war files, which are used to distribute Web applications.
20. **A**. Deployment descriptors are specified using an application's web.xml file.
21. **C**. The name of a servlet's class is specified using servlet-class (`web-app/servlet/servlet-class`).
22. **D**. Servlet initialization parameters are specified using `web-app/servlet/init-param`.
23. **B**. The `ServletContextAttributeListener` interface is used to handle events that occur when an attribute is added or removed from the application's `ServletContext`.

24. **D**. The `HttpSessionActivationListener` defines the `sessionWillPassivate()` method.

25. **A**. Application event listeners are specified using `web-app/listener/listener-class`.

26. **C** and **D**. Distributable applications may involve the use of more than one servlet container/JVM. A is wrong because Servlet init. params are defined in the web.xml file and cannot be altered for each Web container. B is wrong because a session is tied to the JVM, not the machine.

27. **B** and **D**. The `setError()` and `sendStatus()` methods are not defined.

28. **A**. The `web-app/error-page` deployment descriptor is used to specify an error-handling page.

29. **D**. The `ServletContext.log()` method is used to write information to a Web application's log file.

30. **D**. The `HttpServletRequest.getSession()` may be used to access a session object.

31. **C**. The `invalidate()` method is used to expunge a session.

32. **B** and **C**. An existing session object will be invalidated if its `invalidate()` method is invoked or the session timeout expires between two requests by the client. If an object's `setMaxInactiveInterval()` method is invoked with an argument of –1, the session will never time out.

33. **A**. Page URLs must be rewritten to include the `jsessionid` parameter so that the session information may be propagated back to the servlet container.

34. **C**. Data integrity is the means used to prove that information has not been modified by a third party while in transit.

35. **A**. Authentication is the means by which communicating entities prove to one another that it is really them; they are acting on behalf of specific identities that are authorized for access.

36. **B**. Access control is the means by which interactions with resources are limited to collections of users or programs for the purpose of enforcing integrity, confidentiality, or availability constraints.

37. **B**. The `web-app/security-constraint` is used to associate security constraints with one or more Web resource collections.

38. **C**. The `web-app/security-constraint/auth-constraint` element identifies the user roles that should be permitted access to this resource collection.

39. **D**. The `web-app/security-constraint/user-data-constraint` element identifies how data communicated between the client and container should be protected.

40. **B**. The `web-app/login-conf element` is used to configure the authentication method that should be used to authenticate application users.

41. **A**, **B**, **C**, and **D**. All four authentication methods are supported by Servlet Containers.

42. **A** and **B**. Local variables and request parameters are thread safe. Access to instance and class variables should be synchronized because they are shared among multiple concurrent requests.

43. **D**. Since it is not single-threaded, it is multiple-threaded, which means any number of instances can access the service method of a single servlet when it doesn't implement the `SingleThreadModel` interface.

44. **B**. Under the `SingleThreadModel` multiple servlet instances can be created, but only one thread can be executing the servlet's service method at a given time.

45. **A**. The javax.servlet.SingleThreadModel interface is used to declare that a servlet must use the single thread model.

46. **D**. <%@ and %> are the opening and closing tags of a JSP directive.

47. **C**. <%! and %> are the opening and closing tags of a JSP declaration.

48. **B**. The jsp:root element is the document element when a JSP is written in XML format.

49. **C**. The jsp:declaration element is used to specify a declaration.

50. **A**. The jsp:scriptlet element is used to specify a scriptlet.

51. **A**, **B**, **C**, and **D**. All are examples of JSP actions.

52. **B**. The import statement within the page directive is used to import packages into a JSP.

53. **A**, **B**, and **D**. The error variable is not a predefined variable.

54. **A**. The include directive performs a translation-time include. The others perform a runtime include.

55. **B**. The web-app/taglib/taglib-location element identifies the location where to find the Tag Library Description file for a tag library.

56. **A**, **B**, and **C**. EVAL_BODY_AGAIN is a return value of the doAfterBody() method.

57. **C**. The value for the bodycontent tag library descriptor element for a custom tag that surrounds content that is used only by the tag handler is tagdependent.

58. **D**. The taglib/tag/attribute/rtexprvalue tag library descriptor identifies whether or not the attribute's value can be dynamically specified.

59. **A**. The taglib/tag/tag-class tag library descriptor element identifies the class of a tag handler.

60. **D**. The business delegate design pattern decouples presentation and service tiers, and provides a facade and proxy interface to business services.

PART

APPENDIXES

APPENDIX A

Servlet API Snapshot

This appendix helps you prepare for the exam by describing the Servlet API. While the chapters explained the various portions of the API in detail, this appendix gives you a simple listing of the classes, methods and fields as a reference.

INTRODUCTION

This appendix describes the javax.servlet package, mostly taken from the content that is generated from the javadocs, which define the actual Java classes and interfaces. You don't have to know the entire API. However, every class and method on the exam is here, and a few more for completeness. Among all the classes and interfaces, the Servlet interface is the central abstraction of the Servlet API. The specification ensures that all servlets implement this interface. This is usually done by extending a class that implements the Servlet interface. While two classes in the servlet API implement the Servlet interface, `GenericServlet` and `HttpServlet`, we will focus only on `HttpServlet`. It's the `HttpServlet` class methods that will appear on the exam.

The Servlet 2.3 API defines the interfaces, classes, methods, fields, and constants that you will use to build servlets. The Web Component Developer Exam is filled with questions on this API. Therefore it is helpful to have an appendix which simply filters the most important parts of the Servlet 2.3 API.

> NOTE
>
> **Servlet API Version** The Java 2 Web Component Developer Exam covers version 2.3 of the Servlet API and version 1.2 of JavaServer Pages.

OVERVIEW OF THE SERVLET API

The Servlet 2.3 API consists of two packages: `javax.servlet` and `javax.servlet.http`. Although the exam also covers JSP 1.2, in this appendix we will focus only on these two servlet packages. The base functionality is defined in the `javax.servlet` package whose classes and interfaces outline a generic, protocol-independent implementation. This means you can use it for non-Web applications, too. Of course, the exam targets the Web, so the HTTP protocol is the only one discussed in this book. The `javax.servlet.http` interface defines classes and interfaces that are specific to the Hypertext Transfer Protocol (HTTP).

THE `javax.servlet` PACKAGE

The `javax.servlet` package defines 12 interfaces, 7 classes, and 2 exceptions. These interfaces, classes, and exceptions are summarized as follows.

Interfaces

The interface include the following:

- `Filter`—Preprocessor of the request before it reaches a servlet. It can also be a postprocessor of the response leaving a servlet. It can modify a request or response (for example, change headers), the request to a resource (a servlet or static content), or the response from a resource.

> NOTE
>
> **Filtering** Request/response filtering was introduced with version 2.3 of the Servlet API. Filter questions are not covered by the exam so they are not discussed in this book.

- `RequestDispatcher`—This is the servlet version of a redirect. It enables requests to be processed and then forwarded to other components of a Web application, such as another servlet, HTML file, or JSP file.
- `Servlet`—Defines the life-cycle methods that are implemented by all servlets.
- `ServletConfig`—This class has the methods for accessing the servlet configuration information such as the servlets name (from the web.xml file), the initialization parameters, and the ServletContext object.
- `ServletContext`—These methods enable your servlet to communicate with its servlet container. This is how you get the MIME type of a file, dispatch requests, or write to a log file. Notice that this information has application scope. The most important features of the ServletContext are application-scope attributes access, logging, and context initialization parameters.
- `ServletContextAttributeListener`— Implementations of this interface receive notifications of changes to the attribute list on the servlet context of a Web application. Supports the handling of the `ServletContextAttributeEvent` class.
- `ServletContextListener`—An interface that supports the handling of the `ServletContextEvent` class. Defines a set of methods that a servlet uses to communicate with its servlet container. It can get the MIME type of a file, dispatch requests, or write to a log file. Notice that there is one context per "Web application" per Java Virtual Machine. The specification defines a "Web application" as a collection of servlets and content installed under a specific subset of the server's URL namespace, such as /catalog, and possibly installed via a .war file.
- `ServletRequest`—This interface forms the base for the class that provides client request information to a servlet. It is protocol-independent.
- `ServletResponse`—This interface forms the base for the class that represents the response sent from the servlet to the client.
- `SingleThreadModel`—An interface that ensures a given servlet handles only one request at a time.

Classes

The classes include the following:

- `GenericServlet`—An abstract class that implements ServletConfig. It defines a generic, protocol-independent servlet.
- `ServletContextAttributeEvent`—This is the event class for notifications about changes to the attributes of the servlet context of a Web application.

- `ServletContextEvent`—This is the event class for notifications about changes to the servlet context of a Web application (parent of `ServletContextAttributeEvent`).
- `ServletInputStream`—Provides an input stream for reading binary data from a client request. You can modify it; it already has the `readLine` method for reading data one line at a time.
- `ServletOutputStream` —An abstract class providing an output stream for sending binary data to the client. You print HTML, XML, or other output to the client using `ServletOutputStream`'s `print()` and `println()` methods.
- `ServletRequestWrapper`—Provides a convenient implementation of the `ServletRequest` interface that can be subclassed by developers wishing to adapt the request to a Servlet. This is where you can modify the behavior of request objects.
- `ServletResponseWrapper`—Provides a convenient implementation of the `ServletResponse` interface that can be subclassed by developers wishing to adapt the response from a Servlet. This is where you can modify the behavior of response objects.

Exceptions

The exceptions include the following:

- `ServletException` —Extends `java.lang.Exception` to provide a base class for defining servlet-related extensions.
- `UnavailableException` —Extends `ServletException` to indicate that a servlet is temporarily or permanently unavailable.

UNDERSTANDING THE `javax.servlet` PACKAGE INTERFACES, CLASSES, AND EXCEPTIONS

Each of the above classes, interfaces, and exceptions are covered in the following subsections.

Interfaces

The following sections describe the interfaces of the `javax.servlet` package.

`RequestDispatcher`

The `RequestDispatcher` interface defines the `forward()` and `include()` methods for use as request wrappers. It enables requests to be processed and then forwarded to other elements of a Web application. It also allows the results of other application elements to be included in the response. A `RequestDispatcher` object is created with the path or name of the resource to be dispatched.

Servlet

The `Servlet` interface defines methods that are implemented by all servlets. A default implementation of these methods is provided by `GenericServlet`.

The following methods are used to control the servlet life-cycle:

- `void init(ServletConfig config)`—Invoked by the servlet container to put the servlet in service.
- `void service(ServletRequest req, ServletResponse res)`—Invoked by the servlet container to enable a servlet to respond to a request.

- `void destroy()`—Invoked by the servlet container to remove the servlet from service.

These methods provide access to servlet configuration information:

- `ServletConfig getServletConfig()`—Returns the `ServletConfig` object that is associated with the servlet.
- `String getServletInfo()`—Returns the servlet's information string.

ServletConfig

The `ServletConfig` interface defines methods for accessing servlet configuration information. Configuration information is passed as a series of name-value pairs.

Methods also provide access to the servlet's name and `ServletContext` object:

- `String getInitParameter(String name)`—Returns the value of the specified parameter.
- `Enumeration getInitParameterNames()`—Returns an `Enumeration` of the names of the servlet's initialization parameters.
- `ServletContext getServletContext()`—Returns the `ServletContext` object corresponding to the servlet.
- `String getServletName()`—Returns the servlet's name.

ServletContext

The `ServletContext` interface defines methods for accessing application-scope attributes. It is limited to a single JVM, and therefore should not be used when clustering is in effect. The `ServletContext` methods provide access to objects that are placed in application scope:

- `Object getAttribute(String name)`—Returns the object corresponding to the named attribute.
- `Enumeration getAttributeNames()`—Returns an `Enumeration` of the defined attribute names.
- `void removeAttribute(String name)`—Removes the attribute from the servlet context.
- `void setAttribute(String name, Object object)`—Sets the object associated with the specified attribute name.
- `String getInitParameter(String name)`—Returns the value of the named initialization parameter.
- `Enumeration getInitParameterNames()`—Returns an `Enumeration` the initialization parameter names.
- `int getMajorVersion()`—Returns the major version of the Servlet API supported by the servlet container.
- `String getMimeType(String file)`—Returns the MIME type of the specified file, if known.
- `int getMinorVersion()`—Returns the minor version of the Servlet API supported by the servlet container.
- `String getRealPath(String path)`—Translates a virtual path into a real path.
- `String getServerInfo()`—Returns the name and version of the servlet container on which the servlet is running.
- `ServletContext getContext(String url)`—Returns the `ServletContext` object that corresponds to the specified URL. The URL must be on the same server.
- `RequestDispatcher getNamedDispatcher(String name)`—Returns a `RequestDispatcher` object that acts as a wrapper for the named servlet.

- RequestDispatcher getRequestDispatcher (String path)—Returns a RequestDispatcher object that acts as a wrapper for the resource located at the specified path.
- java.net.URL getResource(String path)—Returns the URL of the resource that is mapped to the specified path.
- java.io.InputStream getResourceAsStream (String path)—Returns the resource located at the specified path as an InputStream object.
- void log(String msg)—Writes the message to the servlet log file.
- void log(String message, Throwable throwable)—Writes the message to the servlet log file along with a stack trace for the Throwable object.

ServletContextAttributeListener

The ServletContextAttributeListener interface defines methods for handling the ServletContextAttributeEvent. These methods are as follows:

- void attributeAdded (ServletContextAttributeEvent scab)
- void attributeRemoved (ServletContextAttributeEvent scab)
- void attributeReplaced (ServletContextAttributeEvent scab)

ServletContextListener

The ServletContextListener interface defines methods for handling the ServletContextEvent. The ServletContextEvent object represents the creation/destruction of a ServletContext.

The contextDestroyed() method handles the destruction of a ServletContext. Lastly, the contextInitialized() method handles the creation of a ServletContext object.

ServletRequest

The ServletRequest interface provides a protocol-independent definition of the methods used to access the information contained in a client request of a servlet. These methods provide access to nearly all of the information contained in the original request.

A ServletRequest object is created by the servlet container and made available to a servlet via its service() method. ServletRequest is extended by javax.servlet.http.HttpServletRequest.

ServletRequest defines several methods for accessing request data:

- Object getAttribute(String name)—Returns the object associated with the attribute name.
- Enumeration getAttributeNames()—Returns an Enumeration of the request's attributes.
- void removeAttribute(String name)—Removes an attribute from this request.
- void setAttribute(String name, Object o)—Sets the value of an attribute of this request.
- String getParameter(String name)—Returns the value of the specified request parameter.
- Enumeration getParameterNames()—Returns an Enumeration of the names of the parameters of this request.
- String[] getParameterValues(String name)—Returns an array of the values of the specified request parameter.
- ServletInputStream getInputStream()—Provides a ServletInputStream that corresponds to the body of the request.

- `java.io.BufferedReader getReader()`—Provides a `BufferedReader` that corresponds to the body of the request.
- `String getCharacterEncoding()`—Returns the character encoding used in the body of the request.
- `int getContentLength()`—Returns the length (in bytes) of the request body. Returns -1 if the length is not known.
- `String getContentType()`—Returns the MIME type of the body of the request, if known.
- `String getProtocol()`—Returns the name and version of the protocol used to make the request.
- `String getScheme()`—Returns the name of the scheme used to make this request (http, https, or ftp).
- `int getServerPort()`—Returns the port number associated with the request.
- `boolean isSecure()`—Returns a boolean indicating whether this request was made using a secure protocol, such as HTTPS.
- `java.util.Locale getLocale()`—Returns the Locale object corresponding to the Accept-Language header.
- `Enumeration getLocales()`—Returns an `Enumeration` of `Locale` objects based on the Accept-Language header.
- `String getRemoteAddr()`—Returns the IP address of the client.
- `String getRemoteHost()`—Returns the host name of the client or the IP address if the host name cannot be determined.
- `RequestDispatcher getRequestDispatcher(String path)`—Returns a `RequestDispatcher` object that acts as a wrapper for the resource located at the specified path.
- `String getServerName()`—Returns the host name of the server that received the request.

ServletResponse

The `ServletResponse` interface encapsulates a response sent from the servlet to the client. A `ServletResponse` object is automatically created by the servlet container and passed to a servlet via its service method. `ServletResponse` defines several methods for configuring, assembling, and sending response information:

- `String getCharacterEncoding()`—Returns the name of the charset used for the MIME body sent in this response.
- `java.util.Locale getLocale()`—Returns the locale assigned to the response.
- `void setContentLength(int len)`—Sets the length of the content body (Content-Length header).
- `void setContentType(String type)`—Sets the content type of the response being sent to the client.
- `void setLocale(java.util.Locale loc)`—Sets the locale of the response and the appropriate headers.
- `ServletOutputStream getOutputStream()`—Returns a `ServletOutputStream` for writing binary data to the client.
- `java.io.PrintWriter getWriter()`—Returns a `PrintWriter` object for writing character data to the client.
- `void flushBuffer()`—Forces any content in the buffer to be written to the client.
- `int getBufferSize()`—Returns the actual buffer size used for the response.
- `boolean isCommitted()`—Returns a boolean indicating whether the response has been committed.

- void reset()—Clears any data that exists in the buffer as well as the status code and headers.
- void setBufferSize(int size)—Sets the buffer size for the body of the response.

SingleThreadModel

The SingleThreadModel interface is implemented by servlets that are required to handle a single request at a time. This interface is intended to make sure a single servlet thread is executed at a given point in time, providing thread safety. This interface defines no methods.

Classes

The following sections describe the classes of the javax.servlet package.

GenericServlet

The GenericServlet class defines a basic implementation of the Servlet interface in a protocol-independent manner. It also implements the ServletConfig and java.io.Serializable interfaces. It is extended by javax.servlet.http.HttpServlet.

ServletContextAttributeEvent

The ServletContextAttributeEvent is generated as the result of changes to the attributes of the servlet context. The getName() method returns the name of the attribute that was changed. The getValue() method returns the value of the changed attribute.

ServletContextEvent

The ServletContextEvent class is the parent class of ServletContextAttributeEvent. It provides notifications about changes to the servlet context of a Web application. The getServletContext() method provides access to the affected ServletContext object.

ServletInputStream

The ServletInputStream class is an abstract class that provides a stream for reading client request data. It extends java.io.InputStream. It is typically used with HTTP POST and PUT requests. An instance of this class is obtained via ServletRequest.getInputStream().

ServletOutputStream

The ServletOutputStream class is an abstract class that provides an output stream (binary) for sending response data. It extends java.io.OutputStream. An instance of this class is obtained via ServletResponse.getOutputStream().

ServletRequestWrapper

The ServletRequestWrapper class provides an implementation of the ServletRequest interface that can be extended and tailored to modify the way that a request is processed. A ServletRequest object is provided as an argument to the ServletRequestWrapper constructor. The methods of ServletRequestWrapper can be overridden to provide the wrapped effect. ServletRequestWrapper is extended by HttpServletRequestWrapper.

ServletResponseWrapper

The ServletResponseWrapper class provides an implementation of the ServletResponse interface that can be extended and tailored to modify the way that a response is processed. A ServletResponse object is provided as an argument to the ServletResponseWrapper constructor. The methods of ServletResponseWrapper can be overridden to provide the wrapped effect. ServletResponseWrapper is extended by HttpServletResponseWrapper.

Exceptions

The following sections describe the exceptions of the javax.servlet package.

ServletException

The ServletException exception extends java.lang.Exception to provide a base class for defining servlet-related extensions. The getRootCause() method provides access to the exception (if any) that results in the throwing of ServletException.

UnavailableException

The UnavailableException exception extends ServletException to indicate that a servlet is temporarily or permanently unavailable. The getUnavailableSeconds() method returns the number of seconds the servlet expects to be temporarily unavailable. The isPermanent() method returns a boolean value indicating whether the servlet is permanently unavailable.

The javax.servlet.http Package

The javax.servlet.http package defines eight interfaces and seven classes. These interfaces and classes are summarized in the following sections.

Interfaces

The interfaces include the following:

- HttpServletRequest—Extends javax.servlet.ServletRequest to support HTTP.
- HttpServletResponse—Extends javax.servlet.ServletResponse to support HTTP.
- HttpSession—Defines methods that provide access to persistent session-state information.
- HttpSessionActivationListener—Implemented to handle the HttpSessionActivationEvent.
- HttpSessionAttributeListener—Implemented to handle the HttpSessionAttributeEvent.
- HttpSessionBindingListener—Implemented by objects that listen for HttpSessionBindingEvent events.
- HttpSessionListener—Implemented to handle the HttpSessionEvent.

Classes

The classes include the following:

- Cookie—Encapsulates HTTP cookies.
- HttpServlet—An abstract class that extends javax.servlet.GenericServlet to provide support for HTTP.
- HttpServletRequestWrapper—Provides the capability to wrap and modify incoming HttpServletRequest objects.
- HttpServletResponseWrapper—Provides the capability to wrap and modify outgoing HttpServletResponse objects.
- HttpSessionBindingEvent—Extends java.util.EventObject to define an event that is sent to an HttpSessionBindingListener when an object is bound or unbound from the current HttpSession.

- HttpSessionEvent—Parent class of HttpSessionBindingEvent.

The javax.servlet.http package does not define any exceptions.

UNDERSTANDING THE javax.servlet.http PACKAGE INTERFACES AND CLASSES

Each of the above interfaces and classes are covered in the following subsections.

Interfaces

The following sections describe the interfaces of the javax.servlet.http package.

HttpServletRequest

The HttpServletRequest interface extends javax.servlet.ServletRequest to support HTTP. An HttpServletRequest object is automatically created by the servlet container and provided as an argument to the HttpServlet's doXXX() methods.

HttpServletRequest provides numerous HTTP-specific methods for accessing the client's request. Some important methods are

- String getAuthType()—Returns the name of the authentication scheme used with the servlet.
- String getContextPath()—Returns the context path of the requested URL.
- Cookie[] getCookies()—Returns an array containing all of the Cookie objects sent by the client.
- long getDateHeader(String name)—Returns the value of the date header as a long value.
- String getHeader(String name)—Returns the value of the specified request header.
- Enumeration getHeaderNames()—Returns an enumeration of all the header names that are associated with the request.
- Enumeration getHeaders(String name)—Returns an Enumeration of all the values of the specified request header.
- int getIntHeader(String name)—Returns the value of the specified request header as an int.
- String getMethod()—Returns the name of the HTTP method associated with the request.
- String getPathInfo()—Returns any extra path information associated with the request.
- String getPathTranslated()—Returns any extra path information after the servlet name but before the query string.
- String getQueryString()—Returns the query string that is associated with the request.
- String getRemoteUser()—Returns the login of the user making this request, if the user has been authenticated.
- String getRequestedSessionId()—Returns the session ID specified by the client cookie or URL-rewriting.
- String getRequestURI()—Returns the part of this request's URL from the protocol name up to the query string.
- String getServletPath()—Returns the part of this request's URL that calls the servlet.
- HttpSession getSession()—Returns the current session associated with this request, or if the request does not have a session, creates one.

- `HttpSession getSession(boolean create)`—Returns the current `HttpSession` associated with this request or, if there is no current session and create is true, returns a new session. Otherwise, null is returned.
- `java.security.Principal getUserPrincipal()`—Returns a `java.security.Principal` object containing the name of the current authenticated user.
- `boolean isRequestedSessionIdFromCookie()`—Checks whether the requested session ID came in as a cookie.
- `boolean isRequestedSessionIdFromURL()`—Checks whether the requested session ID came in as part of the request URL.
- `boolean isRequestedSessionIdValid()`—Checks whether the requested session ID is still valid.
- `boolean isUserInRole(String role)`—Returns a `boolean` indicating whether the authenticated user is included in the specified logical "role."

HttpServletResponse

The `HttpServletResponse` interface extends `javax.servlet.ServletResponse` to support HTTP. An `HttpServletResponse` object is automatically created by the servlet container and provided as an argument to `HttpServlet`'s `doXXX()` methods.

`HttpServletResponse` also defines a number of response error code constants. It provides numerous methods for manipulating the response sent to the client.

The following are important `HttpServletResponse` methods:

- `void addCookie(Cookie cookie)`—Adds the specified cookie to the response.
- `void addDateHeader(String name, long date)`—Adds a response header with the given name and date.
- `void addHeader(String name, String value)`—Adds a response header with the given name and value.
- `void addIntHeader(String name, int value)`—Adds a response header with the given name and integer value.
- `boolean containsHeader(String name)`—Returns a `boolean` indicating whether the named response header has already been set.
- `String encodeRedirectURL(String url)`—Encodes the specified URL for use in the `sendRedirect()` method. It appends the session ID in it.
- `String encodeURL(String url)`—Encodes the specified URL by including the session ID in it.
- `void sendError(int sc)`—Sends an error response to the client using the specified status.
- `void sendError(int sc, String msg)`—Sends an error response to the client using the specified status code and descriptive message.
- `void sendRedirect(String location)`—Sends a temporary redirect response to the client.
- `void setDateHeader(String name, long date)`—Sets a response header with the given name and date.
- `void setHeader(String name, String value)`—Sets a response header with the given name and value.
- `void setIntHeader(String name, int value)`—Sets a response header with the given name and integer value.
- `void setStatus(int sc)`—Sets the status code for this response.

HttpSession

The HttpSession interface defines methods that provide access to persistent session-state information. These methods are used to get and set attributes into the session scope (getAttribute() and setAttribute()). Methods are also provided to get access to the session creation time, last access time, maximum timeout interval, and session ID. The invalidate() method is used to terminate an HTTP session.

HttpSessionActivationListener

The HttpSessionActivationListener interface defines methods for handling the HttpSessionActivationEvent. These methods are sessionDidActivate() and sessionWillPassivate().

HttpSessionAttributeListener

The HttpSessionAttributeListener interface defines methods for handling the HttpSessionAttributeEvent. These methods are attributeAdded(), attributeRemoved(), and attributeReplaced().

HttpSessionBindingListener

The HttpSessionBindingListener interface defines methods for objects that listen for HttpSessionBindingEvent events. The valueBound() method is invoked when an object is bound to an HttpSession. The valueUnbound() method is invoked when an object is unbound from an HttpSession.

HttpSessionContext

The HttpSessionContext interface was deprecated as of the Servlet 2.1 API. It is the predecessor of HttpSession.

HttpSessionListener

The HttpSessionListener interface defines methods for handling the HttpSessionEvent. The sessionCreated() method is used to handle the creation of a new HttpSession object. The sessionDestroyed() method handles the destruction of an HttpSession object.

Classes

The following sections describe the classes of the javax.servlet.http package.

Cookie

The Cookie class encapsulates HTTP cookies. It enables cookies to be retrieved or set. Cookies are retrieved via HttpServletRequest.getCookies(). Cookies are set via HttpServletResponse.addCookie(). Both version 0 (Netscape) and version 1 (RFC 2109) cookies are supported. Created cookies are version 0, by default. The Cookie class implements the Cloneable interface.

HttpServlet

The HttpServlet class is an abstract class that extends javax.servlet.GenericServlet to provide support for HTTP. It is extended to create custom servlets. It supports the HTTP GET, POST, PUT, DELETE, OPTIONS, and TRACE requests via protected methods of the form doGet(), doPost(), doPut(), doDelete(), doOptions(), and doTrace(). These methods take an HttpServletRequest object and an HttpServletResponse object as their parameters.

These protected doXXX()methods are overridden to handle specific request types. Remember that the service method dispatches to the appropriate doXXX() method.

HttpServletRequestWrapper

The HttpServletRequestWrapper class provides the capability to wrap and modify incoming HttpServletRequest objects. It extends ServletRequestWrapper and implements HttpServletRequest.

The request to be wrapped is passed to this class's constructor. Since this class implements the methods of HttpServletRequest, all of the request methods can then be invoked on the wrapped object. These methods can be overridden to produce the new wrapped results.

HttpServletResponseWrapper

The HttpServletResponseWrapper class provides the capability to wrap and modify outgoing HttpServletResponse objects. It extends ServletResponseWrapper and implements HttpServletResponse.

The response to be wrapped is passed to this class's constructor. Since this class implements the methods of HttpServletReponse, all of the response methods can then be invoked on the wrapped object. These methods can be overridden to produce the new wrapped results.

HttpSessionBindingEvent

The HttpSessionBindingEvent class extends HttpSessionEvent (which extends java.util.EventObject) to define an event that is sent to an HttpSessionBindingListener when an object is bound or unbound from the current HttpSession.

The String getName() method returns the attribute name of the object.

The HttpSession getSession() method returns the associated HttpSession object.

HttpSessionEvent

The HttpSessionEvent class is the parent class of HttpSessionBindingEvent. It is used to provide notifications of changes to sessions within a Web application. It defines one method, getSession(), that returns the HttpSession object of the affected session.

SUMMARY

In this appendix, you reviewed the details of the Servlet API. You learned the purpose of the classes and interfaces of the Servlet API, and covered important methods of these classes and interfaces. This is something you can refer to now and again. Also, you should scan this the night before you sit for the exam.

Suggested Readings and Resources

1. Exam objectives for the Sun Certified Web Component Developer For J2EE Platform, http://suned.sun.com/US/certification/java/exam_objectives.html.
2. The Java Servlet 2.3 Specification, http://jcp.org/aboutJava/communityprocess/first/jsr053/index.html.
3. The Java Servlet 2.3 API, http://java.sun.com/products/servlet/2.3/javadoc/index.html.

APPENDIX **B**

JSP Syntax

This appendix helps you prepare for the exam by providing you with a syntax reference to the main features of JSP. Chapter 7, "JavaServer Pages (JSP) Technology Model," discussed JavaServer Pages in depth. Here, this appendix gives you a simple listing of the syntax elements with brief examples. Sometimes it is useful to have a quick reference.

This appendix comes from Sun's specification and documentation (see `http://java.sun.com/products/jsp/syntax.pdf`). I've tried to make it more readable by keeping the most essential information and tossing out the rest.

While Sun provides you with the full JSP specification and a more detailed syntax card, this appendix has a quick look format. The JSP and XML syntax come straight from the specification, but the explanations and examples are edited for readability.

> NOTE
>
> **JSP Version** The Java 2 Web Component Developer Exam covers JavaServer Pages version 1.2.

Syntax Rules

There are a few general syntax rules to keep in mind:

- All tags are case sensitive.
- A pair of single quotes is equivalent to a pair of double quotes. This is generally true in HTML tags as well. Note that single quotes must be matched with single quotes, and doubles with doubles.
- Outside of quotes, spaces don't count, but inside they do. Also, spaces are not allowed between an equals sign and an attribute value. This is consistent with current XML/HTML tagging practices in that spaces are supposed to be used only to separate attribute-value pairs from each other and from the name of the tag. In my opinion, spaces should not be significant between operators (for example, scriptlet delimiter and equals sign) the same way Java syntax is handled in general, but I'm in the minority on this issue.
- JSP tags and their XML equivalents cannot be mixed (well) within a page. You don't throw JSP inside an XML tag. Likewise, you must be very careful if you try to use an XML tag inside, say, a scriptlet. The following is wrong:

```
<% customerCount=8;
<myTagLibrary:customer count="8">
System.out.print(customerCount); %>
```

- A page in one syntax can include or forward to a page in the other syntax.
- How do you quote JSP? You would do this in an online JSP tutorial, for example. You have to escape some of the syntax so the engine knows to pass it through as text and not interpret it. Notice that without the JSP beginning tag, the engine treats it as text, so you can have as much Java code pass through as text. You might do this if your Web page is a Java tutorial. You can tell the container "ignore this Java; I want it to print on the page" by simply escaping part of the start tag. Here are some examples: `<\%`, `%\>`, `\'`, `\"`. So the following will be added to the output stream and not translated:

```
<\% customerCount=99; %>
```

Format Conventions

These are the formatting conventions used in this appendix, the same ones used by Sun:

- `code` = fixed
- **`bold`** = default
- *`italics`* = user-defined
- `|` = or
- `[ ]` = optional
- `{ }` = required choice
- `...` = list of items
- `+` = can repeat

HTML OR OUTPUT COMMENT

These are plain HTML comments that are passed through to the client. The client doesn't process these. There is nothing special about them and the servlet container ignores them, passing them through as text. Notice how you can use a scriptlet to insert text in the comment before it is sent off to the client. For example, you can datestamp a comment.

JSP Syntax

```
<!-- comment [ <%= expression %> ]-->
```

XML Syntax

None.

Example

```
<%@ page language="java" %>
<html>
        <head>
           <title>Hidden Comment</title>
        </head>
        <body>
           <h1>Hidden Comment</h1>
           <!--
             Any text between these delimiters
             is passed through by the
➥processor and is
             included in the response
             including this: <%="scriplet"%>.
           -->
        </body>
</html>
```

Which produces

```
<html>
        <head>
           <title>Hidden Comment</title>
        </head>
        <body>
           <h1>Hidden Comment</h1>
           <!--
             Any text between these delimiters
             is passed through by the
➥processor and is
             included in the response
             including this: scriplet.
           -->
        </body>
</html>
```

HIDDEN COMMENT

The text within a hidden comment (`<%-- --%>`) is ignored by the JSP container. Unlike HTML comments, within which you can embed scriptlets, you don't place scriptlets in a hidden comment. The JSP container does not process anything between the `<%--` and `--%>` characters. A hidden comment is not inserted into the response.

JSP Syntax

```
<%-- comment --%>
```

XML Syntax

None.

Example

```
<%@ page language="java" %>
<html>
        <head>
           <title>Hidden Comment</title>
        </head>
        <body>
           <h1>Hidden Comment</h1>
           <%--
             Any text between these delimiters
             is ignored by the processor and
➥is not
             included in the response
           --%>
        </body>
</html>
```

Declaration

A declaration declares variables or methods that you can use afterward in the JSP page. The declaration must precede these variables' use in the JSP page. You can place numerous declarations between the delimiters. The following rules apply:

- Terminate the declaration with a semicolon. This is the same for scriptlets, but the opposite of an Expression.
- You don't have to declare variables or methods that are already declared in imported packages.
- Since a static include file is treated as original JSP source, declarations in these must precede use. Conversely, declared variables are accessible from include files if the include directive comes after the declaration. Be careful with this. It is easy to get spaghetti code because the references to variables in the included code have to come after a declaration for those variables. Conversely, when you use includes, be mindful of what is declared in the include file. The scope of a declaration does not include dynamic resources included with `<jsp:include>`.

JSP Syntax

```
<%! declaration; [ declaration; ]+ ... %>
```

XML Syntax

```
<jsp:declaration>
   declaration; [ declaration; ]+ ...
</jsp:declaration>
```

Example

```
<%! String firstName = new String("Patricia");
%>
<%! int customerCount = 84; %>
```

Expression

A JSP expression can be any valid Java expression. The container evaluates it, converts the result to a String, and appends this String to the output stream. The only surprise with this element is you do not use a semicolon to terminate the statement. If you remove the equals sign from the opening delimiter, you have a scriptlet and must use a semicolon even though it is the same Java expression.

JSP Syntax

```
<%= expression %>
```

XML Syntax

```
<jsp:expression>
   expression
</jsp:expression>
```

Example

```
<%@ page language="java" %>
<html>
        <head>
           <title>Hidden Comment</title>
        </head>
        <body>
           <h1>Expression </h1>
           <%="This expression is simply a
➥String." %>
        </body>
</html>
```

SCRIPTLET

This contains a code fragment, containing valid Java statements and/or local variable declarations. These statements and declarations are being placed in a method (the `_jspService` method).

JSP Syntax

```
<% code fragment %>
```

XML Syntax

```
<jsp:scriptlet>
   code fragment
</jsp:scriptlet>
```

Example

```
<jsp:root

xmlns:jsp="http://java.sun.com/JSP/Page"
            version="1.2">
        <jsp:directive.page
➥import="java.util.Date" />
        <jsp:scriptlet>
            Date date = new Date();
            String message = getDate(date);
        </jsp:scriptlet>
        <jsp:text>
             <html>
                <head>
                   <title>Expression in XML
➥Syntax</title>
                </head>
                <body>
                   <h1 align="center">
                     <jsp:expression>
➥message</jsp:expression>
                   </h1>
                </body>
             </html>
        </jsp:text>
        <jsp:declaration>
            String getDate(Date date)
            {
                String message = "The date
➥is: " + date;
                return message;
            }
        </jsp:declaration>
        </jsp:root>
```

Which produces this

```
<html >
      <head >
        <title >Expression in XML
➥Syntax</title>
      </head>
      <body >
        <h1   align="center">
             The date is: Fri Jun 21 09:47:22
➥PDT 2002
        </h1>
      </body>
</html>
```

INCLUDE DIRECTIVE

An include directive inserts all the text in the named file into the JSP page at the point of the tag. Notice that it is as if this text is part of the JSP, so it is processed along with the rest of the JSP. This is called a static process. In other words, the container copies the text referenced in the file and does not process it in any way before being inserted into the JSP page. The included file can be any text, including pieces of JSP, HTML, XML, or plain text. Once this text is included, it is parsed as if it had been in the original JSP page.

Notice how this static include compares to the HTML equivalent: `<!--#include file="somefile.html" -->`. This HTML include is performed by the browser, which also inserts the result of this fetch into the HTML page. However, in the HTML include case, the referenced resource can be static (HTML, stylesheet) or dynamic (like a servlet or JSP page). If it is dynamic then whatever that resource sends back is what is placed inline at the point of the include tag.

JSP Syntax

```
<%@ include file="relativeURL" %>
```

XML Syntax

```
<jsp:directive.include file="relativeURL" />
```

Example

```
<jsp:root
    xmlns:jsp="http://java.sun.com/JSP/Page"
    version="1.2">
<jsp:text>
    <html>
        <head>
            <title>Example Include</title>
        </head>
        <body>
            <h1 align="center">
              <jsp:directive.include file="
➥message.txt" />
            </h1>
        </body>
    </html>
</jsp:text>
</jsp:root>
```

message.txt contains

```
This text was included from another file.
```

The output is (minor tweaks to spacing for printing)

```
<html >
        <head >
                <title >Example Include</title>
        </head>
        <body >
                <h1   align="center">This text
➥was included from another file.
                </h1>
        </body>
</html>
```

PAGE DIRECTIVE

This tag is the most powerful one of the bunch. It defines attributes that apply to an entire JSP page. Please see Chapter 7, "JavaServer Pages (JSP) Technology Model," for a complete explanation with examples.

Notice that you can use the page directive more than once. However, you can only use each attribute once. Imports are the only exception. Also, you can place it anywhere on the page. I strongly recommend grouping these tags together, normally at the top or bottom of the file.

JSP Syntax

```
<%@ page
    [ language="java" ]
    [ extends="package.class" ]
    [ import="{package.class | package.*},..." ]
    [ session="true|false" ]
    [ buffer="none|8kb|sizekb" ]
    [ autoFlush="true|false" ]
    [ isThreadSafe="true|false" ]
    [ info="text" ]
    [ errorPage="relativeURL" ]
    [ contentType="mimeType [ ;
       charset=characterSet ]" |
       "text/html ; charset=ISO-8859-1" ]
    [ isErrorPage="true|false" ]
    [ pageEncoding="characterSet | ISO-8859-1" ]

%>
```

XML Syntax

```
<jsp:directive.page pageDirectiveAttrList />
```

Example

```
<%@ page import="java.util.*" %>
```

Or

```
<jsp:directive.page language="java"/>
```

TAGLIB DIRECTIVE

The taglib directive tells the container that you will use custom tags. It names the tag library and specifies their tag prefix. You can use many taglib directives in a single page, but the prefix defined in each must be unique.

JSP Syntax

```
<%@ taglib uri="URIForLibrary"
➥prefix="tagPrefix" %>
```

XML Syntax

No direct equivalent, but you can specify a tag library in <jsp:root>.

Example

```
<%@ taglib uri="/que_taglib_message"
prefix="message" %>
<%@ page language="java" %>
<html>
        <head>
            <title>Tag Library</title>
        </head>
        <body>
            <h1>Tag Library</h1>
            <message:insert definition="appendix"
                                 parameter="syntax"/>
          </body>
</html>
```

<jsp:text>

A jsp:text element allows you to add text that you want sent to the client unaltered within the XML tags. The text you place in here is appended literally to the output stream.

JSP Syntax

None. There is no direct syntax. Anything that is not JSP syntax is "text."

XML Syntax

```
<jsp:text>
   your text
</jsp:text>
```

Example

```
<jsp:root

xmlns:jsp="http://java.sun.com/JSP/Page"
    version="1.2">
<jsp:text>
     <html>
        <head>
           <title>jsp:text Example</title>
        </head>
       <body>
           <h1 align="center">
                This is a jsp:text example.
           </h1>
        </body>
     </html>
</jsp:text>
</jsp:root>
```

<jsp:include>

The <jsp:include> element allows you to include text in a JSP page. There are two kinds. One is static (text is simply inserted as if it were part of the original JSP page) and the other is dynamic (text is processed first and then only the result is inserted into the JSP page). If it is dynamic, you can use a <jsp:param> clause to pass the name and value of a parameter to the resource.

JSP Syntax

```
<jsp:include page="{relativeURL | <%=
➥expression %>}"
   flush="true|false" />
```

Or

```
<jsp:include page="{relativeURL | <%=
➥expression %>}"
   flush="true|false" >
   <jsp:param name="parameterName"
      value="{parameterValue | <%= expression
➥%>}" />+
</jsp:include>
```

XML Syntax

```
<jsp:include page="{relativeURL | %= expression
➥%}"
   [ flush="true | false" ] />
```

Or

```
<jsp:include page="{relativeURL | %= expression
➥%}"
[ flush="true | false" ] >
   [ <jsp:param name="parameterName"
      value="{parameterValue | %= expression
➥%}" /> ] +
</jsp:include> }
```

Example

```
<jsp:include page="company_logo.html" />
<jsp:include page="salesTax.jsp">
   <jsp:param name="state" value="CA" />
   <jsp:param name="amount" value="359.92" />
</jsp:include>
```

<jsp:plugin>

This tag tells the browser to load an applet or bean. You have to specify both the applet/bean and the plug-in. If the client can't find the plug-in, the browser should display a dialog to initiate the download of the plug-in software.

JSP Syntax

```
<jsp:plugin
   type="bean|applet"
   code="classFileName"
   codebase="classFileDirectoryName"
   [ name="instanceName" ]
   [ archive="URIToArchive, ..." ]
   [ align="bottom|top|middle|left|right" ]
   [ height="{displayPixels |  <%= expression
➥%>}"]
   [ width="{displayPixels |  <%= expression
➥%>}"]
```

```
    [ hspace="leftRightPixels" ]
    [ vspace="topBottomPixels" ]
    [ jreversion="JREVersionNumber | 1.2" ]
    [ nspluginurl="URLToPlugin" ]
    [ iepluginurl="URLToPlugin" ] >
    [ <jsp:params>
       [ <jsp:param name="parameterName"
          value="{parameterValue | <%=
➥expression %>}" /> ]+
    </jsp:params> ]
    [ <jsp:fallback> text message if plugin
➥download fails
       </jsp:fallback> ]
</jsp:plugin>
```

XML Syntax

```
<jsp:plugin
   type="bean|applet"  code="classFileName"
   codebase="classFileDirectoryName"
   [ name="instanceName" ] [
➥archive="URIToArchive, ..." ]
   [ align="bottom|top|middle|left|right" ]
   [ height="{displayPixels | %= expression %}"
➥]
   [ width="{displayPixels | %= expression %}"]
   [ hspace="leftRightPixels" ] [
➥vspace="topBottomPixels"]
   [ jreversion="JREVersionNumber | 1.2" ]
   [ nspluginurl="URLToPlugin" ]
   [ iepluginurl="URLToPlugin" ]  >
   [ <jsp:params>
      [ <jsp:param name="parameterName"
         value="{parameterValue | %=
➥expression %}" /> ]+
   </jsp:params> ]
   [ <jsp:fallback>  text message if plugin
➥download fails
   </jsp:fallback>  ]
</jsp:plugin>
```

Example

```
<jsp:plugin type=applet
➥code="houseViewer.class"
➥codebase="/html">
   <jsp:params>
      <jsp:param name="property_listing"
➥value="A33IN" />
   </jsp:params>
      <jsp:fallback>
         <p>Unable to load applet</p>
      </jsp:fallback>
   </jsp:plugin>
```

<jsp:useBean>

The `<jsp:useBean>` element locates or instantiates a JavaBeans component. If it does not exist, the container will attempt to instantiate it from a class or serialized template. You can access a JavaBeans component, but not an enterprise bean directly. However, you can call a JavaBean that in turn calls an EJB.

JSP Syntax

```
<jsp:useBean id="beanInstanceName"
   scope="page|request|session|application"
{
   class="package.class" [ type="package.class"
➥]|
   beanName="{package.class | <%= expression
➥%>}"
      type="package.class" |
   type="package.class"
}
{ /> | > other elements </jsp:useBean> }
```

XML Syntax

```
<jsp:useBean id="beanInstanceName"
   scope="page|request|session|application"
{
   class="package.class"  [
➥type="package.class" ]  |
   beanName="{package.class | %= expression %}"
      type="package.class" |
   type="package.class"
}
{ /> | > other elements </jsp:useBean>  }
```

Example

```
<jsp:useBean id="houseLotBean" scope="session"
➥class="session.Realestate" />
<jsp:setProperty name="houseLotBean"
➥property="id"
value="33245" />
```

<jsp:setProperty>

This element sets the value of one or more properties in a bean, using the bean's setter methods. Of course, the `<jsp:useBean>` tag must be declared first. The most frequent mistake with this tag is to not match the value of name in `<jsp:setProperty>` with the value of id in `<jsp:useBean>`.

JSP Syntax

```
<jsp:setProperty name="beanInstanceName"
{
   property="*" |
   property="propertyName" [
➥param="parameterName" ] |
   property="propertyName"
               value="{stringLiteral| <%=
➥expression %>}"
}
/>
```

XML Syntax

```
<jsp:setProperty name="beanInstanceName"
{
   property="*" |
   property="propertyName" [
➥param="parameterName" ] |
   property="propertyName"
               value="{stringLiteral | %=
➥expression %}"
}
/>
```

Example

```
<jsp:setProperty name="houseLotBean"
➥property="id" value="33245" />
```

Another example that takes the values of all form fields coming in from a form and assigns them to bean properties that have the same names as these form fields:

```
<jsp:setProperty name="request" property="*" />
```

<jsp:forward>

This element forwards the request object (which has all client request information) from one JSP page to another resource. The target can be an HTML file, another JSP page, or a servlet, as long as it is in the same application context as the forwarding JSP page. Notice how the lines in the source JSP page after the `<jsp:forward>` element are not processed.

The biggest problem you'll have with this one is trying to forward after some output has been sent to the client. This happens if you are not buffering output (page directive buffer="none"). If you forward in this situation you will cause an IllegalStateException.

JSP Syntax

```
<jsp:forward page="{relativeURL | <%=
➥expression %>}" />
```

or

```
<jsp:forward page="{relativeURL | <%=
➥expression %>}" >
   <jsp:param name="parameterName"
      value="{parameterValue | <%= expression
➥%>}" /> +
</jsp:forward>
```

XML Syntax

```
<jsp:forward page="{relativeURL | %= expression
➥% }">
   <jsp:param  name="parameterName"
      value="{parameterValue | %= expression
➥%}" /> +
</jsp:forward> }
```

Example

```
<jsp:forward page="page_moved_page.htm" />
```

<jsp:getProperty>

This tag is how you retrieve a value from a bean using its getter method.

JSP Syntax

```
<jsp:getProperty name="beanInstanceName"
➥property="propertyName" />
```

XML Syntax

```
<jsp:getProperty name="beanInstanceName"
➥property="propertyName" />
```

Example

```
<jsp:useBean id="tax" scope="page"
➥class="state.Tax" />
Current tax rate is:<jsp:getProperty name="tax"
➥property="taxRate" />
```

SUMMARY

In this appendix, you reviewed the basic syntax of the JSP specification. The list is short with quick examples, but it is nice to have a concise reference at times. You can refer to the chapter on JSP for more details. Also, you should refer to the specification for the last word.

Suggested Readings and Resources

1. Jakarta has a more extensive syntax card that you can grab with Tomcat at `http://jakarta.apache.org/tomcat/index.html`.
2. Sun's nice JSP syntax card at `http://java.sun.com/products/jsp/tags/10/tags.html`.
3. The Java Servlet 2.3 API at `http://java.sun.com/products/servlet/2.3/javadoc/index.html`.
4. The most current version of the JSP specification at `http://java.sun.com/products/jsp/download.html#specs`.

APPENDIX C

Resources

This appendix helps you prepare for the exam by providing references to information about Java in general and servlets and JSP in particular. While the chapters provided many references, too, this appendix gives you a simple listing of my favorites.

REFERENCES

The amount of reference information available is staggering, but only a little of it is presented in a way that is easy to digest. So, most of my references here were chosen based on reliability and quality of presentation. It is difficult to filter through so much material. The big search engines are an interesting lot. Some do and some don't group results well, and they never offer an opinion so these engines make it really hard to prioritize and rate references. But I was surprised by what I found at Netscape, which is good otherwise. If you search for Java (`search.netscape.com/search.psp?search=java`) you get uneven results. Netscape returned the usual suspects at Sun, but threw in a link to an obscure product by a vendor I never heard of as the third reference. Why did Netscape think that I was interested in that? Give that company's marketing team a bonus, but shame on Netscape. My favorite search engine is Google (`http://directory.google.com/Top/Computers/Programming/Languages/Java/`) because it ranks results by actual use, not tricky keywords that every spam company has mastered. The next two that I use to peruse the Java landscape are Yahoo! (`http://dir.yahoo.com/Computers_and_Internet/Programming_and_Development/Languages/Java/`) and Lycos (`http://dir.lycos.com/Computers/Programming/Languages/Java/`). These are strong in scope, but their ranking mechanisms are mediocre. They contain only a few bad links and they usually give at least a minor descriptive comment.

Once you leave the big search engines, you can use the more focused lists. This tier of references is at Java developer sites like jGuru (`www.jguru.com`) and Java Skyline (`www.javaskyline.com`). These have meaningful descriptions, opinions, and bias which do help you cut to the chase. There are a slew of them, but my favorite are the two I just mentioned.

Then there are book store sites like Amazon (`www.amazon.com`) and Bookpool (`www.bookpool.com`). Review books here before you buy because there are tons of reader comments. I haven't been surprised by flaming posters. You might read one of their useless comments like, "Alain Trottier is a jerk because when we worked together…" Why do they bother to tell us about their career problem in a book review?! But I admit it's been a pleasant surprise to read the large number of helpful book reviews. Now, these are nice to see when they write something like "This book is great but I hate this one aspect," and "This book has good explanations but is full of code errors," or "This book steered me wrong on three exam objectives." While I have to be careful not to judge the book by one unhappy customer, I do find the facts (found two code errors on page 39) they sometimes provide insightful.

The following references are what I use most often. They are a moving target, so the book Web site is more current.

> **NOTE**
> **Online Version** Since resource names are like a good API (don't change), but the URLs are like the implementations (change often), please visit the book's Web site to get the most current version.

Reference List

The primary set of references that I use is small, but effective. Table C.1 presents Sun references.

> **NOTE**
> **The Source** You have to start with Sun. Download their specs and docs because you will use these far more than anything else.

TABLE C.1
Links to Sun

Name	*Description*	*Resource*
Sun's Java homepage	This is your top Java link. You should check weekly to see what new and cool things Sun says are happening to Java.	`http://java.sun.com/`
J2SE 1.4	J2SE is the foundation, so you need this to learn about servlets and JSP.	J2SE 1.4.0 Product Page (`http://java.sun.com/j2se/1.4/index.html`) Java 2 SDK, Standard Edition, version 1.4 Summary of New Features and Enhancements (`http://java.sun.com/j2se/1.4/docs/relnotes/features.html`) Technical Article: Project Merlin: Front and Center, A Technical Overview of the J2SE (`http://java.sun.com/features/2001/06/golden.j2se.html`)
J2EE 1.3	J2EE is a collection of APIs built on top of J2SE. These APIs include servlets, JSP, and EJB components.	J2EE Information (`http://java.sun.com/j2ee/`) J2EE Tutorial (`http://java.sun.com/j2ee/tutorial/`) J2EE Downloads (`http://java.sun.com/j2ee/download.html`)

Name	*Description*	*Resource*
JSP 1.2	JavaServer Pages is very similar to Microsoft Active Server Pages. It's a way to place Java code in an otherwise normal HTML page. A few of the advantages of using JSP are that they are easier to code than servlets, have XML capabilities, are automatically converted into servlets, and that they have access to server-side Java objects to return dynamic content to a client.	JavaServer Pages Technology (`http://java.sun.com/products/jsp/`) JSR 152 (JSP 1.3) (`http://jcp.org/jsr/detail/152.jsp`) JavaServer Page—Tomcat@Jakarta (`http://java.sun.com/products/jsp/tomcat/`) JSP Implementations & Specifications (`http://java.sun.com/products/jsp/download.html`) JavaServer Pages Tag Libraries (JSTL) (`http://java.sun.com/products/jsp/taglibraries.html`) Technical Article: Web Application Development with JSP and XML Part III: Developing JSP Custom Tags (`http://developer.java.sun.com/developer/technicalArticles/xml/WebAppDev3/`)
Java Servlets 2.3	Java Servlet technology is regular Java except you extend certain classes so the Web server can pass requests to and receive responses from the servlet. This is Sun's version of CGI.	Java Servlet product page (`http://java.sun.com/products/servlet/index.html`) JSR 154 (Servlet 2.4) (`http://jcp.org/jsr/detail/154.jsp`) Java Servlet Downloads and Specification (`http://java.sun.com/products/servlet/download.html`)
Java Web Service Developer Pack (Java WSDP)	The Java Web Services Developer Pack (Java WSDP) is an all-in-one download containing key technologies to simplify building Web services using the Java 2 Platform. The technologies comprising the Java Web Services Developers Pack include JAXM 1.0.1 EA2 JAXP 1.2 EA2 (with XML Schema support) JAXR 1.0 EA2 JAX-RPC 1.0 EA2 JavaServer Pages Standard Tag Library (JSTL) 1.0 Beta 1 Ant Build Tool 1.4.1 Java WSDP Registry Server 1.0 EA2 Web Application Deployment Tool Apache Tomcat 4.1-dev Container	Java Technology and Web Services (`http://java.sun.com/webservices/index.html`) Java Web Services Tutorial (`http://java.sun.com/webservices/tutorial.html`) Java Web Services Download (`http://java.sun.com/webservices/download.html`) Technical Article: Java Web Services Developer Pack Part 1: Registration and the JAXR API (`http://developer.java.sun.com/developer/technicalArticles/WebServices/WSPack/`) Technical Article: Deploying Web Services on Java 2, Enterprise Edition (J2EE) (`http://developer.java.sun.com/developer/technicalArticles/WebServices/wsj2ee/`)

continues

TABLE C.1 *continued*
LINKS TO SUN

Name	*Description*	*Resource*
Extensible Markup Language (XML)	XML is a universal syntax for describing and structuring data independent from the application logic. XML can be used to define unlimited languages for specific industries and applications.	World Wide Web Consortium (W3C) (`http://www.w3.org/`) XML.ORG (`http://www.xml.org`) O'Reilly's XML.COM (`http://www.xml.com`) Java Technology and XML (`http://java.sun.com/xml/`) Java XML Pack (`http://java.sun.com/xml/javaxmlpack.html`) Java Technology & XML Downloads and Specifications (`http://java.sun.com/xml/download.html`) XML FAQ (`http://java.sun.com/xml/faq.html`)
The Java API for XML Processing (JAXP)	JAXP is how Java processes XML using Document Object Model (DOM), Simple API for XML (SAX), and XML Stylesheet Language for Transformations (XSLT). JAXP enables applications to parse and transform XML documents independent of a particular XML processing implementation.	JAXP Documentation (`http://java.sun.com/xml/jaxp/docs.html`) JAXP Downloads and Specifications (`http://java.sun.com/xml/downloads/jaxp.html`) JAXP FAQ (`http://java.sun.com/xml/jaxp/faq.html`)
Java Developer Connection	Sun's developer network. Membership is free for some tech support, forums, training, early access, newsgroups, and bug reporting. Basically, it's almost an insiders' group.	`http://java.sun.com/jdc`
Java History	This is how it all started.	`http://java.sun.com/features/1998/05/birthday.html`
Code Convention	This is how Sun recommends you write your code. My biggest divergence with them is in cryptic identifiers (such as, int instead of integer—I've heard they did that to avoid confusion with the object Integer and that it made it easier to cross over from C/C++. I don't buy it.) and the placement of curly braces (We line up everything else, why not these?!).	`http://java.sun.com/docs/codeconv/html/CodeConvTOC.doc.html`
Glossary	Look here first if you want the official definition for a given term.	`http://java.sun.com/docs/glossary.html`
Certification	The home page for the SCWCD exam.	`http://suned.sun.com/US/certification/java/java_web.html`

Table C.2 contains rundowns for vendors dedicated to Java.

TABLE C.2
VENDOR LINKS DEDICATED TO JAVA

Name	*Description*	*Resource*
Microsoft's Java homepage	Home page for Microsoft Technologies for Java. Some very smart people there have useful things to say about Java.	`http://www.microsoft.com/java/default.htm`
Oracle	Oracle is pushing Java hard and has many downloads and products for Java.	`http://otn.oracle.com/tech/java/content.html`
IBM	Big Blue is serious about Java. I especially love their Alphaworks free samples.	`http://www-106.ibm.com/developerworks/java/` IBM's awesome Alphaworks—`http://www.alphaworks.ibm.com`
BEA	Wow! The company most dedicated to Java on the planet. Unlike its bigger partners, BEA doesn't spend resources on non-Java products.	`http://dev2dev.bea.com:80/index.jsp`

Table C.3 lists magazines that devote their contents to Java.

TABLE C.3
GLOSSY MAGAZINES DEDICATED TO JAVA

Name	*Description*	*Resource*
Sys-Con	These guys are my favorite when it comes to Java and related publications. They pack each issue. I even like the ads in their industry leading *Java Developers Journal.*	`http://www.sys-con.com`
JavaPro	Closer to earth. Fawcett (publisher) keeps the newbie in mind.	`http://www.fawcette.com/javapro/`

Table C.4 covers Web sites dedicated to Java.

TABLE C.4
WEB SITES DEDICATED TO JAVA

Name	*Description*	*Resource*
jGuru	Java Guru is fun and has the best lists of Q&A and FAQs.	`http://www.jguru.com`
Gamelan	It's been around for a long time, so lots of articles, but it's not organized well.	`http://softwaredev.earthweb.com/java`
JavaWorld	This Web site features a variety of useful Java information and resources.	`http://www.JavaWorld.com`

continues

TABLE C.4 *continued*
WEB SITES DEDICATED TO JAVA

Name	*Description*	*Resource*
DevX	JavaZone has articles and a solid code repository . (click Sourcebank)	`http://www.devx.com/java/`
Java Skyline	You don't see this on many lists, but they have a stellar collection of links.	`http://www.javaskyline.com`
JSPinsider	Nice resource for JSP.	`http://www.jspinsider.com/index.view`
Servlets.com	Jason Hunter is a Java star and author. His site is all servlets and looks like it was built by a one-man army. What he does for O'Reilly is very good.	`http://www.servlets.com/index.tea`
JavaLobby	Rick Ross is on a crusade with moxie. I wonder what Microsoft did to incur such wrath?	`http://www.javalobby.org/`
Serverside.com	Articles and lots of chat.	`http://www.theserverside.com`
JavaRanch	A potluck of Java goodies.	`http://www.javaranch.com/books.jsp`
Jars	Tons of code with ratings.	`http://www.jars.com/`
Java Boutique	Many articles and links, but zany colors.	`http://java.internet.com/`
JavaPrepare	A nice little site that focuses on Java certification. Lists mock exams too.	`http://www.javaprepare.com/scwd`
CityJava	World's biggest Java User Group (JUG).	`http://www.cityjava.org/`

There are many books on Java. Don't buy all of them. Get this list of books and read nothing else for the next year or two. If you take my advice you will easily surpass the geek in the next cubicle who buys/scans 50 books a year.

- *Java in a Nutshell* and *Java Examples in a Nutshell: A Tutorial Companion to Java in a Nutshell*, both by David Flanagan. Another wonderful Nutshell from O'Reilly.
- *Thinking in Java* by Bruce Eckel (Prentice Hall). We have someone who actually thinks about what we are trying to do. This book has won many awards and is mentioned often in the literature. Mr. Eckel's book is becoming a classic.
- There are several nods here for Sun's outstanding Core Series (Prentice Hall) including

  Core Java 2, Volume 1 and 2 by Cay S. Horstmann, Gary Cornell.

  Core Servlets and JavaServer Pages by Marty Hall.

  Advanced JavaServer Pages by David Geary.

  Core J2EE Patterns: Best Practices and Design Strategies by Deepak Alur, John Crupi, Dan Malks.
- This is the guy who turned the world of building things into patterns with a pair of classics (Oxford University Press).

  The Timeless Way of Building by Christopher Alexander.

A Pattern Language: Towns, Buildings, Construction by Christopher Alexander, Sara Ishikawa, Murray Silverstein.

- These four (Gang of Four or just GoF) told us that programming is a form of building so software has patterns, too.

  Design Patterns by Erich Gamma, Richard Helm, Ralph Johnson, John Vlissides (Addison-Wesley).

- This is a gentle explanation of the GoF's thinking. The GOF book is hard to digest. This one couches design patterns in a more palatable voice.

  Design Patterns Explained: A New Perspective on Object-Oriented Design by Alan Shalloway, James R. Trott (Addison-Wesley).

- A very strong title from O'Reilly.

  Java Servlet Programming by Jason Hunter, William Crawford.

- An excellent book from New Riders.

  Java for the Web with Servlets, JSP, and EJB: A Developer's Guide to J2EE Solutions by Budi Kurniawan

SUMMARY

In this appendix, you are presented with several references. These are my favorites and don't represent anyone's opinion but mine. There are only a few so I recommend you click through them all in one evening. You'll get a good sense of the best of what is out there. Then bookmark the few you really like.

As for the books, you can't miss with these. Just buy them. I rotate books by giving my old books to my students. They love this because it is new to them and probably still a good title. Then I have a wife excuse to buy another honey-I-really-need-this-one book :->

APPENDIX D

Setting Up a Servlet Environment

This appendix helps you prepare for the exam by guiding you through setting up a servlet environment on your machine. You need a servlet engine that conforms to the Servlet 2.3 and JSP 1.2 specifications from Sun.

This appendix describes how to obtain, install, and set up a simple Web application server that supports JavaServer Pages technology (JSP) servlets. The application server chosen for this appendix is Tomcat (`http://jakarta.apache.org/tomcat`), the Java servlet and JSP container included with the Java Web Services Developer Pack ("Java WSDP"; `http://java.sun.com/webservices/downloads/webservicespack.html`). It is also available from the Apache Web site. This appendix is intended as an introduction to installing application servers, especially Tomcat. The material here provides a basis for installing other application servers.

While this appendix and the entire book use Tomcat, you can use any container. The code in this book will work on any application server that supports the Servlet 2.3 and JSP 1.2 standards. There are several places you can look to get a list of commercial and open source Java/J2EE application servers that provide servlet and JSP capabilities.

> **EXAM TIP**
>
> **Enterprise JavaBeans** You do not need Enterprise JavaBeans for this exam.

SELECTING AN APPLICATION SERVER

One of the best places to look for application servers is javaskyline. If you jump over there, you will find an extensive list of commercial and open source Java/J2EE application servers that provide servlet and JSP capabilities (`http://www.javaskyline.com/serv.html`). I recommend choosing one based on three things:

- **Price**—Get a free one since the best free ones are comparable to the average commercial ones.
- **Servlet Version**—This has to be servlet version 2.3. Most of the engines on Java Skyline's list support earlier versions, but the exam is on version 2.3, so stick with that.
- **JSP Version**—This has to be JSP version 1.2. Most of the engines on Java Skyline's list support earlier versions, but the exam is on version 1.2.

The current kings of the application server space are BEA's WebLogic, JBoss's JBossServer, and IBM's Websphere. All three of these products are outstanding. The definition of a J2EE server is becoming muddy again. Basically, a Web server that can handle servlets, JSP, and EJBs is a J2EE application server. For this exam you can ignore EJB. So, there are plain Web servers like Apache. If you add on servlets and JSP you have a minimal application server or, said differently, a dynamic content generating Web server.

If you want a "full" J2EE implementation that will get you an excellent Web application development and deployment platform then your choice will support middleware (EJB and JMS), database connectivity (JDBC), transactions (JTA/JTS), presentation (servlets and Java Server Pages), and directory services (JNDI). If you also get support for Web services (Universal Description, Discovery, and Integration [UDDI]; Simple Object Access Protocol [SOAP]; and Web Services Description Language [WSDL]) you will have the best feature set there is for a Java based application server.

JBoss, one of the leading Java Open Source groups, integrates and develops these services for a full J2EE-based implementation. JBoss beat out BEA and IBM to sweep the JavaWorld Editors' Choice 2002 Award for Best Java Application Server.

JBoss is one of those successful open source products. It is a J2EE 1.3-based application server that is free. Since it is open source, you can experiment with the technology. It has surpassed all others in downloads recently (company says 100,000/month!). JBoss provides JBossServer, the basic EJB container and JMX infrastructure; JBossMQ, for JMS messaging; JBossMX, for mail; JBossTX, for JTA/JTS transactions; JBossSX, for JAAS based security; JBossCX, for JCA connectivity; and JBossCMP, for CMP persistence. JBoss enables you to mix and match these components through JMX by replacing *any* component you wish with a JMX-compliant implementation for the same APIs. JBoss doesn't even impose the JBoss components that are modular. Please see `http://www.jboss.org/` for this excellent product.

BEA WebLogic Server is the one most big companies have settled on. It has Web services support, J2EE Connector Architecture support, updated J2EE services, EJB caching enhancements, deployment descriptor editing tools, and much more. It is designed well and the company behind it is the most dedicated Java company on the planet. You can download a 30-day trial version free (`http://commerce.bea.com/downloads/weblogic_server.jsp`).

BEA's closest rival is IBM's WebSphere Application Server (`http://www-3.ibm.com/software/info1/websphere/index.jsp`). You can download an evaluation version that won't have everything crippled like some companies do. I think WebSphere is the best application server on the market, but you pay a handsome price for it. Also, IBM does things its own way. If you look at the servlet code and libraries, it is a mixed bag of Sun and IBM proprietary classes. Regarding its outstanding IDE VisualAge (`http://www-3.ibm.com/software/ad/vajava`), I wish they would let you click a button that would let you toggle between pure Sun and vendor-specific libraries. Otherwise you can end up with servlets that only work on their server. VisualAge works very well with WebSphere. This is a good thing especially when you use complicated EJBs. WebSphere has much support for the growing Web services movement, including Universal Description, Discovery, and Integration (UDDI); the Simple Object Access Protocol (SOAP); and Web Services Description Language (WSDL).

While these three products are the best available and there are many others worthy of consideration such as iPlanet (`http://www.iplanet.com/`), this book uses Tomcat because it is the most straight forward implementation of the Servlet 2.3 API and JavaServer Pages specification 1.2. Therefore let us now download and install Tomcat.

NOTE

Servlet 2.3 API The Servlet 2.3 API defines the interfaces, classes, methods, fields, and constants that you will use to build servlets. The Web Component Developer Exam is filled with questions on this API.

Obtaining and Installing Tomcat

Tomcat is an open-source project released under the Apache Software License. It is the servlet container used in the reference implementations (this is how it should be done according to Sun) for the servlet and JSP technologies. Tomcat 4.0 employs the Servlet 2.3 and JSP 1.2 specifications.

This section presents a step-by-step guide on how to set up Tomcat, the free servlet and JSP application server, and create your first dynamic page. It doesn't explain what servlets and JSP are or how to use them; the chapters of the book will help you with that. Although the description is based on using Tomcat on Windows, most of the issues discussed in this appendix will also apply to installing Tomcat on other platforms and even to many other application servers.

The developers wrote Tomcat entirely in Java. Only the Web server connectors were written in C/C++. This makes sense because the connectors can't be guaranteed to run in a JVM; most don't. Therefore, in order for Tomcat to run, you need to install the Java 2 SDK standard edition. You need more than the JRE because Tomcat needs to compile servlets and JSP pages. It needs the compiler that comes with the SDK but which is missing from Java Runtime Engine. I strongly recommend you go with the J2SE 1.4 SDK (`http://java.sun.com/j2se/1.4/download.html`). You do have the option of using IBM's development kit, but I recommend using Sun to keep things simple.

Obtaining Tomcat

Tomcat is the servlet container that is used in the official Reference Implementation for the Java Servlet and JavaServer Pages technologies. The Java Servlet and JavaServer Pages specifications are developed by Sun under the Java Community Process. Tomcat is developed in an open and participatory environment and released under the Apache Software License. Tomcat is a collaboration of some of the best developers from around the world. You too can participate in this open development project. To learn more about getting involved, go to `http://jakarta.apache.org/site/getinvolved.html`.

The Tomcat homepage is at `http://jakarta.apache.org/tomcat/`. In addition there is an open source effort to document Tomcat. Please go to `http://tomcatbook.sourceforge.net/` to see this online book about Tomcat.

The latest version of Tomcat can be found at `http://jakarta.apache.org/site/binindex.html`. Jakarta provides three types of downloads for its products. They are the release, Milestone, and nightly builds. You can play with the first two, but don't bother with the nightly build because you'll never know if it's your servlet or Tomcat that is coughing. Get the release or Milestone builds, as they implement the correct versions of the servlet and JSP specification required for the certification exam. You should only use the nightly builds for experimental purposes—testing, trying out the new features, or something to that effect—and never in your production or development environments.

The Jakarta folks also make the actual source code available for you to use. You will learn much by perusing the source and poking around. How does it convert JSP into servlets and then compile it on the fly? You can answer this interesting question by going to `http://jakarta.apache.org/site/sourceindex.html` and downloading the source.

You can either download the files from `http://www.apache.org/dist/jakarta/` by following the links on this page or use one of the Apache mirror sites. The release of Apache Tomcat is available in both binary (`http://jakarta.apache.org/builds/jakarta-tomcat-4.0/release/v4.0.4/bin`) and source (`http://jakarta.apache.org/builds/jakarta-tomcat-4.0/release/v4.0.4/src`) versions.

Download the appropriate binary depending on your operating system. On a Windows platform, you will need a file like (file name will be different for each version) jakarta-tomcat-4.0-YYYYMMDD.zip. On a Unix platform, you will need jakarta-tomcat-4.0-YYYYMMDD.tar.gz. I am developing on a Dell Windows laptop, so I have downloaded the jakarta-tomcat-connectors-4.0.2-01-src.zip file.

> NOTE
> **Notice!** Tomcat is an open-source implementation of Java servlet and JavaServer Pages technologies. It is being developed under the Jakarta project at the Apache Software Foundation. Tomcat is free and can be used for commercial purposes under the ASF license. You can download it from the Apache Web site in both binary and source versions.

Installing Tomcat

Installing Tomcat is painless. You merely unzip the package, copy the files to a home directory, set a few environment variables (Strings containing information such as drive, path, or filename that control the behavior of various programs. See later in this appendix) and start Tomcat to test the installation of this servlet container.

Decompress or unpack the binary distribution into its home directory (conventionally named `"jakarta-tomcat-4.0"`). The Tomcat scripts and documentation use the symbolic name `"${catalina.home}"` to refer to the full pathname of the release directory.

> NOTE
> **Notice!** Before you can run Tomcat, you first need to download and install a Java Development Kit. You can download a Java Development Kit (JDK) release (version 1.2 or later) from `http://java.sun.com/j2se/`. Once downloaded, you install the JDK according to the instructions included with that release. Remember to add the directory to the bin directory to the path environment variable. Also you must create an environment variable JAVA_HOME that points to the pathname of the directory into which you installed the JDK release.

> NOTE
> **Notice!** If you installed a previous version of Tomcat, you should uninstall all of its components before installing the newer version. You should be able to simply delete the directory. However, if you have an installation program (some distributions have installation programs) then use the Control Panel. To open a Control Panel item, click Start, point to Settings, click Control Panel, and then double-click the appropriate icon. Then to remove the old Tomcat
>
> 1. Open Add/Remove Programs in Control Panel.
> 2. Click Change or Remove Programs, and then click the entry for Tomcat.

Starting Tomcat

Once you have installed Tomcat, you should test the installation by running it. You normally start Tomcat by executing the startup script in the bin directory.

You can do this several ways. I have a shortcut on my desktop to both the start and stop scripts. This is an easy way to go. On my system the shortcut is `C:\dev\java\jakarta-tomcat-4.0.1\bin\startup.bat`. Once you set an environment variable CATALINA_HOME to the path of the directory into which you have installed Tomcat (`C:\dev\java\jakarta-tomcat-4.0.1` for my current install), you can execute the shell command (or user interface command):

- `%CATALINA_HOME%\bin\startup` (Windows)
- `$CATALINA_HOME/bin/startup.sh` (Unix)

You can also use the command prompt. First change your current working directory and execute the following shell command for Windows:

1. `cd %CATALINA_HOME%\bin`
2. `startup`

You can do likewise in Unix, changing your current working directory and executing the following shell commands:

1. `cd $CATALINA_HOME/bin`
2. `./startup.sh`

Testing Tomcat

Once you have started Tomcat, you will test it. Tomcat comes with several example servlets and JSP pages. Point to the default Web applications included with Tomcat 4.0 by browsing to `http://localhost:8080/`. If all goes well, you will receive Tomcat's home page. If you see the default page in your browser then you have correctly set up Tomcat. That first page (default is index.html) is located at `$CATALINA_HOME/webapps/ROOT/index.html`.

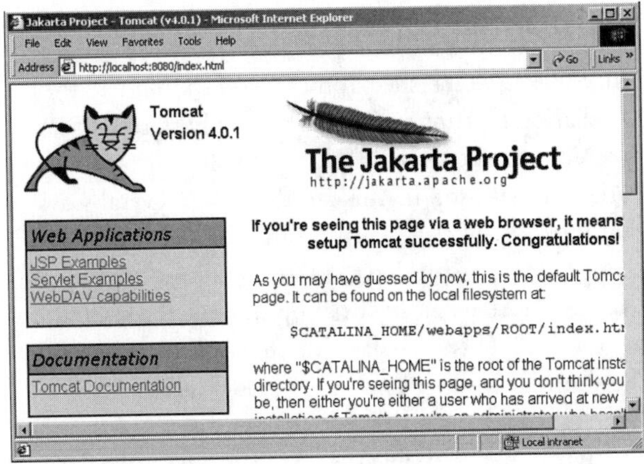

FIGURE D.1
Tomcat default home page.

> **NOTE**
> **Notice!** Before you start Tomcat, you should first stop your other Web servers. Be careful as some servers don't like to go away. When you kill an old Apache, for example, it doesn't always completely stop sometimes, causing a BindException Address already in use error when you try to start Tomcat. Technically, you can run as many Web servers on your machine simultaneously as you please. Since each one should be listening to a different port, there should be no problem. However, avoid any confusion by stopping the others so you can focus on Tomcat.

Once at this default page you should execute a JSP and a servlet example that come with Tomcat. Serving up a default HTML page doesn't guarantee that the servlet engine is configured properly. For JSP Examples go to `http://localhost:8080/examples/jsp/index.html`. For servlet examples go to `http://localhost:8080/examples/servlets/`.

Stopping Tomcat

Once you have installed Tomcat, you should test the installation by running it. You normally start Tomcat by executing the startup script in the bin directory. Later you will stop it. You can do this in several ways that look just like the startup procedures except for the script filename (shutdown). As I mentioned previously, I have a shortcut on my desktop to both the start and stop scripts. This is an easy way to go. On my system the shortcut to stop Tomcat is `C:\dev\java\jakarta-tomcat-4.0.1\bin\shutdown.bat`. Once you set an environment variable CATALINA_HOME to the path of the directory into which you have installed Tomcat 4.0, you can execute the shell command:

- `%CATALINA_HOME%\bin\shutdown` (Windows)
- `$CATALINA_HOME/bin/shutdown.sh` (Unix)

You can also use the command prompt. First change your current working directory and execute the following shell command for Windows:

1. `cd %CATALINA_HOME%\bin`
2. `shutdown`

You can do likewise in Unix by changing your current working directory and execute the following shell commands:

1. `cd $CATALINA_HOME/bin`
2. `./shutdown.sh`

Changing the Port

Tomcat is configured to use port 8080. Sometimes another process is using that port. You change Tomcat's port by opening the file `$CATALINA_HOME/conf/server.xml`. Find "8080" and change it to something else. Mind you that it has to be greater than 1024, as the ports lower than that are reserved (for example, FTP is 22). Once you change the port, restart Tomcat.

If you changed the port to 2345 then you would browse to `http://localhost:2345/`. So, the old parameter looked like this:

```
    <!-- Define a non-SSL HTTP/1.1 Connector
➥on port 8080 -->
    <Connector className=
➥"org.apache.catalina.connector.http.
➥HttpConnector"
        port="8080" minProcessors="5"
➥maxProcessors="75"
        enableLookups="true" redirectPort="8443"
        acceptCount="10" debug="0"
➥connectionTimeout="60000"/>
```

But you changed it to look like this:

```
<!-- Redefine a non-SSL HTTP/1.1 Connector on
➥port 8080 -->
    <Connector className=
➥"org.apache.catalina.connector.http.
➥HttpConnector"
        port="2345" minProcessors="5"
➥maxProcessors="75"
        enableLookups="true" redirectPort="8443"
        acceptCount="10" debug="0"
➥connectionTimeout="60000"/>
```

One last note: Sometimes Tomcat seems to not know it needs to recompile a JSP. See Chapter 10, "Web Applications," about this matter. You can force Tomcat to recompile JSP pages by deleting everything in the work (folder `%CATALINA_HOME%\work`). Don't delete the folder itself, just the contents.

SUMMARY

There are many servlet and JSP implementations on the market and more are on the way. Tomcat is wonderful because it is done well, it is clean, it is free, and it won't muddy the waters with EJB, which isn't on this exam. You can download it from the Apache Web site. You can even get involved and help move that project ahead if you want a worthy challenge.

Suggested Readings and Resources

1. Skyline's list of commercial and open source Java/J2EE application servers that provide servlet and JSP capabilities: `http://www.javaskyline.com/serv.html`.
2. JBoss is at `http://www.jboss.org/`; go there for this excellent open source application server.
3. BEA WebLogic is at `http://commerce.bea.com/downloads/weblogic_server.jsp`.
4. IBM's WebSphere is at `http://www-3.ibm.com/software/info1/websphere/index.jsp`.
5. For Tomcat add-ons and related projects go to `http://sourceforge.net/search/` and search for Tomcat.
6. jGuru's FAQ page on application servers: `http://www.jguru.com/faq/home.jsp?topic=AppServer&page=1`.
7. JavaWorld's yearly Editors' Choice Awards (ECA): `http://www.javaworld.com/javaworld/jw-03-2002/jw-0326-awards.html`.
8. JavaMatters' very nice table of application servers: `http://www.javamatters.com/javaApplicationServers.html`.

APPENDIX **E**

What's on the CD-ROM

This appendix is a brief rundown of what you'll find on the CD-ROM that comes with this book. For a more detailed description of the *PrepLogic Practice Tests, Preview Edition* exam simulation software, see Appendix F, "Using the *PrepLogic Practice Tests, Preview Edition* Software." In addition to the *PrepLogic Practice Tests, Preview Edition*, the CD-ROM includes the electronic version of the book in Portable Document Format (PDF), several utility and application programs, and a complete listing of test objectives and where they are covered in the book. Finally, a pointer list to online pointers and references are added to this CD. You will need a computer with Internet access and relatively recent browser installed to use this feature.

PrepLogic Practice Tests, Preview Edition

PrepLogic is a leading provider of certification training tools. Trusted by certification students worldwide, we believe PrepLogic is the best practice exam software available. In addition to providing a means of evaluating your knowledge of the Training Guide material, *PrepLogic Practice Tests, Preview Edition* features several innovations that help you to improve your mastery of the subject matter.

For example, the practice tests allow you to check your score by exam area or domain to determine which topics you need to study more. Another feature allows you to obtain immediate feedback on your responses in the form of explanations for the correct and incorrect answers.

PrepLogic Practice Tests, Preview Edition exhibits most of the full functionality of the *Premium Edition* but offers only a fraction of the total questions. To get the complete set of practice questions and exam functionality, visit PrepLogic.com and order the *Premium Edition* for this and other challenging exam titles.

Again for a more detailed description of the *PrepLogic Practice Tests, Preview Edition* features, see Appendix F.

Exclusive Electronic Version of Text

The CD-ROM also contains the electronic version of this book in PDF. This electronic version comes complete with all figures as they appear in the book. You will find that the search capabilities of the reader comes in handy for study and review purposes.

APPENDIX **F**

Using the *PrepLogic Practice Tests, Preview Edition* Software

This Training Guide includes a special version of PrepLogic Practice Tests—a revolutionary test engine designed to give you the best in certification exam preparation. PrepLogic offers sample and practice exams for many of today's most in-demand and challenging technical certifications. This special Preview Edition is included with this book as a tool to use in assessing your knowledge of the Training Guide material while also providing you with the experience of taking an electronic exam.

This appendix describes in detail what *PrepLogic Practice Tests, Preview Edition* is, how it works, and what it can do to help you prepare for the exam. Note that although the Preview Edition includes all the test simulation functions of the complete, retail version, it contains only a single practice test. The Premium Edition, available at `PrepLogic.com`, contains the complete set of challenging practice exams designed to optimize your learning experience.

EXAM SIMULATION

One of the main functions of *PrepLogic Practice Tests, Preview Edition* is exam simulation. To prepare you to take the actual vendor certification exam, PrepLogic is designed to offer the most effective exam simulation available.

Question Quality

The questions provided in the *PrepLogic Practice Tests, Preview Edition* are written to highest standards of technical accuracy. The questions tap the content of the Training Guide chapters and help you review and assess your knowledge before you take the actual exam.

Interface Design

The *PrepLogic Practice Tests, Preview Edition* exam simulation interface provides you with the experience of taking an electronic exam. This enables you to effectively prepare you for taking the actual exam by making the test experience a familiar one. Using this test simulation can help eliminate the sense of surprise or anxiety you might experience in the testing center because you will already be acquainted with computerized testing.

Effective Learning Environment

The *PrepLogic Practice Tests, Preview Edition* interface provides a learning environment that not only tests you through the computer, but also teaches the material you need to know to pass the certification exam.

Each question comes with a detailed explanation of the correct answer and often provides reasons the other options are incorrect. This information helps to reinforce the knowledge you already have and also provides practical information you can use on the job.

Software Requirements

PrepLogic Practice Tests requires a computer with the following:

- Microsoft Windows 98, Windows Me, Windows NT 4.0, Windows 2000, or Windows XP
- A 166MHz or faster processor is recommended
- A minimum of 32MB of RAM
- As with any Windows application, the more memory, the better your performance.
- 10MB of Hard Drive space

Installing *PrepLogic Practice Tests, Preview Edition*

Install *PrepLogic Practice Tests, Preview Edition* by running the setup program on the *PrepLogic Practice Tests, Preview Edition* CD. Follow these instructions to install the software on your computer.

- Insert the CD into your CD-ROM drive. The Autorun feature of Windows should launch the software. If you have Autorun disabled, click Start and select Run. Go to the root directory of the CD and select setup.exe. Click Open, and then click OK.
- The Installation Wizard copies the *PrepLogic Practice Tests, Preview Edition* files to your hard drive; adds *PrepLogic Practice Tests, Preview Edition* to your Desktop and Program menu; and installs test engine components to the appropriate system folders.

Removing *PrepLogic Practice Tests, Preview Edition* from Your Computer

If you elect to remove the *PrepLogic Practice Tests, Preview Edition* product from your computer, an uninstall process has been included to ensure that it is removed from your system safely and completely. Follow these instructions to remove *PrepLogic Practice Tests, Preview Edition* from your computer:

- Select Start, Settings, Control Panel.
- Double-click the Add/Remove Programs icon.
- You are presented with a list of software installed on your computer. Select the appropriate *PrepLogic Practice Tests, Preview Edition* title you want to remove. Click the Add/Remove button. The software is then removed from your computer.

Using *PrepLogic Practice Tests, Preview Edition*

PrepLogic is designed to be user friendly and intuitive. Because the software has a smooth learning curve, your time is maximized because you start practicing almost immediately. *PrepLogic Practice Tests, Preview Edition* has two major modes of study: Practice Test and Flash Review.

Using Practice Test mode, you can develop your test-taking abilities as well as your knowledge through the use of the Show Answer option. While you are taking the test, you can expose the answers along with a detailed explanation of why the given answers are right or wrong. This gives you the ability to better understand the material presented.

Flash Review is designed to reinforce exam topics rather than quiz you. In this mode, you will be shown a series of questions but no answer choices. Instead, you will be given a button that reveals the correct answer to the question and a full explanation for that answer.

Starting a Practice Test Mode Session

Practice Test mode enables you to control the exam experience in ways that actual certification exams do not allow:

- **Enable Show Answer Button**—Activates the Show Answer button allowing you to view the correct answer(s) and full explanation for each question during the exam. When not enabled, you must wait until after your exam has been graded to view the correct answer(s) and explanation.
- **Enable Item Review Button**—Activates the Item Review button allowing you to view your answer choices, marked questions, and facilitating navigation between questions.

To begin studying in Practice Test mode, click the Practice Test radio button from the main exam customization screen. This will enable the options detailed above.

To your left, you are presented with the option of selecting the preconfigured Practice Test or creating your own Custom Test. The preconfigured test has a fixed time limit and number of questions. Custom Tests allow you to configure the time limit and the number of questions in your exam.

The Preview Edition included with this book includes a single preconfigured Practice Test. Get the compete set of challenging PrepLogic Practice Tests at `PrepLogic.com` and make certain you're ready for the big exam.

Click the Begin Exam button to begin your exam.

Starting a Flash Review Mode Session

Flash Review mode provides you with an easy way to reinforce topics covered in the practice questions. To begin studying in Flash Review mode, click the Flash Review radio button from the main exam customization screen. Select either the preconfigured Practice Test or create your own Custom Test.

Click the Best Exam button to begin your Flash Review of the exam questions.

Standard *PrepLogic Practice Tests, Preview Edition* Options

The following list describes the function of each of the buttons you see. Depending on the options, some of the buttons will be grayed out and inaccessible or missing completely. Buttons that are appropriate are active. The buttons are as follows:

- **Exhibit**—This button is visible if an exhibit is provided to support the question. An exhibit is an image that provides supplemental information necessary to answer the question.

- **Item Review**—This button leaves the question window and opens the Item Review screen. From this screen you will see all questions, your answers, and your marked items. You will also see correct answers listed here when appropriate.
- **Show Answer**—This option displays the correct answer with an explanation of why it is correct. If you select this option, the current question is not scored.
- **Mark Item**—Check this box to tag a question you need to review further. You can view and navigate your Marked Items by clicking the Item Review button (if enabled). When grading your exam, you will be notified if you have marked items remaining.
- **Previous Item**—View the previous question.
- **Next Item**—View the next question.
- **Grade Exam**—When you have completed your exam, click to end your exam and view your detailed score report. If you have unanswered or marked items remaining, you will be asked if you would like to continue taking your exam or view your exam report.

Time Remaining

If the test is timed, the time remaining is displayed on the upper-right corner of the application screen. It counts down minutes and seconds remaining to complete the test. If you run out of time, you will be asked if you want to continue taking the test or if you want to end your exam.

Your Examination Score Report

The Examination Score Report screen appears when the Practice Test mode ends—as the result of time expiration, completion of all questions, or your decision to terminate early.

This screen provides you with a graphical display of your test score with a breakdown of scores by topic domain. The graphical display at the top of the screen compares your overall score with the PrepLogic Exam Competency Score.

The PrepLogic Exam Competency Score reflects the level of subject competency required to pass this vendor's exam. While this score does not directly translate to a passing score, consistently matching or exceeding this score does suggest you possess the knowledge to pass the actual vendor exam.

Review Your Exam

From Your Score Report screen, you can review the exam that you just completed by clicking on the View Items button. Navigate through the items viewing the questions, your answers, the correct answers, and the explanations for those questions. You can return to your score report by clicking the View Items button.

Get More Exams

Each *PrepLogic Practice Tests, Preview Edition* that accompanies your training guide contains a single PrepLogic Practice Test. Certification students worldwide trust PrepLogic Practice Tests to help them pass their IT certification exams the first time. Purchase the Premium Edition of PrepLogic Practice Tests and get the entire set of all new challenging Practice Tests for this exam. PrepLogic Practice Tests—Because You Want to Pass the First Time.

CONTACTING PREPLOGIC

If you would like to contact PrepLogic for any reason including information about our extensive line of certification practice tests, we invite you to do so. Please contact us online at `www.preplogic.com`.

Customer Service

If you have a damaged product and need a replacement or refund, please call the following phone number:

800-858-7674

Product Suggestions and Comments

We value your input! Please email your suggestions and comments to the following address:

`feedback@preplogic.com`

LICENSE AGREEMENT

YOU MUST AGREE TO THE TERMS AND CONDITIONS OUTLINED IN THE END USER LICENSE AGREEMENT ("EULA") PRESENTED TO YOU DURING THE INSTALLATION PROCESS. IF YOU DO NOT AGREE TO THESE TERMS, DO NOT INSTALL THE SOFTWARE.

Index

A

B

C

D

E

F

G

H

J

K - L

N

O

P

Q

R

S

T